Health and Social Care

for Adult Pathway

NVQ 3 *Candidate Handbook*

Eleanor Langridge
Patricia J Knight
Stephanie Shields
Clare Waite

Nelson Thornes
a Wolters Kluwer business

Published in 2006 by:
Nelson Thornes Ltd
Delta Place
27 Bath Road
CHELTENHAM
GL53 7TH
United Kingdom

06 07 08 09 10 / 10 9 8 7 6 5 4 3 2 1

A catalogue record for this book is available from the British Library

ISBN 0 7487 9615 0

Cover photograph: Tony Sweet/Digital Vision EF (NT)
Illustrations by Angela Lumley
Page make-up by Northern Phototypesetting Co. Ltd, Bolton
Printed and bound in Great Britain by Scotprint

Contents

Introduction

This textbook has been written for care students and practitioners who are studying for a National Vocational Qualification in Health and Social Care for adults at level 3. Students on other courses that require knowledge and understanding of the principles and practice of health and social-care work will also find this book useful.

The contents of the book

The book is divided into 10 units, each providing full and detailed coverage of the relevant unit on the level 3 NVQ Health and Social Care award for adults. This includes coverage of the four core units (HSC31, HSC32, HSC33 and HSC35) and six optional units (HSC328, HSC335, HSC336, HSC343, HSC344 and HSC351). Please note that the level 3 NVQ Health and Social Care award offers almost 100 optional units. We have chosen to cover six optional units that we believe will have the most application across different job pathways. The full range of units that we have chosen is listed in Table 1 below.

To gain a National Vocational Qualification in Health and Social Care for adults at level 3 you need to demonstrate competence in all of the four core units and any four of the many optional units that are available.

Table 1 NVQ units covered in this book

NVQ unit number	Unit title
HSC31	Promote effective communication for and about individuals
HSC32	Promote, monitor and maintain health, safety and security in the working environment
HSC33	Reflect on and develop your practice
HSC35	Promote choice, well-being and the protection of all individuals
HSC328	Contribute to care planning and review
HSC335	Contribute to the protection of individuals from harm and abuse
HSC336	Contribute to the prevention and management of abusive and aggressive behaviour
HSC343	Support individuals to live at home
HSC344	Support individuals to retain, regain and develop the skills to manage their lives and environment
HSC351	Plan, agree and implement development activities to meet individual needs

The structure of the book

As mentioned above, the book is organised and structured around 10 NVQ units. Each unit in the book is divided into sections that follow the elements and performance criteria of the NVQ unit. The beginning of an element is clearly signposted with an Element heading. There are a number of other features in each unit including the following.

The main text of the unit

The main text covers the essential knowledge base for the element being covered. That is, it tells you what you need to know and understand in order to practise competently in that particular area of care. The main text is linked as closely as possible to the expected outcomes of the NVQ unit you are studying. You will see that glossary terms are highlighted and there are a variety of diagrams, photographs, cartoons and other visual material to illustrate and support the points being made in the main text. Each unit contains information about links to the **knowledge, understanding and skills criteria (KUS)**.

KUS 2, 14

To help you make these links, you will find yellow stickers in the margin that tell you which criteria are covered.

Practical examples

This feature provides a care-focused example to make you think about how the knowledge you have been developing could be used in practice. Each practical example provides a realistic scenario and a few questions for you to respond to. Your answers to the questions cannot be used as evidence of your competence for the NVQ award as they do not relate to your real work. However, you will develop your learning further by answering the various questions that you find throughout the book.

Practical Example

Communication

Mrs Simmons is a 90-year-old woman who has been admitted to a nursing home following discharge from hospital. She had a stroke and now has communication difficulties. Mrs Simmons was previously independent and healthy and lived at home; now she appears confused and upset and she wants to go home.

➤ *How do you start to assess communication needs and preferences?*
➤ *Who do you obtain information from?*
➤ *What non-verbal behaviour might you see in the individual?*
➤ *What communication methods might Mrs Simmons use?*
➤ *What communication aids might be used?*

Key points

This is a summary of the main points and themes covered in each unit. There is a Key Points feature at the end of each element. You can use this to reinforce your learning when you have finished reading a section. Alternatively you could use it to jog your memory if you need to clarify a topic quickly.

> **Key points – reflect on your practice**
>
> - Learning is a lifelong process.
> - The aim of CPD is to maintain quality care standards and competence.

Are you ready for assessment?

This feature appears at the end of each unit. It aims to direct your thinking towards the assessment that you have to undertake to demonstrate your practical competence as a care worker for that area of work. The assessment features encourage you to identify and think about what you will have to do to prepare for and carry out an assessment successfully.

Unit
HSC33   Are you ready for assessment?

Take part in continuing professional development

You will need to show that you can use continuing professional development to improve your practice. You will need to identify areas for development in your skills, knowledge and understanding, and compile a plan for your own development.

Direct observation by your assessor

Observation is the required assessment method to be used to evidence some part of each element in this unit.

Other types of evidence

You will need to present different types of evidence in order to:

- cover criteria not observed by your assessor

Preparing to be observed

You need to show your assessor that you have identified areas within your knowledge, understanding and skills which you can develop further. You must also show your assessor that you have negotiated a plan for this development which includes seeking out and accessing opportunities.

Check your knowledge

This feature also occurs at the end of each unit. It consists of a small number of comprehension questions. These are designed to test your understanding of the material you have worked through in the unit. It is worth trying to answer all of these questions as this will improve your learning and understanding. However, completing the questions does not provide evidence that you can use to gain your NVQ award. The evidence you use to claim competence must be produced through real work in your care setting.

Check your knowledge

- What legislation is relevant in record keeping?
- Where do you find out about individuals' communication needs and preferences?
- Describe the specific aids that can be used to support communication.
- Describe how you would communicate sensitive information.
- Why is it important to support individuals to communicate?
- Why is it important to update and maintain records and reports?

Glossary

You will find this feature at the end of the book. The glossary gives a brief explanation of important words and phrases that are highlighted in bold in the main body of the text.

We have used the term 'individual' throughout the text to refer to those people you support because this is the term used in the NVQ. Throughout the book the term 'practitioner' is used in preference to 'professional' as this more appropriately describes the variety of people who have a professional relationship with the individuals they support and work with in health and social care settings.

Legislation

There are legislative differences relating to health and social care in England, Scotland, Northern Ireland and Wales. Please check that you know about the regulations that apply in your area of work. Your manager/supervisor or assessor will advise you about this.

Finally

Good luck with your level 3 NVQ Health and Social Care award for adults. We hope the book provides you with interesting, supportive, motivating and stimulating learning materials which help you to succeed in achieving your goal of an NVQ level 3 award.

About the authors

Eleanor Langridge has 23 years' experience in the health and social care sector having initially qualified as a registered nurse and midwife. For 13 years she has worked as a teacher/trainer in further education colleges, social services and training organisations. She gained a Masters Degree in Education Management with Distinction at University College Chichester. She is an experienced assessor and internal verifier and has worked for City and Guilds as an external verifier. She is currently the managing director of an independent training company and City and Guilds NVQ Assessment Centre. She has also worked as a consultant for the Youth Justice Board for England and Wales and the North-East London Health and Social Care Sector where she was commissioned to write the Education and Training Strategy and accompanying training materials to support the implementation of the Single Assessment Process for Older People.

Patricia Knight worked for four-and-a-half years as a nursing auxiliary, became a State Registered Nurse (SRN) in 1978, and worked as a staff nurse on the ophthalmic ward at Burnley Victoria Hospital. She qualified as a State Certified Midwife (SCM) in 1979 and worked as a midwife at the Edith Watson Maternity Unit at Burnley General Hospital until 1992. She then took on the role of NVQ Centre co-ordinator at the hospital, and qualified as an assessor and internal verifier in 1994. She completed the Certificate in Education, and Return to Midwifery Practice courses during 2003. She left the hospital in 2004 and currently works as an active lead internal verifier for a local training company. Patricia also has qualifications in several holistic therapies.

Stephanie Shields qualified as a nurse in 1983 and midwife in 1985. She worked in an acute hospital setting until she became involved in NVQ Care Assessment in 1996. She achieved her BSc (Hons) Professional Development in Nursing and MSc Health and Social Service Management before entering further and higher education. She has since achieved an MSc in education and since the mid 1990s she has worked as a tutor and assessor on health and social care programmes including NVQ Care.

Clare Waite trained as a nurse in 1988, and mainly her work involved caring for the older person. She has 10 years' experience working with candidates doing NVQ level 2 and 3 in Care and currently works as an NVQ co-ordinator within the learning and development department of the Gloucestershire Hospitals NHS Foundation Trust.

Acknowledgements

The authors and publisher would like to thank the following for permission to reproduce materials and photographs in this book:

British Deaf Association; Makaton; Mind; Outreach 3 Way.

Crown copyright material is reproduced with the permission of the controller of Her Majesty's Stationery Office, Licence no. C2006009492.

© AJ Photo/Science photo library, p.146; © Brand X Pictures/Alamy, p.222; © Bubbles Photo Library, p.33, p.42, p.75, p.83, p.106, p.109; David Buffington/Photodisc 40 (NT), p.289; David Buffington/Photodisc 69 (NT), p.239; © Dynamic Graphics Group/ IT Stock Free/ Alamy, p.10; © Elmtree Image/Alamy, p.255; © Faye Norman/Science Photo Library, p.64; © Helen King/Corbis, p.10; Image 100 GC (NT), p.119; Ingram S V1 CD2 (NT), p.241; © Janine Wiedel Photolibrary/Alamy, p.7, p.261; © Jeff Greenberg/Alamy, p.280; John Foxx V9 (NT), p.174; © John Henley/Corbis, p.3; Keith Brofsky/Photodisc 40 (NT), p.127, p.280; Keith Brofsky/Photodisc 68 (NT), p.265; © Lauren Shear/Science photo library, p.143, p.150; © Libby Welch/Alamy, p.287; © Mark Sykes/Alamy, p.47; © Michael Donne/Science photo library, p.4; © Mika/zefa/ Corbis, p.177; © M. Thomsen/zefa/Corbis, p.80; Paul Doyle/Alamy, p.237; © Philip Wolmuth/Alamy, p.208; Photodisc 16 (NT), p.18; Photodisc 33 (NT), p.18; © Photo-fusion Picture Library/Alamy, p.272, p.281, p.284, p.321; Ryan McVay/Photodisc 66 (NT), p.32; © Stockbyte Platinum / Alamy, p.123; Tom Le Goff/Digital Vision HU (NT), p.18; TRB Foto/Photodisc 68 (NT), p.252; © Tremelet/Science photo library, p.110; Yoav Levy/Phototake/Alamy, p.192.

All other photos by Martin Sookias.

Every effort has been made to contact copyright holders and we apologise if anyone has been overlooked.

I would like to thank my husband Peter and daughter Katie for all their love, support and encouragement. I would like to thank all the people I have cared for and the NVQ candidates I have worked with over the years for all I have learned from them. **Eleanor**

I would like to acknowledge my partner Robert Gibson who has supplied me with meals and many cups of tea and biscuits whilst I have been writing the chapters for the book. I thank him for his patience and support, and for believing in me. **Patricia**

I would like to thank my children Jonathan and Hannah for their support and encouragement. **Stephanie**

Principles of good practice

What is the difference between the level 2 and level 3 NVQ in Health and Social Care?

Some readers will have already completed the level 2 NVQ Health and Social Care (or Care) by the time they read this textbook, while for others this may be the first time they have undertaken an NVQ. If this is your first experience of undertaking an NVQ then you are starting at level 3 due to the nature of your work role and responsibilities. It is helpful to spend some time considering how the level 3 NVQ award differs from the level 2 award.

As a care worker undertaking a level 3 award you are likely to have some supervisory responsibility and/or you will be undertaking more non-routine tasks or specialist tasks with less direct supervision in your workplace. For example, you may be working as a senior carer or support worker in a social care setting or a health care assistant in a hospital or in a general practitioner (GP) setting. The work you are doing will require you to have some specialist or technical knowledge and skills, e.g. supervision skills or the ability to take blood samples. In your role you will also be expected to make some decisions and perhaps support other less experienced workers in your workplace.

Although the core units relate to the same areas of practice as the level 2 award, your role and responsibility requires that you demonstrate a greater level of competence in these areas. For care workers undertaking NVQ level 2, their role and responsibilities are predominantly about being competent at undertaking routine tasks and being able to identify problems and report them to the appropriate person.

As a care worker undertaking a level 3 NVQ your role and responsibility requires you to be competent undertaking both routine and non-routine tasks, i.e. acting on your own initiative, as well as taking the first steps in dealing with problems that you identify before reporting them to an appropriate person. You may also take a supervisory role in your workplace and be the responsible person on shift and so will be that 'appropriate person' that colleagues report to. You may be responsible for supporting colleagues to develop their knowledge and skills through coaching and supervision.

Care workers working at this level also have a responsibility to act as a role model to the individuals they support and to less experienced colleagues. You will be reminded of this responsibility at different points throughout the book as it is an important part of demonstrating competence at NVQ level 3.

Your skills will have developed with experience and appropriate training, and if you have completed your NVQ level 2 in Health and Social Care (or Care) hopefully this too has improved your practice, understanding and self-confidence. Demonstrating knowledge and understanding at level 3 requires you to go beyond the descriptive answers to the 'what?', 'where?', 'how?' and 'who?' questions that are predominantly required to achieve the level 2 NVQ. Although these questions will still be asked by your assessor, they will ask more 'why?' questions, as the knowledge specifications for the level 3 NVQ units require you to demonstrate a greater depth of understanding and application of knowledge to your work.

This is best demonstrated through a more comprehensive explanation for your actions or the outcome in a situation. Therefore, your answers will be more analytical as you explain the reasons why something happens, give reasons for your actions, consider 'what if ...?' scenarios and explain the potential implications of not taking action. For example, if you are asked why it is important to involve the individual and the key people in their lives in the assessment and care planning process, your answer should demonstrate your understanding of the concept of empowerment, the importance and benefits of inclusion and co-operation, as well as the reasons why it is important for you to promote the individuals' rights and choices. To consider the benefits of inclusion and co-operation for example, you will need to consider the alternatives. You need to weigh up the value of including the individual and excluding them. Then consider the impact that each may have on the individual achieving their desired outcomes. This will lead you to a conclusion about what approach is likely to achieve the desired results and therefore why one approach is preferable to the other.

This describes part of the analytical process where you ask yourself questions in order to reach a conclusion. This enables you to reach a decision that has been based on your consideration of the available options and their relative importance. Analysis also helps you to think through a situation and reach an understanding, i.e. to understand the how and why. Analysis requires you to draw on other experience and the pool of knowledge that you have about a subject and to consider if this fits with, or is different to, the situation you are considering.

Being able to analyse your practice will enable you to not only explain that there are policies and procedures in your workplace to guide the work undertaken with individuals, it will also enable you to explain how these actually work in practice. Policies and procedures can only do so much. It is the way in which care workers consistently apply these in practice that makes the difference to individuals' lives and the quality of care they receive.

Another difference about studying at level 3 NVQ is the expectation that you will build on your ability to reflect and utilise this to develop your skills, knowledge, under-standing and most importantly your practice.

Working with people requires a high level of skill in communicating and building relationships with individuals and others. Each individual you encounter is unique, so to be effective in these essential skills it is important that you take time to reflect on your work with individuals and others. Reflecting on what happened, what you did, what they did and how you responded to one another will enable you to learn from each interaction. You can then add what you have learnt to your knowledge pool ready for an opportunity to apply your learning in another encounter. In your role many of the tasks you undertake will not be routine and this means that you will need to be able to apply your knowledge and understanding more and more to help you deal with situations that arise. Therefore, being able to reflect on your practice and apply what you have learnt will enhance your practice as well as your confidence.

Reflection also helps you to consider alternatives. When you consider a situation that you have been involved with, reflection helps you to think about other ways you could have dealt with it and whether a different approach may have resulted in a different/more successful outcome. In unit HSC33, page 84, you will find a model which provides a framework or structure for reflection and which hopefully will help you to become a more reflective care practitioner.

As previously mentioned, demonstrating competence for level 3 NVQ Health and Social Care requires you to both apply the values and principles of good care practice prescribed by organisational policies and procedures and to act as a role model for others in the care setting. Your competence in doing this should be clearly visible in the way that you promote the rights, choices, preferences, equity and confidentiality of the individuals you support and your work with others within your care setting.

Each level 3 NVQ unit emphasises the need for these values and principles to be embedded in, or provide the foundation for, your practice. Before you begin reading through the units, take time to consider the different ways in which your practice would demonstrate to the individuals you support and to your assessor that you promote the following rights when supporting individuals and others:

- To be respected.
- To be treated equally and not to be discriminated against.
- To be treated as an individual.
- To be treated in a dignified way.
- To privacy.
- To be protected from danger and harm.
- To be cared for in a way that meets the individual's needs and takes account of their choices.
- To be able to access information about themselves.
- To communicate using the individual's preferred methods of communication and language.

Some care workers find this a difficult area to consider as they 'just do it'. In your role, however, you not only need to understand how and why your practice demonstrates these values and principles, you also need to be able to identify when others do not have these principles embedded in their practice so that you can support them to learn from you and develop their own skills and practice.

Working in health and social care brings with it daily opportunities, challenges, frustrations and rewards. We hope this book will help you to recognise and grasp the opportunities, feel better equipped to rise to the challenges, understand and work through the frustrations and reap the rewards of providing better quality care to those you support, while achieving your own goals and realising your potential.

Assessment of National Vocational Qualifications

Before you start your National Vocational Qualification (NVQ) it is important for you to become familiar with the assessment process and the way in which your NVQ is structured.

What is assessment?

In order to achieve your NVQ you will be assessed in your workplace. You will be assessed or measured against national occupational standards in Health and Social Care. These standards describe the performance and knowledge requirements of workers in the health and social care sector and have been developed by experts and experienced practitioners from the specialist area. Awarding bodies (organisations that are responsible for awarding/providing qualifications) use these standards to design agreed nationally recognised qualifications, for example NVQ 3 Health and Social Care. This means that across the UK people will be undertaking the same qualification, and this will ensure that you can continue your NVQ should you move employer before you complete the award. It also means that the NVQ is a nationally recognised award.

Assessment is important so that both you and your employer know that the required standard has been reached. Your assessor will observe how you go about your work and will also find out if you understand the reasons why you carry out tasks in the way that you do as well as what to do if things change. In other words, they will assess your knowledge as well as your performance. It is not enough to either perform well but not understand what you are doing, or to understand the theory but not be able to practise. The key aspect of the NVQ is that you must be able to perform at the required standard and to know why you are doing what you are doing. Once your assessor has seen your practice at work and you have demonstrated you have the necessary background knowledge, they will make a decision about whether there is sufficient evidence to prove that you consistently meet the required standard and have demonstrated your competence.

The structure of NVQs

The NVQ is broken down into units. These units are concerned with broad activities, for example communication. The units are all numbered and they have the letters HSC in front of the number; this is because they are Health and Social Care units. Some of the units are called core units. The core units cover activities that are relevant to all health and social care workers whatever the care setting – for example health and safety. There are a small number of core units but there are many optional units because the various health and social care settings can be very different. Your assessor and employer will guide you regarding your choice of optional units. Remember, you can only choose an optional unit which relates to the job that you are doing because you have to demonstrate your competence in real work situations. Each unit of the NVQ specification has a brief explanation of the unit followed by a section called Scope. The aim of the Scope section is to provide guidance on how the unit relates to the work setting. It also helps you to identify the sort of work you might be doing with individuals. This helps to ensure the unit is relevant to your work. There is a list of terms which are relevant to the unit, followed by examples. Use this information to give you ideas about how the unit applies to your own work and to help you identify assessment opportunities. You will be expected to show evidence of any aspects of the Scope that relate to your work.

There is a statement at the beginning of each NVQ unit which summarises the values underpinning the unit. This reinforces the importance of the values and attitudes of all workers in health and social care settings. A worker would not be considered competent if they did not demonstrate these values. It is essential to apply them in all aspects of your work.

Some of the key words and concepts which appear in the NVQ are explained in the glossary. It is important to read this section carefully to make sure you understand how the words and phrases are being used.

The units are further broken down into elements. There are 2–4 elements in a unit. For example, in unit HSC31 (Promote effective communication for and about individuals) there are four elements of competence which are numbered HSC31a, HSC31b, HSC31c and HSC31d.

Within the element there are performance criteria (sometimes called PCs). The performance criteria state what you have to do in order to show that you are competent in that particular element.

At the end of each NVQ unit there is a list of the knowledge that is required for that unit.

Who is involved in the NVQ process?

Many people are involved in the NVQ process.

You are the candidate. All individuals who are undertaking an NVQ are referred to as candidates and your awarding body will give you a candidate number.

You have an assessor – this person must be occupationally competent to assess you. In other words, they should be suitably experienced and they must also have a qualification in assessment. You may already work alongside this person, they may be in the same team as you or you may work with them occasionally. This will depend upon the organisation that you work for and the nature of the work that you do.

You might have a peripatetic assessor – this person will not be based with you but will come into your work area to assess you.

Wherever your assessor is based, it is vital that you develop a positive working relationship and you should have regular contact throughout your NVQ.

In addition to your assessor you might also be watched by an expert witness. This person must also be occupationally competent and familiar with the health and social care standards but will not necessarily be a qualified assessor. The expert witness can provide testimony to your practice which will contribute to the evidence presented to your assessor.

At different points as you progress to the qualification the assessment records are passed on to the next stage of the process called internal verification. The role of the internal verifier (IV) is to maintain the quality and consistency of the assessment process. The IV does this by sampling evidence, checking that documentation is completed properly and ensuring that you have been assessed, as required, by a suitable assessor. Once the IV has sampled your work they will either agree with the decision of your assessor and add their signature, or they will identify areas that need further work or clarification. The IV could be employed in the same organisation as you, or if you are doing your NVQ at a college or with a training provider, they may be based there.

The external verifier (EV) is appointed by the Awarding Body. EVs monitor the overall quality of the Assessment Centre. They do this by visiting Assessment Centres usually twice a year and conducting a thorough audit. They will examine candidate evidence and talk to candidates, assessors and IVs.

Achieving the NVQ

You do not 'pass' or 'fail' an NVQ. Instead, in order to achieve your NVQ you have to demonstrate that you consistently meet the required standards of practice. To show this you must collect evidence which confirms this. Your evidence could include the following:

- *Observation* – this type of evidence is required in all of the elements of the core units of your NVQ. It will also be required in the optional units unless your assessor has agreed that you may use testimony from an expert witness as an alternative. Your assessor will observe you as you work and check that you are working in accordance with the health and social care units that you are undertaking. A written or verbal (audio recorded) statement describing what was observed will be produced.

- *Expert witness testimony* – a written or verbal (audio recorded) statement provide by an occupational expert which will give testimony to your practice carrying out a specific activity in your workplace. This person needs to be known to your assessor and agreed and prepared for their role.

- *Work products* – your assessor can examine items such as records or forms that you have been responsible for completing as part of your day-to-day work.

- *Confidential records* – records which you complete but which contain confidential information can be part of your evidence, but they must not be placed in your portfolio. They should stay in their usual location and be referred to by your assessor in their records. Confidential records are items such as care plans, individual plans and reviews.

- *Witness testimony* – a written or verbal (audio recorded) statement from a person who has knowledge and experience of your work practice. This could be a co-worker or other allied practitioner, individuals you support or their relatives, or key people. Your assessor will help you identify the best use of witnesses.

- *Reflective accounts, case studies, projects, assignments* – your explanation of work that you have undertaken. This is particularly useful to cover aspects of the knowledge specification or, occasionally, events which might happen rarely or are difficult to observe.
- *Questioning* – your assessor could ask you to answer written or oral questions which will be recorded and kept in the evidence portfolio.
- *Simulation* – a simulation could be used where it is difficult to obtain the evidence from a real work situation. This form of evidence is only permitted as part of the evidence in Element HSC32c covering emergency situations.

Getting started

In order to start your NVQ you will need to be registered with an Awarding Body. You can register through an Assessment Centre. An Assessment Centre could be a college, an NHS Trust, an employer or a private training organisation. The Assessment Centre is approved by the Awarding Body to offer particular qualifications. The assessment and verification processes within the assessment centre are monitored by the Awarding Body. This helps to promote fairness and maintain the high standard that is required of any person working within health and social care. When you have successfully completed your NVQ in Health and Social Care, your assessment centre will give you a certificate from the Awarding Body.

Once you are registered for your NVQ you will be assigned an assessor and an internal verifier. You will receive a full induction to the qualification and you should then meet with your assessor and discuss your level of experience and knowledge. Depending on your existing skills and knowledge, you may need to attend a training programme or receive coaching while you work. When you are ready for assessment you will agree a plan which will outline how you will start to gather evidence relating to the units of your NVQ.

Any plan must be agreed by you and your assessor. You should agree and record target dates and specific units that you are planning to achieve. Your plan will state how you are going to obtain the evidence that you need and identify the types of evidence that are going to be gathered.

All assessment plans will contain the following information:

- WHAT will be assessed.
- HOW it will be assessed.
- WHEN it will be assessed.
- WHO will be involved.

Once you have gathered your evidence you will place it in a folder – this is your portfolio of evidence. Some centres may use an electronic portfolio system which means your documentation will be kept on a computer rather than in an actual folder. Your assessor will advise you of the system in use at your centre and how to put your evidence together. Your portfolio should be organised and all your evidence must be referenced into the health and social care standards. This is done by giving your evidence a page number and by linking your evidence to the specific unit/element/PC or knowledge point that it relates to. Once you have obtained the evidence your assessor will examine it and check that it is:

- *Valid* – the appropriate and required assessment methods have been used.
- *Authentic* – it is your own work, all signatures and dates are included and any testimonies are written by appropriate people.
- *Current* – the evidence indicates current standards of practice, legislative requirements and practice policy.
- *Sufficient* – there is enough evidence to demonstrate that you have met the required standard. You have covered all the performance criteria, knowledge and any additional evidence requirements for the unit.

Your assessor will give you feedback and review your progress to make sure that you understand how you are getting on with your NVQ. Feedback should be recorded.

At the end of each unit of this book there is a heading 'Are you ready for assessment?'. In that section there are questions relating to the unit and suggestions regarding relevant evidence for the particular unit. The information provided in that section should help you to see whether you have a clear enough understanding of the subject and how you might prepare for assessment in the workplace.

Conclusion

Often the most demanding part of doing an NVQ is becoming familiar with the paperwork and the way that the qualification is structured. As you progress through each unit the process becomes more straightforward. Keep motivated and if you are experiencing difficulties ask for help.

Undertaking a qualification in the workplace is hard work and requires a great deal of commitment. However, achieving a formal qualification in health and social care is very important. It is a recognition of the skill and knowledge that you need to fulfil your role and it gives individuals confidence in the service you provide.

Promote effective communication for and about individuals

This unit covers all aspects of communication. This includes identifying ways of communicating on difficult, complex and sensitive issues, supporting others to communicate, and ways of updating and maintaining records and reports.

The unit contains four elements:

⌣ **HSC31a** *Identify ways to communicate effectively*

⌣ **HSC31b** *Communicate effectively on difficult, complex and sensitive issues*

⌣ **HSC31c** *Support individuals to communicate*

⌣ **HSC31d** *Update and maintain records and reports*

Introduction

⌣ What is communication?

Communication is the process of sending and receiving messages between two or more individuals in order to achieve a desired action or effect. Communication is a two-way process and involves talking and listening, writing and reading. Effective communication is important in care settings as it helps people to:

- Build good interpersonal relationships.
- Work together as a team.

When two or more people interact **interpersonal communication** occurs. This involves exchanging information by talking, listening, observing and responding to one another.

⌣ Cycle of communication

Communication is a cyclical process:

- A decision is made by a sender to communicate a message.
- This message is encoded in the appropriate way, for example in written or spoken word, symbol or body language.
- The sender then selects the correct communication medium to send the message, for example making a telephone call, writing a message.
- The message is then decoded by the receiver.
- The meaning of the message is correctly interpreted.
- The receiver provides feedback.

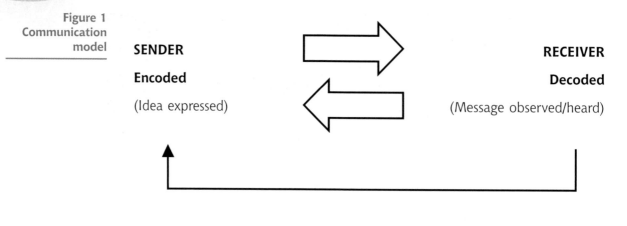

Figure 1
Communication
model

HSC31a *Identify ways to communicate effectively*

Element

Individuals' communication and language needs

KUS 4, 5

We all have different styles of communication and in the care environment it is important that you obtain information about how individuals communicate. Effective communication is essential to the delivery of high quality care to individuals. Communication can help to support individuals and their families. The need for effective communication in health and social care is recognised in the NHS Plan 2000, the Care Standards Act 2000, the Essence of Care 2003, and in the Registration and Inspection Standards 2004.

Effective communication requires careful planning and is seen as:

- An interaction between two individuals (telling someone what to do or just listening is not enough).
- Reducing uncertainty (about diagnosis or outcomes of care etc.).
- Sharing meaning between individuals.
- A process of exchanging information.

Communication begins when you first meet an individual and begin to establish a rapport with them by showing interest and by getting to know them as a person. This will help to build a trusting relationship where the individual will feel comfortable sharing information with you. How the individual communicates can also be observed. You can observe the non-verbal behaviour displayed, for example facial expression, vocal tone, gesture and body positions, body movements, touch and personal space. These can indicate how the individual is feeling and will also support verbal communication.

Questions are also an important part of the assessment process and open-ended questions allow individuals to elaborate on their communication needs. Questions can help individuals and their families to relate communication needs, including the impact of any communication difficulties, environmental barriers and any resources required.

Figure 2
Non-verbal
behaviour

Therefore it is important that you listen to the individual so that all communication needs are understood and met. To do this you need to concentrate on what they are saying and listen for key words and issues on which to comment and ask questions.

Record keeping

KUS 1, 4, 5

Once you gather information you need to record it. Record keeping is an integral part of health and social care practice. The Data Protection Act 1998 defines a health/social care record as any electronic or paper information recorded about an individual for the purposes of managing his or her health care. Good record keeping helps:

- To provide continuity in promoting an individual's communication and language needs.
- When making arrangements to be put in place to meet the individual's communication and language needs.

The focus on record keeping is important as the individual's rights and empowerment are promoted through involvement in care. This has been brought about through the Patient's Charter (Department of Health (DoH) 1991) and more recently through Patient Focus and Public Involvement (Scottish Executive 2001) and Essence of Care (DoH 2003). According to the Nursing and Midwifery Council (NMC), precise record keeping can help enhance care for individuals by promoting continuity and consistency. These records should be:

- Factual.
- Current.
- Comprehensive.
- Consistent.
- Written chronologically (in date order).

Individuals have a right to view and receive written records according to the Access to the Data Protection Act 1998 and How to Access Your Health Records 2003. The Data

KUS 1

Protection Act 1998 gives the individual access to their paper-based and computer-held records. The Freedom of Information Act 2000 grants everyone the right to access all information not covered by the Data Protection Act 1998, for example information which does not contain individual identifiable details.

Figure 3
Individuals have a right to view the written records of their care

Preferred communication

KUS 1

One of the most important ways of conveying respect for individuals' dignity is through effective and sensitive communication. Communication not only conveys respect but it is often the only way of assuring individuals that we are interested in their experience, perceptions and needs. Each individual should be afforded equal opportunities no matter what their communication and language needs are.

KUS 6

Different individuals may have a number of different communication and language needs, and a wide range of communication aids are available to meet those needs.

KUS 6, 7

It is important that you find out from the individual what their preferred language and method of communication is. Then it is important to ensure that these communication aids are available.

Individual's preferred spoken language

Individuals whose first language is not English can be at a major disadvantage in gaining access to health care. Using an individual's preferred spoken language can also assist in expressing health and social care needs. If the individual's first language is not used this can create a barrier to communication.

Use of signs and symbols

KUS 2, 3, 10, 11

British Sign Language (BSL) is the first or preferred language of around 250,000 deaf people in the UK. It is a language that involves using the hands, body, face and head. Finger spelling is just one element of British Sign Language.

Figure 4
Finger spelling

Source: www.learntosign.org.uk/fingerspelling

Makaton is a language programme that is widely used in the UK to enable people with learning and communication difficulties to communicate. It is used for individuals in schools, education and training centres, hospitals and community facilities. Makaton signs and symbols provide a visual representation of language that increases understanding and makes communication easier. Makaton does not try to replace speech; it aims to encourage the development of communication and speech is part of that process.

Figure 5
Makaton symbols

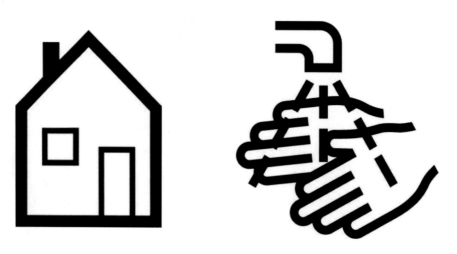

© The Makaton Vocabulary Development Project 2005

Use of pictures and the written word

Communication through pictures and written words is preferred by some individuals over spoken language. Prepared materials may help individuals describe what they are experiencing or what has happened to them. Using pictures and the written word can help individuals express their own perceptions of their problems.

The Picture Exchange Communication System (PECS) is proving to be beneficial in developing communication in people with autistic spectrum disorders. It works by identifying pictures to denote objects desired by the individual. Communication is established when these pictures are exchanged by the individual for their desired object. The TEACCH (Treatment and Education of Autistic and Related Communication Handicapped Children) method is also widely used.

Objects of reference

This is the use of objects as a means of communication. These objects can be made to represent the things about which we all communicate, such as activities, events, people and ideas. Objects of reference can be used by individuals who are deaf or blind and those with short- and long-term memory difficulties, for example **Alzheimer's disease**.

Objects of reference can be used before progressing to more complex forms of communication, for example signs or symbols. They can also be used as an aid to memory, perhaps helping to sequence daily activities. Objects of reference can help individuals to make choices about these activities.

Communication passports

Communication passports are a way of supporting adults who cannot easily speak for themselves. They present the person positively as an individual and not just as a set of problems or disabilities. They also provide room for the person's character, views and preferences to be recorded. Communication passports also record the individual's preferred method of communication. Communication passports are probably most frequently used by adults with learning difficulties as they enable the individual to take control of their communication and increase their independence.

Human and technological aids

There are a wide range of aids to support individuals who have communication difficulties. Individuals with communication difficulties can use more than one of these aids. Some individuals may use interpreters to help communicate their needs. Technological aids range from those that can only communicate single or a few messages to complex devices or portable computers. Electronic aids may be used alongside or instead of other communication systems such as paper based charts and signing systems. The individual will normally use more than one method of communication, for example someone using an electronic aid will reinforce its messages with gestures and head movement.

Different messages are selected using a combination of keys or a dynamic screen display. Many users of electronic aids use a symbol or picture to associate the images with larger messages. Individuals who can spell can use more complex machines which allow messages to be typed in and the machine will then turn these into speech using speech synthesis. Aids such as Message Mate can hold up to 20 or 30 messages and have a fixed vocabulary. More complex aids such as the Liberator have the ability to hold a large number of messages. Portable computers are used as electronic communication aids by running specialist software.

**Figure 6
Sign language**

Methods of communication

In order to communicate effectively, you must identify the different styles and methods of communicating to meet the needs and preferences of individuals and key people. About 7% of the meaning of a message is communicated by the words used, 38% is communicated by voice and tone and about 55% is conveyed non-verbally, for example by gesture, posture and facial expression.

Verbal communication

Verbal communication refers to all aspects of speech. This can mean the language used, tone of voice, rate of speech, volume of speech, intonation and accent. Speech is the highest form of human communication and is used in conjunction with facial expressions, eye contact, gesture, signals and touch. Communication is most effective when simple, clear words are used together with a moderate tone of voice.

Without the use of spoken language individuals and key people find it difficult to classify and order information in ways that can be understood by others. The choice of words by individuals is influenced by many factors, for example age, socio-economic group, race, educational background and gender.

It is important to remember that words do not have the same meaning for all individuals and/or key people. There are two levels of meaning in language:

- **Denotation** is the generalised meaning assigned to a word.
- **Connotation** relates to the more personalised meaning that is implied in addition to the literal meaning of the word or phrase. For example, the word 'chat' (i.e. a conversation) suggests an open and informal exchange. Then think about the word 'gossip' – this word has a less positive feeling.

Do not assume that the meaning of a message is the same for sender and receiver until understanding is checked by using feedback.

Communicating with individuals and key people from ethnic and socio-economic groups other than our own can present challenges. To help communication you should develop an awareness of the **values** of their specific culture and adapt your communication style and skills so that they are compatible with that culture's norms.

People who speak English as a second language find it difficult to translate expressions for which there is no English equivalent, or slang terms or phrases that have double meanings. Individuals who learn English as an adult may continue to think in their native language, translating words into a familiar dialect. Therefore you should allow extra time for information processing especially when an individual is upset or anxious.

Different age groups in the same culture may attribute different meanings to the same words. For successful communication, the words used should have similar meaning to all individuals in the interaction.

The oral delivery of a verbal message expressed through tone and inflection of voice is called **paralanguage**. Voice inflection (pitch and tone) suggests mood and can support or contradict the verbal message. When the tone of voice contradicts the words, the message is less likely to be understood. For example, an increase in volume can indicate anger and aggressiveness, or a teenager saying 'whaaaatever' can indicate dismissive and rebellious behaviour.

There are gender differences in communication patterns. Men are more likely to initiate an interaction, to talk more, interrupt and use hostile verbs. However, men are less likely to disclose personal information.

Women view the process of communication as a connection to others and use more active listening skills than men. For example, women use more encouraging phrases such as 'Uh-huh' and 'I see'.

Non-verbal communication

Non-verbal communication refers to all the body signals and includes posture, position, eye contact, facial expressions, gestures and body language. The function of non-verbal communication is to give clues and help clarify what is communicated. You can use non-verbal communication to build rapport with individuals and key people. Observing their non-verbal behaviour may reveal information that might affect your relationship, for example worried facial expression and lip biting may suggest that the individual is worried. By picking up on these non-verbal cues you can improve communication. For example, an individual may tell you that everything is fine and yet you observe a worried facial expression and lip biting. By staying with the individual and reassuring them, you can build up trust and they may share their concerns.

Figure 7
Non-verbal
communication

Proxemics relates to the personal space that individuals perceive should be maintained between them and others. Each culture has a different idea of the appropriate distance. In Western cultures the distance for personal conversation is 18 inches to 4 feet. The distance reserved for communication between individuals who have a personal relationship is 0–18 inches. At this distance vision is impaired and the main senses used are smell and touch. It is important for care workers to understand that if an individual's personal space is disregarded then this can appear threatening.

KUS 3,
12

There are cultural variations in non-verbal communication. Sometimes a non-verbal gesture that is acceptable in one culture can be perceived as rude in another. For example, putting a thumb and forefinger together can signal approval in the UK, but in Brazil the gesture is obscene.

Different cultures also have a rule about eye contact. Some individuals will avoid eye contact when listening and use eye contact when speaking. For example, in the UK, USA and northern Europe direct eye contact conveys confidence, but in Japan prolonged eye gaze is considered rude.

Touch is one of the most powerful ways to communicate non-verbally. However, you should ensure that cultural boundaries are not broken. For example, Muslim men do not touch women who do not belong to their family.

Gender differences also play a part in non-verbal communication. Women use more facial expressions, for example they smile more frequently, maintain eye contact and use touch more often. Men prefer a greater interpersonal distance between themselves and others. Western men use gestures freely.

Body language is an important part of non-verbal communication and is sometimes referred to as **kinesics**. Body language can help to clarify the meaning of words. Posture, rhythm of movement and gestures can help to convey a message. For example, slow movement and a slumped posture with head down can convey low self-esteem.

Figure 8
Negative body
language

Figure 9
Positive body
language

Eye contact and facial expression are important in signalling feelings. Making eye contact when speaking or listening can mean that the individual is confident. A smile may be used to express joy.

Practical Example

Communication

Mrs Simmons is a 90-year-old woman who has been admitted to a nursing home following discharge from hospital. She had a stroke and now has communication difficulties. Mrs Simmons was previously independent and healthy and lived at home; now she appears confused and upset and she wants to go home.

➤ *How do you start to assess communication needs and preferences?*

➤ *Who do you obtain information from?*

➤ *What non-verbal behaviour might you see in the individual?*

➤ *What communication methods might Mrs Simmons use?*

➤ *What communication aids might be used?*

Key people and communication aids

⸜ Families and friends

KUS 6, 7

Families and friends help to form part of the therapeutic relationship in health care. It is important to involve them when gathering information about the individual's communication needs. By understanding the individual's place in the family group and family history you can build a rapport.

Families usually come into contact with health and social care practitioners during periods of illness, crisis and injury in a variety of settings. Learning about family communication is important for several reasons:

- It provides an awareness of the important relationships in an individual's life. These relationships can provide support for the individual and yourself during communication.
- The advice and information gained can help to identify the communication and support needs of the individual, particularly when there are communication difficulties.

KUS 13

Family members can also be used as interpreters. However, the individual may not feel able to talk freely to a family member about health and personal matters, therefore communication may be limited. There may also be conflicts of interest. It is not advisable for children to be used as interpreters as this is considered unethical and unprofessional.

Family and friends have a role in reducing the tension between the individual and yourself until the therapeutic relationship develops.

⸜ Other workers

If the individual has been transferred from another care setting then other workers, for example speech and language therapists or interpreters and translators, can provide information about how the individual communicates, their support needs and how these are met.

Health and social care records

Care records often contain information about how an individual communicates and details of their support needs.

Interpreters and translators

An individual whose first language is not English, or who is deaf, blind, partially sighted or has difficulty reading standard English print may require the services of an interpreter. The employment of interpreters has become increasingly common in health and social care settings in response to a more culturally diverse population. You need to find out from your organisation how to contact interpreters.

Interpreters may also be used to aid communication in the case of deaf individuals who use sign language. Hands-on signing is used by the deaf and blind individual who follows the signs by placing their hands over those of the signer.

Communication aids

There are a wide range of communication aids for individuals who have communication difficulties (see pages 5–7).

Information on communication issues for the individual and key people

You will often begin a relationship with an individual by exchanging names. Non-verbal communication such as a smile or handshake can help support verbal communication. Therefore it is important for you to gather basic information on how the individual likes to be addressed. From this first encounter you convey to the individual that the relationship will be a partnership.

You must develop a working relationship before you can address the individual's health and social care needs. In the next phase you should provide basic information about the purpose and nature of the therapeutic relationship, for example a procedure to be undertaken.

Once you have clarified what information is required, you should find out where this can be obtained. For example, information may be available from your manager, other professionals and care records.

You should also clarify how the information is to be given to the individual and if any support for communication is needed. You should also be aware of the information to be given to the interpreter or translator. Interpreters and translators will communicate the facts to the individual and also alert you if misunderstandings occur.

If communication needs change then these needs should be reported to your manager or another professional, e.g. speech and language therapist, so that an individual's needs can be reassessed. Additional support for the individual can then be obtained and you can maintain the therapeutic relationship.

A change in approach is also required if the individual has an adverse reaction to the information being given, for example they might be embarrassed if the details relate to an intimate procedure that is to be carried out.

You should also be aware that the care environment can be stressful. The individual may display a stress reaction. They may appear anxious or angry, or have physical symptoms of illness, for example aches and pains, loss of appetite, frequent colds, chest pain and high blood pressure.

Key points – identifying ways to communicate effectively

- Individuals receiving care have different communication needs and preferences.
- Culture, sensory impairment or language difficulties can influence how an individual communicates.
- Information about communication needs and preferences can be obtained from a number of sources including the individual, family, carers, health and social care professionals and records.
- Information on communication needs should be recorded by you in the individual's records and updated when changes occur.
- Use support to meet individuals' communication needs, for example technological aids, signs and symbols and interpreters.
- Effective communication occurs when you meet communication needs.

Communicate effectively on difficult, complex and sensitive issues

In health and social care settings there are a range of difficult, complex and sensitive issues that you may have to communicate to individuals. This can include distressing, traumatic, personal, frightening and threatening issues. They may also pose a risk to and have serious implications for individuals and key people. These communications can be difficult for the individual to understand and therefore health and social care workers will need to use special skills in these situations.

KUS 12,
16

Use of the environment

Creating a physical environment that enables effective communication is important. This is especially true when you have to communicate difficult, complex and sensitive issues. A comfortable private setting where you and the individual can sit facing each other is essential. The seating should be arranged so that there is a comfortable distance between yourself and the individual. The room should be well ventilated and well lit so that it is a comfortable setting to be in. Location of the room is important and others should not be able to overhear the conversation. Perhaps there is a room in your care setting that is used for this purpose already and is suitable for you to use as well.

It is important that interruptions are minimised, so you should inform other members of staff that you are not to be disturbed. Any phones (including mobiles) and pagers should be switched off or diverted.

Some care settings have environments that make communication more difficult. Health and social care settings, for example residential/nursing homes and day centres, can be noisy and offer little privacy. Communication should take place in a quiet room designated for that purpose. If this is not possible, draw the curtain around the bed and sit facing the individual. In the individual's home you are always the guest and it is usually the individual who selects the room where communication takes place.

When selecting the environment you should also take into account the specific needs of the individual. Perhaps the individual is frightened or distressed and requires privacy or the company of a member of staff to provide reassurance before you communicate with them.

KUS 2, 3

Support for communication

After you have prepared the environment you should make sure that you are aware of all the details about the issue to be discussed. This should include how much the individual already knows about the issue and how much they want to know. You can then start at the appropriate point according to the individual's knowledge.

An assessment of the individual's communication needs should have taken place prior to the meeting. You should consider the support that the individual requires. This may include having their family or other members of the care team present. Check with the individual to find out who they want to have with them. You should also be aware that by making a special effort to ensure that the individual is accompanied, you will alert them that a difficult or complex issue is going to be discussed.

If your assessment has shown that the individual requires support for communication in the form of an interpreter or translator, you should make the necessary arrangements well in advance of the meeting. There should also be arrangements to support the individual if required, for example by using:

- Signs and symbols.
- Pictures and written words.

- Objects of reference.
- Communication passports.

KUS 8,
15

Styles and methods of communication

Since the information you are going to give to the individual/key people is on difficult, complex or sensitive issues, you will need to find the most effective way of conveying your message. Information should be given in a way that conveys:

- clarity
- empathy
- warmth
- accuracy
- sincerity.

You can help to encourage the above by creating a relaxed conversation and being aware of your appearance. Studies have shown that the clothing worn can help to convey a particular image of a health and social care professional. Uniform differs between health and social care settings, but the most professional image recognised by individuals is the traditional uniform, e.g. the doctor's white coat. You should also recognise the difficulties that can occur when working in a setting where uniform is not worn. For example, it is often difficult to maintain a professional image when staff wear T-shirts and jeans.

Certain situations can make us all feel tense and this can affect our ability to communicate effectively. In order to feel more relaxed you should be well prepared for the conversation with the individual. By being well prepared, choosing your words carefully and by being conscious of your body language you can put an individual at their ease. This will help the exchange of ideas and information and will develop a relationship where the individual will feel able to ask questions and seek support.

Communication is a mixture of verbal and non-verbal functions that are integrated for the purpose of sharing information. When you exchange information with an individual you also convey messages about how to interpret the communication. For example, the message of caring can be conveyed by making eye contact, not frowning, having a relaxed posture, not fidgeting and making appropriate encouraging verbal responses.

In a professional caring relationship the verbal and non-verbal components of communication are an essential part of that relationship. This is particularly true if you are communicating with an individual who uses sign language. For example, it is not enough to make the sign for 'smile' to convey the message that you are happy, you also have to show a smile at the same time.

Through use of non-verbal communication you can communicate interest and respect for the individual, for example the use of eye contact, body posture, touch, smiling and head nodding at appropriate parts of the conversation.

Verbal communication

Verbal communication involves speech and its component parts of words, clauses, sentences and sequences. Verbal communication is used to convey ideas, share experiences, to check information and to order the world in which we live. Culture plays a large part in our use of language. Communicating with individuals from other ethnic and socio-economic groups can present difficulties, for example if information is not available in a range of languages or uses jargon and complex terms. To overcome these issues you should become aware of the specific individual's culture and adapt your style and communication skills to meet the norms of that individual. If the individual uses English as a second language you should allow sufficient time between messages for the individual to understand, or you should arrange for an interpreter to be present.

KUS 3

Other factors that can influence verbal communication are:

- *Slang and jargon*. Different age groups may attribute different meanings to the same word. For example, an adult may interpret 'wicked' as being evil, but a teenager will interpret the word as being good, exciting. Remember also that health and social care professionals use terms for different aspects of health that may be difficult for the individual to understand, especially if they feel stressed or are in an unfamiliar environment. Be careful not to use terminology that the individual will find difficult to understand.

- *Pitch and tone*. The interpretation of a verbal message can be affected by the way it is delivered, through tone of voice and inflection. It is an important part of language as an individual can misinterpret the meaning despite the good intentions of staff. For example, you might say to an individual, 'I would like to hear how you feel about that', but you may say it in a high-pitched or harsh voice or in a way that sounds rushed. The same statement will be interpreted in a completely different way by the individual if expressed in a soft, unhurried voice. In this case the individual will interpret that you have a genuine interest in how they feel.

- *Gender*. The most effective communication can occur if the provider and the receiver of care are of the same gender. It has been shown that men often use less verbal communication than women use. Women may disclose more personal information as they view conversation as a connection with others.

It is important to remember that verbal communication is not always clear and that non-verbal clues may help to support meaning. However, it is part of your job to check that the meaning of the message is understood. Health and social care professionals should be skilled in the process of entering into conversations, gaining the individual's attention, preparing and giving information and adopting behaviours that will maintain and facilitate that communication. For example, taking turns at speaking will enable both individuals to get their point across. It is important that health and social-care workers do not jump in too quickly when speaking to individuals. Individuals need to feel that their point of view is being taken seriously. Encourage the individual to continue the communication by using sounds such as 'm-hm' or saying 'I see' etc. Silences are important in the conversation and the individual can be encouraged to say more about the subject if you use positive body language, for example maintaining eye contact. Often silence is very effective, but people remain wary of using it and are anxious to fill the gaps in conversation. Silence can be used when an open question is asked – you lean back and give encouragement such as smiling, and the individual will provide further information to fill the silence.

Non-verbal communication

The main function of non-verbal communication is to give clues about what is being said.

This includes:

- *Facial expressions* – these can convey emotional states such as happiness, sadness, fear, surprise, disgust and anger. All of these are universal facial expressions and it is useful in health and social care to recognise these expressions as they can help add to the message conveyed.

- *Eye contact* – this is important but the degree that it is used can vary. Too much or too little eye contact can feel uncomfortable. Eye contact can help to assess the individual's needs, provide support and evaluate reactions. By using eye contact you can help individuals to disclose information to you and therefore improve communication. People who are more anxious will use less eye contact and they will maintain eye contact for less periods of time. It has been shown that females use eye contact more than males.

- *Body movements* – these can convey information, for example hand and arm movements. They can facilitate the transmission of information. Nail biting or twisting rings can indicate nervousness. Messages about how you feel are communicated by the way you walk, turn your head or sit down, and can indicate if you are happy, bored, angry or tired. Nodding your head can indicate that you are listening to the individual.

- *Posture* – this can convey our attitude, emotion and status. Open posture indicates we are approachable and closed posture, with arms folded, will indicate we are guarded and defensive. Leaning towards the individual will show that you are interested, while slouching will indicate that you have lost interest.

- *Gestures* – for example pointing, can help to transmit messages. Gestures can also help to convey emotion, such as clenched fists to indicate anger. Gestures vary from culture to culture and it is necessary to become familiar with cultural norms so that you do not cause offence.

- *Touch* – this plays an important part in human communication. Touch can enhance relationships with others to build rapport and to provide comfort.

- *Use of space* – this is important, as how we position ourselves in relation to others indicates our attitude towards them. In friendly situations we will sit side by side or at right angles. Sitting directly face to face can appear more threatening.

You can use non-verbal communication to build a relationship with individuals and to help deliver the message. Of all the methods of non-verbal communication facial expression is perhaps the most powerful. By observing the facial expression of the individual you can assess the effects of the message.

**Figure 10
Facial expressions**

Non-verbal communication is important in health and social care as:

- Some individuals may not be able to communicate verbally.
- You may be seen as an authority figure, therefore the individual may be less verbal and non-verbal communication can help to improve the relationship. For example, eye contact, leaning forward, smiling, head nodding and pleasant facial expression.
- Fear and uncertainty may make the individual more sensitive to non-verbal cues.
- Individuals may look for non-verbal communication to back up the verbal message and to help them recall and understand the information they were given.

Non-verbal communication has several functions:

- It can replace speech, for example touching an individual when they are distressed provides reassurance and comfort.
- It complements the verbal message, for example nodding your head can help to reinforce a positive message.
- It regulates and controls information, for example turn taking and eye contact can help the individual to feel that their message is important.

- It provides feedback, for example head nodding can indicate to the individual that you have understood the information.
- It helps to define relationships between people, for example wearing a uniform can convey a professional relationship.
- It can convey emotional state, for example smiling can indicate that the individual is happy.

Style of communication

The style of communication that you use can influence an individual's behaviour. Since we all have different communication styles it is important to identify your own style and learn how to modify it when necessary to improve communication with individuals. Personality can influence your communication style, for example you might be described as outgoing or shy. If an individual is shy they may find it difficult to communicate their feelings or personal information. Perhaps one way to identify your communication style is to recognise how others perceive you. Factors that can influence this are:

- Gender.
- Age.
- Manner of dress.
- Skin tone.
- Work role.
- Hairstyle.
- Gestures and confident mannerisms.

If an individual is outgoing and verbal then it will be easier to have a therapeutic conversation. It is your job to try and help quieter individuals to communicate. This can be achieved through encouraging **active listening**, showing empathy and acknowledging the difficulty that the individual has in expressing their feelings. You should also praise their efforts and use more than one method of communication. This will convey to the individual that you care, it will make them feel that they have worth and will help to sustain the relationship.

You should also be aware of the effect that your job role can have on communication. The relationship between the sender and receiver in communication can affect how the information is interpreted. When roles are unequal in terms of power, the more powerful person tends to dominate the interaction. It is important in your job role that you enhance the quality of your relationship with individuals by following through on verbal commitments, paying attention to detail and providing reassurance. It is also important to recognise that there is a change in emphasis in health and social care towards person-centred care. This means that you work in partnership with the individual. Communication can be enhanced using this type of care as no one person dominates the interaction and a positive relationship can develop.

Methods of communicating

KUS 15

Once you have chosen and prepared the setting and found out all the background information, communication with the individual can take place. Since the information may be of a difficult, complex and sensitive nature, you should give care and consideration to how the information will be disclosed. Think about the method and style of communication and the support required by the individual.

KUS 13

During the interaction, use simple language to ensure that the individual can fully understand what you are saying. An individual's emotional state can affect the amount of information that they can absorb. Avoid using jargon that could be misleading or may be misinterpreted. Even words which you do not consider to be jargon may be unfamiliar to the individuals you support. You should be aware of the individual's language capabilities and use similar words and terminology when you talk to them. Non-verbal communication will be important as posture, style and manner can affect the progress and outcome of the interaction.

It is important to check that the individual understands the information and to allow time for questions. If the individual does not ask any questions allow time for these at a later date when they have had time to think about the information you have given them. Remember also that not all direct questions have to be answered by a direct answer. Sometimes you should think about why the individual is asking that question as it may uncover some concerns.

If there is a lot of information to cover then it would be better to have a number of short meetings rather than one long one. Remember that the individual's needs come first and all interactions should be tailored to meet these needs. Therefore you need to pace the meeting accordingly and never appear to be in a hurry. Always tell the truth in a caring and sensitive way – this will also help to build a trusting relationship. Remember that some of the information given at this meeting may have to be repeated as the initial shock of what is being discussed may inhibit the processing of information.

At the end of the meeting always check whether the individual or any family or carers present have any questions and try to answer those before bringing the meeting to a close.

Reactions and support

Since the communication may be about difficult, complex or sensitive issues you should be aware that individuals may become upset or distressed. This is to be expected and is not necessarily connected to the way you have given the information. It is important to accept and acknowledge their reactions. You need to give the individual time to express their reactions. Perhaps you can help by asking questions, for example, 'What are you thinking/feeling?' or, 'What are your concerns?' By using open questions the speaking role is handed to the individual and they are able to provide you with more information. Think about the information required and start the question with 'what', 'when', 'which', 'why', 'when' or 'how'. After you ask the question you can lean back, and once the individual answers you can use non-verbal communication, for example, nodding and smiling, and stay silent. The individual will then offer more information. If closed questions are used the individual will only answer yes or no and further information will not be obtained. Do not give premature reassurance in an attempt to provide comfort as this might mislead the individual and may lead to a loss of trust in you and/or other professionals and damage your relationship with them. Reactions can include:

- Increased rate of breathing.
- Crying, frowning.
- Changes in tone and pitch of voice, higher pitch or shouting.
- More dilated pupils.
- Aggressive body posture, leaning forward with fists clenched.
- Sweating.

If an individual is anxious they may be less able to envisage options and make choices. Acute anxiety will also cause an individual to become more aware of physical symptoms, for example pain, and you should help to reduce anxiety by acting in a calm manner and reporting any symptoms as indicated by your job role. By observing and monitoring the individual you can note the effects of the anxiety experienced and if there are any improvements or a deterioration in condition. Sometimes the individual will act in a hostile manner by saying things that they do not mean, for example blaming the staff for not acting quickly enough. You can help deflect verbal hostility by being open to the expression of negative feelings and supporting the hostile person without condoning the behaviour. Conflict may arise out of misunderstandings. To avoid this happening it is important to check the individual's understanding regularly, clarify what has been said and then recheck. You could do this by asking them what their view or understanding is.

KUS 2, 14

If appropriate, ask the individual, family and carers if you can provide support. This may take the form of contact details of support groups or organisations, for example CRUSE, the Samaritans, Citizens Advice Bureau, Age Concern, British Heart Foundation and local support groups. You may also have access to specialist health and social care professionals who can provide support, for example counsellors, specialist nurses, community psychiatric nurses, GPs and consultants. Perhaps you could give written information about these services at a local and national level and if appropriate make the appointment. Or you could contact someone on behalf of the individual, for example a relative who could provide practical support. Reassure the individual that it is common to ask for further support and advice. However, try to promote the individual's independence and encourage them to make their own arrangements for appropriate support.

KUS 2, 3

If the reaction of the individual gives you cause for concern and they indicate that they are likely to cause harm to themselves or others then you should remain calm and provide emotional support using active listening and counselling skills. Practical support can also be given, for example using touch, making a telephone call or contacting someone on behalf of the individual. It is also part of your job role to summon immediate help from a senior colleague and to report and record the individual's reaction and your response and support according to local policies. Remember that emergency services may also be required.

The individual, family and carers may need some time in private to collect their thoughts and feelings before they leave the room. The individual may require a follow-up meeting with you or someone else from the care team. It is often difficult for the individual to ask for this as they may not want to be a nuisance or they may feel foolish.

After the meeting you should document what has been said and the individual's reactions. Record whether any family members or others were present and their reactions to the issue. Also record details of any support offered and the follow-up plan. This will facilitate other members of staff to care for the individual. Always tell the individual who else you will be contacting and check any concerns about confidentiality. Recording and reporting procedures must comply with confidentiality agreements and legal and organisational requirements.

Practical Example

Reactions and support

The Gables, a residential care home for adults with learning difficulties, is closing and residents are being moved to smaller houses where they will become tenants. There have been months of consultation with residents and families to reach this point. However, it is now time to start preparing individuals to visit the new houses and choose where they want to live.

You are a senior carer and Charlotte Dawson's key worker. Charlotte is a 54-year-old woman with Down's Syndrome who has been a resident for the past 16 years. She has limited verbal communication and uses Makaton. She has become increasingly forgetful and at times she is quite confused. Her GP suspects she has the early signs of dementia.

➤ *What information would you gather so that you can begin preparing Charlotte for the move?*

➤ *What factors would you need to consider in relation to her communication needs when working with her?*

➤ *What possible reactions might Charlotte have to this change?*

➤ *What support might she need with communication?*

➤ *What information would you document?*

Key points – communicating effectively

- The environment is important in order for effective communication to take place.
- Individuals may need support to meet their communication needs.
- The methods and styles of communication should meet an individual's needs.
- Communication should be sensitive to the individual's needs and concerns, especially when communicating difficult, sensitive or complex information.
- The individual may require support to deal with their reaction to the information.
- The information given and the individual's reaction should be recorded.

Element
HSC31c

Support individuals to communicate

When you support someone it is important to understand why people behave as they do and how people are different. There are three theoretical approaches commonly used in health and social care when we think of the person in relation to communication (these are psychodynamic, behavioural and humanist).

Theories in communication

KUS 8

The psychodynamic model was developed by Freud. He believed that people develop a view of themselves according to deep-rooted childhood experiences.

However, investigating feelings that the individual may have is a difficult and time consuming task. Therefore, as part of your job role, you should report and record the individual's reactions. Referral can then be made to the appropriate professional to enable appropriate counselling support to be given to the individual.

The behavioural model developed by Skinner examines the nature of learning that has taken place. If it has been positively rewarded then the behaviour is more likely to occur again.

The humanistic model is the belief that a hierarchy of needs is present for every person. Perhaps the most famous theorist to use this model is Maslow who developed a hierarchy of needs.

Maslow believed that factors that motivate people lie on an ascending scale. Once one group of needs is satisfied the individual will be motivated to move on to the next stage. For example, the individual will not be concerned about communicating their safety needs if their biological and physiological needs are not met.

Figure 11
Maslow's
hierarchy of needs

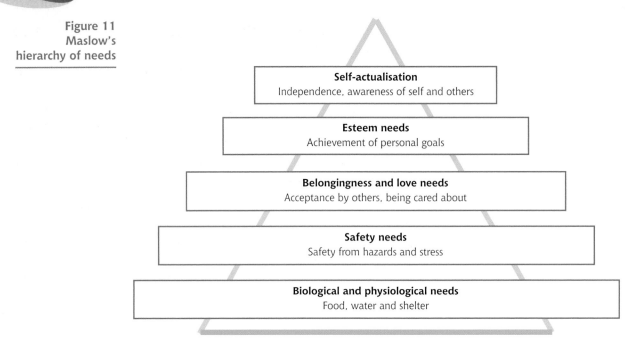

Carl Rogers believed that self-actualisation can happen when a relationship occurs and the person feels fully accepted and valued and genuine empathy is shown.

This model is seen in use with older people or individuals who have learning disabilities. The health and social care worker can show empathy and acceptance and this will help to promote a relationship where the individual feels valued.

Effective relationships

KUS 8

An important part of supporting individuals is helping them to express their preferred methods of communication. This will include providing any specific aids to communication or an interpreter if required. This will help to maintain independence, individuality and self-esteem. Choice in the nature of the support required can also help to promote effective relationships and overcome barriers to communication.

In health and social care it is important to establish effective relationships. For example, by overcoming barriers to communication and providing alternative methods of communication, for example interpreters, the individual will feel encouraged to express their feelings and emotions.

Confidentiality is also important in effective relationships and you should be aware of local and national policies regarding information sharing. This will help you to keep accurate records of the support required for communication.

KUS 8, 9

You need to recognise that there are number of social factors that may influence the effectiveness of your relationship with the individuals you support. These factors may include:

- *Age*, e.g. if an individual is older you may find it hard to relate to them and the experiences that they have had.

- *Gender*, e.g. a female may find it more difficult to share her feelings with a male worker.

- *Social class*, e.g. differences in social class may mean that the health and social-care worker finds it difficult to understand the individual's point of view on culture, diet, housing conditions and educational status.

- *Ethnicity*, e.g. a Muslim female will find it difficult to communicate well with a male health and social care worker.

- *Language*, e.g. if the individual's first language is not English then an interpreter must be obtained each time an interaction is to take place.

- *Power*, e.g. the individual will have less power in a health and social-care setting than the worker. This may cause the worker to feel that they know about the individual and what is best for them. This will lead to an unequal relationship and the individual may not be able to express what they want or feel.

Environment

KUS 12, 16

Being able to communicate clearly is a challenge in health and social-care settings, but by making small changes you can support individuals. The first aspect you should consider is the creation of the right environment. Look around and remove any distractions, for example a television that is blaring in the background which stops you hearing what the individual is saying. Also check that the furniture is positioned correctly in the room so that it does not impede communication. Make sure there is no furniture between yourself and the individual that could be a barrier.

**Figure 12
Creating the right environment in order to communicate effectively**

Recognise individuality

The ability to communicate effectively is more than just sticking to the rules of communication. You will need to look at each person as an individual with different needs. It is your responsibility to recognise and provide the support that individuals require in order to communicate.

Verbal communication

You will need to be aware of the language that an individual uses and whether any help is required. Speak in a clear voice using an appropriate language and provide support if required, for example an interpreter.

Non-verbal communication

Observe the body language and gestures of the individual. You should also pay attention to the tone and intonation and volume of the individual's voice. Again this can convey how the individual is feeling, for example they may be anxious, angry or sad. You can then provide the appropriate support to the individual.

Encourage feedback

Poor communication can lead to misunderstandings and can cause difficulties. Check that you have understood what the individual has told you. Perhaps you could use a phrase such as, 'Now let me check, have I got this clear?'

Obtain support

When the individual requires support in order for communication to occur, you should obtain information before the individual arrives detailing the support required. If this is not possible then you should talk to the individual, family, friends, other professionals, and refer to their care notes to clarify the additional support required.

KUS 6, 7

It is part of your job role to obtain appropriate support. This can include sign language, communication technologies and an interpreter. You should find out where help is available and how to access it. There may be procedures in your organisation that describe how to obtain help and who to approach, for example the local health authority to obtain an interpreter, or a support group, e.g. local centre for the Royal National Institute for the Deaf (RNID).

You may need to talk to colleagues to help to organise this support for the individual. Remember that all information should be recorded and confidentiality maintained according to organisational and national guidelines.

Support for others in the communication process

In health and social care you need to help others to understand what the individual wants to communicate and their preferred communication methods. This will enable effective communication between all those involved. These can include:

- Family, friends and others significant to the individual.
- Other members of the care team.
- Other professionals.
- Interpreters, translators and speech and language therapists.

Family, friends and others significant to the individual

In health and social care today the care needs of the individual are increasingly complex. This can result in family and friends having many encounters with different members of the individual's care team. You need to help families and friends to feel recognised as people whose ideas and concerns about communication are sought. You should make short summaries of what has been said in relation to communication. In this way you have recognised and responded to those thoughts and fears arising from communication.

If the individual requires help with communication and is using communication aids, tell family members and friends how these should be used. Also tell them if any specialised training is required, for example in the use of computers. This will help the individual engage and interact with those who are significant to them and continue to express emotions and feelings.

Other members of the care team

All information on the communication needs of the individual should be given to members of the care team. This will help them to build a relationship with the individual and will also help the individual to communicate feelings, fears and needs.

This information may be given verbally at a report time, but it should also be recorded in the individual's care plan. These records should be reviewed as stated in organisational policy and when any changes occur.

Other professionals

This can include professionals from your own organisation or those that will provide specialist treatment outside your organisation, for example speech and language therapists or interpreters and translators.

It is important that professionals receive verbal and written information about how individuals communicate. You should ensure that confidentiality is maintained and that you follow local and national policies on sharing information. Some organisations use one document where all professions record their information about an individual. This will help communication as everyone is aware of changes and the support required for that person.

You can also use a computer to support the exchange of information about an individual's communication. This will help to exchange ideas about an individual's care and needs and improve communication between the individual, yourself and other professionals. Updates on any changes in communication can also be made quickly using this method. When using this technology be careful to maintain confidentiality and follow policies in relation to this.

You can also receive help to improve communication by asking professionals how to provide support for individuals and answer any questions they have. This can be specialised support, for example interpreters.

Interpreters

KUS 13

An interpreter can be used to provide support for individuals to communicate. However, you should exercise caution when choosing an interpreter – family members should not be used. Family relationships are often strained and it can be difficult for the individual to discuss intimate matters.

Frequently the health authority, social services department or police have a list of interpreters. You will need to work closely with the interpreter to ensure that they know the correct name of the individual and their preferred form of address. Liaise with the interpreter and the individual's key worker and brief the interpreter about what is going to be discussed. It would also be best practice for you to stay with the interpreter when they speak to the individual.

Translators

Translators are there to help individuals access health and social care. They are there to act as **advocates** for the individual and to inform the professional of the individual's cultural and information needs. The translator can help provide written and verbal information to the individual and reduce anxieties that the individual may have.

Speech and language therapists

Speech and language therapists work with a wide range of individuals in health and social-care settings. Individuals may have problems with communication or difficulties chewing and swallowing. These can include individuals who have had accidents, those who have a speech defect, for example stammering, or those who have difficulty eating because of illness. A speech and language therapist will assess each individual and plan a programme of treatment. They will also work as part of a multidisciplinary team in health and social care.

Providing communication support

Darius is on holiday from Greece. He is 29 years old and has been admitted to hospital complaining of abdominal pain. It has been found that Darius requires an operation. Darius does not speak English and he is finding it difficult to understand what is happening. He is accompanied by his girlfriend who does not speak English and his young son aged 11. His son does understand English.

➤ *Explain how you would help Darius communicate.*

➤ *How would you help the doctors to communicate with Darius?*

➤ *How could Darius's family and girlfriend help?*

Encouraging individuals to communicate

KUS 2, 3

When supporting communication it is important that you encourage individuals to engage with others. This will help the individual to express their feelings and needs and maintain relationships.

By being able to express their feelings and needs, the individual can maintain their sense of identity, self-esteem, dignity and self-respect.

Support the individual to communicate by overcoming barriers and finding alternative communication methods. This will help the individual to engage with others and express feelings.

You should support the individual who has language difficulties, for example, loss of speech. This support can be given by liaising with professionals, for example speech and language therapists. The individual could also use pictures and pen and paper to support communication.

Another way of providing support for the individual to communicate is by ensuring that the environment is appropriate. You should try to reduce noise, and plan the environment before communication takes place.

If the individual has dementia you should ensure that aids work, repeat information and re-orientate if necessary.

If the individual is deaf-blind you should encourage them to use communication aids, to verbalise speech and to use sign language.

By giving this support the individual will be able to express how they are feeling and this can help to maintain relationships.

Speech problems

There are a number of speech problems that you may encounter as a health and social care worker.

Dysphasia and aphasia

KUS 9

Dysphasia is impairment in communication, and aphasia is the inability to communicate. Individuals with dysphasia or aphasia may have difficulty talking, understanding and listening. They can be mildly or severely affected and everyday tasks can be difficult to carry out, for example answering the phone. The damage to the brain that results in dysphasia or aphasia can be as a result of a stroke where the blood supply to the brain is interrupted. However, it is important to remember that individuals with these conditions can think clearly and understand what they are feeling. Speech therapy is important and you can help by speaking slowly, using gestures or drawings. Communication should also take place in an environment that is not too noisy and one where there are few distractions.

Dyspraxia

Dyspraxia can affect all areas of development including language. The cause of dyspraxia is brain injury and symptoms can include unsteady gait and difficulties performing routine tasks such as washing and dressing. People with dyspraxia will also have problems remembering messages and instructions and they will have poor handwriting. Working with a speech and language therapist you can help the individual overcome difficulties, for example it could help them with reading and writing activities.

Dementia

Alzheimer's disease is the most common cause of dementia. Individuals can experience communication problems and memory loss and will therefore find it difficult to remember information, instructions and messages. As the disease progresses the symptoms that the individual experiences can become more severe and the individual can become isolated. You can help the individual to improve their memory by reminiscence therapy.

Key points – supporting individuals to communicate

- You should arrange the environment to support communication.
- An individual can be supported through verbal and non-verbal communication.
- Communication can also be supported through communication aids.
- Family, friends and others significant to the individual can be supported by providing information about communication needs and helping them to use these.
- Communication with professionals can be a two-way process and information should be updated regularly.
- Individuals can be encouraged to communicate effectively, and barriers to communication can be overcome.

Update and maintain records and reports

Legal and organisational requirements and procedures for record keeping

KUS 5

Record keeping is central to good quality care as it facilitates the exchange of information between health and social-care professionals thus enabling them to provide appropriate and timely services to individuals. Professionals can also access records in order to see the clinical and care needs of the individual. The Access to Health Records Act 1990 and the Data Protection Act 1998 have resulted in individuals having easier access to records. Individuals have become more willing to complain about their care and this could lead to legal proceedings. Therefore good record keeping is essential. Cases can be won or lost on the basis of record keeping. According to the law and the Nursing and Midwifery Council (NMC), if an incident is not recorded in the notes then it did not happen.

In order to provide good quality care you should record what has happened during the period of time you have cared for the individual to enable others to take over that care. The law states that you should record information within 24 hours.

Good record keeping:

- Promotes high standards of care.
- Helps continuity of care.
- Facilitates good communication between staff within and from other organisations.
- Gives an accurate account of care and support needs.
- Helps to identify problems.

Records can be used as evidence in court cases and are essential reference documents when investigating a complaint. Therefore the records should be factual, accurate and current, and they should contain detailed information about the individual in your care. You need to check your organisation's policies on record keeping.

Access to records

The Access to Records Act 1990 gives an individual the right to receive and review their records. This has since been updated by the Data Protection Act 1998 which gives an individual the right to see and receive all computer-held and paper-based records about themselves. The Access to Records Act 1990 now only applies to the records of deceased individuals.

KUS 5

Since 2005, the Freedom of Information Act 2000 has granted rights of access by anyone to all information that is not covered by the Data Protection Act 1998. This usually applies to all information that does not contain details identifiable to an individual. In Scotland two publications, 'Partnerships for Care: Scotland's Health White Paper 2003' and 'How to Access Your Health Records (2003)', give details on the individual's rights to access health records.

All health and social care professionals have access to records and often use the same documentation to record details of care. You should check with your organisation or a senior member of staff for guidance on the correct format for recording documentation.

Computer-held records

Computer-held records are easier to read and are less bulky than handwritten records. In some hospitals records are now written on hand-held devices at the individual's bed. This can help the individual become more involved in the assessment and treatment of their health and social care needs.

Confidentiality is important with computer-held and faxed records and guidance on this is contained in the Computer Misuse Act 1990. Records held on a computer system must be password protected and you need to ask your manager about who has access to the system. Your contract of employment will contain guidance regarding your responsibility to maintain confidentiality, record keeping and not sharing your computer password. Breaching confidentiality is likely to result in disciplinary action.

Figure 13
Computer-held
records

Retention of records

Organisations are required to keep individuals' care records for a specific period of time. This will be determined by the government, for example the Human Rights Act 1998 and the Caldicott Report 1997 state that records are to be kept for eight years.

KUS 4

Recording information about communication and language

Recording health and social care information is an important part of your role. This includes recording details about individuals' communication and language needs and preferences to ensure that this information is passed on to all involved with supporting them.

KUS 17, 18, 19

All records about the individual's needs must be:

- Factual, accurate and written with the involvement of the individual where possible.
- Written as soon as possible after an event (e.g. an assessment, treatment or change in condition) has occurred.
- Written clearly and legibly, identifying the care planned, decisions made, care delivered and the information shared with others about the individual's needs.
- Signed by you and must show the date and time. You should ask your employers whether your name should be printed next to your signature.
- Jargon free with no abbreviations as these may not mean the same thing to all staff.
- Written in a way that the individual would understand.
- Entered consecutively in date order.

You should also ensure that you:

- Identify any problems with communication and record the action you have taken to rectify them.
- Identify any conflicts with communication and state how you have rectified these; give details of others involved and the steps agreed with the individual to overcome these problems.
- Report your findings to a senior member of staff and to other care workers to enable continuity of care.
- Store away your record to ensure that confidentiality is maintained as recommended by Essence of Care 2003 and the National Minimum Standards (Care Standards 2000).

It is important to remember that no one type of recording documentation is used across all care settings. If you are new to the setting you should ask your employer what documentation is used and how it should be completed.

Figure 14 Recording information

Assessing and recording communication needs

Mr Shah is admitted to the hospital following a stroke. You have been asked to complete records on the assessment of his communication needs.

> ➤ *How do you involve Mr Shah in this assessment of communication?*
> ➤ *When do you write up these records?*
> ➤ *What could you find on assessment of his communication needs?*
> ➤ *How do you record these?*
> ➤ *Who would you report to?*
> ➤ *What other professionals could be involved in the care?*
> ➤ *Where would they record their findings?*
> ➤ *Who has access to these records?*
> ➤ *How do you maintain confidentiality?*
> ➤ *What legislation is involved?*

Accessing records

Check which members of staff have access to records. You should access records only when you are clear that you have permission from your employer.

If the individual is holding their own records you should gain their permission to access these. This is particularly true if the individual is using a device that holds their records around their neck.

When recording information you should make sure that you access the correct records for the individual. Records should be made in a detailed way that accurately reflects the care you have given. All records should be made according to legal and organisational procedures and requirements. The records must be stored according to local and national policies. Records need to be kept in an office and stored within a locked filing cabinet where staff can access them. However, paper-based records become bulky and extra storage space is required for them. Paper-based records are also easily accessed and confidentiality can be breached.

If it appears that records are being misused, or you have difficulty accessing and updating records and reports, or confidentiality is breached you must inform senior members of staff. Usually breaches in confidentiality are a disciplinary matter and are dealt with immediately.

Reporting changes in communication and care needs

KUS 17, 18, 19

Care needs may change as a result of a change in the condition of an individual. It is important that you record any signs or symptoms that may indicate this change together with any decisions or actions you have made as a consequence. You should also record any conflicts that may have occurred and the subsequent action taken. All changes in communication should be recorded in the health and social care records. These should be recorded immediately or, if dealing with an emergency situation, within 24 hours of the change occurring.

- Records should be written in the presence of the individual so that a more accurate account of their changed communication or care needs can be made.
- Information about communication should be dated, the time must be recorded and you should sign the record.
- All changes in communication should be recorded in terms that the individual would understand.
- Your records should document the nature of the change, who you contacted and the care recommended.
- You should also record the effects of the care.
- Records should be reviewed again when required. You should check your organisation's policy on this.

Involving and supporting individuals

In some settings individuals hold their own health care records, e.g. those receiving maternity care, older people living at home. This helps them to become involved with their care as recommended by Essence of Care 2003. Individuals can be involved with and contribute to their assessment of communication needs and the support that has been recommended. Individuals should be told about their responsibilities in keeping these records safe. Check with your employer regarding how to gain individuals' consent to access these records.

Key points – updating and maintaining records

- Legislation covers the access, recording and storage of health care records.
- Guidelines should be followed when completing records.
- Records should be updated as soon as any changes occur.
- Confidentiality should be maintained.
- The individual should be involved in completing their records.

Unit HSC31

Are you ready for assessment?

Promote effective communication for and about individuals

This unit is about how you support individuals to communicate effectively. It includes how you communicate difficult, complex and sensitive issues that may be distressing, traumatic, frightening, threatening, pose a risk to or have serious implications for the individuals or key people such as family, friends or carers.

It is also about how you support individuals to communicate with others as well as supporting family, friends and other practitioners to communicate with the individual. It covers the potential barriers to communication and how these can be overcome. It is also about how you access, update and maintain records and reports on communication and maintain confidentiality using any form of communication.

Most of the evidence you need to cover the performance criteria and knowledge specifications can be gathered during your assessment in other units from your qualification, especially the optional units and also unit HSC35. You should consider this when planning these other units with your assessor.

Your assessment will be carried out mainly through observation by your assessor and this must provide most of the evidence for the elements in this unit. Evidence of your knowledge and understanding will be demonstrated through observation, your assessor examining work products, e.g. reports, minutes of meetings, as well as through answering oral and/or written questions.

Since this NVQ is all about how you work directly with people, there will be many opportunities for observation by your assessor. The scope of the NVQ unit is a helpful reminder of all the different aspects of communication that you are likely to use and will be helpful when planning your assessment. However, if observation by an assessor could intrude on the privacy of individuals then some performance criteria may require alternative sources of evidence of your work practice, such as expert witness testimony, in addition to other observations by your assessor.

Direct observation by your assessor

Your assessor will need to plan to see you carry out the performance criteria (PCs) in each of the elements in this unit. The performance criteria that may be difficult to meet through observation are:

- HSC31a PC 5
- HSC31b PC 9

Preparing to be observed

You must make sure that your workplace and any individuals and key people involved in your work agree to you being assessed. Explicit, informed consent must be obtained before you carry out any assessment activity that involves individuals or which involves access to confidential information related to their care.

Other types of evidence

You may need to present other forms of evidence in order to:

- Cover criteria not observed by your assessor.
- Show that you have the required knowledge, understanding and skills to claim competence in this area of practice.
- Ensure your work practice is consistent.

Your assessor may also need to ask you questions to confirm your knowledge and understanding and ensure that you can apply this to your practice.

Before your assessments you should read carefully the performance criteria for each element in the unit. Try to cover as much as you can during your observation but remember that you and your assessor can also plan for additional sources of evidence should full coverage of all performance criteria not be possible.

Check your knowledge

- What legislation is relevant in record keeping?
- Where do you find out about individuals' communication needs and preferences?
- Describe the specific aids that can be used to support communication.
- Describe how you would communicate sensitive information.
- Why is it important to support individuals to communicate?
- Why is it important to update and maintain records and reports?

Promote, monitor and maintain health, safety and security in the working environment

*T*his unit covers the health and safety of the care environment. It considers your role in promoting, monitoring and maintaining a healthy, safe and secure working environment for all those within it. It focuses on the identification of risks and hazards and the actions you take to minimise these on a day-to-day basis as well as in the event of an incident or emergency.

It contains the following elements:

⌒ **HSC32a** *Monitor and maintain the safety and security of the working environment*

⌒ **HSC32b** *Promote health and safety in the working environment*

⌒ **HSC32c** *Minimise the risks arising from emergencies*

Introduction

Health and social care is provided in a wide range of settings, e.g. a hospital, the individual's own home, or the local swimming pool when an individual is undertaking an activity. Maintaining the health and safety of the environment is an essential part of carrying out individual care and support. Care providers have a duty to care for those individuals they support and to make accurate and objective assessments of any risks that may compromise their safety and security. Employers also have a legal duty to minimise health and safety risks to workers. You have a responsibility to minimise the risks to yourself and others through being adequately and appropriately trained, adhering to organisational policies and procedures and demonstrating safe working practices at all times. As there are many different working environments you will have to alter your assessment of health and safety in each environment.

In 2002–2003, 9550 workers in the National Health Service (NHS) reported injuries that lasted for more than three days, and over half of these were as a result of handling, lifting or carrying. Although this figure shows a decrease on previous years, it is still a significant number and the NHS is only one care environment. The second most common type of injury resulted from slips, trips or falls. Good health and safety working practices must be adhered to by everyone in the care environment if injuries are to be minimised. The number of individuals whose well-being is compromised by poor health and safety standards is difficult to quantify. However, the impact on their care can be substantial, whether that's a longer stay in hospital, admission to hospital or limiting their independence and increasing their support needs. You therefore play a crucial role in keeping yourself, individuals and others with whom you work or are responsible for, safe and secure and minimising the risks present in the environment.

As part of your role you are responsible for role modelling good health and safety practice both in your own personal practice as well as when supervising others. To do this you need to have a clear understanding of health and safety legislation, organisational policies and procedures and how these are applied in day-to-day practice. It is important to remember the rights of the individuals involved when actively promoting health and safety. A balance must be struck between allowing personal freedom and protecting individuals from harm and between promoting health and allowing individuals to take responsibility for their own decisions. Therefore you must also be familiar with your organisation's policies and procedures for the promotion of equality, diversity and discrimination.

Monitor and maintain the safety and security of the working environment

Legal and organisational safety procedures

Wherever you work you will have to be aware of your organisation's procedures for maintaining safety and security. Policies and procedures will ensure that legal health and safety standards can be met. The following legislation exists to help promote these standards and is applicable in all working environments.

Table 1 Safety legislation

Health and Safety at Work Act 1974

Your health, safety and welfare are protected by law. Your employer has a duty to protect you and keep you informed about health and safety. These are direct quotes from the legislation:

'it shall be the duty of every employer to ensure, as far as reasonably practicable, the health, safety and welfare at work of all his employees'

'it shall be the duty of every employee to take reasonable care for the health and safety of himself and other people who may be affected by his act or omission at work'

Control of Substances Hazardous to Health Regulations 1994 (COSHH)

The COSHH Regulations are an extension to the Health and Safety at Work Act 1974 and apply to every workplace.

They control people's exposure to hazardous substances arising from workplace activities.

Hazardous substances must be labelled corrosive, irritant, harmful or toxic and may also carry warning diagrams. It is illegal to carry out work involving any substance hazardous to health without an assessment of the risks.

Manual Handling Operations Regulations 1992

The regulations require employers to avoid the need for hazardous manual handling, so far as is reasonably practicable; assess the risk of injury from any hazardous manual handling that cannot be avoided; and reduce the risk of injury from hazardous manual handling, so far as is reasonably practicable.

Employees have duties too. They should follow appropriate systems of work laid down for their safety; make proper use of equipment provided for their safety; co-operate with their employer of health and safety matters; inform the employer if they identify hazardous handling activities; take care to ensure that their activities do not put others at risk.

Social Security Act 1998

All organisations have a responsibility to supply and provide a means of recording and reporting any accidents or injuries. This is usually an accident report book or accident report form.

Management of Health and Safety at Work Regulations 1999

Employers must assess the risks to employees and make arrangements for their health and safety.

Food Safety Act 1990

Provides the main framework for all food law in the United Kingdom. It makes it an offence to provide food that is injurious to health because it is contaminated or not fit for human consumption.

Health and Safety (First Aid) Regulations 1981

Employers need to make provision for their employees to have access to first aid.

Data Protection Act 1984 and 1998

This covers the confidential storage, retrieval and handling of verbal, written and electronic information to protect the rights of the individual. It sets out guidelines and identifies good practice on the disclosure of information and breaching of confidentiality where this serves to protect the individual or others from harm.

Lifting Operations and Lifting Equipment Regulations 1998 (LOLER)

Applies to any lifting equipment used for lifting or lowering loads, e.g. hoists. The equipment must be safe for the purpose of lifting and all necessary precautions must have been taken to eliminate or minimise risks.

The Regulations require that lifting equipment provided for use at work is:

- Strong and stable enough for the particular use and marked to indicate safe working loads (including attachments such as slings).
- Positioned and installed to minimise any risks.
- Used safely, i.e. the work is planned, organised and performed by competent people.
- Subject to ongoing examination and, where appropriate, inspection by competent people. If equipment is used for lifting people then it must be examined at least six-monthly or at intervals laid down in an examination scheme drawn up by a competent person. Following an examination a report must be submitted to the employer to take appropriate action.

Your organisation has a responsibility to devise appropriate policies and procedures that ensure compliance with legal requirements and you must be familiar with these and how they inform your role and responsibilities. These might include the procedures shown in Table 2.

Table 2 Policies and procedures that ensure compliance with legal requirements

• **Manual handling**	Be sure that you move and handle objects and individuals safely, use designated equipment to help reduce the load and risk of injury.
• **Fire/evacuation policy**	Be sure that you know your organisation's fire and evacuation policy and procedure, and where you could access this information. You should also know the location of fire exits and fire fighting equipment and how to call for help.
• **Waste disposal policy**	Be sure that you know how waste is disposed of: what is the system for disposal of infected/soiled items, sharps such as needles, or for ordinary household waste? Be familiar with the use of different-coloured bags for the disposal of different types of waste.
• **Risk assessment**	Be sure that you understand the risks attached to each activity that you undertake and assess the risks regularly to see if these have increased or decreased.
• **Infection control policy**	Be sure you are familiar with policies that are designed to prevent the spread of infection, such as how to wash your hands properly and what special handling might be required for the care of individuals who may have an infection, e.g. those with MRSA. (See Figure 9 on page 56 on effective hand-washing technique.)

Identifying rights of entry

KUS 2, 3, 8

Security is one of the most important things to consider when monitoring and maintaining the health and safety of an environment. Look at who is coming in and out of the premises: do they have the right to be there? When entering an environment a stranger should identify themselves, preferably using a photograph identity card, and explain their need to be there. This is particularly important when visiting individuals in their own homes as they should feel comfortable about allowing visitors in. When visiting individuals it is important to remember that you are the visitor and therefore the individual has a right to decide whether you can enter the property.

**Figure 1
Security is
important**

When working within hospital or care settings rights of entry can be monitored more strictly, although security may at times be more difficult to monitor simply due to the amount of people entering and leaving the environment. Many places use closed-circuit television cameras (CCTV) to monitor visitors, especially if there are a number of entrances to a building. Security cameras are also useful if a security breach occurs, as it may be possible to refer back to footage to identify intruders. In areas such as maternity units, intensive care and mental health units, security can be particularly stringent and there may be additional locked doors or security guards on duty during visiting hours.

KUS 4, 15, 16

It is your responsibility to challenge a person who does not display proper identification and question their right to be there. You should be prepared to ask people to provide you with proper identification, but you must also be careful not to take unnecessary risks with your own personal safety. Ensure that you know your organisation's procedures for dealing with unidentified visitors and how to summon help if you need to.

Practical
Example

Unidentified visitors

Anna is at work in the care home where she has worked for the last five years. She is taking a woman in a wheelchair from the dayroom to her bedroom. When passing the reception area she notices a man she has never seen before going through individuals' records in the filing cabinet. He appears to be looking at various records and making notes. He has no visible signs of identification on him. Anna is on duty with three other staff and she knows that one is in the kitchen downstairs and the other two are on the top floor. As well as the individual that she is escorting, there are three other people in the dayroom down the corridor.

➤ *What should Anna do?*

➤ *What is Anna's immediate priority?*

➤ *Who is at risk?*

Assessing the risk

Before you start any workplace activity you must assess the risk to yourself and individuals you may be working with. An assessment of risk is a careful examination of what could cause harm in your workplace. These risks are known as hazards and you must assess whether there is a chance, however great or small, that someone will be harmed by the hazard.

Every day at work you assess risk on an informal basis without even thinking about it. You probably act without considering the safety aspects attached to what you are doing. For example, you wash your hands between patients to minimise the risk of infection spreading from one patient to another. Before serving food you take proper precautions according to your organisation's policy to ensure a clean environment, and that food is stored and served in a hygienic manner to prevent any transmission of infection. However, it is also necessary to have a formal approach to managing hazards in the workplace in order to meet organisational and legal requirements.

It is your responsibility as an employee to take notice of anything that you consider could be a health, safety or security risk and report this to your employer. Your employer will make an assessment of that risk and decide what action to take.

KUS 3, 4, 14

The government leaflet '5 steps to risk assessment' identifies the basic steps towards assessing risks in the workplace. These are:

- Look for and list the hazards.
- Decide who might be harmed and how.
- Evaluate the risks arising from the hazards and decide if existing precautions are adequate or whether more should be done.
- Record the findings.
- Review the assessment regularly and revise if necessary.

It is important to remember that when dealing with individuals, risk assessment and evaluation is an ongoing process. You will need to re-evaluate the risks attached to the tasks you are undertaking as their condition changes. For example, if an individual living at home suddenly becomes immobile you will need to think about how to move them around their home safely without putting them or yourself at risk.

You must also remember that it will not always be possible to completely eliminate all risks and the law accepts this. The Health and Safety Act 1974 states 'as far as reasonably practicable', so providing you have assessed and implemented the five steps above and taken every reasonable precaution to prevent an accident occurring, this will be considered acceptable.

Whilst you may make every effort to prevent accidents and eliminate hazards you will also have to consider the needs and wishes of individuals. Not everybody will be willing to co-operate with the health and safety measures you may wish to use. If an individual wishes to continue living in their own home even though they are unsteady on their feet and therefore at risk of having a fall, that wish must be considered. Even though it might be unsafe for them to remain there, individuals cannot be forced into compliance with assessments. Individuals should be enabled to make informed decisions with a clear explanation of the implications of their decision. Their wishes, preferences and choices must be considered against the balance of the risk. If they wish to remain in their own environment, every practicable step should be taken to eliminate as many hazards as possible.

Allowing individuals and key people to express their needs and preferences and assess any risks associated with these will encourage them to recognise and understand the risks and take and/or share responsibility for minimising the risks to their health, safety and well-being.

Monitoring the work area

Responsibility for health and safety lies with both the employer and the employee. You and your employer must monitor your work areas to ensure that they conform to health and safety regulations. Risk assessments are one way of identifying these risks and deciding on the best practices for managing them.

Not only is there a responsibility to observe health and safety in the environment, there is also the need to monitor actual working practices.

Working practices can be defined as:

- Activities.
- Procedures.
- Use of materials or equipment.
- Working techniques.

All working practices must be monitored according to the procedure laid down for your working environment. Different working environments could include:

- Within the premises of an organisation.
- On the premises of another organisation.
- In someone's home.
- Out in the community.

Whatever your working environment you will be able to identify the working practice appropriate to you.

Equipment

KUS 6, 12

When using equipment you must ensure that you are using it correctly in accordance with the manufacturer's instructions. Training should be given on the use of individual equipment and if necessary this training should be updated to take into account any changes or new developments. The types of equipment might include those shown in Table 3.

Table 3 Equipment that might be used in a care setting

Manual handling equipment	Mobility aids, hoists, sliding sheets.
Protective equipment	Gloves, aprons, goggles, personal alarms, mobile phones.
Electrical equipment	Computers, televisions, domestic appliances.
Fire-fighting equipment	Extinguishers, fire hoses, alarms, fire blankets.
Medical devices	Cardiac monitors, blood pressure monitors, thermometers, intravenous infusion pumps.

If you are not sure how to use a piece of equipment then you have a responsibility to let your employer know, as you will be putting yourself and others at risk if you use it incorrectly. Your employer should provide adequate training to ensure employees know how to use equipment safely.

Each piece of equipment should have instructions about how to use it and you should also refer to these. It is essential that you operate equipment properly and that the correct storage procedures are followed when the equipment is not in use. If this is not done equipment may deteriorate and its function may be impaired.

Materials

Materials can be regarded as hazardous or non-hazardous. The Control of Substances Hazardous to Health Regulations 1994 ensure that hazardous materials in the workplace are managed correctly and safely.

Substances hazardous to health include:
- Cleaning chemicals.
- Lotions.
- Potions.
- Dust.
- Anything toxic/corrosive.

The hazard could reach you, an individual or your colleagues via any of the following ways:

- Inhalation.
- Ingestion.
- Body contact.
- Absorption.
- Injection.

KUS 11, 12

Your responsibility is to make sure that you are aware of any dangers attached to hazardous materials that you are working with. Each identified hazardous material should carry a warning sign that should alert you to its toxic/corrosive components.

**Figure 2
Hazard warning
signs**

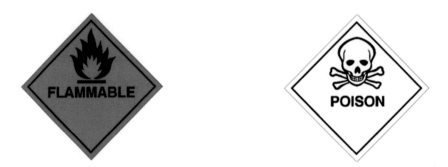

Once aware of the dangers of a particular substance, you should know how to protect yourself and other individuals against it. Make full use of personal protective equipment provided by your employer. If a material has been identified as hazardous a risk assessment will have been completed and there will be protocols on how to manage that substance in the event of a spillage. All employees should be aware of the procedures for clearing up spillages of hazardous and non-hazardous materials so that the correct protocol is followed.

KUS 12

You are required to dispose of waste products safely and quickly. The Environmental Protection Act 1990 imposes 'a duty of care' on producers of waste. Organisations are required to accept responsibility for waste management from the point of origin to ultimate disposal. You should know your employer's policy on the disposal of waste, particularly if you work in a large hospital where different types of waste will accumulate, and you should make sure that you carry out the correct procedure.

Observing and reporting on health and safety issues

KUS 3, 4, 11

The Health and Safety at Work Regulations 1999 require that employers identify and monitor risks, and that they provide proper training and equipment to promote safety. Proper safety procedures must also be in place in the event of an accident occurring, and all employees should be aware of these and how to put them into action.

As an employee you are not only responsible for your own health and safety, but also the health and safety of people in your care, staff and other individuals in your work environment. You should actively support and encourage others to observe health and safety precautions. If you feel that colleagues have not been adequately trained, or are not competent to use certain equipment or to implement certain procedures, you should advise them to seek extra help and support them in doing so. Colleagues who are less confident or inexperienced may look to you to guide them in an emergency.

Figure 3
Learn to use
safety equipment

KUS 18

Health and safety procedures also require that if new concerns about health and safety issues are raised you report these to the appropriate people. The term 'appropriate person' will be defined by the area in which you are working. Concerns should always be reported in the first case to your direct manager. If you are working in an individual's home you may also mention this to them and their family especially if their own safety will be affected. You should discuss these concerns with your manager and devise a plan to tackle the issue. It is important to document your concerns on the appropriate records used by your organisation. This formalises the issue and therefore requires a manager to investigate the concern. Failure to mention your concerns could result in an accident occurring and individuals being harmed.

Key points – monitoring and maintaining safety and security in the working environment

- Make sure you are familiar with your organisation's procedures for safety and security.
- Be aware of relevant legislation and how it applies in practice.
- Each individual is responsible for their own health and safety.
- Always wear an identification badge.
- Check visitors' rights to entry.
- Be able to recognise potential hazards.
- Use personal protective and other equipment according to guidelines and procedures.

Figure 4
An
accident/incident
report form

ACCIDENT / INCIDENT REPORTING FORM IR1	NAME OF REPORTING ESTABLISHMENT:	BASE:

1 About injured person

SURNAME of person injured	INJURED'S STATUS	OCCUPATION
OTHER NAMES	▫ EMPLOYEE ▫ CONTRACTOR ▫ SELF-EMPLOYED ▫ WORK EXPERIENCE ▫ PUPIL / STUDENT ▫ SERVICE USER ▫ VOLUNTEER ▫ VISITOR ▫ MEMBER OF PUBLIC ▫ OTHER please state:	**EMPLOYER** – If working for a contractor, give name and address of employer
INJURED'S HOME ADDRESS AGE		
POSTCODE TEL NO ▫ MALE ▫ FEMALE		

2 About the incident

CATEGORY OF INCIDENT: a) ACCIDENT b) DANGEROUS OCCURRENCE c) WORK RELATED DISEASE d) CHALLENGING NEEDS e) VIOLENCE AT WORK	DATE OF INCIDENT TIME OF INCIDENT include am or pm	EMERGENCY RESPONSE ▫ AMBULANCE ▫ FIRE ▫ POLICE ▫ NONE ▫ OTHER (please state) ....
WHERE DID IT HAPPEN? ▫ AT THE REPORTING ESTABLISHMENT ▫ ANOTHER O3W PREMISES/SITE ▫ SOMEONE ELSE'S PREMISES/SITE ▫ PUBLIC PLACE	PLACE ON SITE WHERE IT HAPPENED (eg room A19)	
ADDRESS WHERE INCIDENT HAPPENED (Omit if O3W)	NAMES OF WITNESSES (and addresses if not known by O3W)	
DESCRIBE BRIEFLY WHAT HAPPENED Attach another sheet if necessary. State what activity the person was doing.		

3 Injuries

DETAILS OF INJURIES / THE EXACT PART(S) OF THE BODY AFFECTED (eg burn to index finger, left hand)	MEDICAL TREATMENT GIVEN ▫ NONE ▫ FIRST AID ▫ GP/PRACTICE NURSE ▫ HOSPITAL IN-PATIENT ▫ HOSPITAL OUT-PATIENT	TIME OFF WORK ▫ NONE ▫ UP TO 2 DAYS ▫ LIKELY 3+ DAYS	CONSEQUENCE OF INJURY ▫ UNCONSCIOUS ▫ NEEDED RESUSCITATION ▫ HOSPITAL 24 HOURS +
		IF RELEVANT, HAS COUNSELLING/DEBRIEFING BEEN OFFERED? ▫ NO ▫ YES	

4 Violence at work

VIOLENCE AT WORK ONLY: Give assailant's name, address, status (see top of Form for status list), sex and approximate age. State if violence was physical, verbal or both.	HAVE YOU (OR DO YOU INTEND) REPORTING THIS TO THE POLICE? ▫ NO ▫ YES
	IF THE ALLEGED ASSAILANT IS A SERVICE USER, HOW LONG HAVE YOU WORKED WITH HIM/HER?
ARE THERE ANY GUIDELINES/PROCEDURES IN PLACE FOR SUCH INCIDENTS? ▫ NO ▫ YES	
WERE THESE PROCEDURES FOLLOWED? ▫ NO ▫ YES	
Signature of person filling in above details	Print name of person filling in above details

5 Actions

MAIN FACTORS THAT CONTRIBUTED TOWARD THE INCIDENT eg conditions, actions, equipment	IMMEDIATE ACTIONS TAKEN TO PREVENT A FURTHER INCIDENT

6 Manager's Comments

I believe the statements made within this report are correct **SIGNATURE OF MANAGER / SECTION HEAD**	PRINT NAME OF MANAGER/SECTION HEAD	DATE SIGNED	SHEETS ATTACHED. If yes, state how many ▫ NO ▫ YES .... sheets

Promote health and safety in the working environment

Minimising and managing risks

This element focuses on how you should actively promote health and safety in the working environment, both for yourself, individuals and your colleagues.

In order to do this effectively you must measure the risk and decide if there is a chance, however great or small, that someone will be harmed by the hazard.

KUS 11, 14, 18

In the workplace you are responsible for identifying risks and taking action to prevent them becoming so severe that they cause accidents. In this way you are actively promoting health and safety. One way to do this is to carry out a formal risk assessment of an identified hazard.

All working environments are different and will pose different threats or hazards. The first step when carrying out a risk assessment is to identify a hazard that has the potential to cause significant harm. Look around your own working environment and try to identify hazards that would fall into this category. Examples of potential hazards are listed below.

Substances hazardous to health include:

- Trailing cables.
- Fumes.
- Heavy objects.
- Uncovered plate of food.
- Wet floors.
- Noise.
- Poor lighting.
- High shelving.

You may have seen one or more of the above or may have identified a completely different set of hazards. It is important to remember that these will vary greatly depending on your working environment. If you study Figure 5, how many hazards can you identify?

**Figure 5
How many
hazards are there?**

When you have identified a hazard you must decide how it has the potential to harm. Who would be at risk from the hazard? This could be you, individuals, other colleagues, visitors or anyone coming into the area who may not be aware of the risk.

You must decide what, if anything, you can do to reduce the risk. This may range from a relatively simple action, for example placing a yellow hazard sign to indicate a spillage/wet surface, to something much more complicated, for example evacuating the area if the spillage is hazardous and may cause breathing difficulties. There may even be a cost implication for your employer if the hazard is severe.

Figure 6
The type of risk
assessment form
that might be
used in the
workplace

| RISK ASSESSMENT FOR

Company Name:

Company address:

Postcode: | ASSESSMENT UNDERTAKEN

(date)
Signed
Date | ASSESSMENT REVIEW

Date |
|---|---|---|
| List the significant hazards: | List the groups of people who are at risk from the significant hazards you have identified: | List existing controls or note where the information may be found. List the risks which are not adequately controlled and the action needed: |

Limits of your role and responsibilities

KUS 17, 18

Whilst you have a responsibility to report hazards and to be aware of risks in the working environment there is a limit to your role or responsibility. Depending on your level of responsibility this will either be to notice and report the hazard or to take action. Identifying hazards, completing risk assessments and implementing changes are examples of one way to reduce risks and promote health and safety. There may also be other ways to demonstrate this.

KUS 9

You may be seen as a role model. More junior or new staff may look up to you; they may turn to you for guidance in certain circumstances where they are unsure how to manage situations. You must be aware of this and make sure that you observe all the proper health and safety procedures. When new procedures and policies are introduced into the working area, as part of your role you will be expected to help implement these changes. You could be asked to demonstrate new procedures to more junior staff, so you should ensure that you have had adequate training yourself in order that you feel comfortable offering advice and teaching colleagues. Part of your role will also be to support individuals and colleagues to assess and manage the risks to their own health and safety and so you need to have a good working knowledge of these areas in order to meet this responsibility. You could do this through coaching the individual, i.e. by demonstrating and explaining how and why, followed by observing and giving constructive feedback to them when they undertake the task. Or you could involve them in risk assessment and management.

As a role model you are in a position of trust, and you must be able to judge the limits of your role and how far your responsibility stretches. You must be able to recognise when to seek further help yourself from senior colleagues and you must not take on tasks which fall outside your responsibility. If you take unnecessary risks, you could endanger yourself, your colleagues and the individuals you provide care for. You expect help and guidance from your manager and you should be prepared to offer this to your colleagues. A role model sets an example. This may not just be to your colleagues but also individuals and visitors coming into your working environment. It is about giving an impression of professionalism and confidence in the work that is being carried out and this includes not only your knowledge but also your appearance and your manner towards others: it encompasses your whole approach to working.

KUS 16, 18

It is very important that you remember the limits of your role and your responsibility and do not take advantage of others by abusing your position.

Promote health and safety in the working environment by observing the policies and procedures yourself. You must always let colleagues know where you are and the work you are carrying out. This demonstrates good communication and team building and is essential in maintaining health and safety in the environment. If there is an emergency situation, for your own safety your colleagues and manager must know how to locate you.

Safe procedures for moving and handling

KUS 13, 18

One of the key aspects of heath and safety is how you implement moving and handling procedures. As mentioned in the first element of this unit, health and social care workers are governed by the Manual Handling Operations Regulations 1992. You must be familiar with your own workplace's procedures for moving and handling and ensure you keep to these. Back injuries in the workplace are a major cause of sickness at work and can result in long-term disability. You may also cause injury to the individuals you are caring for.

Moving and handling are part of your everyday working life. You are moving, carrying and supporting objects all the time. These could be small items like books, files and trays or larger items such as beds, trolleys, chairs etc. You may also be required to move individuals if they are unable to move themselves or to assist them with a partial move. Before you move anything you must consider the risk to yourself or others and ask yourself the following questions:

- Do I need to move this object or person?
- If I do need to move this object or person how can I make it easier?
- Is there equipment available to help me?
- Do I need another person to help me?

You may need to move an object in a number of different ways, for example pushing, pulling, lifting to carry the object or to lower it to the ground. There are special manual handling techniques and equipment to use when moving people: you must be adequately trained to use these techniques and equipment.

Points to remember

Load:

- What are you moving?
- How heavy is it?
- Is it an awkward shape?
- Can you get a good grip on it?
- If it is an individual can they move themselves?
- Is the load likely to do anything unpredictable?

Environment:

- Where is the load situated?
- Will you have to stretch up or bend down to pick it up?
- Is there enough light – can you see what you are doing?
- What is on the floor – is it slippery, can you stand firmly?
- Will you have to twist into a confined space to reach it?

Task:

- Where is the load going?
- How far does it need to be transported?
- How often does it need to be moved?

Individual:

- Can you move this load?
- Can you move the load alone?
- Do you require help?
- Who is going to help me?

**Figure 7
The wrong way to
lift and move
things**

**Figure 8
The right way to
lift and move
things**

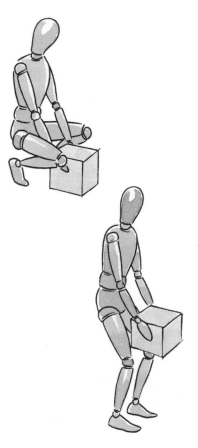

There are many ways to reduce the stresses and strains that moving and handling objects may cause. You can use the different types of equipment provided by your employer to help you, such as hoists and sliding sheets. You should use trolleys to move objects long distances rather than carrying them. Make sure that you adjust items to the right height so you do not have to strain your back by bending, e.g. beds. If you raise a bed or other object for manual handling, always put it back to the original position. Ensure that tables and trolleys with wheels work properly and that you are not twisting to control them. Make proper use of stair lifts and wheelchairs to avoid unnecessary handling of individuals.

You must also be aware that when working, colleagues will look to you to lead and co-ordinate the move. It is essential that you give clear instructions to avoid any misunderstandings that could cause an accident. You must assess together what you are going to do and be very clear on how to achieve it. If you are using a piece of equipment you must make sure that your colleagues are familiar with and know how to use it. Equally, when working with individuals and helping them to move, you must be clear that they understand what is happening. If the individual can move themselves then they should as this will reduce the amount you need to do. This will also encourage their independence. You need to allow sufficient time and space for any manoeuvre so that you or the individual does not feel rushed as this can create undue stress and increase the risk of injury.

You must always consider the individual's dignity and not leave them exposed or feeling vulnerable. If using a hoist you need to take time to position it correctly. If you need to take an individual from one place to another, e.g. from bedroom to bathroom, it is better to transport them in a wheelchair and use the hoist when you get there, e.g. in the bathroom. You must never leave an individual alone while they are in a hoist, so it is important to plan the activity well before you start.

Practical Example

Moving and handling an individual safely

Michael is a 102 kg man who has recently had a right below-knee amputation. He is also mildly confused. He has fallen on the floor whilst trying to get out of bed to go to the toilet. He is now lying on the floor. He has been incontinent of urine. He tells you that he is not hurt, but needs help to get up.

➤ *What risks are there?*
➤ *What must you do before thinking about moving Michael?*
➤ *How would you help Michael into the chair?*
➤ *Who would you report this to?*

MRSA – good hygiene in infection control

Recently the problem of effective infection control through safe working practices has been highlighted by the rise in the occurrence of Methicillin-Resistant *Staphylococcus Aureus* (MRSA). The infection has become a serious problem in care settings worldwide. This has partly been due to the overuse of antibiotics with the result that this bacterium now has a resistance to some antibiotics. However, a significant factor in the spread of this common bacterium (it is carried by a significant percentage of the population without any ill effect to them) has been the presence of low standards of hygiene and poor use of infection control techniques in care settings. The presence of MRSA means a prolonged recovery for the individual as it takes longer to treat any infection. It may be fatal for individuals who already have a weak or compromised (inefficient) immune system as they have fewer natural reserves to fight infection.

KUS 8, 18

Contrary to many people's worries MRSA-positive individuals are not a risk to other individuals, staff, visitors or members of their family, including babies, children and pregnant women. The Department of Health has stated that there is no justification for discriminating against people who have MRSA by refusing them admission to a nursing or residential home or by treating them differently from other residents. Individuals with MRSA should be helped with hygiene if their mental or physical condition makes it difficult for them to manage these areas independently.

As a senior care worker you may need to reassure others about MRSA and the perceived risks as well as acting as an effective role model in demonstrating good hygiene practice.

**Figure 9
Effective hand-
washing
technique**

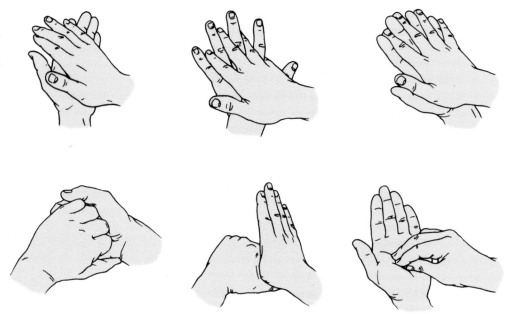

KUS 11, 12

Risk assessment and good hygiene practices are the key to managing MRSA-positive individuals and minimising the risks of cross-infection to staff and other individuals. Good practice points include:

- A risk assessment undertaken by a competent person to determine how MRSA will affect the individual and the potential cross-infection risks to others.
- The individual's care plan must indicate if they are MRSA positive and it should include clearly written management guidelines.
- All care staff must be familiar with organisational policies and procedures regarding infection control including MRSA prevention and management.
- All workers must adhere to effective hand-washing and general hygiene precautions (see Figure 9).

The Department of Health also advises the following:

- MRSA-positive individuals may share a room as long as neither they nor the person with whom they are sharing has open wounds, drips or catheters.
- MRSA-positive individuals with open wounds should be allocated single rooms if possible.
- MRSA-positive individuals may join other residents in communal areas such as sitting or dining rooms as long as any wounds or sores are covered with an appropriate dressing which is changed regularly.
- MRSA-positive individuals may receive visitors and go out of the home, for example to see their family or friends.
- Care workers with eczema or psoriasis should not perform intimate nursing care for MRSA-positive individuals.
- Care workers should complete any procedures for other individuals before providing care interventions, e.g. dressings or personal care, for MRSA-positive individuals.
- Any clinical procedures and dressings on an MRSA-positive individual must be undertaken in the person's own room.
- Care workers must ask for and follow expert infection control advice from the consultant in communicable diseases control and/or an infection-control nurse for any MRSA-positive individual who has a post-operative wound, drip or a catheter.

Avoiding potential accidents

In any care environment there is always the potential for an accident. Individuals may be injured and people in your care are particularly at risk.

Certain people are more vulnerable than others. Older people, small children, confused individuals or those who suffer with a mental or physical disability are more at risk of an accident. You must show that you take appropriate action when there is the likelihood of an accident or injury occurring.

The potential for an accident may sometimes seem small, but even those activities that seem safe may be more hazardous than you think. For example, you should be aware of sharp corners on worktops or tables as these may be easily knocked as you walk past; they could cause quite severe bruising to colleagues or individuals. You may work frequently with sharp objects such as knives, scissors or needles, and you should take care to put these away properly so that they cannot cause injury. Needles, as well as being sharp, carry the added risk of possibly transmitting infection if they have been used. Needle-stick injuries can have severe implications for health-care workers and can be serious. You must make sure that all sharps are disposed of immediately in the designated sharps areas.

KUS 14, 18

The risk that individuals will fall is another significant hazard that you need to be aware of. This risk is considered so severe, especially in older people, that it represents standard six of the National Service Framework for Older People (2001). (See also unit

HSC343.) The after effects of a fall can cause reduced mobility, a fracture, pressure injury, loss of confidence and at worst death. Individuals who have fallen need increased care and this has time and cost implications as well as implications for the independence of the individual involved.

KUS 9, 11

Try to eliminate the dangers of falling by being constantly alert to hazards, such as unsuitable footwear ('sloppy slippers'), slippery floors, trailing flexes etc. It is your responsibility to remove these hazards or, if the hazards cannot be removed, to warn people they are there by putting up signs. Individuals may be particularly at risk if they are unsteady and frail or have reduced **cognitive awareness** or sight. These dangers exist not only in the care environment but also in the individual's home.

KUS 10, 15

Individuals who are confused are less likely to recognise danger signs and this increases the risks to their security. There are many reasons for people being confused, e.g. a lack of familiarity with the environment, depression, sleep deprivation, infection (especially a chest or urinary infection), dementia or a side-effect of the medication they are taking. They may wander into areas that are not safe or out of fire exits, setting off alarms. If an individual is in their own home this may not pose such a problem as they will be familiar with their surroundings and comforted by them. Some people who are confused become aggressive if constrained. You must judge the risk to each person individually, and as a team you should agree a course of action to protect the individual and allow them some freedom as well. You have a responsibility to protect individuals against potential accidents especially when they are unable to do this themselves. You should always know where individuals in your care are so that you can anticipate any potential problems.

KUS 12

Other potential accidents in the workplace may include spillages of hazardous body fluids. You must be aware of your organisation's policy and procedure for clearing up spills of blood, urine, faeces, vomit or any other body fluids that could cause harm or transmit infection. You should also know how to dispose of these properly according to the waste-disposal policy. Make proper use of personal protective equipment when dealing with any body fluids. This could include wearing gloves, aprons and goggles to prevent splashes entering the eyes. If you do not use protective equipment you are more likely to transmit infection from one individual to another (see page 43).

Completing health and safety records

No matter how hard you try to avoid them, accidents will occur. When they do you must know the correct way to report and record them.

In addition to carrying out risk assessments there may be other health and safety records that you need to complete regularly. This will vary depending on your working environment. There should be routine checks of equipment to ensure that it is working correctly. This will be conducted either by outside contractors or by your organisation's works department. Equipment is usually checked annually and then a date is placed on it stating when it was checked. This applies to all equipment: electrical, gas appliances and medical equipment. If there is then an incident involving a piece of equipment, you can refer back and see when it was last serviced.

In addition to these routine maintenance checks you may also be required to carry out health and safety checks on a daily or weekly basis. Some medical equipment requires checking and recalibrating frequently to ensure it works correctly. If you check these items then you will document your results, and this forms part of the safety record for that item. Some specialised mattresses and beds need to be checked on a daily/weekly basis to make sure they are safe for individuals. Manual handling equipment such as hoists is required to be tested by a competent person every six months. Security procedures and fire alarms also need to be tested and records completed. There are many routine health and safety records that are completed on a regular basis.

KUS 3, 4, 13

If an accident or incident does occur, as well as carrying out the correct emergency procedures you must know how to report these and who to report them to. Incidents could include:

- Intruders.
- Chemical spillages/contamination risks.
- Lost property.
- Missing individuals.
- Individuals locked out.
- Aggressive/dangerous encounters.
- Bomb scares.

Accidents could involve:

- Falls.
- Hazards in the environment.
- Illness.
- Disability.
- Weaknesses.
- Sensory and **cognitive impairment**.
- Frailty.

KUS 16

Looking at the above list some incidents appear far more serious than others. Be aware that they must all be reported. Some can be handled within your own department and some must be dealt with by your organisation. Your organisation will have standard incident/accident forms to be completed. Make sure you know how to access these and how to complete them. When you complete them ensure that all details are correct and state the facts. You should record the accident/incident that occurred, the date, time and place and personal details of those involved so that they can be contacted later if necessary. These documents may be used as evidence if the incident is so serious that further action such as a claim for damages is made, so it is very important that you complete them correctly.

KUS 3, 4

In some instances the accident/incident is so serious that it has to be reported under RIDDOR 95. RIDDOR 95 stands for Reporting of Injuries, Diseases and Dangerous Occurrences Regulations 1995, which came into force in April 1996.

This is a statutory requirement applicable to all employers, and it means that employers must report work-related accidents, diseases and dangerous occurrences.

The purpose of this is to identify where the greatest risks occur and to look at serious accidents. The Health and Safety Executive (HSE) enforce RIDDOR and offer advice on how to prevent accidents. The things that must be reported are work-related:

- Deaths.
- Major injuries.
- Reportable diseases, e.g. tuberculosis.
- Dangerous occurrences.
- Gas incidents.

The Regulations apply to all working environments, and hopefully this type of occurrence will be rare within the care environment.

Whatever your working environment you must be aware that accidents will occur even though you have completed a risk assessment and reviewed it regularly. You are not expected necessarily to prevent all accidents from occurring, but you should take reasonable care or yourself and others. If you are familiar with all of your organisation's procedures and policies you should feel confident to do this.

Key points – health and safety in the working environment

- You are responsible for actively promoting health and safety in the workplace.
- Identify the risks and hazards in your workplace and recognise which individuals are at risk.
- Know how to undertake and record a risk assessment.
- Understand your responsibilities as a role model for others as well as your limitations in relation to health and safety.
- Demonstrate good hygiene practice to limit the possibility of cross-infection.
- Be able to move and handle objects and individuals safely.
- Know the correct procedures for reporting and recording incidents.

Minimise the risks arising from emergencies

Health and environmental emergencies

Although every effort is made to minimise risks in any care setting there are times when an **emergency** or **incident** may occur. This could involve the individuals in your care, their relatives, your colleagues, visitors or workers in the environment. The type of emergency and the resources available to help you deal with it will vary depending on where you work. For example, if you work in a hospital you will have quicker access to help from other people and specialist equipment will be available. In the community you may be working alone and there will be a delay in help arriving and little access to any specialist equipment. You need to be aware of the types of emergency that you may have to deal with and be able to recognise the signs and symptoms and what action to take in each case. In all emergencies the priorities are the same: to preserve life, prevent the situation from worsening and promote recovery.

If an emergency occurs you may be the first person on the scene to deal with it or raise the alarm, or you may be summoned by someone else to assist them. You will be able to deal with an emergency better if you take a structured approach (see Figure **10**).

**Figure 10
A structured
emergency
response
procedure**

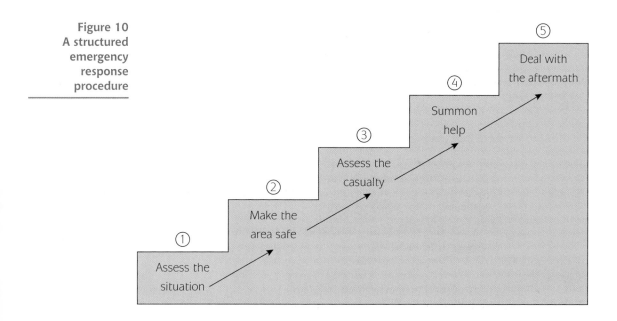

- *Step 1: Assess the situation.* If you hear an alarm, or a colleague shouts for help then you need to act quickly. You must be calm, quick and controlled. If you know the policies and procedures for the different emergencies that could occur you will be much more confident in your ability to cope.

- *Step 2: Safety.* Make sure that you follow the procedures to maintain the health and safety of everyone involved. Before approaching the emergency check the safety of the area. Is it safe for you to go in? If the emergency is environmental it may not be safe to go in, for example in a suspected fire or gas leak. Prioritise – you need to work out what your priorities are in any emergency situation. First you need to protect your own safety. If you have assessed the situation correctly and made sure it is safe then you can help others. You must not go into a situation if you would be endangering your self. You should call for assistance and let the professionals, such as the fire brigade or ambulance service, deal with the situation.

- *Step 3: Make an initial assessment of the casualty and give emergency aid.* You need to check the situation quickly and calmly. Ask yourself the following questions: How many people are affected by the emergency? Are they injured and if so are you able to initiate the relevant first aid? If you need to evacuate the area you must have an accurate picture of numbers involved, routes available to you and the ability of the individuals to move themselves. You also need to make sure that you prevent further injury to individuals. If you have more than one casualty in a situation then you should give priority to the most seriously injured person. You must also try to maintain the privacy and dignity of the individuals at all times. In any emergency there will be an element of panic. You need to be able to offer reassurance using a calming but confident voice. Individuals will inevitably be upset by what is happening, so you should reassure them that the situation is being dealt with and is under control.

- *Step 4: Summon assistance*. In all emergency situations you will need assistance. You must call for help immediately. This may involve shouting to other colleagues or setting off alarms or emergency buzzers, or in some cases calling the emergency services. No one can manage an emergency alone and you should not try to as doing so could cause further injury or worsen the situation.

- *Step 5: Dealing with the aftermath*. Once the situation has been dealt with it is important to make the area and individuals within it safe and secure. You will need to report and record all that has happened and complete any required documentation. You will also need to ensure that individuals and others involved are given time to talk through what happened in a more relaxed atmosphere, perhaps over a hot drink. With colleagues this may be a more formal debriefing where the incident or emergency is discussed in depth and conclusions or recommendations about handling similar incidents in future are made. It is also an opportunity for people to discuss their feelings and to receive constructive feedback on their actions. This will help people to feel more confident about dealing with future incidents. It is important that discussion following these events provides you with an opportunity to reflect on the incident, what you learnt and any development needs identified.

KUS 5, 7

Taking a structured approach will help you to manage your own anxieties better. It will also enable you to take appropriate action to keep yourself and others safe while working effectively and efficiently to deal with any immediate danger. Your safety in an emergency situation is not a luxury, it is a necessity. Without the ability to function effectively or if your actions are unsafe or reckless, the individuals you are trying to help will be in even greater danger. You may have a senior position within your workplace and so you have a responsibility as a role model for others. In an emergency, therefore, they will look to you to take the lead and provide them with clear guidance and support. Emergencies may be related to an individual's health, e.g. a fall, heart attack or choking, or an environmental emergency which could potentially affect the whole workplace, e.g. a fire, gas leak or an intruder.

KUS 16, 17, 18

Health care emergencies

A number of different types of health emergencies can occur in the workplace. Health emergencies that require first-aid intervention must be dealt with by someone who has received appropriate, up-to-date first-aid training. Reading about how to deal with a health emergency is no substitute for actually practising what to do under expert guidance on a first-aid course and having your competence assessed by an appropriately qualified person. Any first-aid course should also include how to manage your own feelings in an emergency situation. If you have not attended a first-aid course then it would be advisable to discuss this with your manager or supervisor and access this as part of your development. Ideally there should always be a qualified first aider on duty in your workplace. In addition there should be policies and procedures detailing what action to take in the event of an emergency and you must ensure you are familiar with these. In this area as much as any other it is important that you recognise and accept the limitations of your own abilities and do not try to act beyond your level of competence in treating other people's injuries.

KUS 18

Signs and symptoms of some common health emergencies

The following information is designed to raise your awareness or refresh your memory about common first-aid situations. It is not intended as a comprehensive guide or a substitute for first-aid training.

Unconsciousness

Often the first sign that an individual is experiencing a health emergency is when they lose consciousness. Although this can happen for a number of reasons it is important that you follow the emergency response procedure and carry out an initial assessment. If the individual is unconscious this means you must check their airway, breathing and circulation (ABC).

Figure 11
Check ABC

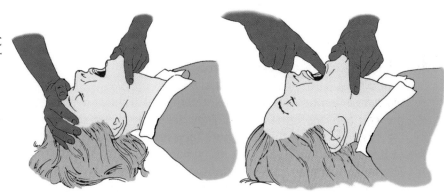

If the individual is not breathing you must raise the alarm immediately. It is vital to seek medical help immediately to ensure the individual is receiving oxygen as without oxygen brain function will begin to deteriorate after three minutes and other organs will also be affected. Delays in treatment can lead to death. If you have been trained on how to give cardiopulmonary resuscitation (CPR) then you should proceed, but ensure you have summoned help before you start as once you start CPR you should not stop until help arrives to support you.

If the person is breathing, they need to be placed in the recovery position (see Figure 12) if you know how to do this and it is safe to do so. If you do not know what to do then you need to summon help immediately. The individual should not be placed in the recovery position if you suspect they have a head, neck or back injury. In these cases they should not be moved unless there is a risk they will choke, e.g. in cases of suspected overdose or poisoning.

Figure 12
Put a breathing
but unconscious
casualty into the
recovery position

The recovery position is used to prevent the injured individual from choking, e.g. if they vomit or there is something stuck in their airway. You can also use this position to turn an unconscious person in bed. You must always support them and turn them towards you to prevent them rolling out of bed.

Choking

Choking is a common problem affecting the individual's airway. It may be caused by an obstruction, such as an object lodged in the airway, or an asthma attack. If the individual's airway becomes obstructed they will experience difficulty breathing. They may have noisy laboured breathing and find it hard to breathe. They will probably be coughing and spluttering, producing excessive saliva and they may find it difficult or impossible to speak. In extreme cases the individual's skin colour will change as they are not receiving an adequate supply of oxygen to their body. You can test this by gently pressing the nail bed. Initially when pressed the nail bed will go pale and then the colour in the nail will return immediately. If they are not receiving sufficient oxygen the nail bed will remain pale. They are likely to become distressed quite quickly as they struggle to breathe. The more they struggle the more distressed they may become, so it is essential that you seek immediate help and reassure the individual throughout. The individual may lose consciousness.

If the individual is choking then you need to do the following:

- Reassure them.
- Sit them down so that they are leaning forward.
- Encourage them to cough hard to try and remove the blockage from their airway.
- If this does not work then you need to give them up to five sharp slaps on their back between their shoulder blades with the flat part of your hand whilst taking care to support their head. Stop as soon as the obstruction clears.

If the back slaps do not work then you need to give five abdominal thrusts and repeat this procedure until help arrives. If the individual becomes unconscious then the emergency services must be called and the first aider should attempt artificial ventilation.

Figure 13
Back slaps and
the abdominal
thrust/Heimlich
manoeuvre

Breathing problems

An individual may also have breathing problems if they are experiencing a cardiac arrest, a stroke (a cerebrovascular accident or CVA) or an asthma attack. In the case of an asthma attack the individual is likely to have been given clear instructions on how to manage their condition. If they are not responding to these measures, e.g. use of their inhaler, then you must summon help. You may need to support them in using their inhaler until help arrives and if they become unconscious then remember the ABC procedures and follow these.

Shock

This is caused by stress or an injury which results in an inadequate amount of oxygen getting to the brain and other vital organs. Shock could be an after-effect of any of the other emergencies mentioned here. The individual may be pale/grey in colour, have a rapid but weak pulse and shallow fast breathing. They might be cold and sweaty, and may complain of feeling faint. You need to improve the blood supply to the vital organs. If you know how to and if it is possible, place the individual in the recovery position as this will help to improve the circulation of blood to the heart and brain. Try to keep them calm, and reassure them. Do not give them anything to drink or eat, and call for help.

Some types of shock, such as anaphylactic shock (severe allergy) and septic shock (severe infection) may present different symptoms, but what you need to remember is that if an individual is unwell they need help.

Heart attack (also called cardiac arrest)

This occurs when the heart stops working effectively and so stops pumping blood and oxygen around the body. The individual may complain of a crushing chest pain and possibly pain down their left arm and/or into the neck. They will be sweaty, breathless and pale. Do not move the individual unnecessarily as this will place a strain on the heart. Try to keep the individual calm and try to improve the oxygen supply – loosen tight clothing and if sitting try to encourage them to lean forward slightly as this will

KUS 7

help their breathing. You need to preserve their dignity and privacy and move others away from the scene as this can be an added pressure. They will need a lot of reassurance from you as they will be frightened, anxious and in considerable pain. If the heart stops pumping altogether they will rapidly become unconscious. As before, assess the individual and provide the appropriate first aid if you are trained to do so, e.g. summon help before starting CPR.

Epileptic fit

In this situation the individual will suddenly become rigid, or have a sudden fall or have convulsions, and they could stop breathing. Some individuals who have had epilepsy for a long time are able to tell when they are about to have a seizure, but you cannot rely on this. If the individual is going to fall try to break their fall but do not catch them as you may hurt yourself. You should protect them from dangers around them but do not physically restrain them during convulsions. You need to preserve their dignity and privacy and move others away from the scene. You should support and protect their head; move furniture and other obstacles to stop them hurting themselves. Once the main seizure has passed you need to move the individual into the recovery position. Although you may have heard that people having a seizure can swallow their tongue, it is not possible to do this; you can do more harm than good by trying to force something between their teeth. After the seizure, the person may be very disorientated and confused, and they will need help, support and reassurance until they are fully alert. You may want to talk to them about what triggered the seizure as this can help to either avoid or limit the possibility of a reoccurrence.

KUS 9

Fall/fractures

The individual may complain of pain or the fracture may be obvious from the way they are lying. It may not be clear whether a fracture has been sustained, but if in doubt you should treat as if it is a fracture until expert help has been obtained. Check the individual all over before attempting to move them. Look for deformity, swelling, pain, shortening of the limb and inability to move the affected limb. Keep the individual calm, still and as comfortable as possible (e.g. keep them warm) until help arrives.

Electric shock

The individual may be unconscious, and you may be able to see burns at the entry and exit points where the electric shock has passed through. Before you approach make sure it is safe – either switch off the electricity supply or knock away the appliance with a non-conductive instrument such as a wooden broom handle. If necessary you may have to initiate CPR, otherwise you should place the individual in the recovery position.

Burns/scalds

These can be caused by, for example, fire, any hot objects, steam, hot water and oil, hot electrical appliances or even from extreme cold. If the burn is superficial the individual will experience more pain as nerve endings are near the surface of the skin. Deep burns are more serious but will feel less painful. You must attempt to cool the area with cold water, using wet towels for at least 10 minutes. If possible remove jewellery (in case of swelling) and clothing from the affected area. Do not remove

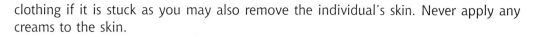

clothing if it is stuck as you may also remove the individual's skin. Never apply any creams to the skin.

Bleeding

First identify where the bleeding is coming from. If it is external then apply direct pressure to the wound. If there is an object embedded in the wound then apply pressure on each side of the object. You should wear protective gloves if at all possible or ask the individual to put their own hand over the wound and then, if possible, raise it above the heart to reduce blood loss. A clean dressing could be applied. The individual will need to receive emergency treatment.

**Figure 14
Elevating a wound
above the heart
will help to slow
blood loss**

Dealing with a health emergency

While working in the kitchen at the care home, Vicky hears a sudden crash from one of the residents' rooms. When she arrives she finds an older woman lying on the floor, she is unconscious and frothing at the mouth. Vicky does not know where any of the other staff are, there is no emergency call bell and the nearest telephone is at the end of the corridor.

➤ *What is Vicky's first priority?*
➤ *How can Vicky obtain help?*
➤ *What should Vicky do to help the lady?*

Environmental emergencies

In addition to health care emergencies you may also have to deal with environmental emergencies. Here are some examples although there are many general incidents.

Fire

KUS 4, 16, 18

Workplaces must follow the fire precautions set out in the Fire Precaution Act 1971 and the Workplace (Fire Precautions) Regulations 1999 and the Health and Safety at Work Act 1974, as mentioned previously. You must know the fire evacuation procedures for your place of work and the location of fire alarms and fire-fighting equipment. It is the responsibility of your employer to make sure that you have adequate fire training and that this is updated on a yearly basis. It is your responsibility to observe proper precautions on a day-to-day basis to avoid increasing the risk of fire. There are some routine practices that you should carry out daily to limit the risk of a fire:

- *Do not block or wedge open fire doors*. The purpose of a fire door is to delay the progress of the fire; this allows valuable time for evacuation. If it is wedged open it cannot provide the seal required to delay the fire.
- *Empty waste-bins regularly*. Fire feeds on oxygen, heat and fuel. Rubbish provides that fuel. If you empty bins regularly the fire will be deprived of its essential needs more quickly.
- *Make sure that you put everything away tidily*. Do not stack boxes or other items in corridors, again these provide fuel for a fire. They are also a hazard and may even be blocking an escape route.
- *Check smoke detectors regularly to make sure they are working*. Replace the batteries when required, but at least annually. Make sure someone has responsibility for doing this and that it is carried out.
- *Many places operate a no smoking policy*. If this is the case in your workplace, you have a responsibility to make sure it is adhered to. Remind visitors and staff of the policy and direct them to designated areas if there are any. If you work in an individual's home then you will not be able to enforce a no smoking policy, but you can encourage the use of deep ashtrays and empty them often, ensure that cigarettes are stubbed out properly and discourage the individual from smoking in bed.

Gas leak

If you smell gas you should open doors and windows. Check the gas appliances to see if they are turned off and check if the pilot lights are out. Turn the gas off at the mains if you know how to. You should know the emergency procedure in your area and phone the appropriate numbers.

Do not turn on the light switches, do not light a match, use door bells or mobile phones or anything that could produce a spark and cause an explosion. Evacuate staff and other individuals until the gas leak is identified and resolved.

Security breach

You must be vigilant about security, particularly at night. Ensure that the security protocol is observed and that relevant doors and windows are locked. Any alarms should be switched on. If you notice that something has been tampered with and there is no obvious explanation for it, e.g. an external door has been opened, you should summon help and be very careful about proceeding any further in case there is an intruder.

Responsibilities in an emergency

KUS 6, 18

Once you are aware of the type of emergencies that could occur in your area, make sure you know how to manage them. Remember that junior staff may look to you to take the lead in the management of any emergency. Ensure you know how and where to access information about dealing with emergency situations and follow the emergency response procedure outlined on page 61.

Support and report to professionals in emergencies

Part of your assessment in an emergency will involve identifying appropriate help and support. Who you call for assistance will depend on the type of emergency. This may include the fire brigade, paramedics, a gas engineer, the police, doctors or nurses. Whoever you need to call, once they arrive you should follow their lead and give them as much support as possible.

You should provide an adequate handover of the situation. If it is a health care emergency medical personnel will need the following information:

KUS 3, 4, 16

- The time that the incident occurred.
- What happened leading up to the health emergency.
- How many people are involved.
- Medical history of the individual including any medication they are taking.
- The name and age of the individual.
- What first-aid treatment you have administered.

The more information you can give, the easier it will be for the emergency services to provide ongoing care.

In the event of a fire/gas emergency, the following information will be needed:

- Location of the incident (gas leak/fire).
- Number of personnel in the building.
- Have any individuals been evacuated and if so where have they been taken?
- Is anyone unaccounted for?
- Has anybody tried to tackle the fire?
- Location of fire-fighting equipment/gas mains.

In the event of a security breach, you should call the police or the security guard if you work in an area where a guard is employed. The police will need to know:

- Who discovered the problem.
- How regularly that area is checked.
- Once they have investigated, you will need to tell them if you think anything is missing.
- Whether anything is damaged.

- Who has been in the area recently so they can be eliminated from the investigation.

It is not always your responsibility to provide all of this information, but you must know where the information is kept, such as stock lists, details of individuals' property etc., so that you can obtain these if needed.

Once the emergency has passed you will need to deal with the after-effects. There are several aspects to this:

KUS 3, 4, 16

- *Legal* – official documentation may have to be completed by law, such as a police or fire report. Although it may not fall within your responsibility to complete these, you may be able to provide important information about what happened. It is a good idea after an emergency to jot down some notes for yourself because you will quickly forget exact details.

- *Organisational* – as well as outside agencies your organisation will have procedures in place to follow up incidents. Records need to be kept of incidents that occur. Reports need to be accurate, complete, factual and legible. Following an incident policies and procedures may be reviewed. Accurate and complete accounts will help this process and may lead to changes to eliminate the risk of a reoccurrence.

- *Personal* – you will need to take into account how others feel about what has happened. When people have experienced a shock they can often be distressed, so you must try to offer comfort where you can. This may include practical support such as providing a cup of tea, or contacting friends and relatives. It may also mean providing emotional support such as listening, or appropriate and acceptable physical comfort, e.g. a hand on the individual's arm/shoulder.

KUS 5

- *Yourself* – as well as taking care of other people's needs remember that you may need to talk to someone about what has happened. You may be upset as a result of the incident or may feel that you did not handle some aspects of it well. You should be offered an opportunity to discuss things, maybe as part of a group with others involved or on an individual basis. Talking experiences through you will help you gain confidence in your ability to deal with problems as well as identify where you might need to get more training or support to enable you to cope better the next time.

Key points – responding to emergencies

- Identify the emergency situations that could occur in your work area.
- Use the emergency response procedure to ensure you take a structured approach to dealing with an emergency.
- Know the organisational procedures to be carried out in any emergency, including basic first aid.
- Know your responsibilities and the limits of these in an emergency situation.
- Know when and how to summon help.
- Remember to keep notes of what happened in case they are needed later.

Unit
HSC32

Are you ready for assessment?

Promote, monitor and maintain health, safety and security in the working environment

This unit is about how you promote health and safety and monitor and maintain a safe and secure working environment. It is about how you ensure that you maintain safe working practices and as a result minimise risks that arise from emergency situations. It covers how you identify risks to individuals, yourself and others and the actions you take to minimise these risks. It is also about the actions you take in accordance with procedures in the event of a health or environmental emergency in order to minimise any risks that may be present.

Your assessment will be carried out mainly through observation by your assessor and this should provide most of the evidence for the elements in this unit. Your assessor must observe you for some part of each element. The scope relating to emergencies and element HSC32c is broad enough to enable you to evidence your competence through your normal work activities. However, if this is not possible then simulation is permitted for this element. You will need to discuss this with your assessor. Evidence of your knowledge and understanding will be demonstrated through observation, your assessor examining work products, e.g. reports, minutes of meetings, as well as through answering oral and/or written questions.

You need to be aware when planning assessments that this unit relates to both the core and optional units and you may be able to evidence performance criteria for these.

Direct observation by your assessor

Your assessor will need to plan to see you carry out the performance criteria (PCs) in each of the elements in this unit. The performance criteria that may be difficult to meet through observation are:

- **HSC32b PC 6**

Preparing to be observed

You must make sure that your workplace and any individuals and key people involved in your work agree to you being assessed. Explicit, informed consent must be obtained before you carry out any assessment activity that involves individuals or which involves access to confidential information related to their care.

Before your assessments you should read carefully the performance criteria for each element in the unit. Try to cover as much as you can during your observation but remember that you and your assessor can also plan for additional sources of evidence should full coverage of all performance criteria not be possible. ▶

Other types of evidence

You may need to present other forms of evidence in order to:

- Cover criteria not observed by your assessor.
- Show that you have the required knowledge, understanding and skills to claim competence in this area of practice.
- Ensure your work practice is consistent.

Your assessor may also need to ask you questions to confirm your knowledge and understanding and ensure that you can apply this to your practice.

Check your knowledge

- What are the main legal requirements for health and safety in the working environment?
- How would you carry out a risk assessment?
- How do you store hazardous materials in your work area?
- What are the main principles of moving and handling?
- How do you promote the health and safety of others?
- What are the limits of your role in an emergency?
- How can you support others to deal with stress?
- How do you dispose of both hazardous and non-hazardous waste in your area?

Reflect on and develop your practice

This unit focuses on the need for care workers to reflect on their work, to use this to evaluate how effective they are within their job role and to take an active role in developing their knowledge and skills.

The unit contains two elements:

- **HSC33a** *Reflect on your own practice*
- **HSC33b** *Take action to enhance your practice*

Introduction

Why is it important to continually develop knowledge and skills?

Learning is something that we do throughout our lives – it is no longer considered to be something we do only when we are younger. **Lifelong learning** is seen as important, whether it is learning with the purpose of gaining qualifications or related to hobbies or leisure interests.

In most areas of the country a wide variety of lifelong learning opportunities are available through local schools and colleges as well as other organisations, for example evening or weekend courses on DIY skills, cooking, dancing, local history etc. The list is seemingly endless! The internet provides the opportunity for learning at a pace and a time convenient to the person.

The interest in lifelong learning is growing in the workplace too, especially within health and social-care work. Research has shown that people who are involved in any kind of learning are more receptive to new ideas and find it easier to adapt to changes that occur in their life and work. Health and social care work involves considerable change and so it is important to continue developing your knowledge and skills in order to remain up to date and competent.

Background to continuing professional development

KUS 3, 4

Since the 1980s health and social-care work has increasingly recognised the need for and value of lifelong learning or **continuing professional development (CPD)**.

Changes in legislation such as the National Health Service and Community Care Act 1990, the Care Standards Act 2000, the NHS Plan 2000 and government White Papers such as 'Modernising the Social Care Workforce' (1998), all emphasised the need for a workforce that is responsive to social change and the expectations of those accessing health and social care services.

Recent legislation is aimed at raising the quality and standard of care. In order to support this process, standards have been set with regard to qualifications, training and development opportunities for people working in health and social care.

All newly employed staff are now required to undertake a structured induction programme that has to be completed within the first 12 weeks of employment, and then progress on to the Care NVQ 2 or 3 depending on their job role and responsibility.

Health and social care workers will eventually be registered to practise with one of the four social care councils. They will be required regularly to demonstrate how they maintain their CPD and currency of work practice, as is the case for other practitioners, e.g. general nurses.

These changes are intended to professionalise health and social care work and provide career pathways linked to qualifications and registration requirements. This should raise the status and value placed on health and social care work. It should encourage people working within the sector and attract others to join this challenging and rewarding area of work.

Element HSC33a   *Reflect on your own practice*

Analysing and reflecting on your work practice

Analysing your work practice involves breaking down the tasks that you do as part of your role so that you can gain a better understanding of each task. To do this you need to think about what actions you take to achieve the task effectively and to the required standards. Many people find it difficult to think about what they do and determine what ensures that they complete the task successfully or competently.

The following questions may help you to do this:

Figure 1
Think about the task in the following way

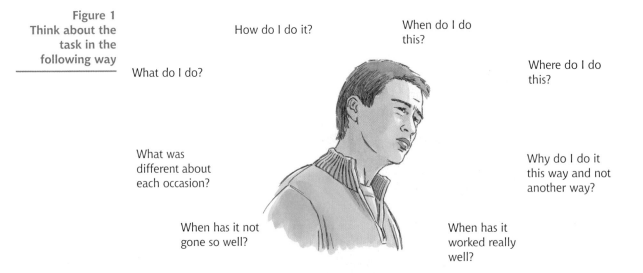

How do I do it?

When do I do this?

What do I do?

Where do I do this?

What was different about each occasion?

Why do I do it this way and not another way?

When has it not gone so well?

When has it worked really well?

Before you can begin **analysing** and **reflecting** on what you are required to do as part of your job role, you will need to be clear about what that role is. Your job description will outline the key tasks that you are expected to carry out as part of your job. It will also have details of your responsibilities to individuals, colleagues and your employer.

To help you analyse your current work practice and your effectiveness in performing your role and meeting your responsibilities you will need the following:

- A copy of your job description.
- Access to or copies of your organisation's policies and procedures relating to your work role and responsibilities.
- Access to or copies of the national standards and guidelines that relate to your area of work as these also set the standards by which you can analyse your competence.

National minimum standards and service frameworks may include, for example, the care standards that apply to your establishment as well as specific government guidance, for example 'Valuing people and supporting people' relates to working with adults with learning difficulties.

Understanding your role and responsibilities

Many job descriptions use NVQ competencies to outline the main tasks within a job role, others may use statements to list the tasks you are required to do. If you are uncertain about any part of your job description or you have been working in your current job for a while and your job description does not closely reflect what you currently do, ask to discuss this with your supervisor. This will be a useful opportunity for you to check that your understanding of your role and responsibilities is the same as that of your supervisor.

**Figure 2
Talk to your
supervisor if you
are unsure about
your job
description**

**OUTREACH 3 WAY
SENIOR SUPPORT WORKER**

SECTION I

LOCATION:	
JOB TITLE:	**Senior Support worker**
QUALIFICATION REQUIREMENTS:	**NVQ 3 preferred**
POST ACCOUNTABLE TO:	**Residential House Manager**
OTHER MAJOR CONTACTS:	**Supported Housing Manager, Chief Executive, CTPLD (Community Team for People with Learning Difficulties)**
GRIEVANCE OFFICER:	**Supported Housing Manager**

SECTION II

Function or purpose: To work as part of the senior management team to ensure that the home is managed in accordance with the organisation's policies, and that all day to day procedures are carried out effectively. To be directly involved in the delivery of personal care and appropriately meeting the emotinal needs of the service users. To provide the necessary stimulation, encouragement, and care, to enable service useers to achieve their individual potential.

DUTIES

- To provide support, advice and assistance with personal care to the service users as required, including toileting, washing, bathing, showering, oral hygiene, shaving, hair care and nail cutting (except where professional attention is needed). Also support service users to maintain their bedrooms i.e. making beds clean and tidy.
- To attend monthly staff meetings which all staff are required to attend. Communicate affectively with colleagues and contribute to the exchange of ideas through staff meetings and regular supervision in order to promote good care practice with the staff team.
- To maintain a professional manner and code of confidentiality in all matter relating to the service, and the service users.
- To assist service users in developing skills related to living independently i.e. shopping, cooking, supporting where necessary in understanding the importance of an adequate nutritional diet, and advising them in accordance with their health.
- Support service users where necessary with GP/Hospital visits and provide medical assistance where necessary.
- To undeerstand the full range of Support Workers, duties and participate in Support Workers, inductions and ongoing training.
- Assist in the organisation and supervision of individual group activities.
- Prepare and distribute medication (following appropriate training) strictly in accordance with the organisation's directives.
- Ensure that personal plans of service users are kept up to date and that appropriate information is recorded.
- **Be conversant with:**
- a) Fire precautions and evacuation procedures at a supervisory level.
- b) Admission and discharge procedures.
- c) The procedure of altering emergency services e.g. engineers, electricians etc.
- Monitor the quality of the service provision as directed, and support the practise of a high level of Health and Safety within a residential setting.
- Work in accordance with Equal Opportunities policy, and promote anti-discriminatory practice and opportunities for service users and employees.
- To support service users, ongoing personal development, the exercise of choice and to foster self reliance and facilitate the development of mutual support. To support service users in taking on the responsibility of citizenship, and maintain and develop a network of relationships within the community.
- Identify and arrange for provision of training for service users as appropriate.
- To facilitate, attend and record meetings with other staff and service users involved in service provision.
- To assist service users in maintaining and developing leisure interests i.e. supporting service users to plan outings and holidays and to escort them where necessary.
- To advocate for the service useers where appropriate.
- Assess, plan, implement, monitor and review care plans and risk assessments and maintain accurate record at all times.
- To liaise with other professionals – CTPLD's (Community Team for People with Learning Difficulties) Work placement officers employers etc, and support multi agency working where appropriate.
- Undertake other duties as required by the organisation.

Person Specification	Essential	Desirable	To be Evidenced by
A QUALIFICATIONS			
1 NVQ Level 2/3	X		Interview
B EXPERIENCE			
1 Experience of work in a care setting	X		Application form/certificate
2 Experience of work with other agencies	X		Application form/interview
3 Full range of personal care tasks	X		Application form/interview
4 Experience of working as a team	X		Application form
C KNOWLEDGE			
1 Awareness of risk management and health and safety requirements	X		Interview
2 Awareness of organisation policies and implications for practice, e.g., Health and Safety	X		Interview
3 Broad understanding of the enabliing role required for supporting adults with a learning difficulty	X		Interview
4 Awareness of the five accomplishments relating to the service for adults with learning difficulties i.e. Community presence, relationships, choice, competence and respect	X		Interview
D SKILLS			
1 Ability to communicate effectively with service users, carers, clleagues and members of the wider community	X		Interview
2 Ability to train/develop skills in others		X	Interview
3 Ability to support service users in developing self esteem and self reliance	X		Interview
4 Understanding of budgets		X	Application form/interview
5 Ability to lead staff without authoritarian approach	X		Interview
6 Able to handle difficult behaviour with service users/colleagues	X		Interview
7 Able to motivate other staff	X		Interview
8 Ability to write reports about service users and to record informaiton accurately	X		Interview
9 Contribute to care management process by supporting or advocating for service users and to record at meetings	X		Interview
E VALUES			
1 Non-judgemental approach	X		Whole process
2 Promotion of equal opportunities and anti-discriminatory practiceX	X		Whole interview process
3 Commitment to best value principles	X		Interview
4 Loyalty to the organisation	X		Interview
F PERSONAL ATTRIBUTES			
1 Willingness to undetake NVQ training	X		Interview
2 Team Player	X		Interview

Think about each of the tasks on your job description and consider the following questions:

- When do I do this?
- How well do I think I do this?
- How confident do I feel doing this?
- How do I know how well I do this?
- Who gives me feedback about my ability to do this task?
- Are there any parts of this task I feel less confident about doing or would like help with?
- Do I consistently do this task to the expected standard?
- How does this affect the people I work with and support?

If you can answer these questions you will begin to get a sense of how competent you are, where your strengths are and any areas of uncertainty where you feel you need to develop your knowledge or skills.

People are often reluctant to admit that they do not know something or are unable to do something as they fear others will judge them unfavourably. However, being able to identify what you need help with shows a professional approach and a commitment to working safely and in the best interests of individuals and colleagues.

KUS 9,11

Like many care workers, you may find it difficult to think about how and why you do things and you might find it particularly difficult to consider what you are good at and why your approach to a task works well. You might think that you can learn more from your mistakes than from the things that you do well. This may be true if you take time to reflect on what happened and get constructive feedback about how you could have done things differently. However, you can learn more from reflecting on those things you do well, especially if you also ask for and receive constructive feedback from others.

You can then add this learning and understanding to your pool of knowledge and skills. As a consequence you will find that when a similar situation arises you will be able to adapt and apply your learning to help you understand and work out a way of dealing with the situation. The ability to transfer your knowledge, understanding and skills to new situations is an important aspect of working with people as everyone you work with is a unique individual and requires an individual response to their needs.

The organisation you work for is likely to have a philosophy or view that the best-quality service is one which strives to provide individualised client care. The organisational policies and procedures will describe how the organisation aims to achieve this through its workers.

Organisational policies and procedures

Organisational policies and procedures are a key information source to help you to understand your role and responsibility. There will be procedures relating to the organisation and its workers meeting legal requirements, for example fire evacuation, checking fridge temperatures and administration of medication. Other policies and procedures may relate to working according to good practice guidelines such as adult protection procedures, reporting and recording procedures etc.

It is relatively easy to analyse if you are competent at these tasks as they are measurable. That is, if it is part of your job to do these tasks then there will be some evidence to show how and when you have completed them. This may be through examining records you have made, e.g. fridge temperature records, medication records or care plan entries. Indeed as part of evidence gathering for your NVQ these records will be good sources to evidence your competence to your assessor.

KUS 1

Other policies may relate to the ethos, philosophy, values or principles by which the organisation provides services to individuals. These may include equal opportunities policies, person-centred planning, promoting independence, supporting activities, individual choice and managing risk.

It is often more difficult to analyse how well we achieve these aspects of our work with others. Sometimes particular situations make this analysis easier, for example supporting an individual to develop or maintain their independence or make informed choices regarding risk. However, the day-to-day promotion of rights, choice, dignity, respect and individuality can be harder to analyse as you may view it as just part of what you do. Demonstrating these attitudes and behaviours with each person that you work with is what makes the difference between doing the job and doing the job well.

KUS 9, 11

As part of your NVQ your assessor will observe how you demonstrate these values and principles in practice in the way that you work with people. They will provide you with constructive feedback and this will help you to recognise your competence in this area of your work. NVQs are one type of national standard that you can use to help you understand your job role and responsibility. There are others that relate specifically to how health and social care services are provided.

National standards and guidelines

National standards and guidelines are important as they provide organisations and individuals working in the health and social care sector with examples of accepted good practice. These examples set the standards or benchmarks which are then used to measure the quality of care being provided to individuals. As a worker it is important that you know and understand what these standards mean in practice as you are expected to meet these when you undertake tasks within your job role.

KUS 3, 4

The Commission for Social Care Inspection (CSCI) (in England) and the Healthcare Commission advise organisations about the expected standards of care and carry our regular inspections to ensure the standards are being met. You may have been involved in an inspection when it was being carried out in your workplace.

If your workplace is registered and receives CSCI inspections then there will be a copy of the Care Standards – National Minimum Standards within your workplace. If you have not read these then you could ask your supervisor for a copy to read as part of your development.

Alternatively you can obtain a copy from the CSCI website: www.csci.org.uk. You can find out about the Healthcare Commission by visiting their website at www.healthcarecommission.org.uk.

The national minimum standards and inspection requirements provide guidelines to help you understand why certain activities take place as well as the reasons for many of the organisational policies and procedures. Together these will provide you with a framework which you can then use to monitor your work practice and evaluate how effective you are within your role.

Monitoring and evaluating your work practice

As a health and social care worker it is important for you to have opportunities to take a step back from your day-to-day work in order to monitor or check the quality and effectiveness of your work practice. This is true regardless of whether you have been working in health and social care for many years or whether you are relatively new to this area of work, as learning is a lifelong experience. Monitoring and evaluation processes can be either formal or informal. Being able to make the best use of these opportunities will help you to reflect on and develop your practice.

KUS 5, 8, 9, 11

Formal monitoring and evaluation processes are more structured and planned. Examples of this are supervision or appraisal with your manager or supervisor or a formal debriefing discussion following a critical incident, such as an abusive incident or an accident. This would take place at a prearranged time and have an agreed framework. The processes are designed to guide you through reflection and evaluation and to give you feedback, with the purpose of stimulating your learning and developing your practice. Self-reflection, however, is a more informal process where you reflect on, for example, how your day went or how you dealt with a particular incident, and you learn for yourself. The formal monitoring of performance and development is generally through supervision, carried out every 4–8 weeks, and an annual appraisal.

Supervision

One of the key ways in which you would reflect on your practice and consider whether you are achieving the required standards and working effectively within your role and responsibilities is through regular discussions with your supervisor.

KUS 5

This discussion time is often called 'supervision'. Supervision is your opportunity to review what you have been doing within your work role. It is also an opportunity to talk through new areas of work and get constructive feedback from your supervisor/ manager on your performance and to consider your ongoing professional development. You may be working in a situation where you are responsible for supervising other staff. As a supervisor you will be viewed as a role model for other workers. The way that you supervise them is important and the principles of supervision listed below apply to how you are supervised as well as how you supervise others.

**Figure 4
Supervising others**

You should agree the items for discussion with your supervisor/manager beforehand so that you can have time to prepare and think about them. Supervision can include a variety of topics although most models of supervision would include the following items:

- The work that has been allocated to the worker (including areas they are uncertain about and would like advice about).
- Discussion about their work, progress and feedback on this (including how well they are working with people).
- Personal learning and development – goals and progress.

KUS 8, 9, 11

Having supervision, or time to think about your work and your own development, is an important aspect of care work. Working with people is complex and having time to reflect helps workers to remain clear about their role and responsibilities and the limits or boundaries of these.

Supervision provides a structured opportunity to step away from work so that you can reflect or think back on particular situations and how you dealt with them. You can reflect on why you did what you did at the time, what you learned from the situation, and how you might use what you learnt to help you deal with similar situations in the future. In addition to this your supervisor will give you constructive feedback on how effectively you handled the situation. Your supervisor will explore how you use your knowledge and skills in your work as well as your attitudes, behaviour and your ability to form effective supportive relationships with individuals and colleagues.

They will give you constructive feedback about your strengths or areas that need further development. The aim is to enable you to identify what actions you need to take to improve your practice. Receiving constructive feedback should also help you to develop your skills of reflection and evaluation. Feedback from others will give you other views or perspectives to consider. All of these things together help you to learn and develop your competence and confidence. A particularly important part of feedback is information from others about the way that you relate to other people.

Being given feedback by others about the way that you do things and relate to other people will help you to learn more about yourself and the impact your behaviour has on other people. Once you begin to gain these insights you can start to understand your relationships with other people and what it is that makes the difference between a care worker and a good care worker.

Remember, it is not just what you do, it is the way that you do it that makes the difference.

As a care worker you will need to develop relationships with a wide range of people that you may not come into contact with in the usual course of your life. To be effective at doing this you need to develop good people skills. For relationships to work both people need to understand one another. So you will need to understand the other person and their needs and circumstances, and you will also need to understand yourself.

KUS 2

Supervision is an opportunity to learn more about yourself and how others see you, and the effect your actions have on those you work with. For people who work with people it is important to be able to recognise and understand the factors that have influenced your beliefs, values and attitudes and the effect or impact these have on your work and relationships with other people. Practice dilemmas and conflicts can occur when your views and those of individuals and/or the organisation differ. For example, different attitudes towards risk taking can create tensions. Supervision provides an opportunity to discuss these tensions and reconcile them so that they do not indirectly lead to discriminatory practice or compromise the quality of support you provide.

Supervision is a confidential meeting, unless agreed otherwise, and you should receive a copy of any notes made during supervision so that you can refer to these between meetings, especially if actions and timescales for completion were identified.

When supervising others it is important to remember to focus on the workers' needs and the desired outcomes for the individuals they support. You need to be clear about what is expected of the worker in terms of role and responsibility and what constitutes effective practice. You also need to know about the organisation's supervision policy and access to any specific training. Supervising another worker will involve you using active listening skills, being able to analyse and paraphrase their comments and reflect them back for further consideration and discussion. Supervision will also involve using your experience, knowledge and skills to develop others. You will find that the process of supervising is a developmental process for both you and the worker.

Appraisal

KUS 5

All workers in health and social care are required to have a personal development plan and this is usually negotiated and agreed with your manager or supervisor at the appraisal meeting each year.

Appraisal is an opportunity to review the previous year as well as to look forward and plan your development for the coming year. You should receive the appraisal document (this could be your personal development plan) prior to the appraisal meeting so that you have time to prepare and reflect on your performance and development over the past year as well as review any goals set. Before the meeting you will need to consider what you would like to achieve and what development opportunities you wish to explore to help you improve your practice in the coming year.

At your appraisal you will have an opportunity to discuss your plans as well as receive constructive feedback from your supervisor.

KUS 8

Your supervisor will also prepare for the appraisal meeting. As part of their preparations your supervisor may observe you working, ask other people for feedback on your work with them or make other checks on your work practice, e.g. review your care plan entries. Getting feedback from a range of different sources will help your supervisor to give you more specific feedback that you can then use effectively to identify how you can improve your practice.

At your appraisal you will be able to plan the development activities you are required to undertake in the next year, e.g. fire training, manual handling update, as well as those that you have identified to meet your aspirations and those that are designed to improve your performance. For example, you may have identified undertaking your NVQ 3 as a development goal. Perhaps this is because you wish to progress into higher-education training, e.g. nursing, occupational therapy or social work.

Personal development plans that are developed through appraisal are important in order for an organisation to prepare and plan an overall training plan which in turn meets the national standards in relation to staff training and development.

So far we have considered how your supervisor or manager gives you feedback on your performance. However, there are many other people who can also provide this valuable information to help you reflect upon and develop your practice.

Reflecting on life experience

KUS 7

Self-reflection is an informal way of monitoring and evaluating your own performance, knowledge, skills, attitudes and behaviour, although most people can find this quite a daunting prospect without some kind of structure or framework to guide them. Health and social-care work revolves around supporting relationships with individuals who are often very vulnerable and have a range of complex needs. Therefore, to effectively support individuals it is important for you to develop self-awareness.

We are all individuals and our identity develops as a result of many different factors mixing together as we grow up and experience new things. As a result of this we all have an individual view of the world which is unique and unknown to other people unless we share it with them.

When we are young our family or primary carers have the greatest influence on the formation of our values, beliefs and views. However, as we grow up we come into contact with a wider range of people from different backgrounds and experiences as well as having our own life experiences. Each of these will, to a greater or lesser extent, shape our unique view of life and may be the driving force in determining the choices we make about our life in terms of our relationships, job or the dreams and aspirations we have.

Other factors that influence our views and beliefs are, for example, friends at different times in your life, school and other educational experiences, where we live, social groups, leisure interests, parenthood, work experiences and bereavement. Since the middle of the 20th century television, music, films, newspapers and magazines have also had an increasing influence on shaping peoples' views, values and beliefs. The internet is another more recent influence due to increased access to computers.

All of these factors will have mingled together to make us who we are today. However, it is important to recognise that our views and beliefs can change as we travel through life and our experiences teach us new things about the world and about ourselves. You may like to consider how your attitudes towards certain things have changed over time.

**Figure 5
Freinds can be a
big influence**

Reflection

You may ask yourself why reflection is important. As a care worker you have a responsibility to support individuals and others, and a lack of self-awareness can lead to you becoming part of the problem and not part of the solution.

KUS 7

You may find it difficult to reflect on your practice and find that when you try to do this you get stuck after describing what happened. Many people have found it helpful to use a framework or a set of trigger questions so that they can structure their reflection. Reflection can then be a really helpful tool in developing your understanding of your work practice and the impact you have on others. One framework for reflection is Gibbs Reflective Cycle which can be used to help you whether you are writing it down, talking it through with someone or thinking it through yourself.

**Figure 6
Gibbs Reflective
Cycle (1988)**

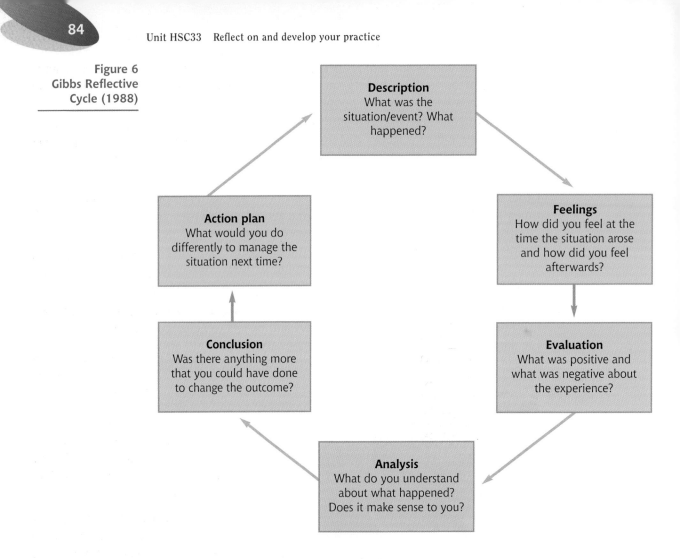

Description
What was the
situation/event? What
happened?

Feelings
How did you feel at the
time the situation arose
and how did you feel
afterwards?

Action plan
What would you do
differently to manage the
situation next time?

Evaluation
What was positive and
what was negative about
the experience?

Conclusion
Was there anything more
that you could have done
to change the outcome?

Analysis
What do you understand
about what happened?
Does it make sense to you?

Practical Example

Reflecting on a situation

Gary works in a small group home with four adults who have learning
difficulties. He was working with a colleague one evening when the fire alarm
went off. He had recently attended a fire training update and remembered
what to do. He took charge of the situation and followed the fire evacuation
procedure correctly. When the situation had been dealt with by the fire brigade
they all went back inside. Gary made everyone a hot drink and sat down with
the residents to reassure them and talk through what had happened. He
praised them for the calm way they coped with the emergency and left the
building. He recorded the incident in the correct records. Later his manager
arrived and gave Gary the opportunity to debrief the incident before he went
home.

Put yourself in Gary's situation and reflect on it using Gibbs' model of
reflection.

➤ *How easy was this model to use?*
➤ *What was the most difficult part?*
➤ *When do you think you could use this?*

KUS 7, 11

Donald Schon considered that reflection took place when workers came across unique situations that they were not able to apply previous learning to. He identified two types of reflection:

- 'Reflection-in-action' takes place during the event while in the process of responding and is sometimes referred to as 'thinking on your feet'. Reflection in this situation is limited as there is neither the space nor time to answer all the questions raised by the situation.
- 'Reflection-on-action' takes place after the event and provides an opportunity to consider the reasons for actions and the impact of those actions on the individuals and the situation.

To be effective, care workers need to be able to utilise both types of reflection so that they can continue to develop their practice and add to their knowledge bank. Reflection should result in some change in the person and their perspective of the situation as well as learning. Supervision and/or post-incident debriefing provide opportunities for these types of reflection, learning and practice development.

KUS 1

Current health and social care practice focuses on providing **active support** to individuals and other people involved with the individual's well-being. An essential part of health and social care work today is promoting an individual's independence to enable them to maximise their potential and enrich the quality of their life experience. Sometimes the wishes of the individuals can challenge the views or beliefs of the care worker. The worker may hold views that are based on prejudices or assumptions and because the worker may have a greater level of influence this can result in the individual's wishes being overridden. So the aim of providing a service which enables individuals to make their own choices and decisions is not met.

This can happen if your own needs, values, beliefs or views override those of the individuals to the extent where you are unable to act in their best interests. It is likely that the individuals you support have a diverse range of needs, circumstances and backgrounds, all of which require you to transfer your knowledge and skills to enable you to adapt your approach and support each one effectively and **equitably**.

Understanding yourself and the factors that have influenced you also helps you to understand other people and the factors that may have influenced their lives and responses to situations they find themselves in as life changes.

Feedback on your work practice

Getting feedback from a range of people that you work with can provide you with insights into how others see you, and this will increase your self-awareness.

A greater self-awareness will enable you to have a more rounded picture of your competence and help you to identify areas of practice that can be developed further.

KUS 8

There may be many different ways in which you receive feedback from other people. Individuals may be given questionnaires to find out what they think about the service they receive; they may also tell you how they feel about your work with them. It is important to enable individuals to participate in giving you and other workers constructive feedback. A central principle of your work responsibilities is to meet individual needs in a way that promotes independence, rights, choices and diversity and enriches life experience. Individuals are therefore best placed to tell you whether the way you support them achieves this. However, some individuals may require

Figure 7
Who in my work
could give me
feedback on my
performance?

assistance to do this and so you will need to consider their preferred communication method. This may use signs, symbols, pictures, technological communication aids or non-verbal communication, i.e. facial expression and gestures. An individual's advocate or family member may also give you feedback.

It is worth remembering that individuals may have some reservations about giving less-than-positive feedback in case this results in them being unfairly treated. Therefore, it is important that feedback is gained sensitively and the individual is reassured about who it will be shared with and how it will be shared, e.g. that the source of the feedback remains anonymous. Colleagues and other workers may also give you direct feedback or you may find this out via your supervisor or manager.

Another form of feedback is through complaints. However, many people think of this in a negative way, although sometimes it is the only way we know that something is not working. All organisations have complaints procedures and these should encourage more specific feedback that can help the organisation and the person involved to identify what action needs to be taken to change and improve what is being provided. Complaints procedures should be accessible to all individuals. For example, they should be available in an appropriate format, e.g. signs, symbols, different languages, audio tape or Braille. Many individuals may feel powerless in the care situation. They may be unaware of their rights or feel intimidated and frightened to make a complaint for fear of reprisals. Sometimes they are living in an inflexible environment with limited or no personal freedom and no opportunity to express their individuality, choices and preferences. This is often called being institutionalised. It is part of your role to enable individuals to use these procedures and to respond to complaints in a positive manner viewing them as a sign of individual empowerment and an opportunity to improve the individual's experience. If individuals feel empowered they will be more likely to voice their concerns, and so the fact that there have been complaints tells us more about how empowered individuals are than the lack of complaints does.

Having used a range of ways to identify your current competence as well as what you need to do to improve and develop your work practice the next step is to devise a plan which will help you to achieve the goals you have set yourself.

Identifying your development needs

KUS 4

You may discuss with your supervisor or manager the actions you need to take to meet the development needs identified through appraisal and supervision. You may formally record your development needs on a personal development plan.

Any development plan should include what actions you will take, the resources you may require to help you, how you can access these, and the timescales for achieving your agreed goals

Health and social care work uses information from research as a basis for practice – this is referred to as evidence-based practice. Workers need to know why they are doing things just as much as how to do things.

Reflecting on your practice and developing your knowledge and skills is not only an important part of being a health and social care worker in the 21st century, it is an essential one.

To make the best use of development opportunities you need to consider what type of activities you learn most from. This will help you to decide what actions to take to enhance your practice. This is explored more in element HSC33b below.

Key points – reflect on your practice

- Learning is a lifelong process.
- The aim of CPD is to maintain quality care standards and competence.
- Reflecting on your care practice is an essential skill when working with individuals with diverse needs and circumstances.
- There is a range of guidance available to help you clarify your role and responsibilities.
- Supervision, appraisal and constructive feedback from others will help you to monitor and evaluate your effectiveness as a care worker.
- Understanding what has influenced your values, motivations and beliefs helps you to be part of the solution rather than part of the problem.

Take action to enhance your practice

Developing yourself using a range of available opportunities

Within your workplace there will be a number of formal and informal opportunities that you can use to help you learn more about what you do. In the first part of this unit we considered the formal processes of supervision and appraisal and discussed how these are both opportunities for you to receive feedback about your performance. These processes are also opportunities for you to discuss with your manager or supervisor areas of your practice that could be improved. This improvement could be through learning more about how to do something, i.e. developing your skills, or through increasing your knowledge and understanding.

The informal processes include comments and feedback from colleagues, carers and the individuals you support. You may ask for this feedback directly or it may be given spontaneously. Either way these are valuable sources of support as they may confirm your competence as well as identify areas for improvement.

KUS 6

There are also a number of opportunities outside your workplace that may help you to reflect on your practice and areas for development. If you attend a training course being run by another organisation you may receive feedback, especially if the course relates to developing skills and the course involves practising those skills, e.g. first-aid course, Makaton course, manual handling or taking physiological measurements (temperature, pulse rate and blood pressure etc.).

Working with other organisations may also provide opportunities to learn and receive feedback, both of which will develop your practice. Your organisation may have arrangements with external organisations to provide a variety of learning opportunities for staff and there will probably be processes in place to help you decide if these are appropriate for you.

Each organisation is different and consequently the arrangements that are in place to support staff development differ. Therefore, it is important that you are able to find out what is available to you and to decide which opportunities suit you and your learning style.

Identifying systems to support development

Supervision and appraisal are two systems available in your workplace that can support your development. However, there are likely to be other systems that can also help.

Think about your workplace and identify the different systems that are available to help you develop your practice.

KUS 6

Many workplaces will have a training plan or training calendar with details of training and development courses or opportunities that are available to staff. Alternatively, information leaflets or flyers advertising courses may be posted on the staff notice board from time to time.

Figure 8
Which systems
can support your
development?

Who can support me to
improve my practice?

What type of support
can they provide?

When can I access this
support?

How can I access this
support?

Where can I access this
support?

Once you have an idea of where you can get support, it is important to think about the areas of practice you need to develop.

Using development support systems

KUS 6, 9, 11

Refer to your personal development plan in order to help you choose the right opportunities to meet your specific development needs. During supervision you could discuss with your supervisor or manager what is available and what would be most helpful to you. It is important to choose the right opportunities so that you get the best out of them and they really do help you to progress.

Attending a training course is one way of developing your skills and knowledge.

To help you make informed decisions about which courses are relevant to you and your development needs you need to know:

- The course aim – the reason for attending.
- The course objectives – what you can hope to achieve as a result of putting into practice what you have learnt from the course.
- The course content – the subjects covered.
- The learning methods used – how the subjects are taught, e.g. small group work, discussion, formal presentation, demonstration, participative activities, role play.
- How the course links to relevant qualifications – links to relevant NVQ units or other qualification requirements.

Once you have identified possible training and development opportunities you should discuss these with your supervisor.

Attending a training course is only one way to develop your knowledge and skills. Reading reports and recommendations from government inquiries where there have

KUS 6, 9, 10

been failures in health and social care practice and case studies about innovative approaches to practice are both valuable ways of developing your knowledge and understanding. Articles in health and social care journals and on the internet are good sources for this type of learning opportunity and they are more up-to-date than books. It is important to find those opportunities that suit you and your development needs.

Adults learn in different ways and so some opportunities may suit you better than others. If you think about your own experience of learning you will probably remember the best learning experience as an enjoyable one and one where you had fun. You may not have even been aware that you were actually learning at the time and only realised afterwards what you had gained from the experience. Most adults can also remember situations, often when they were younger, which put them off learning, where it was a struggle and they were left feeling that they were no good at learning. Those negative experiences can affect how you approach workplace learning as an adult. However, as an adult you have a broader range of experience to bring to your learning and this, plus a different purpose (i.e. developing your skills and knowledge in something which interests you), can help you to overcome some of your anxieties.

KUS 9, 11

Adults find it easier to learn if what they are learning about is relevant to what they do. This can relate to problems or situations they deal with or goals they wish to achieve. Being actively involved, having their experiences valued and being listened to are also important. Another important factor in creating a positive learning environment includes having some control over how and when the learning happens. It is also important that people feel safe enough to express themselves without being judged or made to feel inadequate. After all, the purpose of any learning situation is to learn new things, and for that to happen it is very likely that people will need to ask questions to clarify their understanding. So it is important to consider where you learn and the atmosphere in which you learn. Most people will find it difficult to learn anything useful if they are physically uncomfortable, for example the space they are working in is too cramped, too hot, too cold, or they are feeling unwell. In addition, learning is more difficult if you are worried and anxious about being asked to do something you are unsure about. In fact many people may be reluctant to attend courses or undertake their NVQ because they lack confidence due to poor learning experiences in the past. If you are to make the most of learning opportunities it is important to understand what helps you to learn and how you learn best.

**Figure 9
How do you
learn best?**

I hear and I forget

I see and I remember

I do and I understand

At some time you may have completed a learning styles questionnaire to help you identify your preferences in relation to different learning opportunities. As you read through the descriptions below, see if you can recognise yourself and your preferred learning style.

Some people are active learners and find that the most stimulating learning experiences are those where they are actively involved in activities and in doing things. This may be through group activities or games. They will find sitting listening to someone talking and explaining something rather boring and are therefore less likely to learn much through that approach.

For others the opposite is true as they find active involvement in energetic activities not to their taste. They tend to be reflective learners and learn best when they are given the opportunity to observe others, to think about subjects and reflect on them.

Theorist learners are those people who learn best when using ideas, models and theories and analysing where they fit in relation to other ideas and what they already know. They like applying logic to learning situations. They prefer to learn through reading books and articles about new subjects. They also like having more in-depth discussions with people and being able to ask questions so that they can test out their thoughts and conclusions. This approach is what they find most useful when learning and it is quite different from the practical learner.

Practical learners enjoy problem solving and thinking about how they can apply their learning to real-world situations now. Theories and more abstract concepts make learning more difficult for them. They like it when real examples are used so that they can relate to these and apply them to what they already know.

Although these descriptions are helpful most people tend to use a mixture of the four different learning styles. This is good as it means that you can potentially learn from a wider range of opportunities instead of only being able to learn from one approach. In fact some subjects lend themselves to particular approaches. For example, you could read about the correct way to take someone's temperature, pulse and blood pressure. However, probably the best way to learn this is to watch someone demonstrate how to do it, for you to practise doing it and for them to check you are doing it correctly.

Learning styles

Lucy has been working as a senior care worker for the past six months. She is keen to develop her practice as she would like to apply for nurse training next year. She has already started her NVQ3 and plans to complete this in a few months' time.

She enjoys more activity-based learning and also reading and reflecting.

She wants to develop her skills using different forms of communication as well as learning more about supporting individuals through loss and change.

➤ *What do you think Lucy's preferred learning style(s) are?*

➤ *What sort of learning opportunities could she access to meet her preferred learning style(s)?*

Having considered how you like to learn you can then find out about the range of learning opportunities that you may be able to access that will suit your preferred style and help you add to your skills and knowledge.

You will need to consider opportunities inside and outside your organisation. Your manager or supervisor will be able to advise and support you to choose appropriate opportunities as well as access them. To ensure you are meeting both the statutory requirements for your job and your future career aspirations you will need to plan your development. Your personal development plan helps you to structure your development clearly. It is also useful when monitoring your progress and identifying development priorities.

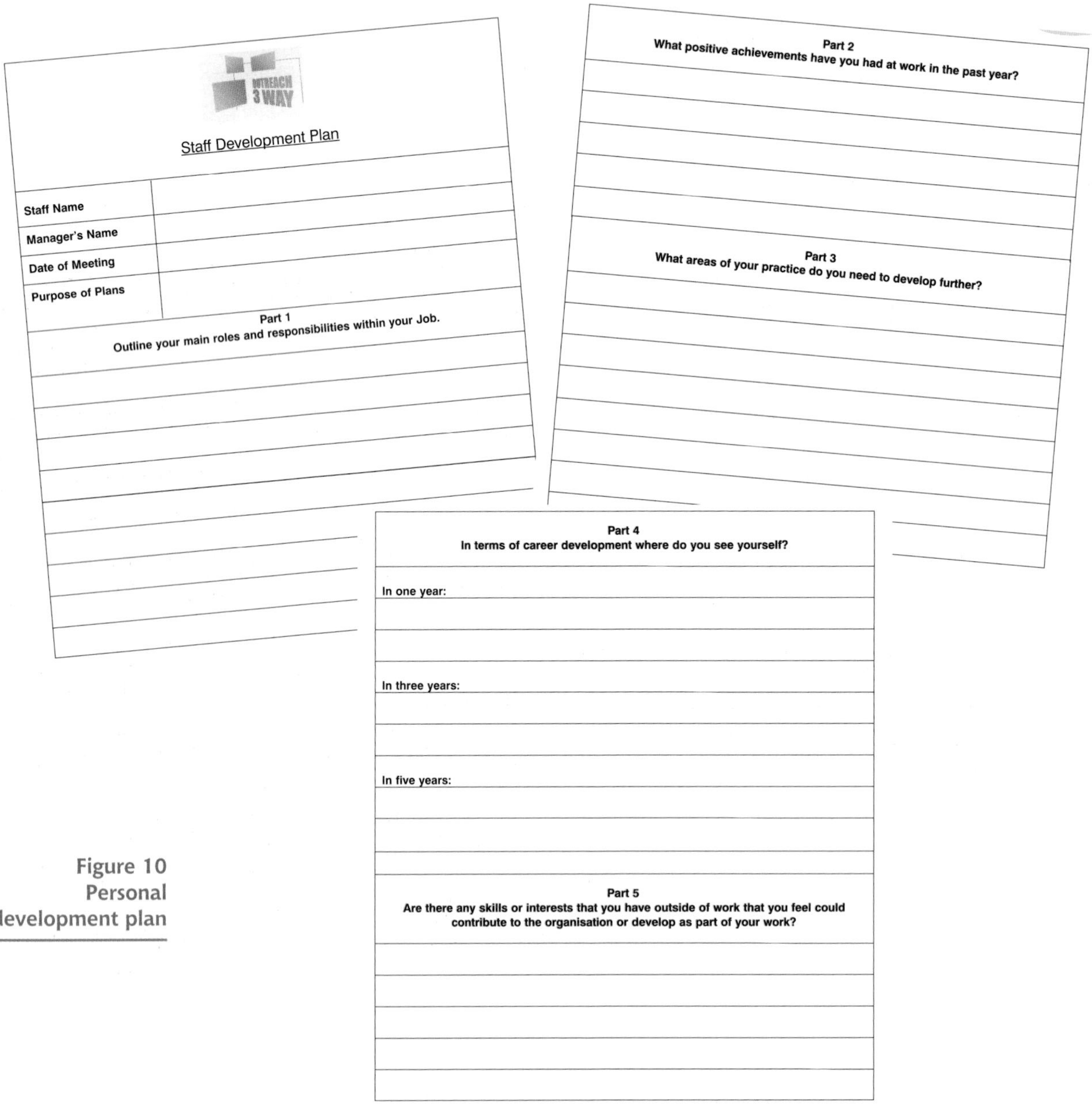

Staff Development Plan

Staff Name	
Manager's Name	
Date of Meeting	
Purpose of Plans	

Part 1
Outline your main roles and responsibilities within your Job.

Part 2
What positive achievements have you had at work in the past year?

Part 3
What areas of your practice do you need to develop further?

Part 4
In terms of career development where do you see yourself?

In one year:

In three years:

In five years:

Part 5
Are there any skills or interests that you have outside of work that you feel could contribute to the organisation or develop as part of your work?

Figure 10
Personal
development plan

Staff Development Policy

1. Outreach 3 Way recognises that staff are its most valuable resource and we are committed to providing development and training opportunities for all our staff.

2. The purpose of staff development is to enhance the ability of staff to achieve the mission of the organisation, to adapt to the changing needs of the organisation, and (when coonsistent with the organisations objectives and vlaues) to ahieve the personal developmental aims of employees.

3. Staff development will be delivered through policies, procedures and practices such as training and supervision that develop an on ongoing basis, the knowledge, skills and understanding of staff members.

4. Staff development applies to all categories of staff whatever their role within the organisation, and an equitable provision will be made for them commensurate to their position.

5. The Training and Development Manager will be responsible for the co-ordination of staff development at an organisational level.

6. This responsibility will be met in the following ways:

- Application of the Staff Development Policy – through support to managers in delivering staff development plans and supervision.

- An annually reviewed Corporate Training Plan.

- A centrally resourced (through the Training and Development Budget) programme of staff development and related activites.

7. The training and Development Manager will provide the central focus for the co-ordination planning and delivery of a range of training activities. The HR Department will provide information to all categories of staff of training opportunities that meet their identified objectives.

8. Each line manager is responsible for the development of their staff. Managers should help staff develop their performance and effectiveness by actively encouraging and supporting appropriate activities, analysing training and development needs, setting clear objectives, and providing development opportunities as appropriate.

9. Development activities might include attendance at seminars, workshops and conferences, development of specialist, technical or amangerial skills, secondments, work shadowing, research, induction, mentoring, participation in internal programmes related to policy implementation, retraining and updating.

10. Line managers will be responsible for the annual review of development objectives with staff.

11. Staff Development is most effective when the individual member of staff takes responsibility for their own development in an agreed and accountable way, using performance indicators and defined competencies as a guide to development needs. All staff should be given appropriate support and encouragement including reasonable time and resources for this purpose.

Staff Development Plan – Procedure

1. Development planning meetings should occur annually.

2. Managers will book a time to meet with staff members to complete their development plan – the meeting should be at a time and in place convenient to both parties, where they will be undisturbed.

. Both the staff member and the manager should have a copy of the (blank) staff development plan before the meeting so that they can consider the questions.

In **Section 1** the member of staff and the manager should consider the main roles and responsibilities of the staff member. These may evolve over time and this should be recognised.

In **Section 2** they should reflect on the positive achievements of the staff member in the past year – this mjight be the achievement of training, a particular piece of work with a service user, a piece of written work, or simply the development of their working practice.

In **Section 3** they should reflect on the developmental needs of the staff member. This section is not intended to be critical of the staff member but rather to outline opportunities for their continued development while working for Outreach 3 Way.

 Section 4 they should discuss the future aspirations of the staff member – this could be to gain promotion, to change services (for ample to move from residential services to day services), or simply to main in post and develop their skills..

ction 5 recognises that staff often have skills or connections outside of r usual working life that may be useful to both themselves and the anisation and may contribute to their development..

 final section of the **Staff Development Plan** should then be completed using the information gathered in the previous sections to inform the development activities – it is important that the development activities are clearly defined and have outcomes. Both the member of staff and the manager should sign the Staff Development Plan and each take a copy.

10. The Development Plan should then be a standing item in supervision so that the staff member's development is monitored and assessed.

Planning your development

KUS 3, 4

There are a number of areas of practice that require regular updating in order that the legal (statutory) requirements and standards within your care setting are met. Statutory requirements usually relate to areas of health and safety such as fire safety, manual handling, first aid, food handling and hygiene. If you need to undertake or update your training in any of these areas then this would be identified by your manager or supervisor as a priority. These priority areas would need to be addressed before other areas of learning and development could be considered.

There may also be priorities within your organisation in terms of work standards. For example, before being given the responsibility of carrying out specific tasks you may be required to undertake training related to that task. This may be in areas such as the administration of medication, taking venous blood samples or person-centred planning. Performance monitoring through supervision and appraisal may have identified areas for improvement in your practice and these may also be identified as a priority.

KUS 7,8,9,11

You may have your own priorities to consider. You may wish to apply for a more senior position within a particular timescale or you may wish to progress your career by applying to undertake, for example, nursing, social work or occupational therapy training at university.

When planning your development you need to consider both external (statutory) requirements and internal requirements, and these will help to determine the importance and order in which development activities are undertaken. Decisions about priorities will be made through discussion with your manager or supervisor. Although workplace learning and development is supported by employers, there is also an expectation that care workers contribute to their own development as well. This may be through a financial contribution and/or giving their own time to undertake development activities.

Having constructed your personal development plan, identified what skills and knowledge you need to develop and your developmental priorities, next you need to decide what learning opportunities will help you to meet your needs.

KUS 8

During supervision you will be able to discuss with your supervisor the options that are available to suit your learning and development needs. Your supervisor will be able to advise you and help you access some of the different opportunities available. Most organisations have processes in place where managers or supervisors are involved in discussions and decisions about appropriate development opportunities.

KUS 9, 11

There is an increasing number of learning resources available via the internet or there are interactive CD-ROMs and this may be a good way of developing your knowledge and understanding whilst working at your own pace and at a time that suits your life circumstances. Health and social care journals may be available within your organisation or you may be able to borrow books and journals from the organisation's own library.

Shadowing a more experienced colleague or senior worker that you respect and who has high quality work standards is an excellent learning opportunity. They are often an excellent role model for learning new skills as well as positive attitudes and behaviours.

**Figure 11
A completed
personal
development plan**

Development Plan Your learning outcomes (what you want to achieve):	Target achievement timescale
1 Improve my recording skills and understanding of Data Protection Act and how this affects my work	July 2006
2 Update fire training	October 2006
3 Develop care plan reviewing skills	July 2007

*	Resources you may require	Monitoring process How: (method) Who: (will be involved) When: (timescale/frequency)	Progress report (include any changes to plan as a result of monitoring) and outcome in terms of changes to practice
1	Copies of record keeping and confidentiality policies Attend record-keeping workshop	Discussion in supervision and review examples of recording Myself and my manager Monthly	Attended workshop and read policies. Agreed with manager to feed back what I had learnt from the workshop to the rest of staff group so that I could reinforce my learning. I feel my record keeping has improved as I have a greater awareness of my responsibilities both legal and organisational.
2	Fire training	Discussion in supervision Myself and my manager 3-monthly	Booked to attend training day in September 2006
3	Develop care plan reviewing skills	Review work activity through examining reviews and discussion in supervision Myself and my manager. Other people involved in reviews, e.g. individuals and other practitioners 3-monthly	

Name: Kate Walters | **Date:** March 2006

By shadowing them or working alongside them you can closely observe what they do and how they do it. You can also ask questions about why they work in the way they do. This way of learning suits many people. It is particularly useful for learning how to do a particular task and also learning how to work with individuals. These are often referred to as the 'soft skills' and include listening, communication and demonstrating empathy. In addition it can help you to recognise how others respect and value individuals and how their attitude and approach empowers and enables the individuals they support. These are essential elements of working with individuals in a helping relationship. These skills, attitudes and behaviours are difficult to learn solely by reading a book, although we can gain some insights by doing this. However, if you work with an individual who demonstrates these skills in their practice you will see the difference it makes to the individual, their quality of life and experience.

KUS 2

Attending a training course is another way of meeting learning and development needs. As discussed above, it is important to look closely at what the course is designed to help you achieve. One of the benefits of attending a course with people from other organisations is that you learn about those other organisations and get ideas from other people. Group work also gives you an opportunity to listen to other views and approaches to working, discuss practice dilemmas and reflect on your practice. This can be stimulating as well as challenging. Training courses may also provide an opportunity to practise new skills in a safe environment and one where it is alright to try out different ways of doing something.

Learning can also come from working with different individuals as they are often experts about their own condition or disability. You will probably learn something new every day without realising it. The individuals you work with have a diverse range of needs and circumstances and each day you will get to know more about them, their needs and abilities. In turn that will alter your practice as you adapt what you do in the light of this new learning.

Opportunities for learning are all around and it is important to choose the right opportunities to meet the goals identified in your personal development plan. There may be specific procedures for accessing the development activities you have identified. These may involve completing an application form or seeking agreement from your manager/supervisor or others involved. After you have accessed and made use of the relevant opportunities it is important to evaluate how well they met your learning and development needs and consider how what you have learnt can be implemented in your practice to improve it.

Matching development needs to opportunities

Before undertaking any development activity it is important to check what you need. It will help if you have a clear idea about what opportunities you are looking for, i.e. what subject areas you need to learn more about, what your preferred learning styles are and what you want to achieve. Your personal development plan can be used here as it should contain all of this information. You can then assess or measure each development opportunity that you identify against your personal development plan goals. This will help you to match what you want or need with what is available. After the event it is important to review and evaluate the effectiveness of those development activities in meeting your goals and expectations. This will help you to make future choices and decisions.

If you attended a course then you will have been asked to complete an evaluation form at the end of the course. This helps you and the trainer to judge whether the course has met your expectations. The evaluation will often include a section asking you to state how you will apply what you have learnt to your work practice. You may also have an evaluation form from your organisation to complete and return to your manager or supervisor for discussion in the supervision meeting following the course.

Table 2 Tasks to assist your personal development

Shadowing senior worker	✓
Attending a first-aid training course	✓
Learning about legislation via the internet or CD-ROM	✓

KUS 7

To review and evaluate development activities you will need to refer to your personal development plan where the purpose of undertaking the development activity is recorded. You will find it helpful to refer to any information you have about the development activity as this may have details of the intended purpose and expected outcomes. You can then use these as the benchmark or starting point from which you can measure how effective the development activity was in meeting your needs. When reviewing and evaluating consider the questions in Figure 10.

Figure 12 Reviewing and evaluating development activities

What did you find most helpful/enjoy about the development activity?

What did you find least helpful about the development activity?

How well did the development activity suit your learning style(s)?

Would you undertake a similar development activity again?

Was it a comfortable learning environment?

Did the development activity meet your expectations and development goals?

What examples of work practice can you provide to show that your practice has changed/improved as a result of your learning?

How can you demonstrate what you gained or learnt from the activity?

Self-reflection and evaluation is important. However, it is also useful to ask people – who you work with for feedback. Sometimes it can be difficult to see how practice changes and you only become aware of it when colleagues or your supervisor comment on it.

Reviewing your development plans

In some organisations personal development plans are reviewed each month as part of supervision. In others the review is carried out annually or after you have completed a development activity such as attending a training course. The frequency of review may be determined by the number of learning and development needs identified and the different timescales set for undertaking development activities to meet these. Whatever the process in your organisation, it is important that you review your personal and professional development regularly with your manager or supervisor.

In reviewing your personal development plan you will need to consider the goals or objectives you have set and decide whether these have been achieved or whether they may need to be altered in light of other factors.

Are the goals or objectives still relevant to your:

- Job description?

- Role and responsibility?

- Learning and development needs?
  - Are the goals or objectives realistic and achievable?
  - Do the timescales for achievement still apply or do they need to be altered?
  - Are there additional learning and development needs that should be included?
  - What other opportunities and sources of support and development can be accessed?

You will review your development plan with your manager or supervisor in light of evidence from your practice and the changes you have made to this as a result of your learning.

Evaluating changes to your work practice

Often when someone learns something new they do one of two things. Either they put what they have learnt into practice straight away, see the benefits, keep repeating the new way of working, and their practice changes so that they almost forget how they used to do it. Alternatively they try it once or twice, find that it takes a little longer (because they are learning) and so revert back to doing it the way they did before and so their practice never really changes. Sometimes the attitude of colleagues can discourage someone from trying out new skills and ways of working. When this happens the person feels reluctant to do things differently as they may be singled out, and so although they know that there is a better way to do something they revert to old habits because it is easier than challenging accepted practice. This is another reason why it is important to gain support from your manager or supervisor when trying to integrate new skills into your work practice. Gaining their support and getting constructive feedback about the changes you are making to your practice will encourage you to continue developing your practice.

How can you identify what has changed in your practice? Reflecting on what you have learnt from any development activity and as a part of that reflection considering how you can apply your learning to your practice is an important starting point.

You may need to make a conscious effort to actually apply a new way of working or a new approach and to recognise an appropriate time to try this. Sometimes this is obvious, for example using a new procedure. At other times it is less obvious and more difficult to do something without thinking about it. For example, you may have learnt a new technique to diffuse a potentially abusive or disruptive situation. When you are confronted by that situation you will need to make a conscious effort to apply what you have learnt and try a different approach as the speed at which it happens and the tension in the situation is likely to pull you to respond in a more familiar way where you feel more confident about your actions and the potential outcome. If you have had the opportunity to practise what you have learnt, for example through role play either on a course or with your manager or supervisor, you are likely to feel more confident about using what you have learnt and applying a different approach. Supportive debriefing after an event will also help you to feel more confident about trying new approaches and putting your learning into practice.

What you have learnt through self-reflection as well as being able to provide examples of how you have changed your practice can be shared with your manager or supervisor as evidence of the value of the development activities undertaken. In addition constructive feedback from colleagues and the individuals you support can also be valuable in evaluating if your work practice has changed and you have achieved the improvements you were seeking to make.

You may need to actively seek that constructive feedback by asking other people, or your manager/supervisor may do this as part of their evaluation. You may also receive feedback spontaneously.

Sometimes it is easy to measure improvements because they are visible. For example, an area for improvement may relate to written recording. You attend a course on record keeping and as a result are much clearer about the legal and organisational requirements and the standards of recording required. You can therefore compare the entries you made in care records before you attended the course with those made after you attended the course and identify the improvements. These can also be quantified by comparison with the organisational standards for recording. Other changes to work practice may be more difficult to quantify especially if they relate to the soft skills such as changes in attitude. Reflection and seeking constructive feedback from others are effective ways of evaluating these more subtle changes to practice.

Evaluating your work practice and reviewing your personal development plan are both likely to lead you to identifying other areas for development, and hence learning becomes a lifelong activity and your professional development is a continuous process.

Maintaining your continuing professional development record

KUS 4, 7

As you review your personal development plan you should also spend time updating your professional development records. It is important to keep accurate records of all development activities so that you meet statutory and organisational requirements. For example, you will need to provide evidence that your health and safety training is up to date. In addition, having accurate and up to date records will ensure that you do not attend the same course twice and so make best use of your time and access to development opportunities. In some care settings you may be asked to present your CPD records for inspection by a regulatory authority such as CSCI.

Within your organisation there may be a prescribed layout and format for your CPD record. You may be provided with a folder and expected to complete certain activities in relation to each development activity you undertake. For example, as well as listing all the different developmental activities you undertake, there may be evaluation forms to complete after you attend a course, or a format for a reflective account to complete

Figure 13 A continuing professional development record

Activity undertaken	Outcome	Date
Attended training course on person-centred care	Attendance certificate Reflective account of learning	23 January 2006
Attended team meeting where community psychiatric nurse explained their role	Discussion with colleagues and made notes in my resource file	15 February 2006
Read article about MRSA	Shared what I had learnt with colleagues at team meeting. Article and notes in my resource file	8 March 2006
NVQ assessment – assessor observed my planning and carrying out an activity with a group of individuals	Assessor feedback and self-reflection following the assessment identified that I need to know more about different communication methods	22 March 2006
Researched different communication methods • did a search on the internet • spoke to my manager • read my NVQ textbook	Wrote an assignment for my NVQ about different communication methods	4 April 2006
De-brief and reflection with manager following an abusive incident at work	Reflective account of incident	5 April 2006

following other types of development activity, such as dealing with an incident. You may also be expected to keep a record of all the articles or books you read related to your work.

You can also keep other types of information that relate to your activities in your CPD record, for example copies of articles you have read, course details and notes that you made at the time. Whatever you include it is more helpful if you take time to reflect and record your comments about what you have learnt, how it applies to your work and how you intend to use this learning to enhance your practice. Your CPD record can also be useful to refer to during supervision and appraisal meetings. Keeping a comprehensive record will also demonstrate your commitment to developing your practice.

Your CPD record is a good place to keep any course attendance certificates as well as qualification certificates. However, as it is an important document you would be wise to keep your record in a safe place so that you can locate it easily when needed, it remains confidential and you reduce the risk of it being mislaid. You will find it useful to add these certificates etc. as your record then becomes part of your development itself. You can review your record and look back at how much you have changed and how your thinking and practice have developed over time. This is encouraging and will help you to gain confidence as well as motivate you to continue developing your practice.

When recording information in any document you need to consider who will have access to it and ensure that confidentiality is maintained at all times. Although you may not think that you will show your CPD record to anyone else, you may be asked to show it if you apply for another job or wish to undertake other training. If you are reflecting on work with an individual you support or with a colleague, do not include any information that may identify them to others.

There are a number of ways to take action to improve and develop your practice. Some activities will involve working with and being supported by other people, and many are within your control where you decide what you need to do to move in the direction you want to go to enhance your professional knowledge and skills.

Key points – take action to enhance your practice

- Your personal development plan should identify areas for improvement, priorities and the desired outcomes from undertaking development activities.
- Identify the range of development opportunities available and how you can access these.
- Match development activities to your identified development goals and your preferred learning style(s).
- Agree development activities with your manager or supervisor.
- Evaluate all development activities to measure how effective they have been in helping you to change and improve your practice.
- Keep accurate, current, comprehensive and confidential records of your continuous professional development.

Unit HSC33

Are you ready for assessment?

Reflect on and develop your practice

This unit is about how you analyse and reflect on what is required of you in order to be a competent and safe worker who can actively support individuals and others you work with. It is about how you use support systems and seek constructive feedback from a range of different people you work with to help you evaluate your practice and identify your learning and development needs. It is also about how you use this information to plan your professional development and access opportunities to enhance your knowledge and skills.

Your assessment will be carried out mainly through observation by your assessor and this should provide most of the evidence for the elements in this unit. Your assessor must observe you for some part of each element in this unit. Evidence of your knowledge and understanding will be demonstrated through observation, your assessor examining work products, e.g. reports, minutes of meetings, as well as through answering oral and/or written questions.

You need to be aware when planning assessments that this unit also relates to core and many optional units and so you may also be able to evidence performance criteria for these.

Direct observation by your assessor

Your assessor will need to plan to see you carry out the performance criteria (PCs) in each of the elements in this unit. The performance criteria that may be difficult to meet through observation are:

- HSC33a PCs 1, 2, 4
- HSC33b PC 1

Preparing to be observed

You must make sure that your workplace and any individuals and key people involved in your work agree to you being assessed. Explicit, informed consent must be obtained before you carry out any assessment activity that involves individuals or which involves access to confidential information related to their care.

Before your assessments you should read carefully the performance criteria for each element in the unit. Try to cover as much as you can during your observation but remember that you and your assessor can also plan for additional sources of evidence should full coverage of all performance criteria not be possible.

Other types of evidence

You may need to present other forms of evidence in order to:

- Cover criteria not observed by your assessor.
- Show that you have the required knowledge, understanding and skills to claim competence in this area of practice.
- Ensure your work practice is consistent.

Your assessor may also need to ask you questions to confirm your knowledge and understanding and ensure that you can apply this to your practice.

Check your knowledge

- Identify at least three sources of information that provide guidance about your role, responsibilities and expected work standards.
- Describe how supervision and appraisal processes help you to identify your development needs.
- Describe how you access and use information about development opportunities.
- Using examples, describe how working with other people has enhanced your knowledge and practice.
- Explain how you monitor your progress towards achieving the development goals in your personal development plan.
- Explain what is meant by reflective practice.
- Using an example, describe how reflection has enhanced your knowledge and practice.
- Describe how learning can be transferred into practice and identify the factors that can support this process.
- Explain why continuous professional development is an important part of current health and social-care work.

Promote choice, well-being and the protection of all individuals

*T*his unit focuses on the development of supportive relationships and the promotion of choice and independence whilst respecting the diversity and differences of individuals. It also discusses the protection of individuals from danger, harm and abuse. Throughout the unit we will be aware of the key people in the individual's life, such as family, friends and other people with whom the individual has a significant relationship.

The unit contains three elements:

- **HSC35a** *Develop supportive relationships that promote choice and independence*
- **HSC35b** *Respect the diversity and difference of individuals and key people*
- **HSC35c** *Contribute to the protection of all individuals*

Introduction

KUS 1

All people are different, no two people are the same. We all have our own particular needs and values and our own individual and social characteristics including age and gender. Individuals also have different religions, culture and personal beliefs and preferences. Regardless of these differences, everyone is entitled to equity of care and treatment and should be treated with the same respect.

It is important to promote the individuals' independence as much as possible in order to maintain their well-being and self-esteem. If individuals are going to make the best choices about their care, they need information and advice about their options. It is important to find out from the individual just what their needs are, and you should respect these. Their needs may change depending on how well the individual is supported by their family, friends and the other people in their lives. The environment itself can also have an effect on the individual, whether this is their own home, a care facility or a hospital. In some cases their needs may not be met, and this will have a serious effect on the way the individuals feel about themselves.

All individuals have basic human needs. In 1943 the psychologist Abraham Maslow suggested that human needs are arranged in a hierarchy of importance that ranged through five levels, and that only when the needs at the bottom were met could the needs in the higher levels be achieved (see unit HSC31).

KUS 12

Human beings have four basic health needs and these are physical, intellectual, emotional and social needs, or P.I.E.S. All groups of people have similar needs that fall under these headings. Different groups of individuals, such as babies and children, adolescents, adults, older people and people with disabilities, will have specific needs and you should be aware of these. Health needs can change over time depending on the individual's personal situation. You should consider this when helping to promote choice and well-being in order that the appropriate care and support can be provided.

Figure 1
The four basic
health needs

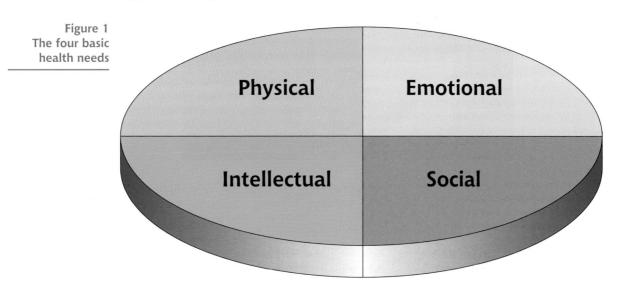

Element HSC35a

Develop supportive relationships that promote choice and independence

Developing supportive relationships

KUS 2, 8

You should develop and maintain relationships that promote the views, preferences and independence of individuals. It is important that you show respect towards all individuals, whether they are individuals that you are caring for, their family, friends or other people in their lives. Protect their privacy and dignity at all times so that they can maintain their self-respect. Help them to feel valued and important. By using a professional attitude and behaviour towards individuals, you will encourage mutual respect and meaningful interactions between everyone concerned.

KUS 2, 4, 8, 12, 16

Developing a good supportive relationship with the individual will encourage effective communication and the sharing of information. It will help you to understand the individual's wishes relating to their ongoing care. It will also enable them to discuss their views and preferences openly with you, and will hopefully assist them in making the right choices. This will help the individual to maintain self-confidence, self-esteem and independence.

Carl Rogers (1902–1987) identified three conditions necessary for creating a safe conversational atmosphere that values an individual. Although these were originally seen as the basis for counselling relationships, they have since been adopted as the

Figure 2
Develop supportive relationships with individuals in order to encourage the sharing of information

basis for supportive and befriending relationships. The three conditions that the carer must show or convey are:

- Warmth – sometimes called acceptance.
- Understanding – sometimes called empathy.
- Sincerity – sometimes called gentleness.

It is not always easy to establish a supportive, caring relationship; it depends on many different factors. In 1957 Biestek identified how the caring relationship is composed of a controlled involvement:

- Sensitivity – the care worker must demonstrate sensitivity to the individual's feelings at all times.
- Understanding – the special kind of understanding that is typical of the caring relationship. The understanding focuses on the individual, who they are and what they may be facing.
- Response – while there may be many practical tasks involved in caring for the individual, responses must always incorporate feelings. These feelings may be communicated either verbally or non-verbally. The response that the care worker makes to the individual should communicate an acceptance of that individual. Acceptance is communicated through warmth, courtesy, respect, concern and interest. Individuals may have beliefs that we do not share or behave in ways that we do not approve of. Some individuals both fear and expect disapproval because they lack self-esteem. It is important to note that acceptance does not mean approval.

Empowerment

To enable the individual to make the appropriate choices for their well-being and independence, they should be involved in all aspects of their care and be empowered to make their own decisions.

KUS 5, 8, 16

Empowerment is an extremely complicated process. It is not just a question of helping or enabling individuals, it is more about assisting them to see the obstacles in their lives and helping them to identify the steps to remove them in order to progress. In order to do this they need to experience the following.

Understanding

To enable the individual to make the appropriate choices and decisions, they will need to be fully informed about the different treatment and care options available to them. They will need to know about specific options that are suitable for their current and future health and well-being needs and requirements. They should be enabled to express their views or concerns, and any questions they have need to be answered by the appropriate person clearly and in a way that they understand. An individual needs to have a clear understanding of the facts before they can make the appropriate choices. You should give them plenty of reassurance and support in order to do this.

Participation

Encourage the individual to participate in the discussions about their care. Occasionally, previous service users are invited to come and talk to an individual and to explain how they coped in a similar situation, whether this is in connection with their health requirements or the services they used. This can give the individual a clearer picture and may help to alleviate any concerns or anxieties they have.

Relationships

As well as their own family, friends and other significant people in their lives, the individual needs to have a supportive relationship with their current carers. They should be informed who their named nurse or key worker is, as well as the names of the other people who will be looking after them.

When it comes to empowerment, the emphasis is on not obstructing it. There are some things that you can do to help individuals to become empowered. You should use effective communication with the individual so that a satisfactory exchange of information takes place, and you must ensure that the confidentiality of this information is maintained. The individual's beliefs and preferences may be different from yours but you need to respect these because they are important to them. The individual should not be discriminated against regardless of their personal characteristics, and they should be treated in the same way as everyone else. You need to support and encourage the individual to regain and maintain their independence to the best of their ability.

Communication

You should support individuals to communicate their views and preferences regarding their current and future needs and priorities. Try to help the individual feel at ease. They need to feel they can trust you and talk freely about any issues that concern them, knowing that any information will be used in their best interests and for their welfare. Each relationship you have is as unique as the individual and will change over time as you both change.

To understand what the individual's choices are, you need to make time to sit and talk with them. Build up a good rapport with the individual and speak in a manner and tone and at a pace which is understood easily by the individual. Use their preferred spoken language wherever possible. If an interpreter or translator is required then these should be made available. It is not always appropriate to use the individual's family or friends as an interpreter because confidentiality could be breached. Occasionally the individual may ask for an advocate to speak for them, and again this will need to be arranged. You could also use gestures, signs, symbols, pictures or other non-verbal forms of communication. It is important that you check that any sensory equipment used by the individual is in good working order. You need to make sure that you are not giving the wrong messages to the individual, for instance saying one thing with words but allowing your body language to say another.

KUS 2, 4, 5, 16, 23

Try not to put any undue pressure on the individual to make choices or decisions. The use of open-ended questions will help the individual to communicate what they want. Some individuals may need more time to consider their choices or may need more explanation about the services available to them and how they can access them. Try to give them this information, or if you are not sure how to do this ask someone more senior to help.

Occasionally the individual's personal choices cannot be met and you need to explain clearly why their requests cannot be granted or why they must be restricted. Let them know if their options are reduced – this may be due to their current problems or related to a particular treatment that they are currently receiving that is essential for their recovery. Remember to inform your manager or supervisor of their concerns or decisions.

Care and support

You need to work with individuals to identify the care and support they can and wish to undertake themselves. It is important that you value and respect all of the individuals in your care. Someone who is new to the care setting may feel that they have lost all of their independence, especially if they are not well. Their current condition may be a physical or a mental one, and the amount of care and support they need may vary. They may not be able to think clearly due to their current physical or emotional state. Where they would normally have been able to care for themselves and to maintain their own basic personal hygiene, dress themselves, feed themselves etc. they may now have to let someone else undertake these tasks. This could cause them anxiety and embarrassment, they may feel that they have lost their independence and also their pride. This loss of independence could lead to a loss of self-esteem and reduced self-confidence. They may no longer feel valued and important and they may lose their self-worth. It is essential that you encourage the individual to demonstrate or explain how much they can manage to do themselves so that a plan of care can be developed and the appropriate support can be arranged.

KUS 3, 15

You should be willing and available to support them with their self-care and encourage them to participate as much as possible. This will play a large part in helping them to maintain some form of independence and as a result will work towards the fulfilment of their physical needs and also their emotional needs. The needs of individuals should be assessed in such a way that makes use of their strengths and aspirations as well as those of their carers.

KUS 14

Identify the care and support that can be provided by the support networks of family and friends and other significant people. These people could play a large part in helping the individual to regain some of their independence by providing them with sufficient care and support to help them achieve it. It is important that this is discussed not only with the individual and their family, but also with other care staff such as the health visitor, social worker, general practitioner or community nurses and any other people who have a role to play in the individual's care and support. There may be other support networks such as self-help groups or voluntary organisations that would be able to work with the individual and their family. These networks can be extremely beneficial in giving much-needed advice, care and support to the individual and their carers.

KUS 4, 14

Some individuals may regain their independence once they have recovered from their current health or social care problems, whilst others may need ongoing care and support from their current service provider and from other service providers in the community. Help to identify the care and support that needs to be provided by yourself and others within and outside your organisation. It is important that all service providers are involved in the discussions relating to the individual so that preparations can be made for their care whether that is ongoing support, discharge or transfer of care, whichever is in their best interest. A variety of care services may be involved in caring for the individual and you should work in partnership with these people as far as your job role allows, taking advice and support from your manager or supervisor.

Figure 3
A multi-disciplinary team meeting

KUS 4

There are many options available to individuals for discharge or transfer of care. The choice will depend on the individual's physical and emotional needs. Residential care homes are provided by social services or the private sector. Older people, people with physical or learning disabilities and other residents live there. Care workers are on duty at all times to provide the help and support required. Some older individuals may decide to move into sheltered accommodation where there is a warden on call in case of emergency. In this situation they will live independently of other people and will be able to make their own choices. They will have the chance to join in with social activities if they choose. The ability of the individual to carry out activities for daily living will have been assessed accordingly. They will need advice and possibly assistance with financial arrangements.

If the individual is to be discharged home, they may need the services of an occupational therapist, who will assess the individual's ability to take care of themselves in the home setting and also decide on the specific aids or equipment that may be required. The individual and their carers will require some form of training, advice and guidance in using the aids and equipment provided so that they feel safe using them and do not harm or injure the individual or themselves.

The kitchen, bathroom or other parts of the house may need to be adapted or altered to suit the individual's needs and requirements, e.g. fitting extra hand rails on the staircase or near the front and back doors, a stair-lift or a ramp to enable them to get in and out of the house if they are in a wheelchair. Regardless of where the individual chooses to live, they need to be aware of all the services available to them and how to access them.

Figure 4
Adaptations can be made to an individual's house

Assessment of need

KUS 7

People working in care are expected to be able to assess and meet the needs of the individual. The assessment of need is required by law. The National Health Service and Community Care Act 1990 stresses autonomy, empowerment and choice, and it covers:

- The needs of individuals with long-term health problems.
- De-institutionalisation.
- A 'mixed economy of care' – care can be provided by local authorities, private and voluntary agencies.
- A priority to promote informal care.
- Increased citizen participation and choice.

'Needs-led' services (based on what the individual particularly needs rather than what services are available).

Active support

KUS 2, 3, 4

You should provide active support to the individuals in your care in order to meet their **holistic** needs and preferences. Work co-operatively with the individual and help them to assert their right to make decisions for themselves. This would hopefully increase their motivation and self-esteem and would help them to achieve some independence. Each individual, whether they are disabled or not, still needs carers who will enable them to do what they can for themselves.

Find out about the amount of active support they need from you or from other service providers so that their ongoing care can be planned accordingly. Active support from you will encourage the individual to determine the best course of action to take. It will also assist them in making any necessary arrangements or preparations if they are to be transferred to another service provider or if they are to be discharged home. For example, the individual may be able to undertake some personal hygiene for themselves but may need help to get in and out of the bath. It is quite possible that they may be afraid of slipping when getting in and out of the bath, and need assistance. They may be able to make simple meals for themselves but need help with more substantial meals and with the shopping.

Always be specific when you are offering choices to the individual, and if you experience any problems or concerns about offering choices then you need to seek advice from someone more able to deal with the situation. Some individuals may try to persuade you to let them have their own way, regardless of what the care plan says they are able and allowed to do. Always confirm information by reading the care plan and/or checking with your manager. Never let yourself be manipulated, for instance the individual might say, 'The other care worker always lets me do it'.

Promotion of rights and choices

Carry out the activities for which you are responsible in ways that promote the individual's rights and choices and their personal preferences. It is essential that the individual's rights, choices and preferences are respected and you should always remember this when performing any activity with the individuals in your care. If you are able to promote their rights and choices within the care setting you will encourage the individuals to feel less vulnerable, and this will allow for a greater understanding and co-operation between you. Become familiar with your local and organisational policies regarding the promotion of rights and choices. Also make sure that you are aware of the responsibilities and boundaries for your own job role and the actions that you can take within it. Give the individual as much support and reassurance as they need so that they feel relaxed and happy with any changes there may be relating to their ongoing care. Remember that every individual has a right to:

KUS 6

- Be respected.
- Be treated equally and not to be discriminated against.
- Be treated as an individual.
- Be treated in a dignified way.
- Privacy.
- Be protected from danger and harm.
- Be cared for in a way that meets their needs and takes account of their choices.
- Access information about themselves.
- Communication – using their preferred methods of communication and language.

Try to give the individual as much support as possible and help them to promote their rights. Offer them the appropriate advice and guidance by explaining what their rights are in the context of their care. You need to take into account their personal needs and preferences, and support them to strive towards regaining and maintaining their independence. Some individual's may not be able to exercise their own rights personally. This could be due to poor communication skills or because of their age or mental or physical condition. In this situation ensure that an advocate is available to speak for the individual. Advocacy for others requires sensitivity and care in order to ensure that the feelings and wishes of the individual are relayed accurately.

**Figure 5
Provide assistance
when it is needed**

KUS 3

Carry out your activities in ways that complement and support the activities of the individual, their carers and other care staff within and outside your organisation. It is possible that conflicts or disagreements may occur between the individual and their carers regarding the individual's rights and choices and the decisions they have made. It is important to remember that the carers also have rights. Listen carefully to what they have to say and ask your manager for support if you feel unable to deal with the situation. Once a mutual agreement has been made, give the individual and their carers all the help that you can to support them in their decision.

Information and resources

You need to support the rights of individuals and others to access information and resources to meet their needs and preferences. It is the right of everyone to receive accurate, up-to-date information about the services and resources available to meet their needs. Once the individual and their carers have made their choices they need to be provided with the necessary information. You may find that they need your help to access this information, or you could obtain relevant information leaflets for them. Your organisation may have a supply of various information leaflets and booklets available and these should be in the individual's own language or preferred format wherever possible. Ensure that the individual receives a full explanation of the resources available to them so that they can make informed decisions.

Resolving conflicts

Try to resolve any conflicts, and seek additional support and advice from your manager or supervisor if a situation arises that you are unable to deal with. Some of these conflicts may be due to a lack of understanding or the absence of clear information and may cause friction between the individual and their carers. Alternatively, the conflict might be due to the individual making excessive demands of the carers. In order to prevent the situation getting out of control you should get the appropriate support to help you deal with it.

Comments and complaints

KUS 8

You should support and respond appropriately to individuals and other people who wish to make comments or complaints about their care. They may want to express their thanks and gratitude for the care they have received whilst in the care setting and want to thank specific people. Alternatively, they might be dissatisfied with some aspect of their care and simply want to let you know that they were not happy about something. Or they may be very dissatisfied and want to make an official complaint. This can be a positive step and will indicate that the individual is sufficiently empowered to make their feelings known. Complaints need to be considered positively as this is one way that organisations receive feedback about what they do and can help them to improve their services.

If an individual does wish to make a complaint about the care that they received (or did not receive), you will need to report this to your manager or supervisor so that they can either talk to the individual concerned or to one of their family about it. It may be possible to resolve the complaint, but if they still wish to proceed then they should be given information about the complaints procedure for your organisation. They should also be given the names and telephone numbers of the appropriate people who will deal with the complaint. All of the relevant documentation must be completed and processed in line with the procedure. The individual should be given support and reassurance that the complaint will be dealt with. It is important that you are familiar with the complaints procedure and that you know what action you should take if someone wishes to complain.

By developing a supportive relationship with all concerned, you will help to promote choice and assist the individual to maintain their independence.

Offering support and promoting independence

Amy is 74 years old. She is a widow and lives with her son and daughter-in-law at their new house. She has her own room and an en-suite bathroom on the first floor. Amy has always been very independent and is a very proud woman. She has recently been in hospital and as a result of her illness she has had to have a colostomy (stoma), which is an operation to form an opening from the colon onto the surface of the body for emptying the bowel. She has recovered well from the operation and, although she has been a little squeamish about the stoma itself, she is coping well. The stoma nurse has given Amy a lot of support since her operation. She has helped Amy to come to terms with the stoma and has shown her how to look after it. The care staff will assist Amy to change the colostomy bag whenever necessary and there have been no problems. Everything is healing well and Amy is eating a normal diet. Amy now feels that she wants to go home as she misses her own things around her. The nurses believe that at the moment Amy will not be able to cope with changing the colostomy bag herself and may need some help. Amy's son and daughter-in-law have been very supportive of Amy during her illness and during her recovery, and they are told that Amy wants to go home. They are informed that although they would have extra help and support from the community staff, they may need to help Amy to change the colostomy bag if necessary. Amy's son said that he would prefer not to have to deal with it as his mother has always been a private, independent person. Amy was beginning to feel that she would never be able to go home and she became very upset. Her daughter-in-law told Amy and the staff that initially she felt she could not cope with the stoma as anything like that made her feel ill. But she said that if someone showed her what to do, she would give Amy all the help and support she needed so that she could return home.

➤ In what way could having the stoma affect Amy's independence?

➤ What advice and support could you give to the daughter-in-law to help her overcome her anxieties and enable her to cope with the situation?

➤ What reassurance would you give to Amy and to her son and daughter-in-law?

Key points – promoting choice and independence

- Develop a good relationship with each individual and provide them with the support they need to communicate their views and preferences regarding their health and well-being.

- Individuals receiving care have different physical, emotional and social needs. Find out what the individual is able to do for themselves and what other services may need to be provided for them.

- Consider the holistic needs, rights and preferences of the individual and provide them with active support to meet these.

- Where necessary assist the individual in obtaining information on services and resources to meet their needs.

- Work towards resolving conflicts and seek additional support and advice to enable the individual to make comments and complaints about their care if they so wish.

Element HSC35b *Respect the diversity and difference of individuals and key people*

Privacy and dignity

KUS 1, 7, 8, 9, 11

Each individual is entitled to the same quality of care. You should respect their privacy and dignity and maintain this at all times. Help and support the individual to feel valued and respected. If the individual were to lose their self-respect and self-esteem, this would have an adverse effect on their overall recovery.

Privacy and dignity are important during clinical treatments and during toileting and personal hygiene sessions, whether the individual is able to carry this out for themselves or if they need assistance from yourself or other staff.

KUS 6, 7

Any meetings or discussions regarding their ongoing care should ideally be held in private, away from other individuals in the care setting. It is essential that all information about the individual is kept safe and secure and that confidentiality is maintained at all times and not breached by anyone. You should be familiar with your own organisation's confidentiality policy and be aware of your responsibility within it. All care staff should follow the requirements of the Data Protection Act 1998 which came into force on 1 March 2000. The Act covers all data held in respect of any individual and covers paper records as well as those held on computer. The Act has eight principles which must be enforced.

The principles of the Data Protection Act 1998

All data must:

- Be secure.
- Not be kept for longer than is necessary.
- Be adequate, relevant and not excessive.
- Be fairly and lawfully processed.
- Be processed for limited purposes.
- Be accurate.
- Be processed in line with the individual's rights.
- Not be transferred to other countries without adequate protection.

The Caldicott Principles

If you work within the National Health Service (NHS), you should also be aware of the **Caldicott Principles**. These could also be applied to other settings.

It was recommended by the Caldicott Committee that every NHS organisation and hospital should appoint an individual to be responsible for maintaining and protecting patient information. This person is known as a Caldicott Guardian. The Committee also recommended six principles relating to the handling of patient-identifiable information. These are:

1. Justify the purpose.
2. Do not use patient-identifiable information unless it is absolutely necessary.
3. Use the minimum necessary patient-identifiable information.
4. Access to patient-identifiable information should be on a strict need-to-know basis.
5. Everyone should be aware of their responsibilities.
6. Understand and comply with the law.

KUS 6, 8, 16

Values, beliefs and preferences

Treat and value each person as an individual and ensure that the support you give takes account of their needs and preferences. Each individual has their own values, and regardless of what these are, they should be given the same respect and privacy as everyone else. The individual's values, beliefs and preferences should be identified during the initial assessment and admission process. All information relating to their personal history needs to be recorded in their case notes. If you observe any particular needs and preferences whilst working with the individual, or if they inform you what their preferences are, you need to let your manager or supervisor know so that these can be recorded in the plan of care. Their personal beliefs and preferences are important to them and also to their day-to-day activities. Any changes to these can cause the individual a great deal of anxiety and distress. For example, religious, cultural or ethical beliefs may influence the individual's diet. Their personal hygiene requirements are important – some individuals prefer to shower in running water rather than sit in a bath, and they may have particular toileting preferences. You need to work with the individual in ways that provide support that is consistent with their beliefs, culture, values and preferences.

Tensions can arise if your personal beliefs and values differ from those of the individuals in your care. Other colleagues may also have different opinions and values. If you think you may have problems accepting an individual's particular preferences you should do something about it. Try to reflect on and challenge your own assumptions and behaviour. It is important to seek advice, counselling and guidance from your manager or supervisor on how to deal with this. Make sure there are no problems with regard to providing care to any individual or groups of individuals. It is important that all individuals feel safe, protected and valued by the staff caring for them.

Values (from *Homes are for Living In*, London: HMSO, (1989)

KUS 6, 12, 15, 16

'Privacy
- *The right of individuals to be left alone or undisturbed, and free from intrusion or public attention into their affairs*

  All individuals are entitled to have some personal space, they may wish to spend some time on their own either in their bed or their room, and you need to respect this by not disturbing them unless absolutely necessary. They also have a right to confidentiality regarding their personal affairs, and should not be expected to answer probing questions about them.

Dignity
- *Recognition of the intrinsic value of people regardless of circumstances, by respecting their uniqueness and their personal needs*

  Regardless of the individual's personal, cultural or religious beliefs they are entitled to be treated with dignity and respect, and you need to assist them to fulfil their needs without being disrespectful towards them.

Independence
- *Opportunity to act and think without reference to another person, including a willingness to incur a degree of calculated risk*

  Individuals are entitled to have their own thoughts and make their own decisions regarding their lives without having to consult anyone else. They may not be aware of any possible risks involved. You need to help them to understand and prevent these.

Choice

- *Opportunity to select independently from a range of options*

  Providing the individual is given all of the options available to them, they should be given the opportunity to make the appropriate choices to meet their needs. You need to discuss these options with them, and give them the appropriate support and guidance to make the right choices.

Rights

- *The maintenance of entitlements associated with citizenship*

  The individual may not be aware of their human rights, and you need to be able to give them the support they need to achieve these.

Fulfilment

- *The realisation of personal aspirations and abilities in all aspects of daily life*

  In order that the individual can reach fulfilment, you need to help them to achieve the goals that they have set for themselves, and give them praise and feedback on their achievements.'

Maintaining independence

KUS 16

You need to provide active support to enable individuals to participate in activities and maintain their independence. Once you find out what activities the individual can undertake for themselves, encourage and support them to complete the activity. Enabling the individual to perform some activities will increase their independence.

Figure 6 Things to remember when providing support to individuals

Support their rights to practise their individual beliefs and preferences

Be sensitive to every individual's needs

Not behave in a manner which offends others, such as by speech, actions or gestures

Address individuals by their preferred name and title

Be willing to listen when they wish to talk

Respect their possessions

Be respectful of their beliefs and lifestyles when planning care

Show an interest in their beliefs

Never question or make fun of their beliefs or customs

Never try to force your own beliefs and preferences on them

Try to encourage other colleagues with whom you work to recognise and respect the individual's beliefs and preferences and to take account of these in everything they do. They need to seek advice from their manager if they feel they are having problems caring for the individual.

Acknowledge diversity

You must acknowledge and respect diversity and difference. It is easy to make assumptions or rely on first impressions about the individuals in your care. Until you really get to know them and begin to recognise their individual characteristics and **diversity**, your assumptions about them may be wrong.

Figure 7 Acknowledge diversity

Discriminatory practice

KUS 5

You need to reflect on and challenge your assumptions, behaviour and ways of working and also those of others. Your actions should respect the individual's expressed beliefs and values; any discriminatory practice should be avoided. Consider how you communicate with individuals. Is it possible that what you say or the manner in which you say it causes them distress or offence? If you think this is the case then you need to do something about it. You should be familiar with your organisation's policies and procedures relating to anti-discriminatory and anti-oppressive practice. Discrimination is a denial of rights and can be aimed at different individuals who could be discriminated against because of their gender, age, sexual orientation or their mental and physical disabilities. If you think this is the case then consider how you can improve what you do so that you can avoid this. Are there any particular practices that you think may be discriminatory against some individuals in the care setting? If you have any concerns about these, or if you think other colleagues may be using discriminatory behaviour or practices towards individuals, discuss these with your manager or

KUS 18

KUS 7

supervisor. Practices that are found to be discriminatory against any particular individuals should be discussed at team meetings and reviewed if necessary. Protect yourself and others from discrimination by taking the appropriate action. Offer support and guidance to individuals who have been discriminated against. Challenge and provide feedback to anyone who has been discriminatory, explain the effects and consequences of their actions. Inform your manager of any discrimination that you encounter or support others to do so. Discrimination is a denial of rights and the unfair treatment of a person based on prejudice and intolerance. Discrimination can result in inequality in access to services. The following Acts are concerned with discrimination:

- Sex Discrimination Act 1975 – makes it unlawful to discriminate between men and women and covers direct discrimination and indirect discrimination.
- Disability Discrimination Act 1995 – aims to prevent discrimination against people with disabilities.
- Race Relations Act 1976 – makes it unlawful to discriminate on 'racial grounds'.

KUS 6, 7, 8

In 1986 the Equal Opportunities Commission outlined 10 aspects that should be written into an organisation's policies if it is to become an equal opportunities employer. The policies should include the following and must comply with the law on discrimination:

- Definitions of direct and indirect discrimination, victimisation and sexual harassment.
- A statement of the organisation's commitment to equal opportunities.
- The name of the person(s) responsible for ensuring the policy is carried out.
- Details for how the policy is to be carried out.
- An obligation upon employees to respect and act in accordance with the policy.
- Procedures for dealing with complaints of discrimination.
- Examples of unlawful practices.
- Details of monitoring and reviewing procedures.
- A commitment to remove barriers to equal opportunity.
- Provision of equal opportunity training.

There are different forms of discrimination, as follows.

Appropriate discrimination

This is where there is obvious reason for the discrimination, for example:

- Providing specific parking spaces in public places for disabled drivers only.

Inappropriate discrimination

This is where the reason is not appropriate or is not necessary, for example:

- Not allowing a disabled individual to take part in an activity just because they are in a wheelchair.
- Advertising for 'men' of specific height, say '6 feet 4 inches', to apply for a job, thereby discriminating against females.

Overt discrimination

This is something that is openly discriminating, for example:

- Only males being admitted to a club, and women being allowed in only at weekends provided they are accompanied by a male.

Covert discrimination

This is something that is difficult to prove, for example:

- Only males of a certain age being offered promotion within a company despite many females being employed.

Ensure that you are familiar with the Equal Opportunity Policy for your organisation. The principle of equity in the care sector means that everyone should be treated fairly and equally. This should apply no matter what their background, and should be reflected in their plan of care. Some individuals may need additional support due to their current physical or mental condition or because of a particular treatment they are receiving. Always respect the diversity and differences of the individuals in your care.

Discrimination

Sunita is 26 years old. She is married and her husband is currently in Pakistan. Sunita and her husband live with her husband's parents in their home in the local community. Sunita gets on well with them. Her father-in-law has arthritis and walks with a stick. Her mother-in-law is an insulin-dependent diabetic and her diabetes is mostly controlled. Sunita is expecting their first child in two months' time. She tends to do most of the cooking, shopping and housework for the family, but she has had to go into the local maternity hospital for rest. Her own parents do not live locally but they come to visit her occasionally. Sunita speaks English well as she has lived in the UK for many years and her sister has two young children who go to the local school.

Once in the maternity ward, Sunita is asked to stay on bed rest for the time being. She shares a room with two English women and on the whole they get on very well. When the meals arrive there is no Asian meal available on the trolley for Sunita. The health care assistant says she will go to the kitchen to get one for her, but the sister says in front of the other two women that there are plenty of English meals available, and that Sunita should eat one of those otherwise they will be wasted. Unfortunately, none of them are suitable for Sunita. The ward sister says that Sunita will have to do without as they are busy on the ward and they do not have time to get a special diet just for her. Sunita is very upset and says that she is hungry and needs something to eat. Eventually a suitable meal is obtained for her. Sunita's relatives arrive to visit her later on and are surprised to find her so upset. She is normally a very happy person, but now she says that she wants to go home and that she will rest at home.

▶

> ➤ How will this situation have affected Sunita's self-respect and well-being?
> ➤ How could Sunita's privacy and dignity have been maintained?
> ➤ What (if anything) would you do about the actions of the ward sister?
> ➤ How could you help Sunita to settle on the ward and get the rest that she needs?
> ➤ How would you reassure her relatives?

Key points – recognising the diversity and difference of individuals

- All individuals have a right to be treated with respect, privacy and dignity regardless of their personal beliefs and preferences.
- To feel valued and respected can help an individual to regain their self-esteem and their self-confidence, which can help with their general well-being.
- Participating in some activities with your support will help the individual to maintain some of their independence.
- Your own beliefs and values and those of others in the care setting may not be the same as those of the individual. Take action to challenge these, and avoid discriminatory practice.
- Whenever necessary seek support and advice if you are experiencing difficulty in promoting equality and diversity.

Element
HSC35c

Contribute to the protection of all individuals

Identifying risks

KUS 9, 18

It is important that you use all available information to identify the risks of actual and likely danger, harm and abuse for individuals, key people and others with whom you work. At the handover meeting you might be given information about an individual in the care setting who may be at risk of danger or harm. You may be asked to observe and monitor the individual during your shift and report any concerns that you have to your manager or supervisor. An individual may disclose to you that they are feeling vulnerable and afraid. You need to take notice of what they are saying. Listen carefully to them and try to find out what is actually worrying them. They may have concerns about one of their carers. Unfortunately it is sometimes the carers who actually abuse the individuals they are supposed to be looking after. This can happen in the

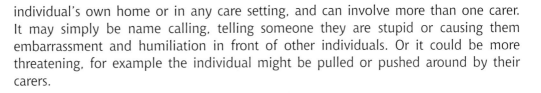

individual's own home or in any care setting, and can involve more than one carer. It may simply be name calling, telling someone they are stupid or causing them embarrassment and humiliation in front of other individuals. Or it could be more threatening, for example the individual might be pulled or pushed around by their carers.

Figure 8
Abuse may
involve aggression
from carers

The individual might be frightened of one of their relatives or other visitors who may have previously threatened or abused them, or may recently have started to be aggressive towards them. Along with other colleagues you will need to take some responsibility for protecting the individuals in your care. Always be alert to any possible situations and try to reduce the risk of harm or danger if at all possible.

Sometimes incidents happen that cause damage or destruction to the environment or to goods and property, and as a result injury or harm to individuals is possible. Be alert for anything that can cause harm or injury or be a danger to individuals in your care or to you and your colleagues.

Protection of individuals

KUS 18, 19, 20

Some individuals may need protection from other people. This may be someone they already know, or a carer, or even another individual in the care setting. Always ensure that your own practice and actions are sensitive to any particular issues or behaviour that may lead to danger, harm or abuse of individuals. Provide the necessary protection whilst balancing the individual's rights and those of others. If you are assisting the individual with their personal hygiene and helping them to dress, be observant to any changes in their physical or emotional condition. You may notice marks on the individual's body that were not there before, or you might find that they have become agitated or withdrawn and do not wish to talk to you. You may not recognise initially that the individual is experiencing any problems and they may keep this hidden from you, but if you have built up a good rapport with them you may notice that their behaviour has changed and that there is obviously something worrying them. Let them know that you are there to help and support them, and that they can tell you if there is anything concerning them. If they do disclose anything to you, explain that you will need to discuss the situation with your manager or supervisor so that the necessary steps can be taken to protect them from any danger, harm or abuse.

If you think that an individual is at risk, or if you suspect that abuse has been a regular occurrence, you must always report it. An individual may tell you that they do not want a particular person to come to visit them. You may have noticed a change in the individual when this person has visited before. It is important that you take notice of this and report it. It is the individual's right to choose who they do and do not want to see. You need to provide the necessary protection for the individuals, balancing their rights and those of key people and taking notice of any restrictions placed upon anyone. There may be a record in the individual's care plan stating that there is restriction on visiting. Be aware of this and do not allow anyone into the care setting who may be a threat to the individual or to others in the environment.

There may be very strict rules on how the care setting is run. Individuals may find that they are restricted and are given no rights or choices. They may have to follow the rules of the establishment regarding what they do and when they do it. Although rights and choices should always be considered and taken into account, the individual's overall protection is essential. If there are rigid, inflexible routines which do not allow for individuality and diversity, this would be considered as institutional abuse.

Some individuals may need to be protected from themselves depending on their physical or mental state. Individuals may not always be aware of danger and may put themselves at risk. Others may self-harm, they may refuse medication and treatment, or they may refuse food and fluids. Others may cut themselves. The fact that they self-harm may be recorded in their case notes and plan of care. It is extremely difficult to protect the individual from harming themselves, and you and other colleagues will need to observe the individual closely at all times to try to prevent them from doing so. Give them all the support that you can to overcome the need to self-harm.

Recognising and challenging inappropriate behaviour

KUS 13, 16, 17, 18, 19, 20

It is essential that you recognise and challenge (appropriately) dangerous, abusive, discriminatory or exploitive behaviour. In your workplace you may often encounter some form of disruptive behaviour aimed at specific individuals. This could include threatening the individual or being abusive towards them. It can also include the use of discriminatory remarks or actions against an individual. This type of behaviour is inappropriate and can cause a great deal of distress not only to the individual who is the target but also to others in the vicinity. As part of your role it may be necessary for you to deal with the after-effects of this type of behaviour on the individuals in your care. They may be frightened, anxious and concerned for their welfare. They may need a great deal of support and reassurance from you and your colleagues to help them overcome their distress. If you observe some form of abusive, discriminatory or exploitive behaviour towards any individual, regardless of whether this is from someone who is receiving care or from a visitor to the care setting, you need to try and find out why they are acting in this way. They could be unhappy about the care that they

KUS 13

or their relative or friend may be receiving. They may not understand what is actually happening and might need a clearer explanation about some aspect of the care being given. They may be worried and anxious themselves and feel that they need to behave in this way in order to get some attention and to get someone to listen to them. They may tell you that they are depressed and that they feel lonely and unable to cope. There may be family problems which are causing them to be angry and aggressive. Talking to them in a calm and reassuring tone of voice may encourage them to talk about their concerns or fears, and this might give you a clearer understanding of why they behaved in such a way. If possible, try to talk directly to everyone involved. Treat them with respect and dignity and do not 'talk down to them'. Although it may be difficult, try to remain calm and in control whatever the situation. Always try to be aware of the build-up of any tension, aggression or frustration between individuals which could involve danger, harm or abuse to you or others in the care setting, and take the appropriate action to prevent it.

Anger and aggression can develop as a result of fear, anxiety or frustration (see also unit HSC336). It can be due to the individual's personal situation or to the fact that everything seems to be getting on top of them. They may no longer feel in control of the situation or of their lives. This in turn may cause them to become increasingly more agitated and aggressive towards other people including you and your colleagues. You will need to use good communication skills to help to alleviate the situation and to give the individuals concerned plenty of reassurance. Look for any possible triggers that may be the reason for their agitation and remove these if possible. It may be that the individual feels that they need more physical or emotional support from their carers or they may have had a disagreement with another individual in the care setting. If this is the case you will need to help them to resolve their differences and hopefully prevent further incidents. Explain to the individuals that compromises sometimes have to be made to enable everyone to feel safe and protected within the environment. You must always take preventive action to help minimise aggression and abuse, and intervene directly if there is any potential risk of danger, harm or injury. Always call for help if necessary. You will need to maintain a calm yet assertive attitude in helping to deal with the situation.

Some behaviour may be dangerous to individuals and to the environment, and if you suspect that this is the case it is essential that you report this to your manager or supervisor so that the appropriate action can be taken to control the situation and prevent danger and harm from happening. You need to be aware of your organisation's policies and procedures for dealing with and reporting dangerous, abusive, discriminatory or exploitive behaviour, and be aware of the steps you should take to control it. Remember that you must never put yourself or others at risk of harm or injury, always get help.

KUS 13

Stress can also lead to inappropriate behaviour. More and more people these days are suffering from the effects of stress. This is often as a result of their busy lifestyle, their social status and their own individual characteristics. It could also be due to the demands put upon them by their families. They may be under pressure at work or they may be suffering from stress because they are unemployed and are not able to provide for their family. This may result in the individual becoming angry and aggressive, and in order to release this tension and frustration they may take it out on other people. They may become very abusive to the **vulnerable adults** in their environment, usually those individuals who are not able to protect themselves.

Danger, harm and abuse

It is important that you recognise the signs and symptoms of **danger**, **harm** and **abuse**, and that you follow your organisation's policies and procedures to report these.

Danger, harm and abuse are all interlinked within this unit. If at any time you believe that an individual or group of individuals is at serious risk of danger, harm or abuse, whether you have been informed about it by someone or you have overheard something, or even if you consider that something does not feel right, always take it seriously. If you forgot to report it and something terrible happened you would never forgive yourself. Danger, harm and abuse are significant and serious problems within our society. For instance, harm and abuse can occur when an individual is deprived of their rights to:

- Privacy.
- Independence.
- Protection and security.
- A decent quality of life.
- Choose for themselves.

Harm and abuse may occur as a result of just a single act or repeated acts. It may be physical, verbal or psychological. It could be as a result of an act of neglect or an omission to act. It can occur in any relationship and can result in significant harm to, or exploitation of, the individual subjected to the abuse, putting the individual in serious danger.

Figure 9
What might make
abuse more
likely?

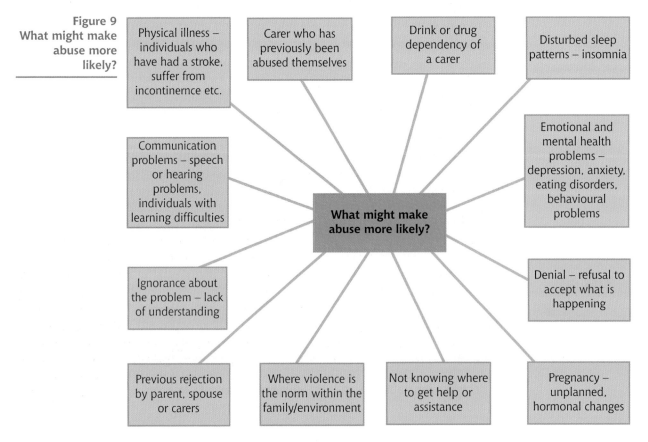

Physical illness – individuals who have had a stroke, suffer from incontinernce etc.

Carer who has previously been abused themselves

Drink or drug dependency of a carer

Disturbed sleep patterns – insomnia

Communication problems – speech or hearing problems, individuals with learning difficulties

What might make abuse more likely?

Emotional and mental health problems – depression, anxiety, eating disorders, behavioural problems

Ignorance about the problem – lack of understanding

Denial – refusal to accept what is happening

Previous rejection by parent, spouse or carers

Where violence is the norm within the family/environment

Not knowing where to get help or assistance

Pregnancy – unplanned, hormonal changes

There are different issues relating to the abuse of adults and children, but one major factor that is common to them both is the abuse of power, where one person is physically, emotionally, psychologically or socially stronger than the other.

Categories of abuse

Physical abuse (assault and neglect)

KUS 19

Definition: Direct infliction of physical pain or injury; unexplained injuries that are caused intentionally, or not prevented by, another person; or the denial of the physical health-related necessities of life.

- Assault: an individual can incur injuries as a result of beating or slapping by another. They can be pushed or kicked, or held in an inappropriate restraint. Cigarette burns or cutting can also be inflicted upon an individual. If incorrect moving and handling techniques are used to move or transfer an individual, abrasions to the skin can occur that could lead to pressure sores and infection. Injuries to joints or fractures could also occur. Assault can also be touching someone in a way that the individual being touched perceives as threatening or harmful.

Figure 10
Neglect is a form of abuse

- Neglect (this can be active or passive): the individual can experience a lack of attention, abandonment or even confinement by family members and society. Neglect can also involve breach of duty of care needs that results in injury or violation of individual rights, for example withholding of nutrition and fluids causing malnutrition and dehydration, or inappropriate use of heat or ventilation where the individual is too hot or too cold. The individual might be denied rest and sleep or could be given inadequate personal care and hygiene and inappropriate or unclean clothing. A lack of privacy, dignity and respect might be shown towards the individual, or there may be a lack of safety precautions or supervision. The individual may be under- or over-medicated or prevented from accessing professional help or treatments.

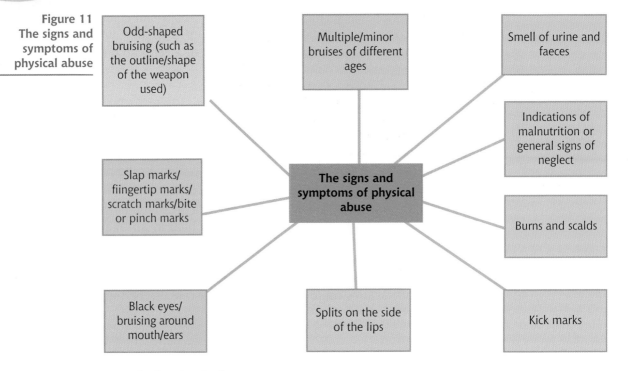

**Figure 11
The signs and
symptoms of
physical abuse**

Psychological abuse

Definition: To negate the individual's choices and independent wishes.

Psychological abuse could include the removal of the individual's decision-making processes and restriction of their choices. The individual could be humiliated, harassed or intimidated, and that may cause them anxiety and fear. They could be socially isolated and starved of love, affection and companionship. They could experience non-verbal abuse and silence or they could be the victim of threatening behaviour or verbal abuse. Aggressive language and behaviour and racist or sexist remarks could be directed at the individual. It is possible that the individual could experience emotional or psychological abuse from others and not be protected from this by their carers.

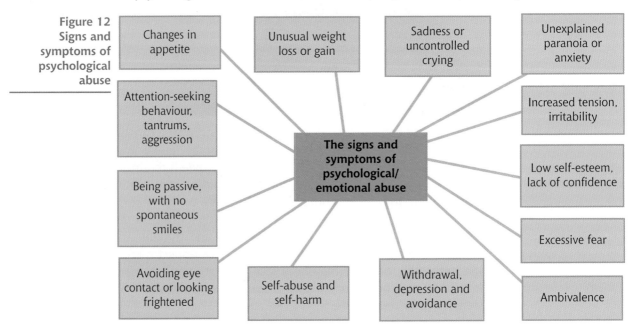

**Figure 12
Signs and
symptoms of
psychological
abuse**

Financial abuse

Definition: Dishonest use of an individual's resources.

An individual could experience the misuse of their money, for instance their pension could be withheld from them or they may not be given any personal allowance. They could be asked to sign cheques for various amounts to be withdrawn from their bank or the Post Office without explanation, and they could find that their personal possessions are taken without their permission.

Figure 13
Signs and symptoms of financial abuse

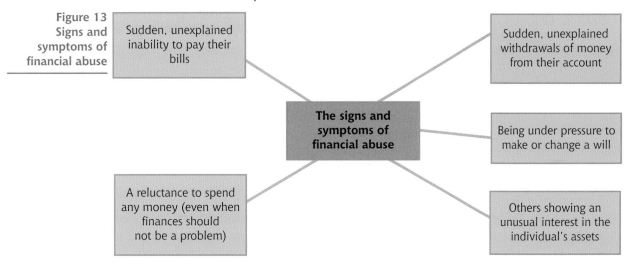

Sudden, unexplained inability to pay their bills

Sudden, unexplained withdrawals of money from their account

The signs and symptoms of financial abuse

Being under pressure to make or change a will

A reluctance to spend any money (even when finances should not be a problem)

Others showing an unusual interest in the individual's assets

Sexual abuse

Definition: The involvement of vulnerable adults or children in sexual activities or relationships which they do not want or understand or, because of their age or mental capability, cannot consent to.

Sexual abuse can take place within a family, in a care environment or in other relationships where the abuse of power is used to intimidate or humiliate the individual. The violation of privacy and the use of personal care tasks or rewards as an opportunity for sexual satisfaction, sexual molestation or rape may also be experienced by an individual.

Figure 14
Signs and symptoms of sexual abuse

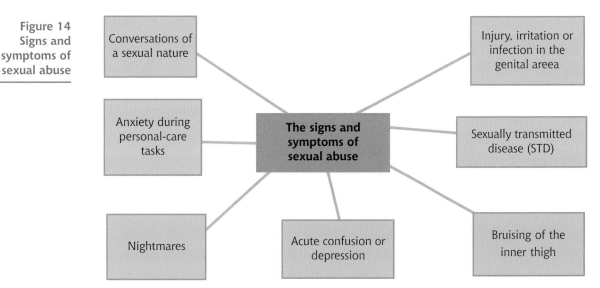

Conversations of a sexual nature

Injury, irritation or infection in the genital areea

Anxiety during personal-care tasks

The signs and symptoms of sexual abuse

Sexually transmitted disease (STD)

Nightmares

Acute confusion or depression

Bruising of the inner thigh

There are many signs that an individual is being abused, the main one being a change in their behaviour. You may notice that an individual who was once outgoing and who normally enjoyed chatting to other people suddenly becomes shy and reserved and does not want to mix with others. This could be an indication that something is wrong. The extent to which the individual will be affected by harm or abuse, either in the short term or the long term, depends on the individual. Some may recover and return to a normal way of life by forgiving and forgetting whatever they may have experienced, whilst others may never recover and will need professional help for the rest of their lives. Alternatively individuals may fluctuate between the two. The support that the individual receives at the time of disclosing and following abuse will impact on their recovery to some extent. Any past experiences they may have had and their own coping strategies, beliefs and self-image will also affect their recovery. You will need to observe and monitor the individual at all times. You may notice changes in their attitude or behaviour, for instance if they are normally quite placid and happy and suddenly they become impatient and demanding, or if their sleep pattern changes or dietary intake changes, then you need to use your organisation's systems and procedures to report these and any other concerns that you may have.

KUS 2, 12

Expression of concerns

KUS 3, 5, 8, 12, 16, 18, 22, 23

Try to develop good relationships with the individuals in your care and with the significant people in their lives so that they can express their fears, anxieties, feelings and concerns without worry of ridicule, rejection or **retribution**. They need to be able to trust you and feel comfortable sharing their problems with you. They need to know that you will listen objectively to their concerns and problems, take them seriously and report these to the appropriate person who will be able to alleviate their fears. Never ridicule an individual for disclosing something which is obviously causing them anxiety and distress, no matter how major or minor the problem may be. Remember to treat the individual with sensitivity, understanding and respect.

Disclosure of danger, harm or abuse

It is important that you respond immediately to disclosures of harm, danger or abuse. If the individual has disclosed some information to you it is essential that you record this information exactly as the individual said it. Avoid actions that could adversely affect the use of evidence in future investigations and in court for instance, do not ask questions or lead the individual into telling you details about what happened. The individual may ask you not to tell anyone because they might think that they will be punished by their abuser if the information gets out. You must always be clear about your role and responsibility to pass information of this type to your manager or supervisor. Never promise a level of confidentiality that is beyond your authority.

Your responsibilities

You need to support individuals and key people to understand your responsibilities to pass on information about actual or likely danger, harm or abuse. Be alert for any situations where an individual tries to confide in you that they are planning to hurt themselves or other individuals. They may think that the information will not go any further, or they may say that they are telling you in confidence. Let them know that any information of this nature has to be reported to your manager or supervisor, and that you cannot keep it to yourself. It is for their safety and protection that you need to report it.

KUS 6, 7, 8, 11

It is the responsibility of everyone who works in the care setting to be vigilant in recognising the signs and symptoms of harm and abuse. The health, safety and protection of all individuals is essential. In whatever capacity you work it is your responsibility to be familiar with policies and procedures relating to the care and protection of individuals. Ensure that you know what action to take if you suspect that harm or abuse has occurred or is currently taking place.

KUS 18

You need to be sure that your own practice does not cause harm or danger to individuals. Maintain good standards of practice at all times, and keep yourself up to date with the knowledge and skills you require to perform your job role according to your organisation's policies and procedures. Always do whatever you can to protect individuals, including yourself and other colleagues, from danger, harm or abuse. Everyone needs to be responsible for their actions and others should not be put at risk of danger or harm. If you see something that may cause a risk to anyone, whether this is an item of equipment or the acts of another individual, you must always take the appropriate action to reduce the danger. Remove and report faulty equipment or call for assistance if you suspect that someone is intent on causing harm to others. Never put yourself at risk, always ask for back-up and assistance from other colleagues.

Supervision and support

KUS 10

It is possible that some situations may be very distressing for you, and you should discuss these with your manager or supervisor. Ask for the appropriate supervision and support to enable you to cope with your thoughts and feelings about any suspected or disclosed danger, harm or abuse that a particular situation may have caused.

It can be difficult to listen to an individual discussing possible abuse and mistreatment. If you get upset about it then it would be advisable to ask another colleague to work with the individual. You should discuss this as soon as possible after the event rather than wait until you return to work for your next shift. You may not immediately recognise that it has upset you, and you may feel alright. On the other hand, it could seriously affect your ability to cope, so it is better to discuss it with someone who can help you.

KUS 11

Your organisation will possibly run courses or workshops on handling aggression and violence or abuse of vulnerable adults, and you need to speak to your manager or supervisor about accessing these to develop your practice.

KUS 6, 7, 8

Completion of records

If it is part of your role to write in the plan of care, always make sure that your notes are accurate, legible and complete according to your organisational guidelines. Ensure that on all entries you record the time, date and names of any colleagues involved before signing and printing your name. If it is not part of your role to write in the plan of care, ensure that you give accurate information to the person making the entry. The individual's plan of care and their case notes are legal documents and may be used for further investigations and in court if the situation arises These are confidential documents and must always be stored safely and securely when not in use, according to local and organisational requirements. When writing your records always complete them in black ink and avoid the use of correction fluid. Any error should be simply crossed through with one line, and you should put your signature alongside it.

KUS 21

It is essential that the records do not contain statements which could adversely affect the use of evidence in any future investigations. The information contained in the records should never be changed, removed or struck out, or added to at any time as this would seriously affect their use if they were required in court in a legal situation.

Practical Example

Abuse

Robert is 65 years old. He is a widower and he was diagnosed several years ago with a depressive illness following the death of his wife. He has been taking anti-depressants prescribed by his GP and has not worked for a few years. His daughter and son-in-law and their three children live nearby and tend to visit him once a week. Although he manages to make some meals for himself he often goes without food. Just recently he has become more depressed and has been quite angry and confused. Once or twice he has fallen in the house and has sustained minor bruises to his head and arms. His daughter is very concerned about him and persuaded him to see the doctor. He was referred for psychiatric assessment and admitted to the local hospital. He was reluctant to leave his home, but agreed to go providing his daughter took care of his house and personal belongings. She agreed to do this, and she said that she would visit him during the week, family, work and time allowing.

The care staff noticed that Robert was becoming very quiet and withdrawn; he had started to pick at his food and was not sleeping very well. They noticed that it was usually when his daughter had been to visit him. One day, one of the care staff noticed that he had a lot of official-looking documents in his room, some of which appeared to relate to his home. Robert asked her when he would be able to go home, because he said that his daughter was going to sell his house because he did not need it. He also told her that he had no money because his daughter was collecting his pension and she always forgot to bring him any money when she came to visit him. His daughter and family had recently been on holiday for two weeks and had sent him a postcard.

➤ *Why do you think Robert has suddenly become quiet and withdrawn, not sleeping and picking at his food?*

➤ *Why do you think he is now telling the care staff about these things?*

➤ *What would you say to Robert, and how could you reassure him?*

➤ *What form of abuse relates to Robert's situation?*

➤ *To whom would you report this situation, and what documentation should be completed?*

Key points – contribute to the protection of all individuals

- Be familiar with the information available to help you to identify the risk of actual and likely danger, harm and abuse.
- Recognise the signs and symptoms of danger, harm and abuse, and report these using your organisation's systems and procedures.
- Develop effective relationships with individuals, support their anxieties and feelings, and respond immediately to any disclosures of danger, harm and abuse.
- Be sensitive to situations, issues and behaviour, and recognise and challenge inappropriate behaviour.
- Seek supervision and support for yourself so that you can cope with suspected or disclosed danger, harm or abuse.
- Complete accurate records and reports, and maintain the confidentiality of information. Avoid the use of statements which could adversely affect the use of evidence in future investigations and in court.

Unit HSC35

Are you ready for assessment?

Promote choice, well-being and the protection of all individuals

This unit is about how you develop supportive relationships with all individuals and promote their choice and independence. It is also about how you provide support to individuals to enable them to communicate their views and preferences. It is about how you support individuals in an anti-oppressive way to ensure they receive care that is consistent with their abilities, beliefs, culture, values and preferences. The unit is about how you contribute to the protection of all individuals in the care setting by challenging discrimination, resolving conflicts and responding appropriately to comments or complaints.

Your assessment will mainly be carried out through observation by your assessor and this should provide most of the evidence for the elements in this unit. Your assessor must observe you for some part of each element of this unit. Evidence of your knowledge and understanding will be demonstrated through observation, your assessor examining work products, e.g. reports, minutes of meetings, as well as through answering oral and/or written questions.

You need to be aware when planning assessments that this unit also relates to the other core units and many of the optional units, and so you may also be able to evidence performance criteria for these.

▶

If your work takes you into the individual's home you need to explain about the assessment and seek the individual's permission for your assessor to visit. If the visit would be intrusive you will need to consider alternative evidence-gathering methods, e.g. expert witness testimony.

Direct observation by your assessor

Your assessor will need to plan to see you carry out the performance criteria (PCs) in each of the elements in this unit. The performance criteria that may be difficult to meet through observation are:

- HSC35a PC 7
- HSC35b PC 7
- HSC35c PC 3, 5, 6, 8

Other types of evidence

You may need to present other forms of evidence in order to:

- Cover criteria not observed by your assessor.
- Show that you have the required knowledge, understanding and skills to claim competence in this area of practice.
- Ensure your work practice is consistent.

Your assessor may also need to ask you questions to confirm your knowledge and understanding and ensure that you can apply this to your practice.

Preparing to be observed

You must make sure that your workplace and any individuals and key people involved in your work agree to you being assessed. Explicit, informed consent must be obtained before you carry out any assessment activity that involves individuals or which involves access to confidential information related to their care.

Before your assessments you should read carefully the performance criteria for each element in the unit. Try to cover as much as you can during your observation but remember that you and your assessor can also plan for additional sources of evidence should full coverage of all performance criteria not be possible.

Check your knowledge

- How can you develop supportive relationships with individuals and help them to make the right choices to promote their independence?
- Why is it important to provide the individual with the appropriate information and advice regarding the services and resources available to them?
- How may your own values, beliefs and preferences affect how you relate to individuals?
- What is meant by holistic needs?
- Why is it important to value individuals and to take into account their individual needs and preferences?
- How can you provide active support to individuals, enabling them to participate in activities to maintain their independence?
- What action would you take if you were having difficulty in promoting equality and diversity?
- How would you challenge dangerous, abusive, discriminatory or exploitative behaviour?
- How would you support individuals following an incident involving abusive or disruptive behaviour?
- Why is it necessary to complete accurate, legible, dated, timed and signed records and reports, and why is confidentiality important?

Contribute to care planning and review

*T*his unit is about all aspects of the care planning process. This includes assessment of needs, development of care plans, implementation and review of these plans. You will be expected to contribute to the assessment of individual needs and preferences in your care setting. You will also be expected to contribute to the development, implementation and review of these care plans.

This unit has three elements:

⌒ **HSC328a** *Contribute to assessing the needs and preferences of individuals*

⌒ **HSC328b** *Support the development and the implementation of care plans*

⌒ **HSC328c** *Contribute to reviewing care plans*

Introduction

All individuals have basic needs that must be met if they are to survive and develop to their full potential. However, individual preferences can vary enormously. Any unmet needs have consequences, for example individuals can feel hurt and be unwilling to ask for further help. Therefore, it is important that you assess needs and preferences and develop, implement and review care plans to enable individuals to feel that their needs are met.

There are four basic needs:

- Physical – food, water, oxygen, sleep, warmth and shelter.
- Social – shared activities, friendships, a sense of belonging.
- Intellectual – sense of achievement, having new experiences.
- Emotional – feeling loved and wanted, feeling love towards others, able to express feelings and emotions.

⌒ **Assessment**

KUS 5, 6

An assessment of individuals' needs is required to provide support to meet those needs. Assessment is a core concept in care and is discussed in key documents, for example Essence of Care (2003), NHS Community Care Act 1990, Care Standards Act 2000, Carers (Recognition and Services) Act 1995, and Registration Homes (Registration & Inspection Standards) 2004. An assessment will help to form a picture of the individual, their circumstances and needs. Assessment will inform the care planning process where appropriate support is identified to meet the individual's needs. In the process the assessor and the individual will bring in their own ideas and interpretations. Therefore, communication is important to enable the assessor to discover the individual's needs and how these can be met. This makes assessment a two-way process.

Types of assessment

There are different types of assessment involved in care planning as follows.

Contact assessment

This is the first assessment when significant needs are first described or suspected. Basic personal information is collected and the nature of the needs is described. The contact assessment acts as the referral document to other agencies. There may be sufficient information in the contact assessment to provide support to the individual. If there are needs in several areas of an individual's life then a more rounded assessment may be required.

Overview assessment

Practitioners, e.g. social workers, nurses and therapists, will carry out an overview assessment if they judge that the individual's needs are such that they require a more in-depth assessment. This will explore personal care, physical well-being, senses and mental health. At the time of the overview assessment the assessor will use information from the contact assessment and their practitioner knowledge and judgement to decide which areas of need require further exploration.

Specialist assessments

Specialist assessments explore specific needs identified in contact or overview assessments. These needs can include difficulties with mobility, housing and nutrition. Specialist assessments may rely on the use of assessment scales or tools to monitor and record the severity of the need. They are carried out by specialist practitioners, e.g. a physiotherapist, palliative care nurse, occupational therapist or psychologist.

Comprehensive assessment

This type of assessment is undertaken when all of the areas of need require more detailed specialist assessment. A multi-disciplinary, multi-agency team would be involved in the individual's care. This is likely to happen if the individual requires intensive short-term or prolonged support. This may include admission to a care home or substantial packages of care at home. A care co-ordinator would be allocated to liaise with all those involved. This could be a practitioner, the individual, their carer or family member.

Assessment is undertaken prior to developing and implementing care plans.

Care planning

KUS 2, 4

Care planning is a cyclical process that is centred on the individual. Care plans are agreed for each individual in the form of a meeting that takes place after an appropriate assessment has been made. Plans are changed when the condition of the individual changes.

The values and principles that underpin all care plans place the user at the centre of the care planning process. Care plans should deliver high quality health and social care and be developed in an anti-oppressive way. For example, they should include the individual and ensure they have access to appropriate information regarding options in their preferred format, they should promote choice and independence, promote the safety of the individual and ensure co-ordination of all health and social care providers. Care plans should deliver continuity of care for the individual and empower and support practitioners working with them. By care planning the health and social care organisation is accountable to individuals, the public and informal carers. Assessment is undertaken prior to the care planning process. Care plans are negotiated and agreed by all those involved, often at a meeting of all the interested parties. Care plans are monitored and reviewed as and when the individual's needs change.

Figure 2
Care planning

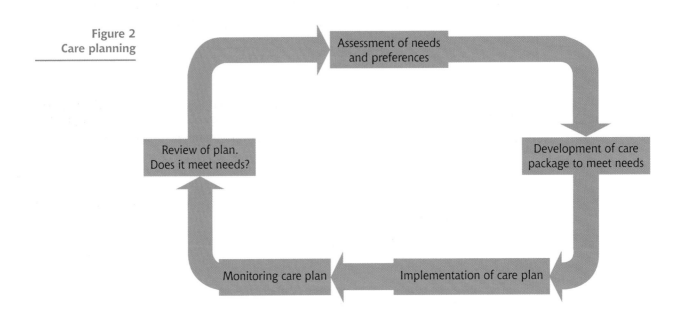

Models of nursing care

KUS 5, 6, 7

Caring is a complex activity and may be demonstrated in a variety of ways. Models of nursing can help you understand the range of approaches to care. In all models priority is given to the individual and assessment is essential to meet the individual's needs. Value is also placed in providing quality care for the period that you are caring for the individual. The choice of the model depends on the assessment and needs identified or factors associated with the health care team, for example environment and resources. It is also important that the individual is at the centre of the care planning process and a variety of practice models are used to facilitate this process.

National service frameworks

These are long-term strategies for improving care in specific areas. They set national standards and identify appropriate interventions for individuals using health and social care services. They will raise the quality of care and bring together the views of individuals, health and social care professionals and families. These frameworks place the individual at the centre of the care planning process.

Social models

These take into account the inner world and experiences of individuals and communities. They also recognise the importance of social factors and social perspectives as well as economic and environmental factors. These models take a holistic view of the individual and their social circumstances while placing the individual at the centre of the care planning process – person-centred care planning. They also involve health promotion and prevention of disease.

Peplau

This developed from working with individuals with mental health issues. The aim was to encourage the individual to examine their feelings to enable them to understand what is happening and to become involved in their care.

Orem

This is used when the individual appears to be able to look after themselves. Responsibility for decision making and caring activities lies with the individual. This means the individual has control of their life as they experience health care.

Roper, Logan and Tierney

This is the model of nursing most commonly used in the UK. It is based on a model of living. The model is made up of:

- Activities of daily living, for example personal cleansing and dressing.
- Life span.
- Dependence/independence continuum.
- Factors influencing activities of daily living.
- Individuality in living.

The activities of daily living are identified as:

- Maintaining a safe environment.
- Communicating.
- Breathing.
- Eating and drinking.
- Eliminating.

KUS 10

- Personal cleansing and dressing.
- Controlling body temperature.
- Mobilising.
- Working and playing.
- Expressing sexuality.
- Sleeping.
- Dying.

These activities make up an individual's life regardless of age, sex or whether or not that person is healthy. They are influenced by life span, for example a baby cannot perform these independently. They are also influenced by the dependence/independence of the individual.

Element HSC328a — Contribute to assessing the needs and preferences of individuals

Roles and responsibilities in assessment

Needs and preferences

The term 'need' has a variety of different meanings which may change over time. Well-being can consist of a wide range of characteristics and therefore needs should include personal and social care, health care, housing, finance, education, employment, leisure, transport and access. Each individual will have a subjective view of what their needs are and what health resources are required to meet these needs. It will be your role to help in the assessment of these needs.

KUS 6

The National Health Service Community Care Act 1990 made assessment of need for community care services a duty for local authorities. Through assessment the services provided are then appropriate to needs.

In 1972 Jonathan Bradshaw defined need as:

- Normative – these are needs identified by professionals.
- Felt – these are wants, desires and wishes of the individual.
- Expressed – how individuals tell you they require services.
- Comparative – needs that are similar for individuals of the same **socio-economic** background in different areas of the country.

To understand this better, here is an example.

Mr Jones is 85 years old, lives alone, is partially sighted and has arthritis and bronchitis in the winter. His GP has identified that he needs a flu injection (normative need). Mr Jones misses being able to read his newspaper and would like to be able to do this (felt need). Mr Jones is finding it more difficult to manage the stairs and would like to move somewhere smaller with no stairs. He telephones the local housing office to ask about accommodation transfers (expressed need). After reading an article in the local newspaper, Mr Jones' son discovers that his father could be receiving a number of benefits and support with shopping and housework (comparative need).

Maslow identified a hierarchy of needs. He believed that human development is controlled by the individual pursuing needs. He identified that some needs are more important than others. For example, once basic needs such as food, water and shelter are met, then the individual will feel motivated to move on to growth needs. These are a feeling of belonging, achievement of personal goals. Self-actualisation is only achieved when all other needs are met. The individual can move up or down this hierarchy when needs change. However, Maslow's theory has been criticised as being oversimplified. More information can be found in unit HSC31.

Legislation

KUS 6, 7, 9

Legislation describes the statutory sector duties and powers that underpin assessment. Community care assessments are the means for deciding whether to provide care as defined in the NHS and Community Care Act 1990. The purpose of community care is to enable the individual to remain in their own home with help and support, for example personal care, meals, equipment and adaptations. Fair Access to Care Services provides a clear framework of eligibility for services and is used by local authorities to determine how resources will be spent equitably.

The government White Paper 'Caring for People' states that assessments should take into account the wishes of the individual and their carer, and the ability of the carer to continue to provide care. To do this the services provided will need to be flexible and the carer and individual should be able to make choices about these services.

Carers are also eligible for assessment of their needs if they provide a substantial and regular amount of care. The legislation that facilitates this is the Carers Recognition and Services Act 1995 and the Carers and Disabled Children's Act 2000.

Further recommendations in response to the need for assessment have been made in Agenda for Change: The NHS Knowledge and Skills Framework 2004. Here, assessment and the process of care planning are related to meeting health and well-being needs. Similar information appears in the Welsh Assembly Government in a Unified Assessment and Care Management process.

Different groups of individuals have different assessment processes, for example:
- Older people have the Single Assessment Process from January 2002.
- Adult community groups in Scotland have the Single Shared Assessment from April 2003.
- Disabled people are entitled to assessment through the Disabled Persons (Services Consultation and Representation) Act 1986 and the NHS Community Care Act 1990.
- Mental health service users are provided for under the Mental Health Act 1983 and the Care Programme Approach.

KUS 7

All care should be given in a way that ensures fair access to care services. In government legislation the emphasis has been on achieving the objectives of the care plan while tailoring choices to meet individuals' needs and promoting choice, for example the

Care Standards Act 2000, Modernising Social Services 1998 and Valuing People 2001. Fair Access to Care was implemented in April 2003. It states that authorities must show that:

- There is consistency in the way need is assessed.
- There are clear objectives in the care plan and that independence is promoted.
- Risk assessment is carried out.
- Regular review takes place.

By offering choice and involving the individual in care planning **empowerment** takes place. Your role will be to ensure that this occurs and that certain groups are not disadvantaged, for example the elderly, those from ethnic minorities and those with mental health issues. By promoting **advocacy** and not allowing your own stereotypes and values to get in the way of listening to individuals, discrimination is reduced. Anti-discriminatory practice should ensure that the individual and others feel they are treated fairly and with respect. All processes in care planning should be sensitive to the racial, cultural and religious background and to disability, sexual and gender needs. These processes should involve the individual in monitoring the design and effectiveness of the care plan. You should ensure that you are familiar with the policies and procedures in place in the organisation relating to anti-discriminatory practice.

Codes of practice

KUS 5

Codes of practice provide guidance on behaviour standards for people working in health and social care, for example for nurses there is the NMC Code of Professional Conduct. This code states that the nurse should ensure that no action or omission within the nurse's responsibility is detrimental to the interests, conditions or safety of individuals. It is therefore the nurse's responsibility to assess need and to develop, implement and review care plans.

The Social Care Councils Code of Practice for Social Workers states that social care workers should promote the rights and the interests of the individual. In relation to care planning this will result in treating each person as an individual, respecting choice, diversity, dignity and privacy and supporting individuals in making choices about the services they use.

Assessment

KUS 2

Assessment is about collecting information on an individual's needs and circumstances. The information should be evaluated and analysed so that eligible needs are identified and an appropriate and timely care plan is put in place.

Assessment lies at the heart of person-centred care and should be approached in a consistent way. Assessment should be based on the individual's account of their needs and wishes. Health and social care practitioners need to work together to ensure that information is shared and not duplicated. This will mean that the individual does not have to repeat information. It will also mean that the services are more responsive to the individual's needs.

Figure 3
Make sure that
information is
shared and not
duplicated

You may be involved in assessing the individual's needs, especially if your organisation is already involved in providing support and/or if you are the individual's key worker. You may also be asked to observe the individual, undertake specific assessment activities and carry out specific tests, for example assessment scale of daily living.

Figure 4
Assessment
should be based
on the individual's
account of their
needs and wishes

KUS 4

Depending on the individual's needs, other practitioners may be involved in the assessment (see Table 1).

Table 1 Practitioners who may be involved in assessing care needs, and their responsibilities

Practitioner	Responsibility
Social worker/team leader	Convene initial assessment meeting and subsequent meetings. Co-ordinate service provision. Set timescales for review. Support individual in assessment of needs and explain process of care planning.
Community care co-ordinator	Attend care planning meetings. Co-ordinate and manage community care services, e.g. home care. Assess the level of service required. Support those involved in implementing care plan and reviewing services provided.
Community matron	Assessment of needs. Act as care co-ordinator in complex cases or where long-term needs are identified. Liaise with other practitioners. Co-ordinate care package delivery.
Community nurse	Assessment of needs. Assess services required. Advise other agencies.
Health visitor	Assessment of individual's needs. Support individual in monitoring and review of needs. Liaise with GP. Provide health promotion information.
Occupational therapist	Assess individual for aids and adaptations to facilitate independent or supported living. Support individual to use adaptations.
Physiotherapist	Assess and treat movement disorders. Co-ordinate and support the individual to restore function.
Voluntary co-ordinator	Liaise with NHS organisations to provide support for individual in community. Support individual in making contact and using these organisations.
General practitioner (GP)	Support the individual during assessment of needs. Co-ordinate services and advise other agencies.
Speech and language therapist	Support the individual in assessment and management of communication. Advise other professionals and agencies in management of communication.
Clinical psychologist	Assessment of intellectual impairment and behaviour difficulties. Advise other professionals and agencies of management strategies. Support the individual in managing these strategies and monitor and review needs.

Access and review information

Your role as a carer is to assess and review information about the individual's needs and preferences.

You need to gather information required for assessment and review from a number of sources:

- The individual.
- The individual's carers, family and friends.
- Other practitioners.
- Assessment scales.
- Records held.

The individual

User involvement in social care is central in policy today (this means that the individual should be involved). The government has reinforced the need to involve those who are or will be potential users of services. Individuals need to be consulted on their needs and preferences. The Health and Social Care Act 2001 makes it a duty for those who receive or will receive care to be involved in the planning of services and changes to services already provided.

KUS 9

The National Service Framework for Older People sets out the principles of involving older people in assessment and care planning processes. The services are also to be designed around needs and preferences. The National Service Framework for Mental Health states that services provided will involve users in planning and delivery of care.

Valuing People states that people with a learning disability should be fully involved in the decision-making process.

This legislation means you must gather information from the individual before any care planning meeting takes place. By doing this you are involving them in decisions about their care and showing respect for life experiences, their needs and preferences. First collate the basic information from the contact assessment or referral. This will indicate the individual's needs and the impact of these on their independence, daily functioning and quality of life. If appropriate, i.e. if you need more detailed information in order to identify appropriate services, you should meet the individual. Explain the purpose of your meeting, how information will be used and gain their consent for information sharing. Collect and collate the information using the organisation's assessment tool. You can then review the information before giving it to other practitioners. You can use electronic tools and data-sharing protocols to provide information to all those involved.

**Figure 5
Collect and collate
the information**

The individual's carers

KUS 4

The carer's perspective is also important as it provides a view of the individual's situation, needs and preferences. The carer can also explain the help and support that the individual is already receiving and whether any further help is required. By involving the carer you are acknowledging the contribution made to the individual's care and the expertise that has been gained. The carer can also inform you of any life events or recent changes that have affected the individual. You might collect this information during a face-to-face meeting or, if this is not possible, other ways of gathering the information should be explored such as via the telephone or in written form. Again you will have to collate the information and review this before the care planning meeting.

Other practitioners

The range of practitioners involved can vary depending on the information you have gathered, evaluated and analysed. Their role is identified on page 146.

Assessment scales

The Department of Health recommends that scales should be used to identify and quantify the extent of a specific health condition in relation to the individual's ability for personal care, mobility, tissue viability, mental health and cognitive ability, for example the Mini Mental Test for memory impairment or the Waterlow Scale for pressure areas.

Records

Information contained in the individual's records is useful in assessing needs and preferences. Records can contain information already expressed by the individual and family and can contain accounts from practitioners involved in care. These may include medical, nursing and therapy notes. Records will also provide you with information on the services already in place to meet these needs and how these have impacted on the individual. The records will provide an account of how needs have changed over time.

You will have to go through the records and collate all relevant information and review this before the care planning meeting. Again this information will need to be shared with all members of the care planning team.

Figure 7
An example of an assessment scale

Guidelines	Patient's Name:
1. Waterlow score update according to patient requirement (minimum weekly)	Unit No.
	Ward:

10+ AT RISK   **15+ HIGH RISK**   **20+ VERY HIGH RISK**

DATE	Month –																	
TIME																		
WEIGHT	Average	0																
	Above average	1																
	Obese	2																
	Below average	3																
CONTINENCE	complete/catheter	0																
	Occasional incont.	1																
	Catheter/faeces incont.	2																
	Double incont.	3																
SKIN TYPE	Healthy	0																
	Tissue paper	1																
	Dry	1																
	Odematous	1																
	Clammy	1																
	Discoloured	2																
	Broken spot	3																
MOBILITY	Fully mobile	0																
	Restless/fidgety	1																
	Apathetic	2																
	Restricted	3																
	Inert/traction	5																
	Chairbound	5																
SEX/AGE	Male	1																
	Female	2																
	14–49	1																
	50–64	2																
	65–74	3																
	75–80	4																
	>81	5																
APPETITE	Average	0																
	Poor	1																
	N.G. tube	2																
	Anorexia	3																
TISSUE MALNUTRITION	Terminal cachexia	8																
	Cardiac failure	5																
	Peripheral vascular dis.	5																
	Anaemia	2																
	Smoking	2																
NEURO	Diabetes, CVA																	
	M.S. paraplegia	4/6																
SURGERY	Orthopaedic below waist	5																
	spinal. >2 hrs on the table*	5																
MEDICATION	Anti-inflammatory Drugs	4																
TOTAL																		
NURSE INITIALS																		

*up to 48 hrs post-operative   Audit date:

KUS 1

All information gathered should be obtained, collated, reviewed, recorded and distributed according to national and organisational policies on confidentiality. Individuals will also have to give written consent to the sharing of information with others involved in the assessment process.

Support required for individuals

Communication is an integral part of the assessment process. Communication skills are central to the relationship that you will build with the individual. In order that the individual can fully participate in the assessment process you will need to assess the individual's communication skills and ascertain if they require extra support.

KUS 8, 12

Extra support can be:

- *An advocate* – used when the individual is confused or is unable to understand what is going on. They can support the individual and acknowledge what their experience is. This is especially important if the individual has had bad past experiences, or is too ill and/or lacks the confidence to express their needs in a room full of practitioners.

- *An interpreter or translator* – used when there is a language difference between the individual and those involved in the assessment process. An interpreter or translator can use the individual's preferred spoken language. They can explain the process and the questions asked and interpret what the individual perceives to be their needs. An interpreter can help maintain the individual's independence and participation as information is provided. Information can be presented in different ways, e.g. verbally, Braille, different leaflets. You should never use a carer or family member as an interpreter especially where medical or personal details are to be revealed.

- *A signer* – used when the individual is deaf, has learning disabilities and communicates using signs and symbols. Again the assessment process can be explained and your questions signed. The individual can then express their needs and wishes.

- *Specialist equipment* – for example, a computer can be used to support the individual to participate fully in the assessment process.

Individual's needs

Your role will be to offer support to individuals and key people.

Key people

When you are involved in the assessment of an individual's needs it is also part of the process to involve key people who have a supportive relationship with the individual. These can include family, friends, carers and others. They can help to identify and communicate the needs and preferences of individuals and identify any risks arising from these. They help to make the assessment inclusive (i.e. the assessment considers the views of everyone concerned with the individual), but you will have to make sure

KUS 4, 8

that no one view dominates over the others. Key people can also help to make the assessment valid and true to life. Information should be recorded about whether there is a current need and how it is presently being addressed.

Individual needs

The individual will have a range of needs that may require your support. These are shown below.

Needs that may require support:

- *Personal care:*
  - Daily living
  - Washing, bathing
  - Dressing
  - Toileting, continence of urine and faeces
  - Pain
  - Oral health
  - Eating, drinking and swallowing
  - Breathing difficulties
  - Foot cae
  - tissue viability, pressure sores
  - Mobility
  - Sleeping patterns

- *Senses:*
  - Sight
  - Hearing

- *Relationships:*
  - Social contact, personal and/or sexual relationships
  - Relationships in general
  - Involvement in hobbies, work and education

- *Environment:*
  - Food preparation
  - Houssework and cleaning
  - Shopping
  - Location and type of housing
  - Access to housing
  - Ability to move around
  - Housing
  - Amenities in housing
  - Heating
  - Personal finances
  - Access to local facilities, e.g. shops

- *Mental health:*
  - Orientation, memory loss
  - Depression and other mental health problems
  - Bereavement and loss
  - Emotional distress

Risk assessment

KUS 2, 3

It is also important that you take into account the risks involved in carrying out activities of daily living, for example washing and dressing. Risk needs to be examined in relation to the holistic assessment of needs. Risk assessments have several things in common:

- The assessment is carried out by a competent person.
- **Hazards** are identified.
- **Risks** are evaluated.
- Control measures are identified.
- The assessment is recorded.
- Action is taken if necessary.
- Reviews are held regularly.

Here is an example of how this can be applied in practice.

Julie is 28 years old and has Down's syndrome. She has recently got a job as a domestic at the local residential home. She needs to walk to the bus stop (which is 10 minutes away). At the end of the journey Julie has to walk to her place of work. This involves crossing three busy roads each way. Her key worker (a competent worker) has completed the risk-assessment training and so carries out the risk assessment. Her findings are detailed below:

Figure 8
Risk assessment is an important part of enabling individuals to become independent

- Hazards identified – crossing three busy roads, walking alone, catching the correct bus, being alone on bus.
- Risks evaluated – injury, death, abuse on bus, getting lost.
- Control measures identified – travel training, practising the route with key worker, abuse awareness training, mobile phone, mentor at place of work etc.

Risks to health might arise from:

- Abuse, e.g. injury.
- Incidents and accidents, e.g. fractures following a fall.

- Neglect, e.g. isolation.
- Deterioration of health of the individual, e.g. injury.
- Deterioration of the situation that the individual is in, e.g. being alone if loss of main carer.
- Self-harm, e.g. injury, death.
- Environment, e.g. illness if damp environment.

Risk can be identified as high, medium and low. The following legislation governs the risk assessment process:

KUS 6

- Health and Safety at Work Act 1974.
- Management of Health and Safety at Work Regulations 1999 Risk Assessment.
- Reporting of Injuries, Diseases and Dangerous Occurrences Regulations (RIDDOR) 1995.

The European dimension on health and safety should also be remembered as the laws above and the 'Six Pack' regulations of 1992 protect the individual and guide the approach taken to health and safety and risk assessment.

Further information on the legislation relating to risk assessment can be found in unit HSC32.

Remember to explore the risks to independence that result from the individual's needs. This evaluation should take into account the likely outcome if help is not provided. Since needs will probably change over time, you should consider the impact of needs on independence in the short, medium and long term. The evaluation of risks should focus on the areas that are central to an individual's independence.

These will include:

- Health and safety, including freedom from harm, abuse and neglect.
- Environmental and community issues, e.g. suitable housing.
- The ability to manage daily routines.
- The individual's **autonomy** and ability to make choices.

KUS 3

- The involvement of family, friends and the wider community. This will include leisure activities, hobbies, employment, unpaid work.

Risk cannot be eliminated as there is no such thing as a completely risk-free situation. A risk assessment should take place when you are devising care plans. Use your organisation's template for assessing risks and measures that should be used to reduce the risk.

You need to produce a plan with the aim of reducing the identifiable risks. Risk is a process that is influenced by a number of factors, for example a change in the individual's health. This means that risk assessment and plans put in place to reduce the risk should be reviewed and updated frequently.

Figure 9
A risk assessment

RISK ASSESSMENT FORM

Name

Key worker

Assessment Completed by:

Organisation
Date Completed:

NATURE OF ACTIVITY Can be broken down into manageable sub-activities	HAZARD/S	PEOPLE AFFECTED	EXISTING CONTROL MEASURES	SEVERITY	LIKELIHOOD	RISK RATING	ADDITIONAL PRECAUTIONS NECESSARY

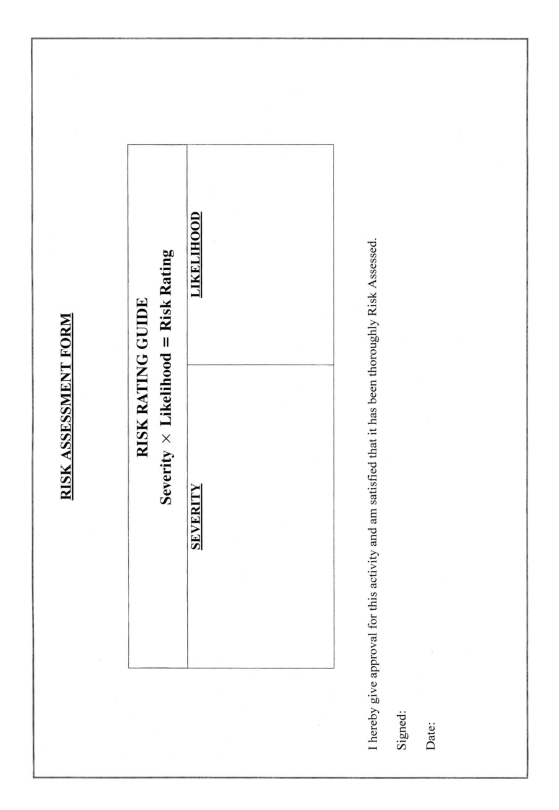

RISK ASSESSMENT FORM

RISK RATING GUIDE

Severity × Likelihood = Risk Rating

SEVERITY

LIKELIHOOD

I hereby give approval for this activity and am satisfied that it has been thoroughly Risk Assessed.

Signed:

Date:

Support individuals and key people to agree assessed needs

Once you have obtained all of the information, you will need to record the needs and preferences identified as well as any associated risks. When writing, take into account the views of the individuals, key people and others involved in the assessment process. A copy of your assessment will be given to all of these people. You can then discuss with them what you have written and how support can be designed to meet the identified needs and preferences and highlight the potential risk involved. Be aware that all services should reflect an awareness of differing racial, cultural and religious backgrounds and values and reflect the individual's perspective. The health and social care worker's and carers' views are only recorded if they differ from the individual's views and/or other needs are identified. Details of the assessment are recorded when it occurs and are written using the individual's own words.

KUS 4, 13

You should also be aware of the needs of carers as some may require access to interpreting/translating services. Key people also require information about the needs of the individual and when these needs change. Often key people such as carers are not recognised as being experts in the care of their relative. They should have this expertise recognised and they should be regarded as partners whose contribution to the assessment of care needs is valued. They should also be able to discuss their needs in relation to the individual and services provided. Many key people do not feel able to talk in front of the individual as they feel they are betraying them. You should take time to talk to key people and to maintain confidentiality.

Often individuals and key people do not understand the role of different professionals and you should take time to explain and answer any questions they have. Perhaps it would be useful to have information available about the services planned.

Others are involved in the assessment process. These may be family, friends and carers. Their views are valid as they know the individual well and can understand and express the needs of the individual. They can help to support the individual during care planning.

KUS 1, 2, 13

Complaints

If the individual, family, friends or others wish to complain about any stage of the assessment process or the needs identified, they should be made aware of the complaints procedure. Any complaint should be resolved locally using the organisation's policy. A copy of this policy should be given to the key people involved. Records of the complaint should be kept. Confidentiality should be maintained at all times. If you cannot resolve the complaint at a local level you should find out how to complain to the local health authority and you should offer support if it is required.

You can also challenge a care assessment. This differs from a complaint and you can listen to the challenge and support the individual through the negotiation and resolution of the challenge.

For example, Mary had her needs assessed and home care services are to call twice a week to bath Mary. However, Mary has started to attend a day centre and has discovered that she could have a bath there. Mary and her family feel that this is a better option and challenge the assessment for baths at home. You support Mary and family in making this challenge and it is agreed that Mary will receive baths in the day centre.

Assessing needs and providing support

Mrs Chan lives in a sheltered housing complex and speaks little English. She is 68 years old and has become increasingly confused. She likes to attend a community centre once a week and visit friends at the weekends. She wishes to travel alone using the local taxi service. However, on several occasions the manager of the community centre has contacted you about Mrs Chan. She has been incontinent of urine, shouted at several members of staff and at times does not appear to know where the taxi is taking her.

Mrs Chan has a daughter who lives five miles away and visits often. Mrs Chan's daughter speaks English as a first language.

➤ *What action should you take?*
➤ *What information should you gather?*
➤ *How would you support Mrs Chan?*
➤ *Who would be invited to the care planning meeting?*
➤ *What needs does Mrs Chan have?*

Key points – assessing the needs and preferences of individuals

- Assessment should involve the individual and key people.
- There are different types of needs and needs can change over time.
- Different sources of information should be used for assessment.
- There are different roles and responsibilities in assessment.
- Communication needs should be assessed and support given.
- The individual, key people and any others involved require support during the assessment process.

Element HSC328b

Support the development and implementation of care plans

Role and responsibilities in developing and implementing care plans

Care planning

KUS 1

After assessing an individual, a care plan is developed to meet the identified needs and preferences of the individual in the best possible way. Care planning should be quick to respond to:

- Age.
- Gender.
- Culture.
- Faith.
- Living conditions.
- Location.
- Disabilities.
- Personal relationships.
- Lifestyle choices.
- Environment.

Care planning is also sensitive to age and does not make assumptions.

Care planning should also focus on the strengths and abilities of the individual and it should build on these. All agencies that are involved in the individual's care should be part of developing and implementing the plan. This is known in the NHS and Community Care Act 1990 as **care management**.

Roles in care planning

Some of the roles identified in the care management process may be undertaken by you depending on your job role. Therefore, it is important that you identify your role and responsibilities in developing and implementing care plans.

Below is a list of the roles and responsibilities of different care workers. Identify which role sounds like yours.

Case worker

This person has responsibility for a case (individual). They are responsible for providing specialist services, for example home nursing.

Key worker

This is the named worker for an individual. They are usually employed by the organisation identified as providing the most relevant services. The key worker will have to liaise with other professionals and the individual's **informal carers**. The key worker will provide a link between the individual and a range of services to meet needs.

Case/care co-ordinator

KUS 4

A case/care co-ordinator is used when several agencies or services are involved in meeting the needs of the individual. The case co-ordinator will also be responsible for providing some services to the individual. They are responsible for co-ordinating the assessment and care planning processes through liaison with all those involved. The care co-ordinator could be the individual, family member or carer.

Care manager

The care manager will have responsibility for the budget used to provide services to the individual. They are also involved in putting some of the services in place and monitoring how well the services are meeting the needs of individuals. The care manager will have good negotiating skills and will be able to manage any conflict between the services. The care manager may be responsible for providing some of the services to the individual.

All of these roles will involve:

- Service provision for the individual, for example home care, social care.
- The management of the networks used to provide support to the individual, for example the individual, members of their family and professionals.

Contribute to discussions on care planning

After the individual has expressed their needs you should contribute to consultations about the development of the individual's care plan. In developing the care plan ensure you have a record of:

- The individual's needs and preferences – a Current Summary Record.
- The objectives of the care plan. This should set out clearly what is to be achieved in the care plan.
- How current support/services meet the individual's current needs and the risks of the individual.
- Additional support/services required to meet the needs and risks of the individual.
- Date of the next review.

Services are matched to eligible needs through **statements of purpose**. These will set out the:

- **Objectives of care**, i.e. desired or required outcomes.
- **Philosophy of care**, i.e. individualised care plans or person centred approach.
- Nature of the service provided, e.g. mental health or learning disability services.
- Type of facilities, e.g. day care, residential.
- Where the facilities are located or area they cover.

- Physical access to the service, e.g. steps/lift available.
- Cost of the service, e.g. charge per week, support available from health authorities.
- Group of individuals for the service, e.g. adults with learning disability only or mixed provision.

Goals/outcomes in care planning

By setting goals the individual can reflect their values and beliefs. Goals will enable the individual and key people involved in care to focus on strengths rather than problems. Once goals are set they allow the individual to move away from a period of dependence to a more independent way of living.

Short-term goals can act as stepping stones to achieving longer-term targets. They can also be monitored and progress charted and adapted if required. This can help the individual to feel fulfilled and have a sense of achievement.

Implementation of care plans

KUS 10, 11

Care planning should lead to an appropriate single care plan. The model used will vary from organisation to organisation but may include:

- A summary of identified needs. This will include the complexity of these needs and the risks to independence.
- A record of whether or not the individual has agreed the plan.
- A record of whether the individual has agreed that the information can be shared with other agencies.
- The objectives of providing support and the outcomes for the individual.
- A summary of how services will impact on identified needs and the associated risks.
- The part the individual will play in addressing needs. This will include their strengths and abilities.
- Details of risk-management strategies. If a certain degree of risk will be accepted by the individual that should also be recorded.
- Details of the part carers will play in meeting needs and any support required.
- A description of the level and frequency of help that is to be provided. The name of the agency providing the service should be recorded as well as their contact details.
- Details of any cost contributions by the individual.
- A nursing plan if appropriate.
- The name of the person co-ordinating the plan and their contact details.
- A contact number in case things go wrong.
- Monitoring arrangements and a date for review.

There may also be specific implementation plans for specialist practitioners, e.g. a diversional therapist.

All individuals who receive services must have a care plan to ensure that the appropriate service is being provided. The detail required in the care plan should be in proportion to the assessed need and service provision. For people who receive one-off support or treatment of a very basic nature, a statement of service delivery and purpose is all that is required, for example 'Meal prepared at lunchtime'.

Individuals have a right to receive a copy of their care plan in the appropriate format and you need to check that this has happened.

Unmet needs

A key element of care planning is the management of unmet needs. There may be conflict and differences when the care plan is developed. You need to be able to negotiate and mediate conflict when it occurs. Unmet needs can be viewed as the differences between the services necessary to deal appropriately with the assessed needs of the individual and those services actually available. Information about unmet need informs the development of future services as individuals' needs and expectations change. For example, a young adult needs someone of similar age to act as a mentor/friend to help them develop social skills and confidence. This may be difficult to find in the short term. However, if highlighted as an unmet need, solutions could be explored for developing future initiatives with young adults in the community.

KUS 1, 2, 12

You can help to support individuals and key people to understand the arrangement for the implementation of care plans. This may involve you obtaining interpreters, translators, signers or specialist equipment to enable communication between individuals and yourself.

Compliments, complaints and challenges

KUS 3

You may find that individuals and key people would like to compliment, challenge or complain about the content of the care plan and its implementation. In these circumstances you need to offer support and advise them of the appropriate procedures to take the matter further.

If they wish to offer a compliment then you need to advise them how they can do this, whether it is by speaking or writing to the manager.

If an individual or key worker has a complaint or wishes to comment on how their needs were assessed, you need to inform them or those representing them using their preferred method. The individual can also complain about decisions regarding the choice of services provided and how long the process took.

Where an individual has services provided by a number of different organisations, you should let the individual know who to complain to. It may also be helpful to inform the individual which organisation is responsible for what aspect of assessment and service.

Where the individual is in receipt of complex or intensive support the best advice may be to raise any concerns or complaints with their care co-ordinator.

For example, the individual's needs may have been assessed and the council decide that they have to limit the number of services being offered. The individual can challenge this assessment, for example if they require help with cleaning but the council only provides services to individuals requiring help with washing and dressing. If the individual wishes to challenge this decision you can support them in accordance with the complaints policy. Initially action will be taken to try and resolve the challenge informally. If the individual is not happy about the results of the informal stage they can move to the formal stage and a complaints manager will be assigned to the case. The individual can also approach the local government ombudsman to seek resolution.

Figure 10
A complaints form

The Acres
Residential Home

COMPLAINTS FORM

Please note that every effort will be made to ensure confidentiality, consistent with a full investigation of the complaint.

1   Name of complainant:
Joseph Hassan

2   Address for correspondence:
1 The Cobbles Close Street Manchester   **Telephone Number:**   0771657239731

3   Details of complaint: (Please ensure that all relevant details are provided, including, where relevant, the date, time and place of the incident giving rise to the complaint. Attach additional sheets if necessary.)
On 20.11.05 when I arrived to visit my mother I noticed that the bedroom was untidy. I asked a member of staff to tidy the room up but she told me that she was too busy. I did not like having to sit in the untidy room to talk to my mother.

4 **Please summarise below any informal action taken to resolve the complaint:**

TEES & NORTH EAST
YORKSHIRE NHS TRUST
LIBRARY & INFORMATION
SERVICE

I understand that a copy of this form may be provided to a member of staff who is the subject of the complaint, or who is otherwise involved.

Signed: .... **Date:** ....

For Office Use Only   *Date complaint received:*

4 **Reasons for continued dissatisfaction:** (Relevant supporting material may be attached.)

I understand that a copy of this form may be provided to a member of staff who is the subject of the complaint, or who is otherwise involved.

Signed: .... **Date:** ....

Please send the completed form to The Manager, The Acres, Chester Road, Manchester

Carry out care plan activities

When you are developing and implementing care plans you need to communicate with other key members of the care team to ensure that everyone knows what is happening and plans are carried out as agreed.

This could include talking about:

- The outcomes of the assessment of the individual's needs and how these needs are to be met.
- The risks that need to be managed and how the team will manage these.
- The goals to be attained.
- The other professionals involved in providing care to meet needs.
- The resources available.

KUS 4, 11, 13

All of this information should be recorded and made available to all members of the team. The benefits of joint agency and multi-disciplinary working in care planning and implementation reflect the complex reality of individual circumstances and needs. Increasingly individuals' needs cannot be met by a single-agency response and so agencies have to work together in the best interests of the individual.

As part of your job role you may be responsible for discussing the care plan with other members of the team. This plan should be kept up to date and discussed with the team. This may happen:

- When a new care plan is drawn up.
- At handover of staff.
- When a new member of the team is employed.
- When a team member has been away or on annual leave.
- When a team member returns from sick leave.
- When changes occur in needs or services required.

You will also have to carry out the care plan activities for which you are responsible, for example washing and dressing the individual.

Training

KUS 8

You may identify that you require training in order to carry out specific tasks identified on the care plan. If this is the case you should inform your line manager and identify relevant factors, e.g. course, cost, venue, dates and provider. Training should be multi-agency and multi-disciplinary to reflect the closer working relationships in assessment and care planning.

Reporting changes

When an agreed care plan is put into place for the individual you should be aware of any changes that occur. It is important to monitor the plan and the services that are in place on an ongoing basis. Many factors can influence an individual's life and affect their needs, circumstances and risks. This will result in the care plan being updated to meet these new needs and to provide continued support for the individual. Monitoring can lead to minor adjustments to the service provision over a period of time in response to changing needs and circumstances.

KUS 15

Factors affecting needs

Many factors in an individual's life can change and these may affect the care received.

- Change in financial circumstances, e.g. loss of job and therefore inability to pay for care.
- Change in housing conditions, e.g. move to residential/nursing home, no longer receives care at home.
- Deterioration in physical condition, e.g. illness, for example a stroke which affects mobility.
- Improvement in physical condition, e.g. following physiotherapy mobility is improved.
- Change in agencies involved in support, e.g. no longer receiving care from a local council.
- Change in the provision of local resources, e.g. review of service from local council.
- Change in nature of informal support by carers, e.g. bereavement of main carer and the individual requires formal support.
- Deterioration in mental health, e.g. progression of dementia to a point at which the individual is now at risk living alone.
- Improvement in mental health, e.g. individual has received treatment for depression and is now able to live independently.

Observing needs

KUS 14

One way of monitoring the individual is to carry out observations. This can help you understand the needs of individuals and become sensitive and perceptive in meeting these needs. By observing individuals you can also help other members of the team to meet these needs. Carrying out observations can alert you to changes in behaviour that may have a physical cause, for example the onset of illness, or they may be an emotional response due to a change in the support from the family or bereavement.

To carry out observations you should know the individual well and be aware of their present needs, preferences and circumstances. You should also understand that individuals will have different reactions to similar situations, for example one individual may settle into a new day centre well while another will find it difficult. You should be able to respect both reactions and take them into account.

When you have made these observations you will need to record your findings and discuss them with the individual and relevant members of the care team so that changes can be agreed with all involved. You should also report your findings to your line manager. This will help you to implement changes in the care plan.

Monitoring using checklists

KUS 11

Checklists can be used to monitor:

- The individual's situation including any changes that would affect needs and preferences.

- The service provided for the individual. This will help you to decide if any change is required to meet needs and preferences.

Checklists can be used with the individual on a regular basis to keep care planning up to date. These can be completed by:

- The individual.
- Yourself and other members of the care team.
- Service providers.

Part of your role will be to ensure these checklists are completed and shared with the individual and support/service providers. You will be involved in ensuring that other members of staff can complete these checklists when required. You should also be aware of any changes made to the services provided. This information will have to be communicated to staff and to the individual.

Other methods of monitoring can include:

- Letters.
- Telephone calls.
- Questionnaires.
- Visits.
- Inter-agency consultation.

Implementing changes

Your workplace will have a policy and procedure for implementing changes to an individual's care plan in your workplace. It will be your responsibility to follow this procedure and to support others in the care planning process to implement these changes according to agreed procedures. By observing and monitoring the effects of the care plan on the individual you can make adjustments as necessary. The people that you should work with to achieve this are:

- The individual.
- Other members of the care team.
- Informal carers/family/friends.
- Care manager.

KUS 8, 11

You should be aware of any training that is required to meet needs. Document any changes and communicate them to everyone involved in care planning. You need to involve the individual in monitoring the care plan and participating in feedback sessions. By doing this you can measure any progress the individual has made and any areas of the care plan that need to be changed. You should encourage other members of the care team to involve the individual. This will help to keep the individual informed of the care provided.

Risks

There may also be risks resulting from the changes. The individual and those who support the individual should be involved in the risk-assessment process. If you become aware of a risk that could occur you should inform the appropriate member of staff and a risk assessment should be carried out or an existing risk assessment updated. Remember the individual's right to take risks and also if there are any conditions that might make the risk worse.

Check your observations with the individual, key people and others that support the individual, for example family and friends. Support individuals, colleagues and key people to identify and monitor any changes in the individual's condition.

It is also part of your role to identify and implement any necessary changes following a reassessment of the individual's needs.

Re-assessing care

David is a 40-year-old man with a learning disability. His father left when he was a baby. Until recently David lived at home with his mother, but she has just died. David attends a local day centre and on two evenings a week he goes to a Gateway Club. David has no other family members to look after him at this time. He has recently expressed to his key worker that he wishes to live independently and to attend a local sports club where he can start to undertake activities such as abseiling. He has also expressed an interest in going to the local pub at weekends.

Staff at the day centre feel David is not able to live on his own and would prefer him to live in residential accommodation. They have expressed concerns to his GP and social worker.

➤ How would you support David to express his needs and preferences?

➤ Who might be involved in consultations about his care?

➤ Why do you think staff consider the best solution for David is living in residential care?

➤ How do you think the situation could be resolved?

➤ Develop a person-centred care plan detailing the activities to meet David's needs and preferences. Include the models of care that can be used.

> **Key points – supporting the development and implementation of care plans**
>
> - Identify your role and that of others in the care planning process.
> - Communication is important in implementing a care plan.
> - Make individuals aware of the compliments and complaints policy.
> - Support colleagues, through communication and training, to implement the care plan.
> - Observe and monitor the individual.
> - A range of factors influence an individual's needs.

Element
HSC328c *Contribute to reviewing care plans*

Care planning review

KUS 11,
14, 15

Statutory review of the care plan and the package of care delivered should occur routinely. According to the document 'Better care, higher standards', initial review should take place six weeks after housing, health and social services are first provided or if major changes to needs have occurred. Review can then take place six monthly or yearly if the individual's condition is unchanged, for example an individual in a health and social care home whose physical and mental health is stable. The frequency of review can also increase, especially for individuals who are vulnerable and/or at risk in some way.

Your organisation will have a policy and procedure for this and there may be formal stages to go through. You need to be familiar with the process so you can support colleagues. The review will check that the individual's needs and preferences are being met and whether these have changed over time. You also have to check your role and responsibilities when providing feedback to the individual and others on the implementation of the care plan.

Purpose of review

KUS 16

Figure 12
The purposes of a review

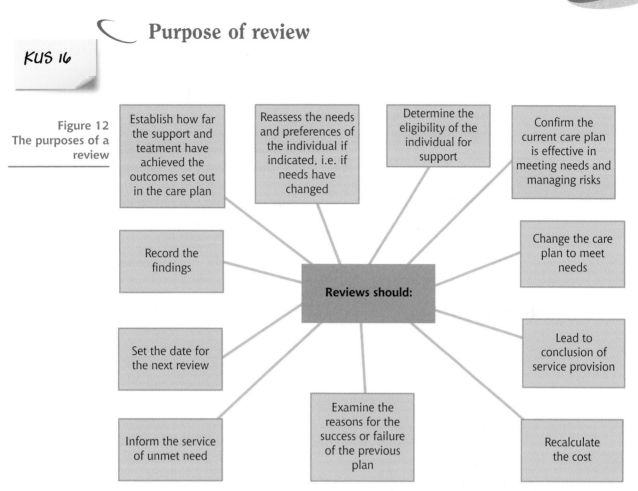

Establish how far the support and teatment have achieved the outcomes set out in the care plan

Reassess the needs and preferences of the individual if indicated, i.e. if needs have changed

Determine the eligibility of the individual for support

Confirm the current care plan is effective in meeting needs and managing risks

Record the findings

Reviews should:

Change the care plan to meet needs

Set the date for the next review

Lead to conclusion of service provision

Inform the service of unmet need

Examine the reasons for the success or failure of the previous plan

Recalculate the cost

Re-assessment of care packages

This is part of the review process and is detailed in the Department of Health document 'Fair access to care services'. Re-assessment can be unscheduled as well as scheduled as the individual's needs may change, for example the individual may have had a stroke and therefore their mobility needs have changed.

When review takes place, information should be gathered using the same process as assessment. You should ensure that the individual's communication needs are supported, for example by providing an interpreter or providing information in the correct format and language.

Parts of the care plan that can change include:

- Health and well-being needs – emotional, mental, physical, social and spiritual.
- Personal demographics – address, environment, living alone, interpreter required.
- Others involved – family, next of kin, main carer, advocate, GP, care manager, other care practitioners.
- The individual's perspective on current needs – significance and amount of support required.

- Clinical background – diagnosis, disabilities, medication.
- Disease prevention – blood pressure, weight, allergies, immunisation, smoking, exercise, alcohol, screening.
- Resources used – equipment, amenities, services.

Part of your role will be to support the individual and care team members to review these and make recommendations about updating the care plan. The care manager or co-ordinator may set the date, time and place for the review meeting. All contributing members of the multi-disciplinary team should be invited. They may either attend or produce a report to be read at the meeting. At this meeting, if you are the individual's key worker it is important that you gather information on how the care plan meets the individual's needs or if there are any unmet needs or service failures, e.g. support not being provided in the quantity, frequency or quality agreed.

Your role may also include the collection of all the notes required for the meeting, reviewing these and ensuring they are ready for distribution at the review meeting.

Feedback

As you are responsible for monitoring the care plan you are able to provide feedback on the individual's needs, preferences and circumstances. You will be able to provide information on how these have changed over time. You should refer to the assessment tools, scales and observations to provide evidence of this.

Part of your role is to support the individual to provide feedback on how the care plan has worked for them. It is also important to include in this feedback session the views of family/carers as they play a vital role in the support and care of the individual. It is important that you inform the individual how their feedback will influence the care plan review and the areas to be discussed.

It is only with feedback from the multi-disciplinary team, the individual and the carers that an effective interpretation of the existing care plan can be made.

Conflict

It is important that any conflict about your feedback and observations is resolved to enable the individual's needs to be met. Opinions are vital so that an effective service can be provided. You need to negotiate the area of conflict and inform senior members of staff. Ensure that the individual is aware of the policy and procedure on complaints before the review takes place. If you cannot resolve the conflict you should then support the individual to comment or complain on the review process. Where a number of agencies are involved in the review process the individual should be advised who is responsible for each aspect of the service.

In complex services the individual should be advised that complaints should be directed through the care manager.

KUS 1, 2, 4, 5

Contribute to care plan revision meetings

The aim of a review meeting is to share information about an individual. This is important information and you are close to the individual, have first-hand experience of how the care plan is working and have expertise. It is important that you make changes according to your role and responsibilities and report and discuss your findings with a line manager before the review meeting. This will enable the individual to receive a quality service and will reduce the fear that the individual is only receiving a service due to a contractual agreement.

KUS 10

Since the individual and key people will be attending the review meeting, you should ensure privacy and confidentiality during the meeting by arranging a suitable environment. Ensure that everyone knows one another and is aware of their purpose for attending. It is also important that the individual knows the process of disseminating the notes and records and who is likely to see these.

During the meeting you should also talk directly to the individual and avoid using jargon. Ensure that everyone at the meeting has an opportunity to discuss needs, preferences and the services required to meet these.

Refer back to the previous review or initial care plan to enable your contributions to be based on evidence-based solutions.

You may also be involved in developing a plan of action and revising and implementing the new care plan. You should therefore be able to assign responsibilities, set time scales and agree the next date for review.

KUS 6

Record keeping and confidentiality

Information held about the individual in the process of care planning is held under legal and ethical obligations of confidentiality. Information is usually provided in confidence and should not be used or disclosed without consent from the individual. It is important that you make any changes in the individual's records according to your role and responsibilities. This information should include details about the review and revisions in the care plan. You will also have to implement any changes in the care plan that are within your role and responsibilities, for example attending developmental activities.

Notes from the review need to record information according to organisation policy and procedure. This should reflect good practice as detailed in legislation. Inform the individual that you will have to record the information discussed during the review. At the beginning you need to ensure that the individual is made aware of whom information will be shared with. They will need to give consent for information sharing. They should also consent to the new revised care plan and sign to say that they are happy for the care plan to be implemented.

Information stored in care plans should also meet organisational policies and follow government legislation. You should record and report information decided at review and pass this on to other members of staff in order that the services agreed are put in place. You should also support the individual to complete paperwork to enable the revised care plan to be implemented.

Review of a care plan

Mr Singh is a 42-year-old man who has long-term mental health problems. He lives with his wife and two young children. Due to his mental health problems he has found it difficult to remain employed for more than a few months at a time. He currently works shifts in a factory four days a week and attends a local day centre for support once a week. He receives weekly visits from a support worker from the community mental health team. Over the past four weeks his wife has noticed that his behaviour has been erratic and he is reluctant to go to work or to the day centre. She contacted the community psychiatric nurse to ask for a review:

➤ *Explain how you would organise a review of the care plan.*

➤ *Who would you involve?*

➤ *What changes do you feel could be made to the existing care plan?*

Key points – contributing to the review of care plans

- Review is a statutory requirement of the care planning process.
- You have responsibilities and a role to play in review of care plans.
- A review meeting should include information from all members of the multi-disciplinary team.
- Feedback should also include the views of the individual and members of their family.
- You can support individuals to make complaints about the review process or services provided.
- Information reported and recorded at review is confidential.

Unit HSC328

Are you ready for assessment?

Contribute to care planning and review

This unit is about how you contribute to the assessment of individual needs and preferences. It is about your role and responsibility in working with others to identify needs and appropriate support to meet those needs. It is about how you support the development and implementation of care plans which meet the individual's needs and preferences. It is also about how you work with individuals and key people to review their needs and identify any changes that may need to be made to the care plan.

Your assessment will be carried out mainly through observation by your assessor and this should provide most of the evidence for the elements in this unit. If your assessor is unable to directly observe you then you may be able to use the testimony of an experienced colleague acting as an expert witness. You will need to discuss this with your assessor. Evidence of your knowledge and understanding will be demonstrated through observation, your assessor examining work products, e.g. reports, minutes of meetings, as well as through answering oral and/or written questions.

You need to be aware when planning assessments that this unit also relates to the core units, in particular HSC31, HSC32 and HSC35, and so you may also be able to evidence performance criteria for these.

You need to take into account that you may need to be observed in the individual's home. Therefore you need to explain about the assessment and seek their permission for your assessor to visit. If their visit would be intrusive you will need to consider alternative evidence-gathering methods, e.g. expert witness testimony.

Direct observation by your assessor

Your assessor or an expert witness will need to plan to see you carry out the performance criteria (PCs) in each of the elements in this unit. The performance criteria that may be difficult to meet through observation are:

• **HSC328c PC 5**

Preparing to be observed

You must make sure that your workplace and any individuals and key people involved in your work agree to you being assessed. Explicit, informed consent must be obtained before you carry out any assessment activity that involves individuals or which involves access to confidential information related to their care.

Before your assessments you should read carefully the performance criteria for each element in the unit. Try to cover as much as you can during your observation but remember that you and your assessor can also plan for additional sources of evidence should full coverage of all performance criteria not be possible. ▶

Other types of evidence

You may need to present other forms of evidence in order to:

- Cover criteria not observed by your assessor.
- Show that you have the required knowledge, understanding and skills to claim competence in this area of practice.
- Ensure your work practice is consistent.

Your assessor may also need to ask you questions to confirm your knowledge and understanding and ensure that you can apply this to your practice.

Check your knowledge

- Which legislation is relevant to assessment of individuals' needs?
- What extra support may be required to help individuals communicate their needs?
- What models of health and social care can be used to assess needs?
- What is your role in developing and implementing care plans?
- How would you support the individual to challenge/complain about the assessment of need?
- When would you review care plans?
- How do you contribute to revising and implementing changes in the care plan?

Contribute to the protection of individuals from harm and abuse

This unit focuses on three areas related to protecting individuals from harm and abuse. The first area is for care workers to be able to recognise and report on the factors that may cause danger, harm or abuse. The second is to work in a way that contributes to minimising dangerous, harmful and abusive behaviour and practices. The third is to contribute to dealing with suspected or disclosed danger, harm or abuse.

This unit contains three elements:

⌣ **HSC335a** *Recognise and report on factors that may cause danger, harm or abuse*

⌣ **HSC335b** *Contribute to minimising the effects of dangerous, harmful and abusive behaviour and practices*

⌣ **HSC335c** *Respond to and report on suspicions of harm or abuse*

Introduction

⌣ Protecting vulnerable adults

KUS 3

Risk is a part of life and taking risks can enhance our life as we discover our abilities and more about ourselves, all of which broadens our experience and makes us who we are. Some risks may affect our physical well-being, e.g. driving a car or undertaking DIY at home, while others may affect our emotional well-being, e.g. forming new relationships. However, the majority of adults have the knowledge and skills to assess the risks they choose to take. They are able to weigh up the potential dangers and benefits of situations. This enables them to make informed choices about what they do and the actions they need to take to minimise the risks and any danger that those choices present.

Whatever health and social care setting you work in you will be working with individuals who have a diverse range of needs and circumstances. The one thing they have in common, however, is their need for some level of support in managing the risks that life presents. For a variety of reasons they may be unable to make informed choices about situations wholly independently.

Given a particular set of circumstances we can all be vulnerable to danger, harm or abuse. Sometimes the vulnerability of the individuals you support is more apparent, although that is not always the case. Defining what is meant by harm and abuse can help you to be clear about your role and responsibilities in relation to protecting individuals.

Defining danger, harm and abuse

Danger can be defined as exposure to possible harm, loss or injury. The danger can occur immediately or in the short, medium or long term.

Harm is considered to be physical, psychological injury or damage and is often associated with abuse.

Harm and abuse are usually considered to be related to the violation of an individual's human and civil rights by another person or persons. Harm or abuse may be physical, psychological, sexual, financial, negligent, reckless behaviour which endangers self or others, and this includes self-harm. It also includes discrimination and bullying. Sometimes the harm or abuse is intentional and sometimes it is unintentional. It may be about doing something (an act of commission) or doing nothing (an act of omission). Health and social care service providers have a legal responsibility to protect individuals from danger, harm and abuse.

Element HSC335a

Recognise and report on factors that may cause danger, harm or abuse

Factors that may cause danger, harm or abuse

KUS 21

There are a number of factors that may cause harm or abuse. However, it is important to remember that although one or more of these factors may be present in an individual's life it does not automatically follow that harm or abuse will occur. As discussed above, we can all be vulnerable to harm or abuse at times given a particular

Figure 1
An individual in a vulnerable position

KUS 21

set of circumstances. For example, a person walking alone in an isolated area may be considered to be in a vulnerable position. This vulnerability may increase if they have no means of contacting others and have no warm clothing, food or water. It may be further increased if it starts to rain, visibility becomes poor and they lose their bearings. Then the temperature starts to fall, it gets dark and they fall and injure themselves. A seemingly controllable situation changes as other factors which they had not considered or planned for come into play.

The care worker's role and responsibility is to recognise when factors and circumstances are coming together to increase an individual's vulnerability and to take action early enough to prevent harm and/or abuse occurring. The factors that make individuals particularly vulnerable can be divided into three categories:

- Those related to the individual.
- Those related to the environment in which they live.
- Those related to the relationships they have with others.

Figure 2
Factors that make an individual vulnerable

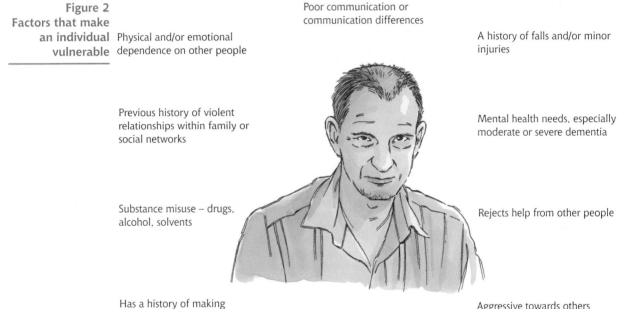

Poor communication or communication differences

Physical and/or emotional dependence on other people

A history of falls and/or minor injuries

Previous history of violent relationships within family or social networks

Mental health needs, especially moderate or severe dementia

Substance misuse – drugs, alcohol, solvents

Rejects help from other people

Has a history of making allegations of abuse in the past

Aggressive towards others

Self-injurious behaviour – self-harm or reckless behaviour

KUS 12, 14, 15, 21, 23

These factors may place the individual in a position where either others have power over them or they are unable to express what is happening to them. The person exerting the power can then intimidate the individual into doing something against their will. For example, where an individual has poor communication skills or a history of self-injurious behaviour, this can create a situation when either injury or changes in behaviour can be explained away or dismissed. In these circumstances the individual is viewed as being unreliable because of their past history or perceived ability. An individual who has experienced long-term abuse may self-harm or behave recklessly as

KUS 13, 23

KUS 21

a consequence of the abuse, believing they are worthless and so have no regard for their own welfare or safety. This increases their vulnerability. Any of these factors can make decision-making more complex for the individual as well as changing their perception of their situation. In turn this can lead to a lack of, or reduced, awareness of what constitutes a danger, particularly in relation to physical danger. For example, an individual who has learning difficulties or dementia may perceive the world differently and be unable to think through the consequences of their actions or inaction. Therefore, if they cross the road without looking and listening for traffic (and without checking as they cross) there is a danger that they will be hit by a vehicle. The potential consequence of this lack of awareness may be that they sustain an injury or death.

**Figure 3
Factors that may
increase the
vulnerability of
individuals**

Living conditions are poor or insecure

Individuals are living in overcrowded accommodation

Individuals are living a long way from family and friends

High staff turnover

Poor management of the care service

KUS 14, 21

The more isolated the individual is from people who know them, the harder it is to recognise the subtle changes that may occur as a result of harm or abuse. An insecure and/or overcrowded environment is likely to be a stressful environment. This increases the likelihood of harm or abuse occurring as people struggle to manage individuals' needs adequately. Poor management and high staff turnover are also likely to mean that tensions created by a diverse group of individuals living together are not managed, and this increases the chance that harm and abuse will go unnoticed.

Figure 4
Providing positive
support to
individuals

Table 1 Factors that relate to relationships (with both formal and informal carers)

Care workers	Informal carers	Both
• Unclear role boundaries between personal and professional relationships	• Situations where there is more than one dependent person within the family or social network • Situations where there are several generations of the same family living together and where this is creating conflicts of personal interests and loyalties • Role reversal or significant change in the relationship between the individual and their carer • A history of abuse in the family – including domestic violence • Where the demands of caring for the individual mean that the informal carer is isolated from practical and emotional support from others	• Unequal power relationships • Increased dependency of the vulnerable individual • Where the carer is experiencing significant levels of stress • Where there is a lack of understanding about the individual's condition and care needs which results in inappropriate care • Where there is dependency on the vulnerable individual • Where the vulnerable individual displays challenging behaviour which the carer finds intolerable or stressful • Where there is a history of the carer being abused or a perpetrator of abuse • Where the carer feels exploited, resentful, angry or guilty • Where there are financial difficulties • Illness or disability of the carer • Where there is significant and long-term stress of the carer

Table 1 shows that there are many factors that relate to the relationship between the vulnerable individual and the people caring for them. Some factors relate to informal carer relationships, some to formal care-worker relationships and some to both. Different factors can also combine and create circumstances that increase the likelihood of harm or abuse occurring.

Institutional abuse has been recognised for some time and public awareness was heightened during and following the closure of many large long-stay institutions for adults with learning disabilities or mental health problems. A number of public inquiries (e.g. the Beech House Inquiry 1996) highlighted the systematic abuse that individuals were subjected to through harsh and rigid routines that became accepted practice and which violated individual rights.

KUS 11, 12, 14, 21

As a result, a set of predisposing factors were recognised as increasing the likelihood of harm and abuse occurring.

Figure 5
Factors that increase the likelihood of harm and abuse

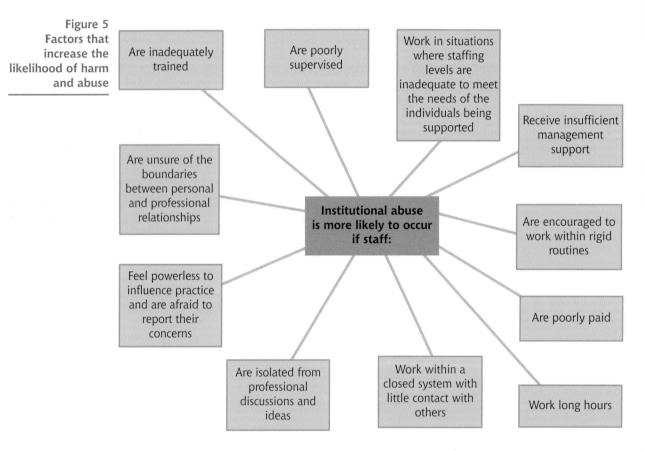

The factors listed in Figure 5 highlight the importance of the effective management, supervision and training of care workers. The national minimum standards for care services seek to identify where these factors are not present and to intervene to prevent harm and abuse. There are also other risk factors to consider.

Risk factors

The individual's capacity for abstract thinking, i.e. the ability to think through the consequences of a situation or the 'what if...?' scenario, is an important factor when considering danger and harm. As we grow up we are generally exposed to situations where we learn what is potentially dangerous and harmful, whether that is a hot cooker, leaving a candle burning unattended or balancing on an unstable surface. All too often we learn through doing those things and bearing the consequences, usually an injury to ourselves. Disability or illness may mean that the individual has not learnt, not been given the opportunity to learn or has forgotten these lessons. In these situations the care worker's role and responsibility is to explain or remind the individual of these to help keep them protected. Determining an individual's capacity for decision making is not an easy process and in some cases it requires specific tests to be carried out with the results interpreted by a psychologist or psychiatrist.

KUS 21

Current health and social care work promotes the rights, choices, involvement and participation of individuals in the life of their community. This presents tensions for health and social care workers as they seek to empower individuals while retaining a responsibility to protect. Where there is confusion about an individual's capacity to consent, this can create a situation of increased vulnerability for the individual as care workers and organisations grapple with the dilemma of rights versus responsibilities. This is particularly an issue and practice dilemma in relation to relationships, particularly sexual relationships and whether these are consensual or not.

KUS 2, 3, 4

There may be situations in which it is obvious that someone is in danger, such as when an individual who is unsteady on their feet is attempting to get out of their chair and walk unaided. The risk is that they will fall and injure themselves. Other situations also present a danger, e.g. water spillage on a bathroom or kitchen floor, while some situations are perhaps less obvious, e.g. a care worker using a piece of equipment they are unfamiliar with and not trained to use. Many of the dangers within health and social care settings relate to health and safety concerns. Organisational policies and procedures which comply with legislation will be in place to manage these dangers and the associated risks.

KUS 1, 5

Signs and symptoms of harm or abuse

There are seven main types of abuse. These are:

- Physical.
- Emotional or psychological.
- Sexual.
- Neglect.
- Financial.
- Institutional.
- Discriminatory.

When reading through these it may appear that recognising and agreeing with others about what constitutes abuse is straightforward. However, that may not always be the case in practice.

Physical abuse

Physical abuse is non-accidental injury or harm to the body.

Signs of physical abuse can include:

KUS 22

- Being hit, slapped, shaken, punched, pulled or dragged.
- Inappropriate restraint, i.e. not in accordance with agreed protocols.
- Being locked up or confined.
- Being deprived of food or drink.
- Being forced to eat or drink.
- Medication misuse, e.g. medication not being given according to doctor's instructions; being withheld; overdosing; infrequent medication review; being given medication intended for another person.
- Aids for daily living being withheld, e.g. glasses, hearing aids, walking aids.
- Being burnt or scalded.
- Care being withheld which causes physical discomfort, e.g. requests to go to the toilet being ignored causing physical discomfort and/or incontinence.

Physical abuse is often accompanied by other forms of abuse such as emotional and sexual.

Emotional or psychological abuse

KUS 22

Emotional or psychological abuse relates to any action that damages an individual's mental well-being. The effects of emotional abuse will reduce an individual's quality of life and their self-esteem to the extent that they will be less likely to achieve their full potential.

Signs of emotional or psychological abuse can include:

- Being ignored.
- Disregarding a person's opinions, life experience or personal history.
- Being bullied and/or harassed.
- Living in fear or in a culture of intimidation, e.g. always being blamed for things.
- Being humiliated, ridiculed or teased, e.g. being insulted all the time and told you are useless.

KUS 23

- Being coerced, pressurised or manipulated into doing something against your will.
- Being subjected to threatening behaviour or loud noise.
- Intentionally withholding emotional support.
- Treating someone inappropriately for their age and/or cultural background, e.g. using 'baby talk' to an adult with learning disabilities or dementia.

Sexual abuse

This is involving any individual in sexual activities which they do not understand, have not consented to or which violate the sexual taboos of family custom and practice. Sexual abuse can occur through either contact or non-contact.

Sexual abuse through contact can include:

KUS 22

- Vaginal or anal rape.
- Buggery.
- Incest.

- Being touched by another person in a sexual manner (including being forced to touch another person in a sexual manner).

Sexual abuse through non-contact can include:

- Being forced to watch pornography or taken to adult entertainment without fully understanding what this may involve.
- Being subjected to indecent exposure, sexual innuendoes, harassment or inappropriate photography.
- Not being given the choice to have a care worker of the same gender to provide intimate personal care.
- Another person looking at an individual's body inappropriately.

Neglect

Neglect is considered to be the deliberate or unintentional failure to meet an individual's needs for care which results in a deterioration in their well-being. This can be acts of omission (not doing something) or acts of commission (doing something on purpose).

KUS 5, 6, 10, 13, 22, 23

Self-neglect will not usually lead to the implementation of adult protection procedures unless there has been a significant act of commission or omission by someone who has some responsibility for the vulnerable adult's care. You need to refer to the adult protection policy and procedures for your geographic area. In these cases other interventions such as assessment and review may be more appropriate. An individual who has experienced harm or abuse may have such low self-esteem and motivation that they self-neglect or they might feel that the abuse (especially sexual abuse) may stop if they are less attractive.

Neglect can include:

- Not responding to an individual's needs or preventing others from doing so.
- Withholding care, including medication or access to medical or care staff and services.
- Not providing the basic standards of care, e.g. meeting basic human needs, warmth, food, drink, safety.
- Being prevented from seeing visitors or spending time with other people.
- Not undertaking appropriate risk assessments and allowing the individual to self-harm or harm others.
- Not intervening when behaviour is dangerous to the individual or to others.

Financial abuse

Financial abuse is the theft or misuse of an individual's money or personal possessions in order to advantage another person.

KUS 22

Financial abuse can include:

- Money and/or belongings being stolen.
- An individual not being given access to their money (including money and benefits being controlled by another person).
- An individual's money being spent without their consent.

- An individual's belongings being removed, bought and/or sold without their knowledge or consent.
- An individual being asked for money under false pretences, e.g. in payment for a service not provided.
- Altering the ownership of property without the individual's knowledge or consent.
- Taking loans out in an individual's name without their knowledge and/or consent.
- An individual being asked to sign financial documents when they have been assessed as not having the mental capacity to consent.
- Money or possessions being borrowed by people who have a care responsibility.

Health and social care workers are in a position of trust when working with vulnerable adults and so all organisations have guidelines within personnel procedures or contracts of employment which detail the expectations and rules regarding gifts and bequests. All staff are expected to adhere to these guidelines and failure to do so is likely to result in disciplinary action.

Figure 6
Health and social-care workers are in a position of trust when working with vulnerable adults

Discriminatory abuse

Discriminatory abuse exists when the values, beliefs or culture within society and/or an organisation results in the misuse of power so that individuals who are different, or perceived as different, are denied the same opportunities as others in society. Discrimination may be on the basis of race, gender, age, sexuality, disability or religion.

Discriminatory abuse also includes:

KUS 1

- Exclusion of an individual from opportunities in society.
- Explaining an individual's opinions or behaviour by blaming them on their age or disability in a derogatory manner.
- Treating an individual in an inappropriate way for their age and/or cultural background.
- Verbal abuse and inappropriate use of language.
- Harassment and slurs.

Institutional abuse

Institutional abuse is the mistreatment or abuse by a regime or the people within an institution. Everyone has a right to feel safe and to be treated with respect and dignity. In situations of institutional abuse the routines, systems and accepted behaviour, i.e. the norms within the organisation, are for the benefit and convenience of the staff and the organisation and not for the individuals being supported.

Institutional abuse can include:

- Inappropriate or poor standards of care.
- Misuse of medication, e.g. sedating individuals to make life easier for staff.
- Inappropriate use of restraint and/or methods of restraint.
- Individuals being denied access to visitors or phone calls.
- Restricted access to the toilet, bathing facilities or a comfortable place to rest.
- Restricted access to appropriate medical or social care.
- Lack of privacy or dignity (including failure to provide access to appropriate privacy).
- Inflexibility in terms of bedtime and mealtimes, choice of food etc.
- Lack of adequate procedures to ensure clear roles and responsibilities of all staff and management.
- The existence of controlling relationships between staff and individuals in their care.
- Repeated acts of poor professional practice.

Types of abuse

Read through the following examples and decide what type of abuse is occurring.

1. *Residents at a home for older people with dementia are not allowed to go to the toilet during mealtimes.*

2. *Lucy, a young woman with learning disabilities, is taken to the local pub by her key worker. At the pub they meet up with three of the key worker's friends. The key worker buys drinks for them all using Lucy's money. The key worker says buying drinks for the others is part of friendship.*

3. *Joan is 87 years old and lives alone. A domiciliary care worker visits her each morning to help her get up, washed and dressed. The care worker also gives her breakfast. To save time the care worker gives Joan her cereal while she is sitting on the commode.*

4. *Philip is 55 years old, has mental health problems and, due to a shortage of available beds, is placed in a residential care home for older people who are physically and mentally frail. Philip is unable to control his behaviour and shouts and swears at everyone. He also hits out at anyone who is near him. Care staff do not know how to support him or meet his needs as they have little experience in mental*

▶

health. The other residents are frightened of him and will not go into the communal areas.

5. William is 28 years old, physically disabled and paralysed from the neck down. He uses a pointer which he moves with his mouth to communicate and control his communication board including his assistance call button. One of the care staff leaves the pointer just out of his reach every time they leave his room.

6. Betty has learning difficulties and lives at home with her parents. She works at the local supermarket three days a week. Tim also works at the supermarket and during the breaks he sits with Betty and talks to her. When they are in the stockroom together he locks the door and then fondles her breasts and puts his hand up her skirt. He also shows her pornographic magazines and says that he will take her away for the weekend so she can really be his girlfriend like in the pictures. He tells her not to tell anyone as it is their secret and if she does he will hurt her. Betty feels uncomfortable when Tim touches her and is frightened of him.

7. Tom is 89 years old. After his stroke his daughter and son-in-law moved into his house to look after him. He is confined to his bedroom most of the time unless someone comes to visit. His daughter has told him that they have to live with him now as the bank had repossessed their house and they are in debt and owe £45,000. He has been unable to find his pension book and his daughter has asked him to sign lots of forms as she told him he was going senile and was not capable of managing his money. His daughter has recently bought a new car and new clothes for herself and her husband. Sometimes Tom is unable to get to the toilet in time and is incontinent. When this happens his daughter shouts and swears at him telling him he is a filthy old man. She makes him sit in his wet and soiled trousers. Tom wants them to leave his house but does not know how to get them out.

Read through the scenarios and for each one decide:

➤ Is abuse present or is it poor care practice?
➤ What factors make the individual(s) vulnerable to abuse?
➤ If it is abuse, what types of abuse are present in the situation?

Health and safety legislation

Health and safety legislation provides guidelines for both employers and employees regarding safe working practices and conditions. The Health and Safety at Work Act 1974 and the Control of Substances Hazardous to Health 2002 (COSHH) regulations provide guidance about responsibilities and how to control potential hazards and dangers. This includes assessing risks, putting controls in place to minimise those risks,

KUS 6, 10

monitoring the effectiveness of those controls and informing and training staff about the risks and their role and responsibility in maintaining the controls (see also HSC32). The national minimum standards also provide guidance about the worker's role and responsibilities in relation to maintaining a safe environment for individuals.

KUS 5, 6, 7

New staff inductions include information regarding health and safety and safe working practice, for example the location of fire equipment, the fire evacuation procedure, what to do in the event of an emergency and procedures regarding admitting visitors to the building. There are also regulations regarding manual handling, safe disposal of waste products, and food handling and hygiene. If workers do not adhere to these guidelines then individuals are potentially at risk of danger and harm. Research has shown that when stress levels are high, whether as a result of unacceptably high work loads or tiredness, these factors are warning signs and may be contributory factors to abuse. They also increase the risk of harm as people who are over-tired are more likely to make errors of judgement. Employment legislation such as the European Working Time Directive 1993 sets limits on working hours and work breaks to try and minimise these and other associated risks. There is also specific guidance related to adult protection.

KUS 5, 6, 7

Legislation and good practice guidelines in relation to adult protection

Since 2002, following the publication of the government guidance document 'No Secrets', in addition to health and safety regulations and guidelines, care organisations are now required to have adult protection policies and procedures in place. These policies are generally multi-agency agreements. This means that all health and social care and related organisations within each county or city have agreed to and work in accordance with these policies and procedures. This is to ensure the consistency of recognition and action. You need to be able to recognise and report any factors that you consider may be dangerous, harmful or abusive to individuals and to take action in accordance with those policies and procedures. All adult protection policies and procedures will contain information about signs and symptoms of harm and abuse and what actions to take in specific circumstances.

KUS 5, 6, 10, 16

Both 'No Secrets' and 'In Safe Hands' (adult protection procedures in Wales) include guidance on training health and social care staff as well as proposals for more rigorous recruitment and selection processes to identify potential perpetrators of abuse before they are employed in the sector. The Care Standards Act 2000 identified the Protection of Vulnerable Adults (POVA) scheme which created a list of people who are considered to be unsuitable to work with vulnerable adults. The POVA guidance included changes to the requirements for the Criminal Records Bureau Disclosures. Unfortunately what is known is that someone who abuses a vulnerable individual is likely to do so many times before they are caught, especially if they leave their employment before the abuse is discovered or they are dismissed. Since July 2004 it has been a statutory requirement for employers to report, for inclusion on the POVA list, people such as these who would previously have gone undetected. Some legal requirements then place responsibilities on employers, while others identify responsibilities for both the employer and the employee.

Workers' roles and responsibilities in relation to protecting adults from the risk of harm and/or abuse

KUS 4

You have a responsibility to act in the best interests of the vulnerable individual. Vulnerability is not a rigid concept and will depend on the individual's capacity and situation. This may create conflict and tensions between people and organisations, so being clear about your role and responsibilities will help you to manage these conflicts in a professional and appropriate manner.

KUS 5, 6

You need to have a clear understanding of your role and responsibilities in relation to risk, abuse and health and safety. You will gain this through reading and understanding your contract of employment and your job description, through the training you receive from induction onwards as well as ongoing supervision and support from your manager or supervisor. Organisational policies and procedures should also provide guidelines regarding expectations in terms of behaviour and responsibilities. Adhering to these procedures especially in relation to safe working practices is essential if you are to protect individuals from danger, harm and abuse.

You need to understand and put into practice the core values of care practice, those of promoting rights, responsibility, equality, diversity and confidentiality, and empowering and enabling individuals to achieve their potential. You also need to understand what abuse is and the signs and symptoms that may indicate abuse. Having clear guidelines to follow will protect you as well as the individuals you support.

KUS 4, 9

Being able to recognise what constitutes danger, harm and/or abuse is the first step in being able to protect individuals. When you read the list that details the factors that make an individual more vulnerable or read the signs and symptoms of suspected or actual abuse you may think it would be difficult to miss an abusive situation. Sometimes the signs are not as clear, and so discussing situations with colleagues and your supervisor will help your understanding as well as establish a collective understanding. However, you need to be aware that you have a responsibility to question and challenge practices that appear to be abusive. Abuse can be unintentional as well as intentional, and abusive practices can become the norm to the extent that workers think that what they are doing is right when in fact it is institutional abuse. Reflecting on your practice is an important part of being a competent and professional care worker.

Reflecting on your own work practice

One of the difficulties that care workers have in this area of practice is deciding the difference between harm and abuse and poor care practice. Your views on this will be influenced by your values, beliefs and past experiences as these have shaped your perception of the world and your interpretation of what happens around you. What may be considered by one person as dangerous or abusive may be viewed quite differently by another. Making decisions about risk taking for yourself is one thing, supporting others to make these decisions is quite another. It is important to recognise and acknowledge the influence that values, beliefs and experiences may have on your attitude towards risk taking and to ensure that these do not unduly influence the individuals you support.

Think about the scenarios in the practical example on page 185. Think about how you arrived at your decisions about whether the situations were abusive or not. What factors, values and beliefs influenced your decisions?

As a care worker you hold a position of trust with the expectation that you will make professional decisions in the best interests of the individuals you support. One of the core principles of health and social care work is to be non-judgemental.

It is often difficult to recognise when personal values, beliefs and experiences influence thinking and decision-making because they are so much a part of who we are. Understanding yourself and reflecting on your practice will help you to achieve this. Remaining non-judgemental and objective when dealing with the emotive subject of abuse and risk taking is not easy and so supervision is extremely important.

Ensure that you make use of supervision and support systems if you are ever in a position where you either suspect or witness abuse or are struggling with decisions regarding risk taking. Supervision provides you with an opportunity to reflect on your practice. It is important for you to analyse your practice regularly and question yourself to determine if there is anything that you do that may be placing individuals at risk of danger or harm or that is abusive. You can ask your supervisor for feedback on this as well.

Contributing to maintaining a safe care environment

When working you are constantly observing the behaviour of individuals and others within the care environment for signs and signals that may indicate they are at risk of danger, harm or abuse.

Understanding the needs and circumstances of the individuals you support and being able to meet these is important. This may be in relation to trigger factors that create stress generally, e.g. persistent noise, or specifically, e.g. for an individual who is autistic the trigger may be certain colours. It may be that if those factors are not minimised or avoided the individuals' stress will build until they are unable to contain or manage their feelings. The way they express their feelings may be perceived by others as aggressive behaviour. Awareness of possible triggers and putting measures in place to minimise the potential for danger, harm or abuse is important. Identifying the triggers early enough through observing behaviour and intervening to diffuse the situation before it escalates will also help to create a safer and more pleasant environment.

Within group living environments, e.g. hospital or care home, this can be difficult as individuals may have little or no choice about the people they live with and this can create tension as needs and preferences clash. As a care worker, ensuring that individuals with very different personalities and needs are not randomly placed in the same space, e.g. the lounge area, will help to reduce this tension and hopefully create a safer environment. If there is little alternative then you need to monitor the situation closely and help individuals to find some common ground.

KUS 6

Maintaining a safe environment includes ensuring that all entrances and exits of buildings where individuals are being cared for are monitored and kept secure. Visitors' signing-in books as well as identity checks are important both for fire regulations and for establishing the credibility of the visitor and their right to be there. Young children visiting a health and social care establishment need to be observed to ensure that they are safe in terms of health and safety and from individuals who may potentially harm them. Individuals you support may be on the Sex Offenders Register and if this is the case then the organisation has a responsibility to ensure the individual is not placed in a situation where they may present a risk to others and which breaches any legal restrictions.

Responding to unsafe or poor practice

KUS 7, 17, 18

If you identify a situation which is either unsafe (i.e. someone is doing something which puts them or others in danger or at risk of harm) or is poor practice (i.e. it goes against the principles of effective care practice) is discriminatory or abusive then you have a duty to act. This relates to anyone within the care environment.

Working as part of a team not only helps to create a safer environment, it also makes it easier to challenge dangerous, harmful or abusive practices.

Being part of an effective team reduces the likelihood of a blame culture where people do not take responsibility for their own actions or they blame the inadequacy of others, the system or the organisation for failures. It will also encourage open and honest relationships between team members, where constructive feedback is accepted as an opportunity for learning and sharing skills and knowledge. This is particularly helpful if situations of poor or unsafe practice arise. In addition, poor or abusive practice can be challenged more successfully if it is also identified by colleagues and reported by the team rather than one worker. This is particularly true in situations of institutional abuse or where the perpetrator (abuser) is more senior in the organisation.

KUS 19

If the situation of potential or actual danger, harm or abuse is one that you can make safe by taking action, you need to do this without delay. For example, you may notice that the cleaner has not used the hazard signs after mopping the floor. This presents an immediate danger and requires swift action so you would put the signs in place and then report the situation to the cleaner's supervisor immediately afterwards. Depending on your position in the organisation and your relationship with the cleaner you may speak directly to them explaining the reasons why the hazard signs must be in place.

Or, for example, you might notice that a piece of equipment that is used once a week is still being used even though it is broken. There is a short-term danger of harm. You must remove the equipment and/or label it indicating to others that it is unsafe and not in use, and report the situation using the appropriate system, e.g. by completing a maintenance request.

KUS 18, 19

Poor practice is generally considered to relate to the direct interactions with individuals, colleagues and others. Depending on your position in your organisation you may have the authority to take direct action to deal with the situation at the time. For example, if you are a senior support worker and a member of the care staff that you supervise demonstrates poor practice, you need to bring this to their attention and deal with it.

**Figure 7
Potential danger**

If you are not in a position to take direct action when you become aware of poor practice then your responsibility is to record the facts of the situation and report it immediately to your manager or supervisor. If you do not feel able to do this because the person demonstrating poor practice is your manager or supervisor, you need to either refer the matter to their manager or follow your organisation's whistle-blowing policy. The whistle-blowing policy will provide details of the procedure to follow in these situations and may involve contacting a confidential telephone service or the regulatory body such as the Commission for Social Care Inspection (CSCI).

Workers' roles in reporting and recording in relation to risk, harm and abuse

As outlined above, you have a responsibility to report and record situations that place individuals in danger of harm or abuse. You will need to refer to your organisation's policies and procedures for specific guidelines. However, there are some general principles that apply:

- Ensure that any action you take does not place the individual or others in further danger of harm or abuse. Danger, harm or abuse may be disclosed to you by another person and it is important that you act in their interests as well.
- Never confront the suspected perpetrator. This may place the individual raising the concern at risk.
- You must know who to report any suspicions or disclosures of danger, harm or abuse to and the time scales for this.
- Your report and records must maintain confidentiality as far as your responsibility and authority allows. If your report is verbal then ensure that this takes place somewhere where you will not be overheard.
- You must not discuss the situation with other members of staff.
- Reports and records must be factual and must not contain subjective opinion unless this is clearly stated as such.

Workers often comment on the difficulty of expressing a 'gut feeling', especially in relation to subtle changes in an individual's behaviour (as discussed in HSC335a, these may be a key sign of abuse). However, if you think hard enough and analyse what makes you have that strong feeling or suspicion, you will find that it is due to various behaviours and these can be described. For example, the report that states 'John is not his usual self today' is unhelpful, as what does 'his usual self' mean? It is more accurate to describe what is different from normal, for example, 'John is quieter than usual today, is reluctant to talk and does not want to go swimming (which he loves and is normally the highlight of his day)'. There could be other explanations for this behaviour, for example John could be ill. Accurate reporting and recording also includes dates and times and details such as where something took place and who else was involved.

Abuse is often carried out on a regular and consistent basis. Accurate reporting and recording by care workers has often been the only way of identifying patterns, and that can lead to abuse being uncovered and the perpetrators being discovered.

KUS 16

Remember, reports and records are legal documents and can be used in a court of law if a disclosure leads to a criminal prosecution. Therefore you are required to ensure that all records are accurate, legible and complete.

Key points – recognise and report on factors that may cause danger, harm or abuse

- There are many factors that can make an individual vulnerable.
- You have a duty to recognise and report potential or actual danger, harm or abuse.
- You need to understand and adhere to adult protection polices and procedures as well as health and safety legislation.
- Reflect on your practice regularly to ensure it is not harmful or abusive.
- You need to understand the impact that values, beliefs and experiences have on attitudes towards risk and abuse.
- Challenge unsafe, poor or abusive practice and know how to do this safely.

Contribute to minimising the effects of dangerous, harmful and abusive behaviour and practices

Working together to protect individuals from potential danger, harm or abuse

Developing and sustaining good communication and relationships with the individuals that you support ensures they are not isolated and this reduces their vulnerability. In addition, ensuring they understand what abuse is and their right to speak out and not be treated in an abusive way also reduces their vulnerability.

KUS 19

Systems such as key working are designed to ensure that the individual has someone they can specifically relate to and who takes a particular interest in their well-being. The key worker is often best placed to notice subtle changes in behaviour which so often indicate that something is wrong. They can also develop a good understanding of individuals' communication differences and interpret these for colleagues.

KUS 2, 15

When developing relationships with individuals it is important to take time to listen to any concerns they have as well as show interest in them and their interests. Spending time talking to and listening to individuals regularly is important. Whether this is while doing an activity together or just relaxing will depend on individual preference. Demonstrating respect, being honest and non-judgemental will encourage trust and these are essential components of an effective relationship.

Understanding the factors that have shaped an individual's life, values and beliefs will help you to understand their attitudes to risk and danger and possible abuse. An individual may have been brought up and conditioned to believe that something you consider to be abusive is normal because they have been subjected to it for as long as they can remember. This increases their vulnerability as they may feel less able to recognise or report the abuse. They may have different attitudes to risk which may challenge your preconceptions of their ability. Spending time getting to know an individual and understanding their motivations better will help you take these factors into account and promote their rights and/or act in their best interests.

KUS 2

By being a positive role model and providing a good model of the professional care worker–individual relationship you can help to protect individuals. Knowing your role and responsibilities as well as the limitations and boundaries of professional caring relationships will help you to be a model for the individuals you work with. If they should subsequently come into contact with other care workers who are abusive then they will be less likely to accept this and will speak out, especially if you have empowered them to do this.

KUS 17

Information about abuse, what it is and what to do if an individual feels at risk, should be available to the individuals that you support. This information needs to be in a range of different language and communication formats, for example as signs or symbols, on audiotapes or in Braille.

**Figure 8
Get to know
individuals and
spend time
talking and
listening to them**

You also need to develop effective relationships with colleagues and others you work with as this also contributes to protecting people. You need to understand their roles and responsibilities and help them to understand yours. Try to understand their values, beliefs and experiences and how this impacts on their practice and interpretation of danger, harm and abuse. Having a common understanding of risk, what constitutes abuse and what action needs to be taken to protect individuals is also important. Evidence from inquiries into situations of abuse consistently found that poor rela-tionships and communication as well as differences in understanding have been significant factors in creating an environment where harm and abuse can occur. Effec-tive relationships are built on trust and so it is easier to raise concerns if you feel you have a number of colleagues that you can speak to and whom you feel will take your concerns seriously.

Effective communication

KUS 15

Communication both with individuals and others is essential if the potential for harm and abuse is to be minimised. Systems for communicating information about individuals must be confidential. However, those who have a responsibility to support individuals must have adequate access to appropriate information. Most organisations will have information-sharing agreements or protocols in place to ensure people are clear about what information can be shared and with whom. The misuse of information is abusive as it removes an individual's rights. There may be a variety of recording systems within your workplace and you have a responsibility to ensure that each is used appropriately. As discussed above, written information can provide vital evidence in situations where abuse is systematic.

You need to know how you can challenge and raise concerns about danger, harm and abuse. The person you refer to first is likely to be your immediate manager. Your report needs to contain all the relevant factual information as well as your signature, time and date. The information must be accurate, legible and complete. You may have a special document to record this information on, e.g. an incident form, see page 48 for an example.

KUS 18

If your manager is the person whose practice you are reporting, you need to refer to your organisation's policy to identify the person you should report to. This could be someone within your organisation or external to it, e.g. CSCI. Remember the importance of respecting individual rights, privacy and dignity in these situations as everyone has a right to these.

Respecting individual rights, privacy and dignity

We have already considered the importance of maintaining confidentiality and not making assumptions in situations of suspected or actual harm and abuse. The facts of the situation need to be gathered as far as possible in order to ensure fairness to all those involved. Assure the individual that you take their concerns seriously and will report them to the appropriate person.

KUS 23

At no time should you dismiss an allegation or someone's explanation as being untrue – it is not your responsibility to make that decision. Any discussions need to be in a private place and information should be shared only with those who need to know (that decision will be made by your manager). In the UK judicial system a person is innocent until proven guilty and so no judgments should be made until the situation has been fully investigated. If the perpetrator of the potential or actual harm or abuse is a care worker it is likely they will be suspended from work pending an investigation. If it is another individual they may be moved in order to prevent further distress, harm or abuse. You must act in a professional manner and ensure that the matter is not a topic for discussion and speculation by others either within or outside the care environment.

It is imperative that you act according to agreed multi-agency adult protection guidelines as this ensures that the incident is dealt with in a way that does not compromise the individual or their recourse to a criminal investigation and/or prosecution.

Workers' responsibilities regarding disclosing information

You may become aware of potential or actual harm and abuse because someone tells you about it (this is known as disclosure). The disclosure could come from the individual, the perpetrator (abuser) or another person. Alternatively, you may become aware of the abuse or harm as a result of your own observations.

KUS 24

In the event of disclosure it is important to remember the following do's and don'ts.

Do:

- Remain calm and try not to show shock, disbelief or anger.

- Listen very carefully to what is being said and respect the individual's wishes.

- Show concern by acknowledging your regret about what has happened, if that is appropriate.

- Reassure the person by telling them they have done the right thing in telling someone and that you take what they are saying seriously.

- If the person disclosing is the individual who has been harmed or abused, reassure them that it is not their fault.

- Be honest about your responsibility to act upon the information disclosed.

- Reassure them that the information will not be shared with other individuals supported within the service.

- Tell them what you are going to do and who you are reporting the disclosed information to.

- Explain that the person you report to will then talk to them about the next steps.

- If appropriate, take urgent action to protect the individual from any immediate danger.

- Be aware, if it is a recent incident, that you need to preserve any material evidence that may be required for an investigation.

Do not:

- Interrupt them or ask questions to gain more details. This will be done later.

- Promise a level of confidentiality that you do not have the authority to maintain as this will mislead the individual.

- Be judgemental.

- Break confidentiality between the person disclosing, yourself and your manager.

- Alert the perpetrator or the alleged victim (if disclosure is by a third party).

KUS 4

It is really important that you do not make assumptions about what has happened. You must report exactly what was disclosed without opinion. Effective action at this point is crucial for both the individual who has allegedly been harmed or abused and for the perpetrator. It is important that procedures are followed correctly throughout so that a proper investigation can be conducted if appropriate. Failure to do so may jeopardise the objectivity of the investigation. This may mean the alleged perpetrator can continue abusing or, if the allegation is unfounded, suspicion may linger.

Identifying sources and signs of danger, harm or abuse

Part of your role and responsibility is to maintain health and safety and so you need to be able to identify potential dangers within and outside your workplace. During the course of your day-to-day work check the environment to ensure that it is safe and secure. For example, you may be checking to ensure that areas where individuals walk are free from hazards or that cross-infection is minimised through effective hand washing. You may work with individuals who require support and supervision to manage their potentially self-harming behaviour, e.g. individuals who misuse substances such as controlled drugs or alcohol, or who physically self-harm using a blade. As a care worker you need to know what particular factors present potential dangers for the individuals you support. Some of those factors may be controllable in terms of close monitoring of the environment while others may be related to the individual and may only become fully known through observation and analysis of incidents and identification of triggers.

KUS 6, 17

If you identify signs or sources of danger, harm or abuse you need to take action. Depending on the nature of the danger, harm or abuse you may need to act immediately or refer to others for advice and support.

Taking action to protect a vulnerable adult

Your day-to-day vigilance regarding health and safety, maintaining professional boundaries, understanding the needs of the individuals that you support and involving yourself in continuous professional development are all ways in which you protect vulnerable adults. However, there may be occasions when you need to take specific action, e.g. if you become aware through observation or disclosure that an individual is either at risk of harm or abuse or has experienced this.

Identifying bad practice and abuse

Sally has just started working on the medical ward of the local hospital. One of the patients, Mr Hawthorn, is 88 years old and a former teacher. He is partially sighted and has a hearing impairment. He was admitted a week ago following a stroke. He has lived alone since his wife died six months ago and when he was admitted it was clear that he had not been looking after himself. His only relative is his son who lives in Canada and he has little contact with him. Mr Hawthorn has been left with some weakness down his right side, difficulty expressing himself and he needs support with walking, washing, dressing and eating. He gets frustrated by his limitations and is at times angry and tearful. Sally has noticed that although Mr Hawthorn calls for help when any of the staff walk past, his requests are ignored. She has overheard other staff making unkind remarks about Mr Hawthorn saying he is a dirty smelly old man. Sally walks onto the ward at the end of lunchtime and sees Mr Hawthorn sitting in a chair by his bed. His lunch tray is on his table at the bottom of his bed well out of his reach. Sally asks Mr Hawthorn if he has finished his lunch. He tells her that no one has told him it was there. Sally sits with him and helps him have his lunch.

After ensuring Mr Hawthorn is comfortable Sally goes to the ward manager and reports the incident. She also reports what she has observed over the previous few days. The ward manager asks her to complete an incident form.

➤ What factors make Mr Hawthorn vulnerable?

➤ Do you think what has happened is poor practice or abuse? Explain the reasoning behind your answer.

➤ What evidence is there to support your conclusions about Mr Hawthorn's situation?

➤ What action should Sally take now? Give the reasons for your answer.

➤ How can this situation be avoided in future?

Key points – minimising the effects of dangerous, harmful and abusive behaviour

- Protecting individuals from danger, harm and abuse is more effective if there is a team approach.
- Developing and sustaining effective relationships and communication is an important factor in early identification of potential or actual danger, harm and abuse.
- All individuals have a right to respect and to the maintenance of their confidentiality, privacy and dignity.
- You need to take all allegations seriously and take appropriate action according to organisational policies and procedures.
- Records need to be accurate, legible, complete, signed and dated.

Respond to and report on suspicions of harm or abuse

Monitoring individuals' well-being

You monitor the well-being of individuals that you support throughout the time you spend with them. You do this by observing their behaviour and body language, listening to them and asking questions. Within your particular workplace you may also undertake specific activities to monitor and measure well-being. For example, at regular intervals you may check an individual's pulse or blood pressure or undertake a urinalysis. The three-, six- or 12-month care plan review is another monitoring process. The purpose of any type of monitoring is to determine if an individual is achieving their potential and is physically and emotionally well. If monitoring reveals that may not be the case then closer monitoring and observation may take place to determine why, so that changes can be made to improve their well-being.

There may be occasions, for example if harm or abuse is suspected or following an abusive incident, when specific monitoring would take place. You may be asked to keep records of an individual's mood, activities and social interaction, how they are maintaining their personal care and cleanliness as well as any unusual behaviour.

One of the significant signs of harm and abuse is changes to an individual's normal behaviour and so monitoring this may provide clues that something is wrong. The better you know the individuals you support the more able you will be to identify changes in behaviour, especially if they feel unable to tell anyone what is happening to them either because they are frightened or have communication differences. Monitoring an individual may mean observing them closely in order to prevent them being harmed or harming themselves. For example, an individual who poses a threat to themselves through self-harming behaviour or is suicidal may be on 24-hour one-to-one observation. Equally, an individual may be at risk from others. In this situation you need to know their whereabouts and that of the person who poses a risk to them and ensure that if they should come together you are on hand to monitor and intervene to prevent harm or abuse.

Taking action in response to suspicions of harm and/or abuse

As described above, you need to remain calm and follow the organisational procedures correctly. These will guide your actions and help you to feel in control of the situation.

There may be some situations that you can deal with directly as they are within your authority, e.g. a risk or danger to physical well-being due to unsafe equipment, situations or practice. You need to deal with a situation of harm and abuse as quickly as possible ensuring that, if distress is caused to an individual, they are supported. You

KUS 7

should demonstrate respect for the other person involved whether they are another worker or a supported individual. You can do this by talking to them in a place that is quiet and confidential. Your attitude throughout should be non-judgemental. If appropriate you need to clarify the facts, i.e. what happened, where it happened, when it took place and who was involved, as the person you refer the incident to will need this information. Inform the appropriate person, e.g. your line manager, as quickly as possible. They will provide further advice and guidance.

If the individual is injured you should seek urgent medical or emergency assistance. If you believe a serious crime has been committed, you need to contact the police. In situations of physical or sexual abuse you have a responsibility to preserve any physical evidence. Record all of your actions, including times, in the appropriate document.

Evaluating available information relating to concerns raised

All allegations need to be taken seriously and reported. When an allegation or incident of harm or abuse occurs it is important to ensure that the facts of the situation and other related information is gathered. There may be observations by others, written reports, physical or material evidence, e.g. torn or soiled clothing, broken furniture. All of the available information must be gathered and kept in a secure place to avoid it being tampered with. You need to evaluate the information to ensure it is as accurate and complete as possible bearing in mind the do's and don'ts outlined on page 194.

This will help to provide a broader picture of events although no judgements should be made at this point. If information sources conflict then additional information will be needed to verify what happened.

Figure 10 Evaluating information

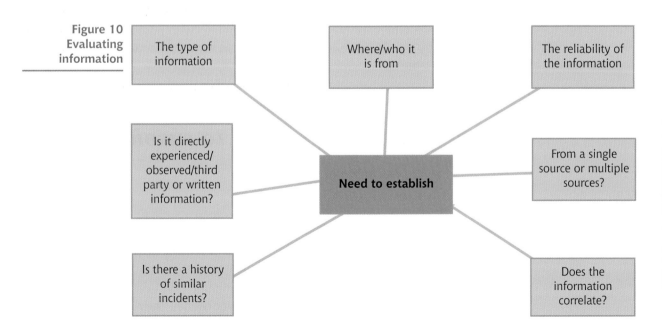

Maintaining the integrity of information and evidence gathered

If an allegation of harm or abuse is made then any investigation, internal or external (i.e. involving the police), will require information and evidence to be preserved in order to help investigators reach conclusions.

KUS 25

All information gathered must be kept confidential and access should be limited to those people who have an agreed need and right to the information. Any written reports must be signed and dated at the end of the writing so they cannot be altered. Information and material or physical evidence must be kept secure. Witness statements given by others must be confidential and must not be shared. Encourage individuals and others to be honest and truthful when stating what happened.

In situations where physical or sexual abuse has occurred, any physical evidence must be left where it is; if it has to be moved it should be handled as little as possible. Nothing should be tidied up or cleaned and you should not touch anything that you do not have to. If a weapon is involved do not touch it (unless it is handed to you by an individual). Handle anything that may be of interest to the police as little as possible to preserve fingerprints, fibres, blood etc. Any physical evidence that has been moved may be placed in a secure dry place. Any clothing that has been in contact with the abused individual should be preserved and kept.

KUS 26

Written records must include information about the physical state of those involved in the incident as well as their attitudes and behaviour and any injuries that can be seen (a physical examination by an appropriate practitioner will need to be carried out following consent). If appropriate you must secure the room in which the incident took place until the police arrive.

If the individual has been sexually abused they will be asked to consent to a physical examination by a forensic surgeon. Any physical contact should be avoided so that cross-contamination does not destroy any evidence.

It is the responsibility of the police to preserve evidence, so anything connected to an incident should be left untouched. If an item has to be touched then it should be placed in a clean brown paper bag or envelope (do not lick it to seal) or, if it is liquid, place it in clean glassware.

You will need to refer to your organisation's policies, or your manager or the police depending on which is appropriate under the circumstances.

Claire works as a home care support worker. In the mornings she visits Grace. Grace is 45 years old and has multiple sclerosis. She lives alone and receives two visits each day, one in the morning and one in the evening.

One morning when Claire visits Grace she is reluctant to undress. She says she feels unwell and when Claire tries to help her she notices that Grace pulls away as if in pain and starts to cry. This is quite unlike Grace and so Claire spends time talking and reassuring her. Grace agrees that Claire can help her to take her nightdress off and have a wash. Claire notices several bruises that are swollen and tender to the touch on Grace's wrists, forearms, abdomen and the inside of her thighs. There is blood on her nightdress. Claire remarks that the bruises look sore and gently asks Grace what happened. Grace bursts into tears and tells Claire that the night-care assistant who visited last night raped her. Claire reassures Grace and Grace tells her everything that happened. Claire tells Grace that she has a duty to report what has happened and also suggests that Grace reports the rape to the police – she agrees. Claire immediately telephones her manager and checks that it is alright to talk. Claire informs the manager of Grace's allegation and the action she has taken. Her manager tells Claire to remain with Grace and says she will come as soon as possible. Claire informs the manager that Grace wants to report the rape to the police.

➤ What action should Claire take next?

➤ How should Claire preserve any evidence?

➤ What information should Claire include in her report?

➤ What are the principles of effective record keeping?

➤ What other agencies are likely to be involved in this situation?

Liaising with other professionals

KUS 17

Evidence from inquiries into adult abuse found that effective communication and liaison between professionals and organisations is crucial if adults are to be protected. Team working and ensuring that suspicions are reported and recorded correctly are essential. It is important you understand your role in adult protection as well as that of others inside and outside the organisation. If you are unsure about your role it is your responsibility to check this with your manager. Attending adult-protection training with workers from other agencies will help you to understand the importance of working together. Some individuals that you support may attend a variety of care services and therefore it is important that any concerns about an individual's well-being or safety are shared with those organisations. Workers from those organisations can be involved in monitoring and reporting changes and be aware of potential vulnerabilities and take action to minimise the risks of danger, harm and abuse. Confidentiality and information protocols need to be agreed.

As discussed above, abuse is often only uncovered when patterns are identified, whether these are patterns of an individual's behaviour or those of the perpetrator. Liaison with other organisations will be more effective in managing the risks and monitoring potential dangers. A co-ordinated approach to monitoring will mean that the individual will be observed more closely and there will be fewer opportunities for them to be placed in vulnerable situations. This will reduce the potential for danger, harm and abuse to go undetected and so provide the individual with a greater level of protection.

Working in accordance with locally agreed adult protection policies and procedures

KUS 5, 7, 17, 26

Following the publication of 'No Secrets' and 'In Safe Hands', the government required local authority social services departments to work with other health and social care organisations in their area to develop, agree and implement multi-agency adult protection policies and procedures. You will find a copy of these in your workplace. You may have attended a multi-agency training event which explained how these work in practice. You may have had the opportunity during that training or in your workplace to discuss with others your role and responsibility in the event of an adult protection issue arising. All policies will include the importance of reporting any suspicions or actual incidents to your manager or an appropriate person as quickly as possible and ensuring that any action you do take is recorded accurately, legibly and in full with times, dates and clear statements of fact. All records should be signed and dated. Any action you do take should not place the individual in more danger or adversely effect further investigations or actions. Those involved have a right to confidentiality and respect and to have their rights, dignity and privacy maintained.

Figure 11
All social care settings should have adult protection policies and procedures

It is your responsibility to read these procedures and to ask for clarification from your manager if there are areas that you are unsure about. If a situation arises, do not be afraid to refer to these procedures as it is difficult to remember everything.

Remember you have a duty of care. That means you are responsible for taking all possible steps to ensure that no harm comes to any individual that you support or others within the care environment. In situations of potential or actual danger, harm and abuse, inaction is not an option.

Key points – responding to and reporting suspicions of harm or abuse

- Monitoring an individual's well-being enables you to identify any signs of danger, harm or abuse.
- Taking action when potential or actual danger, harm or abuse is identified is not an option, it is a requirement.
- Any information gathered must be evaluated and recorded accurately.
- Evidence must be preserved according to your organisation's procedures.
- You must liaise with other professionals to ensure the safety and integrity of evidence.
- Your actions must be in line with local adult protection policies and procedures.

Unit

HSC335

Are you ready for assessment?

Contribute to the protection of individuals from harm and abuse

This unit is about how you contribute to the protection of individuals through recognising the potential causes, signs and symptoms of danger, harm and abuse. It is also about how you ensure that you work in accordance with adult protection policies and procedures, are able to make accurate reports and records, and maintain the rights, privacy, dignity and confidentiality of all those involved. It is about how you use supervision and support systems to reflect on your practice to ensure that your actions are not dangerous, harmful or abusive.

Your assessment will be carried out mainly through observation by your assessor and this should provide most of the evidence for the elements in this unit. If your assessor is unable to observe you directly then you may be able to use the testimony of an experienced colleague acting as an expert witness. You will need to discuss this with your assessor. Evidence of your knowledge and understanding will be demonstrated through observation, your assessor examining work products, e.g. reports, minutes of meetings, as well as through answering oral and/or written questions.

▶

Direct observation by your assessor

Your assessor or an expert witness will need to plan to see you carry out the performance criteria (PCs) in each of the elements in this unit. However, due to the nature of the unit it may difficult for your assessor and/or expert witness to directly observe the following performance criteria:

- **HSC335a PC 4**
- **HSC335c PCs 3, 4**

Preparing to be observed

You must make sure that your workplace and any individuals and key people involved in your work agree to you being assessed. Explicit, informed consent must be obtained before you carry out any assessment activity that involves individuals or which involves access to confidential information related to their care.

Before your assessments you should read carefully the performance criteria for each element in the unit. Try to cover as much as you can during your observation but remember that you and your assessor can also plan for additional sources of evidence should full coverage of all performance criteria not be possible.

Other types of evidence

You may need to present other forms of evidence in order to:

- Cover criteria not observed by your assessor.
- Show that you have the required knowledge, understanding and skills to claim competence in this area of practice.
- Ensure your work practice is consistent.

Your assessor may also need to ask you questions to confirm your knowledge and understanding and ensure that you can apply this to your practice.

Check your knowledge

- Describe the factors that make the individuals you work with particularly vulnerable to harm and abuse.
- Explain how danger, harm and abuse can affect an individual's well-being and behaviour in the short, medium and long term.
- Explain how power can be misused by people who support vulnerable adults as well as by those who wish to harm and abuse individuals.
- Explain what action you would take if you suspected or witnessed an individual being harmed or abused.
- Describe what action you would take if you suspected a colleague was harming or abusing an individual.
- Describe how beliefs, values and experiences may affect attitudes and opinions about what is risky, dangerous, harmful and abusive.

Contribute to the prevention and management of abusive and aggressive behaviour

T his unit covers the prevention and management of abusive and aggressive behaviour. It is also concerned with handling incidents of aggressive and abusive behaviour, and the reviewing and recording of these in accordance with statutory and agency frameworks.

The unit contains three elements:

- **HSC336a** *Contribute to preventing abusive and aggressive behaviour*
- **HSC336b** *Deal with incidents of abusive and aggressive behaviour*
- **HSC336c** *Contribute to reviewing incidents of abusive and aggressive behaviour*

Introduction

Abusive and aggressive behaviour may be verbal or non-verbal, and could be social, physical or emotional. It may involve the individual or people who are significant to the individual, and it could include other people in the vicinity. It may also involve you and other colleagues. For that reason it is vital that you remain alert to any possible situation or behaviour which could lead to harm, danger or the risk of injury to any individual in your care setting. There is often a reason for a person's behaviour. It could be due to the effects of stress, physical or mental illness, or to social and environmental factors. For instance, an individual may have been used to living on their own and pleasing themselves. Once in the care setting they find themselves in the company of individuals that they would not normally choose to spend time with. They have to conform to the rules of the care setting and it may not meet their individual needs and preferences. The environment may be noisy or crowded, there may be insufficient space or they may feel that their privacy is being invaded. They may be frustrated that they are no longer able to please themselves, or they may not understand just what is happening to them. This can cause the individual to feel irritated and agitated.

Some people may be able to recognise that they are becoming aggressive and abusive, whereas others may not. They may deny that there is anything wrong. The emphasis for the management of abusive and aggressive behaviour must be on prevention and de-escalation, and controlling the situation before it gets out of hand.

Individuals currently receiving care are much more aware of care services and their rights. Not everyone's personal expectations can be met, and this has often led to the

KUS 5, 9

build-up of aggressive and abusive behaviour which is often directed towards care staff. Individuals may become angry and project this anger towards other people. Alternatively, your own behaviour and attitude may be a causative factor. If this is the case you need to reflect on your practice and seek appropriate support to change.

Element
HSC336a

Contribute to preventing abusive and aggressive behaviour

Communication

The main part of your role will involve communicating with individuals in the care setting. You will come into contact with many different individuals, all with their own particular personality and complex needs. You will have to deal with a variety of situations involving different individuals during your working day. Some of these individuals may be those you are supporting in the care setting and others may be visitors or other care staff. It is important that you develop a good relationship and effective communication with each individual that you come into contact with during your work. You may find that you are able to communicate with some individuals better than others. However, it is essential that you communicate with all individuals in a manner that is appropriate to them. Communication is more than just talking, it involves facial expression, gestures, touch, tone of voice, space and position. To be able to build up a good **interpersonal interaction** with another individual you need a great deal of skill and ability.

KUS 8

There are different stages to an interaction:

- Stage 1 – Introduction; light, general conversation. Body language is important during this stage and will determine whether the conversation progresses.
- Stage 2 – Main contact, significant information disclosed. Active listening is important during this stage.
- Stage 3 – Reflect, wind up and end positively. Being aware of when to end an interaction is another skill.

KUS 8, 12

You will need to be able to recognise how the individual wishes to, or is able to, communicate, and you should try to communicate with them in a manner which is appropriate to them. It is your responsibility to encourage effective communication with an individual and to establish what they are trying to communicate. Communication can be divided into two parts, for instance what we say and what we do not say. Understanding people involves understanding their non-verbal communication as well as what they actually say. This is essential if you are going to be able to contribute to preventing abusive and aggressive behaviour in your workplace.

Effective communication

Effective communication is important in the care setting, and you need to ensure that your communication techniques are appropriate to all individuals. For communication to be effective there needs to be an adequate exchange of views and information between individuals. The following elements are required:

- A sender – the person who starts the communication.
- A message – what the sender wants to communicate.
- A medium – the way in which the communication takes place, for example verbally or non-verbally, in a face-to-face conversation or by telephone.
- The receiver – the person who hears, reads or sees the message and interprets it.
- Feedback – the receiver needs to show the sender that the message has been received and understood.

KUS 6, 8

Figure 1
Effective
communication is
important in the
care setting

Everyone is different and you will need to adapt your style of communication to meet the varying needs and situations. It is essential that the individual is able to understand what you are saying and that you understand them. Take into account any language differences or difficulties and any physical constraints that may prevent effective communication. It is possible that the individual is distressed and does not wish to listen to you. You will need to make the appropriate adjustments to your communication methods to allow appropriate communication to take place.

KUS 8, 13

You need to consider:

- *Language.* Some words may mean different things to different individuals due to their ethnicity, gender, sexuality, culture, religion or age. Use simple language, avoid using jargon or slang, and speak slowly. Organise an interpreter or translator if at all possible.
- *Hearing impairment.* For individuals who are hearing impaired, make eye contact, speak slowly and clearly and adjust your pace, tone and volume to aid effective interaction. Make sure that you are facing them and that they can see your face clearly in case they lip read. Use gestures or pictures to reinforce what you are saying. If they use sign language, ask someone who can sign to help them communicate.
- *Visual impairment.* For individuals who are visually impaired, you must avoid startling the individual, let them know calmly and quietly that you are there, and introduce yourself. Again speak in a clear tone and at a pace that the individual can understand.

Figure 2
Use an interpreter
or translator if
necessary

● Disability. Consider the disability – it may be physical, emotional or mental. If the individual is in bed or in a wheelchair, sit down near to them so that you can maintain eye contact (if culturally appropriate). This will prevent them from feeling 'talked down to'. If individuals have an emotional or mental disability you will first need to build up a rapport with them and help them to feel safe with you so that they trust you. Show concern for them and speak calmly and reassuringly. Be aware of your body language but do not let this appear threatening. If the individual is confused, such as with dementia, you will need to be patient with them and say the same thing in different ways to help them to understand what you are trying to convey.

KUS 8

Taking these things into consideration will enable you to establish a good relationship with the individuals in your care and with other people with whom you come into contact. Communication is about forming and maintaining relationships, giving and collecting information and conveying it accurately and clearly, ensuring that it is understood by everyone concerned. This will encourage an open exchange of views and information. Effective communication is also concerned with making individuals feel valued, and it will help you to work as part of a team with other colleagues.

Trust is an essential ingredient of an effective relationship. The inconsistent messages from verbal and non-verbal communication can lead to poor relationships. The individual may not trust the worker and the worker might be unaware of this, which may lead to aggressive behaviour.

Constraints to communication

KUS 7

In order for people to communicate effectively, the following conditions are necessary:

● Normal physical and psychological development from early childhood to the present, having the ability to speak, listen and understand clearly what is being said. For individuals who have sensory problems such as poor hearing, sight or difficulty with speaking, you should consider the most appropriate means of overcoming these by using sensory aids, gestures, signs or pictures.

● A common language between the sender and the receiver. The ability to read and understand the written word. For individuals using a different language, interpreters and translators need to be available. Literature and information must be written in the individual's language and ideally printed in a size that they can see.

- Good mental health. Individuals with mental health problems can be confused and disorientated, they may have a high level of anxiety or worry or be unwilling to communicate. An inability to comprehend what is being said may cause distress and frustration.

- Environmental interference. The individual may not be able to hear or be heard due to excessive noise. The individual might be embarrassed to speak openly about their problems and may require more privacy. They may feel closed in and distracted due to the fact that several other individuals are in close proximity to them.

Constraints or barriers to communication can occur in most care settings. There are many factors that can contribute to this and you need to be able to recognise these and deal with them appropriately. You may find that some individuals in your care have specific communication difficulties/differences. Figure 3 shows some of the barriers to communication.

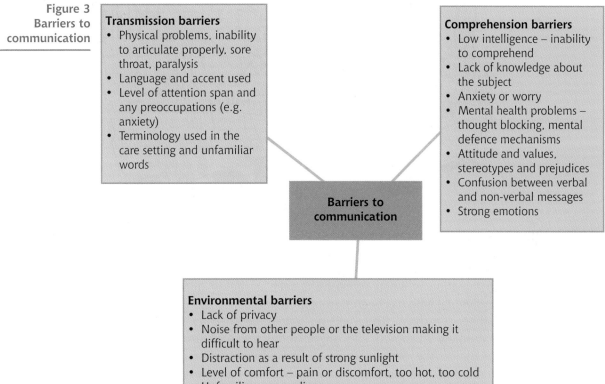

Figure 3 Barriers to communication

Transmission barriers
- Physical problems, inability to articulate properly, sore throat, paralysis
- Language and accent used
- Level of attention span and any preoccupations (e.g. anxiety)
- Terminology used in the care setting and unfamiliar words

Comprehension barriers
- Low intelligence – inability to comprehend
- Lack of knowledge about the subject
- Anxiety or worry
- Mental health problems – thought blocking, mental defence mechanisms
- Attitude and values, stereotypes and prejudices
- Confusion between verbal and non-verbal messages
- Strong emotions

Barriers to communication

Environmental barriers
- Lack of privacy
- Noise from other people or the television making it difficult to hear
- Distraction as a result of strong sunlight
- Level of comfort – pain or discomfort, too hot, too cold
- Unfamiliar surroundings

Try to recognise these constraints and minimise these as much as possible. So, for example, if the area is noisy take the individual to a quiet place for some privacy. If the lighting is inappropriate or the environment is too hot or too cold then try to make improvements so that it is more comfortable for the individual. Listen calmly to what the individual has to say, offer them support and reassurance, and provide them with the means to use the communication methods familiar to them. Being unable to communicate can cause intense frustration and anger. You need to provide the appropriate support and reassurance to encourage the individual to share their views and opinions.

Effects of discrimination and oppression

It is essential that you do not discriminate against any individual or groups of individuals, or become prejudiced against people, **stereotype** them into specific groups, or jump to conclusions about them.

**Figure 4
Do not label
people**

Stereotypes and biases (prejudices) affect communication in a negative way. Discrimination is when someone is seen as being different from other individuals. An individual who has been stereotyped or labelled has absolutely no control over the way others see them. They will no longer be seen as an individual and could become extremely frustrated and angry about the way they are being treated. You should recognise the differences in all individuals and respect them for their individuality. Individuals have a right to freedom from **oppression** or injustice, and should be treated fairly and equally.

KUS 13

The rights of everyone

All individuals have a right and a need to be treated fairly, regardless of their age, gender, social class, intelligence or racial and cultural beliefs and preferences. It is against the law to discriminate against individuals or groups of individuals. You need to be familiar with your organisation's Equal Opportunities Policy and all policies relating to discrimination. Try to support individuals in whatever way you can to sustain their rights and help them to feel valued as individuals. Treat the individual in a fair and equal manner and recognise that they may have specific requirements or needs. Help them to achieve a sense of calmness and well-being.

KUS 1, 2

Individual rights

KUS 3

Everyone who works within the health-care environment will be working within the provisions of the Human Rights Act 1998 which came into force on 2 October 2000. This guarantees the individual rights shown in Figure 5.

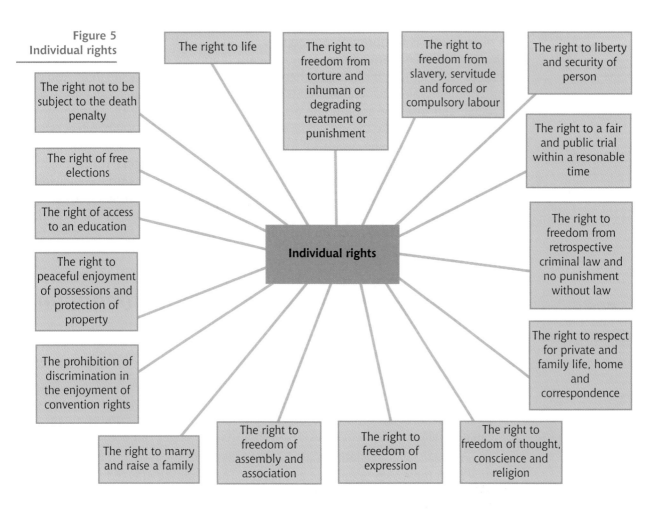

Figure 5
Individual rights

KUS 12

Remember – never express irritation or anger towards the individuals in your care. Your attitude will affect their behaviour. If you ever feel frustrated or angry you need to reflect on this and seek advice from your manager or supervisor on how to deal with your emotions in a constructive manner.

Environment

To enable effective communication and meaningful interaction to take place, you should ensure that the environment meets the specific needs and requirements of all individuals in your care. Ensure that there is adequate lighting, ventilation and space for individuals to sit and talk. Always provide privacy for those who need to talk in private and support for those who need it. If the environment is noisy, or if there are interruptions from other people, the individuals will find it very difficult to have a meaningful interaction and they may become irritated and angry. The space that individuals have to live in has an impact on their behaviour, as do décor and colour.

For example, if an individual has autism then the constancy of their environment may be particularly important to their well-being.

KUS 12

Appropriate action

Part of your role is to observe and monitor the individuals in your care and also the interaction between them and other individuals. If you are monitoring an individual's behaviour do not make it obvious, otherwise you may aggravate a situation. You need to be constantly alert to any situations that may be causing upset or distress to an individual, and take the appropriate action to stop this. You may be able to provide a distraction that will take the individual's mind off what is causing them to feel agitated and angry. It may become necessary for you to remove the individual from the area for their safety and well-being or to remove any possible triggers which might be causing them distress. Be clear and confident in your interactions with the individuals. It is essential that you remain calm and supportive and ensure the safety of yourself and other individuals at all times. It is important to provide assistance for the individuals to communicate effectively, but do not infringe on their rights.

KUS 11

Triggers to abusive or aggressive behaviour

There are many reasons why something may trigger aggressive or abusive behaviour in the care setting. It may be due to the individual in your care or from significant others who may be visiting them. Some of these reasons are:

- *Frustration* – this is the cause of much aggression due to obstacles in personal achievement, or an experience of failure or not being able to do the things they can normally do for themselves. Frustration-related anger can occur.
- *Misunderstanding* – the individual may not fully understand what is happening and may form their own opinion of a situation. This could be affected by the individual's own health problems or particular capabilities.
- *Restrictions* – loss of freedom and mobility, a feeling of loss of independence and self-worth. Lack of choice.
- *Attention seeking* – possibly a means of gaining attention if they feel neglected.
- *Fear or embarrassment* – aggression may be a defensive reaction to threatening intrusions of personal space, or due to a lack of reasoning or common sense.
- *Facilities* – lack of personal space and inadequate facilities.
- *Institutionalisation* – where there are strict rules, regulations, routines and inflexibility imposed by those in the care setting. This causes the individuals to become institutionalised, their lives being run by the timings of the care setting rather than their needs.

Individuals can become upset and angry if they feel that something is not going right for them and they may react to this in an abusive and aggressive way. You need to be alert for possible triggers that may cause someone to behave in this way. Figure 6 shows possible signs that may indicate that someone is becoming angry.

**Figure 6
Signs of anger**

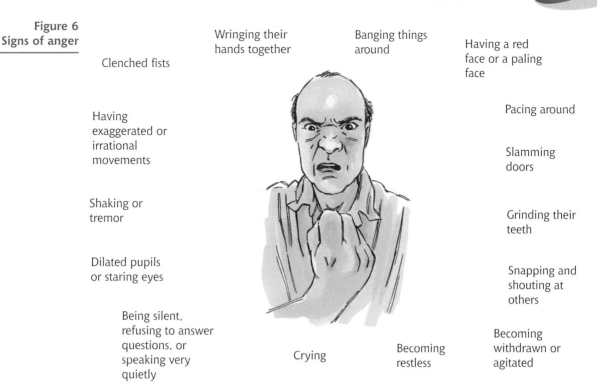

Clenched fists

Wringing their hands together

Banging things around

Having a red face or a paling face

Having exaggerated or irrational movements

Pacing around

Slamming doors

Shaking or tremor

Grinding their teeth

Dilated pupils or staring eyes

Snapping and shouting at others

Being silent, refusing to answer questions, or speaking very quietly

Crying

Becoming restless

Becoming withdrawn or agitated

KUS 1, 9

If you notice an individual displaying any of these signs of potential aggressive or abusive behaviour, you need to take immediate action to prevent harm or injury to anyone in the vicinity including the individual. If the aggressor is a visitor, it may be necessary for you to ask them to leave the area. You may need to call someone to assist you. Individuals may behave in an aggressive way because they do not know what they should do. They may be feeling powerless and uncertain about their future. They may be finding it difficult to express what they are actually feeling, and their behaviour may be a cry for help.

If you have built up a good rapport with the individuals and you are familiar with their attitudes and behaviour, it should be easy to recognise if things seem to be going wrong. Try to encourage the individual to express their feelings and discuss what is troubling them. It is possible that you will be able to ease the situation for them, but do not put yourself at risk. Ask for support from other colleagues if necessary, and always make an accurate record of the event in the incident report book.

When you complete an incident report you must make sure that the information is accurate, legible and complete, and that all the facts are stated clearly. Record as much information as possible, such as what the incident was, who was present, where it took place, the time and date, names of any witnesses and, of course, your name and signature.

Protection of individuals

You need to minimise the effects of aggression and abusive behaviour. Offer reassurance and support to the individual at whom the behaviour was directed and try to ascertain the reason for the aggression. You will need to reassure others in the vicinity as they will also have been affected by the situation. They may not understand what has been going on and will feel vulnerable and afraid. Take care to protect yourself and other individuals in the vicinity, and move them from potential harm or danger if possible.

Handling a difficult situation

Jane is a married woman with two young daughters. She is 32 years old. Currently she is in hospital for a minor operation but has had a setback as she has developed an infection. Although it is not serious, it has prolonged her stay in hospital for a few more days. Her husband has been off work looking after the children as they are not yet at school. He arrives to see her for afternoon visiting with the two little girls. Jane is pleased to see them all. A short time into the visit, the nursing staff observe that Jane appears to be getting upset, her husband seems to be shouting at her. One of the care staff goes to the bedside to see if she can help. Jane's husband tells her to go away and leave them alone, saying that it is nothing to do with her. Jane is crying and she does not answer when asked what is wrong. Her husband begins to get angry and throws Jane's handbag on the bed. The children start to cry and the woman in the next bed rings her bell for the nurse.

➤ *How would you handle this situation?*

➤ *What do you think could have caused the husband's anger?*

➤ *Why do you think the woman in the next bed has rung her bell?*

➤ *What effect might this incident have on the children?*

➤ *What records would you make regarding the situation?*

Key points – your contribution to the prevention of abusive and aggressive behaviour

- Use appropriate communication with individuals to encourage the exchange of views and information.
- Avoid discrimination and oppression, and acknowledge individual rights.
- Maintain the environment to facilitate effective communication.
- Take the appropriate action to minimise the effects of abusive or aggressive behaviour, and maintain calm.
- Provide safety and protection for individuals at whom the behaviour may be directed.

Deal with incidents of abusive and aggressive behaviour

Abusive and aggressive behaviour

KUS 6

You need to be able to recognise expressions of anger, hostility and aggression in the workplace. These can come in a variety of forms which may involve:

- *Verbal abuse* – where someone is shouting at another individual or calling them names and trying to humiliate them.
- *Intimidation* – where someone is trying to frighten an individual or cause them to be upset and anxious.
- *Quiet threats* – you may not always recognise these. Some people can be very clever at not letting others see what they are doing or saying. They can make quite serious threats towards an individual without initially raising your concerns. Be aware of any gestures or facial expressions that could indicate that someone is being threatened.
- *Sexual or racial harassment* – where an individual is targeted and intimidated by others because of their gender, sexuality or race. The individuals may be the victims of discrimination.

The anger or hostility may come from the individuals who are in your care, their family, friends or colleagues, or other members of staff. You may have encountered some type of abusive or aggressive behaviour aimed at either yourself or another individual. Or possibly you may have had to support another individual at whom the behaviour was directed. Whatever the case it can be very distressing for all concerned. There may have been spontaneous acts that lead to acts of violence or physical harm. Alternatively, there may be situations where no actual physical harm occurred, but the incident left you and others feeling frightened, anxious or confused. You may be working with an individual who has learning disabilities, who becomes angry and violent towards the care staff because he is frustrated that he cannot do something. He may also try to cause harm and injury to himself because of it. You need to know how to deal with the situation and ask for help if necessary to help the individual to calm down. Occasionally an aggressor will simply take it out on the environment, causing unnecessary damage, which will affect other individuals. They may choose to throw chairs or other items of furniture, or cause damage to another individual's property. They may use these tactics to get attention or they may be extremely angry about something that has happened. You need to remove other individuals from the vicinity to ensure their safety, and then get immediate assistance.

KUS 9

Aggression in itself is a threat of violence. It is a normal biological or physical response, but it may be misdirected. Aggression is usually treated with great **ambivalence**. Individually directed violence is usually frowned upon and is seen as being antisocial, whereas aggression and violence in a war situation is often treated as something glorious and socially acceptable. Almost all recreational games are based on an attack–defence format. Healthy anger may be that which falls into the parameters of social and cultural rules for a particular society.

The differences between anger and aggression can be defined as follows:

- Anger is extreme displeasure usually caused by some kind of external stimulus.
- Aggression turns anger into hostile or destructive feelings towards individuals or objects.
- Anger can be healthy, aggression is not.
- Anger is often taken out on an individual who has not caused the problem and cannot do anything about it.

KUS 11

There are many causes of anger and aggression, some of these are shown in Figure 8.

Figure 8
Causes of anger and aggression

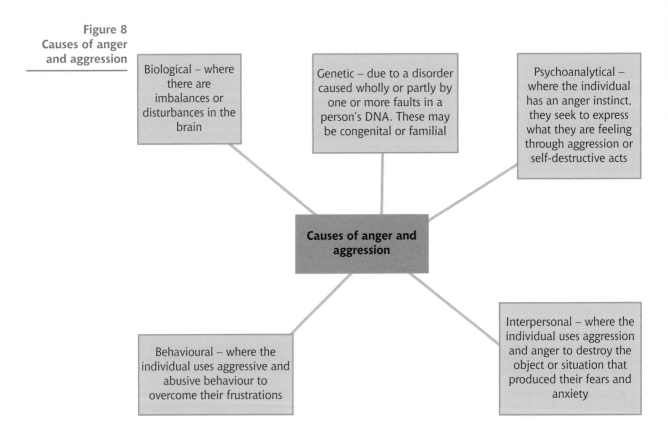

Biological – where there are imbalances or disturbances in the brain

Genetic – due to a disorder caused wholly or partly by one or more faults in a person's DNA. These may be congenital or familial

Psychoanalytical – where the individual has an anger instinct, they seek to express what they are feeling through aggression or self-destructive acts

Causes of anger and aggression

Behavioural – where the individual uses aggressive and abusive behaviour to overcome their frustrations

Interpersonal – where the individual uses aggression and anger to destroy the object or situation that produced their fears and anxiety

KUS 12

Constructive action to minimise abusive and aggressive behaviour

During your working day you may come across incidents involving anger and aggression. Some situations may be mild and will dissipate almost as soon as they begin. Others may start quietly and become intense in a short period of time. You need to be alert to both situations and take immediate action to minimise the risk of the situation escalating. Try to communicate with the individual in a calm and reassuring manner. Be conscious of the tone and pitch of your voice, speak slowly and softly to the individual as this can have a calming effect. Try not to raise your voice or get angry. Ask if they are alright or if there is anything that you can do to help. It may be that by paying them some attention and offering support you can appease the situation. Explain to them that their anger or irritation could cause upset not only to themselves but also to others in the vicinity. Others may not be aware of the situation and could become extremely upset and distressed. Ask them if they need to speak to someone in private, away from other people. Remain polite and respect their privacy and dignity. It is essential that you do not retaliate with anger yourself or tell the individual not to be silly or to calm down. This could be a trigger which makes their anger worse. Ask your colleagues for assistance to deal with any abusive or aggressive incidents, and never put yourself or others into a situation which could be dangerous.

Identification of risk

Other colleagues may disclose to you at the handover meeting that there seems to be a situation developing or that an individual is worried that a relative or friend is coming to visit who is angry about something which has happened. Or you may notice that an individual who is normally quite placid appears to be getting agitated. It might be something that you can deal with, such as pain or discomfort, or it could be due to their physical or emotional condition. However, sometimes a situation may erupt suddenly without you being aware of it. Identify the potential risks to the individual, others, yourself or colleagues, and take immediate and appropriate action to deal with it. For example, if you find that the individual is becoming angry and upset because they have previously asked someone for some pain relief which has not been given, you need to make sure that you get it for them as soon as possible. Imagine how you would feel if you had to wait for pain relief! Give them reassurance and support and help to make them comfortable. If you are aware that an individual is expecting a visitor whom they think may be angry about something, ask them if they need to go somewhere private to talk to the visitor, or if they want you to stay with them. They may prefer not to see the visitor at all.

KUS 1, 2, 8

Effective relationships

If you have previously built up a good relationship with the individual or with their family and friends, you will find it easier to handle the situation. They may already trust you and be willing to tell you what the problem is. If they wish to speak to someone else, you should inform your manager or supervisor so this can be arranged. You need to maintain an effective working relationship with the individual as this is important for the well-being of everyone involved. They need to feel safe and secure from harm or injury. If the individual feels that they are being treated unfairly, unreasonably or are being discriminated against, you will need to keep them calm and prevent the situation from escalating. They may have a different opinion to yours or disagree with some aspect of their care or treatment. Alternatively they may have a problem with the environment, or their grievance may be due to outside influences. They may be under pressure from other members of their family or significant others in their lives to do more for themselves, yet they may not be ready to do so. The individual may have family problems which they feel they need to sort out and they may decline any form of assistance. Whatever the situation, you need to be assertive and express your views in a clear, calm, direct and confident manner without denying the individual their rights.

KUS 1, 3

Rights of expression

Individuals should have equal rights of expression.

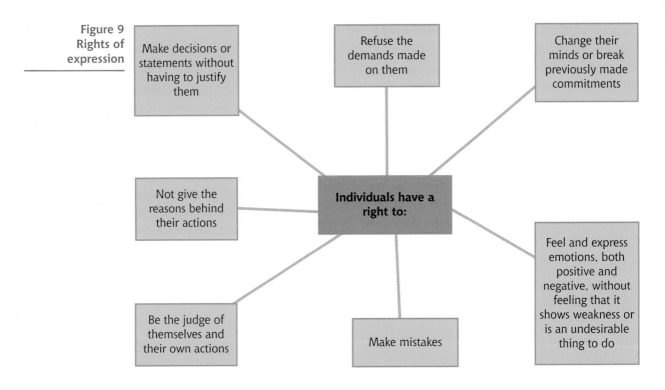

Figure 9
Rights of
expression

Make decisions or statements without having to justify them

Refuse the demands made on them

Change their minds or break previously made commitments

Not give the reasons behind their actions

Individuals have a right to:

Feel and express emotions, both positive and negative, without feeling that it shows weakness or is an undesirable thing to do

Be the judge of themselves and their own actions

Make mistakes

KUS 10

Being assertive helps you to be in control of the situation and it helps you to handle it in a professional manner. Assertiveness is about offering alternatives and choices about how to respond to a situation, looking at something from a different direction or negotiating a different approach. You need to show the individual respect and try to maintain their dignity throughout the incident. By being assertive you will be able to handle difficult situations and challenging behaviour more effectively. You need to remember that your facial expression and body language can give a different impression to other individuals. You may feel that you are being assertive, yet your actions (such as folding your arms, pointing, waving your arms about and shouting) may come across as aggressive. This will inevitably increase the aggression and agitation and make the situation worse. You must be in control of your own emotions. Being faced with an aggressive outburst or situation can be very frightening to everyone involved. Your body will inevitably prepare for the 'flight or fight' response, and you will literally have to think on your feet. You will have to ask yourself. 'Can I deal with this situation, do I need help from others in the vicinity, what risks are involved?' You should have received training on how to handle difficult and aggressive situations and how to deal with challenging behaviour. You need to use the skills you were taught, but be aware that real-life situations are more threatening and frightening than role-play on a course. You need to use both verbal and non-verbal techniques when being assertive, depending on the situation you are faced with. For example, it may be necessary for you to speak loudly and firmly to someone in order to calm them down. You may have to tell them to stop what they are doing, give them short instructions about what you want them to do, explain that you want to help them to sort out the problem. Try not to argue with the individual as it could lead to an increase in their aggressive behaviour. Sometimes, lowering the pitch and tone of your voice, speaking slowly and evenly will help to calm you as well as draw the individual's attention so that you can get them to listen to what you are saying. You must be aware of your organisation's policies and procedures on dealing with abusive and aggressive behaviour. You will need to assess whether the situation is likely to become violent which could result in harm or injury. You need to keep yourself and other individuals safe, and if the situation appears to be getting out of hand shout for help or send someone to get help if possible. Get away from the situation if it is getting worse and call people who are trained to deal with these incidents. Speak to your manager or supervisor as soon as possible after dealing with this type of situation, and have a debriefing session. Make sure that you make a complete and accurate record of the incident. You should know the contact numbers for security, police or other services that you can call upon. Try to memorise the numbers – it would be difficult to look them up in an emergency.

KUS 12

Figure 10
Assertive gestures, such as smiling and staying calm, may help to calm an individual

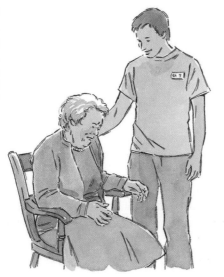

**Figure 11
Aggressive
gestures may
inflame the
situation**

Depending on the circumstances, you could try to calm the situation down by using simple gestures to help the individual to relax and calm down. Not everyone will appreciate you putting your arm around their shoulder or holding their hand, so make sure you have assessed this beforehand. Try to find out what is wrong and explain that you will try to help them. Hopefully they will respond to your calm approach and listen to what you are saying.

KUS 10

Remember that if you remain assertive when dealing with abusive, aggressive behaviour, you will maintain control of the situation. Use good communication skills, listen carefully to what the individual has to say and show them respect. This will encourage the individual to respond to your requests. If you become aggressive you will make the situation much worse and you will gain nothing. Alternatively, you may appear weak and afraid and not in control of the situation. The individual will easily get the better of you, they will find it simple to manipulate and dominate you. This is submissive behaviour, you will let other people win. Which behaviour do you think would be most suitable for you to use when dealing with challenging and aggressive behaviour?

It is the employer's duty to make sure that the work environment is safe for all employees, in line with the Health and Safety at Work Act 1974 (see unit HSC32 for more details on employer and employee responsibilities).

Table 1 The differences between aggressive, assertive and submissive behaviour

Aggressive behaviour	Assertive behaviour	Submissive behaviour
• Showing anger	• Showing confidence	• Showing fear
• Wanting to win	• Negotiating – everyone wins, there are no losers	• Letting other individuals win
• Understanding only your own needs	• Understanding and acceptance of other individuals' needs as well as your own	• Only understanding and accepting other individuals' needs
• A mental attitude that you are far more important than other individuals	• A mental attitude that knows it is better to negotiate in order to get the best outcome for others and yourself	• A mental attitude that considers other individuals are more important than you
• Making excessive demands, not listening to other individuals	• Active listening	• Not speaking, only asking a few questions to find out what is wanted
• A lack of respect for others	• Having respect for others and yourself	• Lack of respect for yourself
• Talking loudly or shouting	• Speaking in a calm, clear voice	• Speaking quietly, hesitating
• Using threatening body language such as folding or waving your arms around, clenching your fists, tensing your muscles, fixed eye contact, staring	• Relaxed body language, arms down by your side, and still, varied eye contact – looking away occasionally	• Submissive body language, avoiding eye contact, looking down, looking tense and afraid

KUS 5

Effective practice

You may have dealt with minor situations in the past or even assisted with more major incidents in your work setting. To develop your practice you need to reflect on these and consider what, if anything, you could have done better to deal with the situation. It is important that you take adequate time to help you deal with your own feelings following any incidents of aggression and abusive behaviour that you may have been involved in. Speak to your manager or supervisor as soon as possible to discuss your feelings about what happened. Talking things over with someone else after the event is the best way of debriefing and it helps to cope. Make accurate reports as soon as possible, recording everything that happened, who and what was involved, where it happened, and, if possible, how the situation started. Always remember to sign and date your records. Remember that if it is written down, then it will be remembered, but if it is not, it may be forgotten. Your records may have to be used if there is a complaint which needs to be investigated, so accurate recording is essential.

Opposing interests

Depending on the type of care setting you work in, individuals in your care may be with you for a short or a long time. They will be in close proximity to groups of individuals that they have probably never met before. They could be from a different culture or have different religious beliefs and preferences. They may have other physical or emotional differences. It is highly unlikely that they will all have the same opinions, and arguments could start. Every individual has the right to be treated equally. You will need to stress to the individuals that although they may have different opinions or interests, it does not mean that they cannot get on. Try to find something they have in common with one another or something that will appeal to all individuals and encourage their interactions.

**Figure 12
Encourage
interaction
between
individuals**

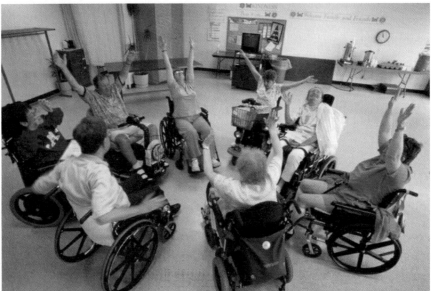

Prompt constructive action

If you take prompt, constructive action when dealing with abusive and aggressive behaviour it will help you manage the situation more effectively. Remember to stay calm, keep others away from the area and reassure them as much as possible. Try to encourage the individual to talk, and respect their personal space. Talking is better than action. Listen carefully to what they have to say, and if appropriate suggest alternative options that may be more acceptable to them. By allowing them to express their feelings or tell you the cause of their anger, you may give them the opportunity to refocus on what is actually important to them and possibly see things in a different light. Make sure that you keep other colleagues informed of your actions and ask for help if necessary. Advise other individuals in the vicinity to remain calm and not to cause unnecessary tension which could adversely affect on the situation. Explain to the aggressor that you find their language and behaviour very upsetting and unacceptable.

Management of physically aggressive behaviour

The management of physically aggressive behaviour should be consistent with statutory and agency requirements. The safest methods of handling situations that involve individuals in your care, yourself, other colleagues or others in the vicinity should be used. Your organisation may hold training workshops for all employees regarding the management of physically aggressive behaviour and you need to make sure you attend these. Discuss this with your manager or supervisor.

It is essential that everyone is familiar with the action they need to take with either violent or non-violent incidents in the workplace. Call for help as soon as possible and ask someone to call for either security or the police, depending on your place of work. Let those who are properly trained in these types of incidents deal with it. Do not allow yourself to be manipulated by anyone or put at risk of injury. Try not to let the aggressor get between you and the door if you are in a restricted area, and ensure that there is nothing available which could be used as a weapon against you.

Again, all records made should be accurate and complete, and the correct documentation should be used. These records must be stored in a safe and secure place in order to maintain confidentiality, according to organisational requirements.

A volatile situation

Andrew is 48 years old. He is divorced but lives with his partner and her two teenage children. He has been diagnosed with depression for several years and has taken regular anti-depressant medication. He recently lost his job and this has seriously affected his confidence and self-esteem. He feels that he can no longer support his family and has become extremely angry and depressed. His partner is very supportive of him and tells him not to worry. Whilst at home he became very aggressive and abusive towards his family and stopped taking his medication. Following a visit to his GP it was decided that he should spend some time in hospital to allow his medication to be reviewed and to help him calm down. He was admitted to one of the mental health wards at the local hospital.

His partner has recently come to visit him and finds him extremely agitated. He is clenching his fists and begins to shout in an aggressive manner. She tries to reassure him and help him to calm down, putting her arm around his shoulder, but he simply shrugs it off and tells her to leave him alone. He gets up from his chair and knocks over the locker next to his bed. This seems to trigger off more anger and he begins to shout at other individuals around him. The nurses are quickly on the scene, and try to calm down the situation. His partner is asked to sit outside the ward until the staff can manage to pacify him. ▶

> *Why do you think Andrew has become angry and abusive?*
> *Why did Andrew not respond and calm down when his partner tried to reassure him?*
> *How would you approach Andrew at this time?*
> *How would you have dealt with the situation and reassured others in the vicinity?*
> *What effect could the situation have on other individuals and also on his partner?*
> *Who would you report to and what records would need to be completed?*

Key points – dealing with incidents

- Take prompt action to minimise abusive and aggressive behaviour, try to identify any possible risks and use constructive action to deal with the situation.

- Maintain effective working relationships with individuals and colleagues, recognise the diversity of views and opinions. Use good standards of effective working practice.

- Be familiar with your local and organisational policies and procedures relating to equal opportunities, discriminatory practice and the management of aggressive and abusive behaviour.

- Safely manage physically aggressive behaviour in accordance with the requirements for your organisation, protecting yourself and others from harm or injury.

- Complete records accurately and legibly and complete and store them securely in a safe place.

Element HSC336c *Contribute to reviewing incidents of abusive and aggressive behaviour*

Reviewing the incident

KUS 5

Regardless of what the situation was, it is important for all of the individuals involved to review the incident and the events leading up to it. If the individual responsible is currently being cared for in the care setting, it would be better if you or another member of staff that they are familiar with supports the individual at this time. Support needs to be given by someone they trust and have developed a rapport with rather than someone they do not actually know and who does not understand the individual and their specific needs and requirements. Encourage them to discuss their behaviour and describe how they were feeling at the time and what they felt caused their aggressive or abusive behaviour. They may not actually understand what they did wrong and it would be up to you or another colleague to try to help them understand what happened. There may be a simple explanation for why they behaved in the way they did. They may have been feeling neglected, anxious or frightened about something which was happening in their lives. Or they may just be seeking attention.

Obviously if the individual who had caused the incident was a visitor to the care setting, they may not wish to discuss what the problem was and it would be more difficult to discover the cause and resolve it. It is possible that the individual has been asked to leave the area, or they may have decided to leave of their own accord. However, they may regret their behaviour and eventually want to talk to someone about it. In this case, the appropriate support and advice should be made available to them, and their privacy and confidentiality should be respected.

Offering time, space and support

KUS 1, 2

Occasionally individuals may need time to reflect on a situation and explore their own feelings about it. It is essential that you do not rush them into talking about it as this may cause them more distress and make the situation worse. The individual should be invited to attend a debriefing meeting with yourself, your manager or supervisor, and other appropriate key people. This should be held in private to demonstrate respect for the individual. Care staff should be aware of the need to be safe from further episodes and the individual needs to know that support is there for them when and if they need it. They may wish to be left on their own to consider the situation, and you should respect this as it is their right. Alternatively, they may prefer you to sit with them, and they may feel reassured that you are willing to listen to them when they are ready to talk. You will need to use your listening skills to check that you understand what they are telling you. Do not make judgements but try to empathise with them. They may be extremely embarrassed about what happened and want to hide away. You will also need to offer time, space and support to everyone involved in the incident, not just to the aggressor.

Exploring the incident

KUS 1, 2, 5

You need to be considerate towards the individual – do not accuse them or show your anger at what happened. Try not to use interrogation techniques with them but encourage meaningful discussions. Let them know how you felt about the situation, that you were concerned that something terrible was wrong and that you wanted to help them to overcome it. They may not realise that they upset other individuals in the vicinity or the care staff. The situation may have been so intense at the time that they did not realise the extent of their behaviour. They may go over the situation again and again before they can fully understand it. They may tell you that something or someone caused them to become aggressive and abusive. Explore what they think may have triggered the aggression. There may have been a specific pattern of events which led up to the incident, something which perhaps could be avoided in future.

It may be that the individual is asked to attend a meeting with the people who were involved. They will need active support to enable them to approach this in an appropriate manner. You will be expected to contribute and to give your views and opinions on what actually happened and what you might have seen or heard. Your records should show an accurate account of the situation and can be used to supplement the discussion which should be held in private.

The incident could have caused particular distress to the individual and you may have to help them cope with this distress in the best way possible. Some of the signs that indicate an individual is experiencing distress are shown below.

Signs of distress:
- Agitation.
- Irritability and frequent bouts of rage.
- Feelings of dread.
- Increased anxiety and panic.
- Shaking.
- Depression.
- Fear of death.
- Nightmares.
- Changes in behaviour.
- Becoming withdrawn, usually quiet or silent.
- Increased smoking.

KUS 9, 11

If you recognise any of the signs shown above in the individual, you must take immediate steps to alleviate any problems which appear to be a causative factor to further distress. If you have built up a good rapport and an effective working relationship with the individual it is possible that you will be aware of some of these causative factors and will be able to give them the appropriate advice and guidance on how to avoid them. For example, the individual may get distressed if they find themselves in a crowded, noisy environment. They may experience increased anxiety and panic. You need to reassure the individual and give them all the support they need to stay calm, and possibly remove them from the area. Your physical presence will be important in helping the individual so that they know that they are not alone and that you are there to help and support them as appropriate. It is easier to deal with distress as soon as it becomes apparent and to give the relevant support in the early stages. Be conscious not only of the individual's non-verbal clues and body language but also of your own when you are communicating with them about the situation. Decide just what help and assistance they need to explore the situation, and be aware of how far you can go within your own job role. Ask open-ended questions and respond to these accordingly. If the individual decides they do not want to talk to you or if they appear to be becoming angry or agitated then you need to let them calm down. Physical touch like putting your arm around their shoulders may or may not be appropriate at the time. Not all individuals respond in quite the same way, so you will have to decide

KUS 12

what the individual prefers. Ideally, you should ask the individual how they want you to support them. Some may tell you to go away and leave them alone.

**Figure 14
Not all individuals
appreciate
physical support**

Alternatively, a friendly arm around their shoulders may be just what they need. They may ask you to sit with them and simply hold their hand. They may break down and begin to cry and welcome your support. It may be a sense of release for them to know that you are interested in them and that they are valued as an individual. Explore constructively with everyone involved the reasons for and the consequences of the abusive and aggressive behaviour.

**Figure 15
Some individuals
welcome the
support of carers**

Referring the incident

KUS 4

Depending on the cause of the aggressive and abusive behaviour and who was actually responsible or involved, the details may have to be shared with other practitioners. Initially you need to report the situation to your manager or supervisor and take their advice about the next stage. For an individual within your care, it may be necessary to involve a medical practitioner, e.g. their GP or hospital doctor depending on your care setting. Other practitioners relevant to the individual's needs and circumstances may also need to be informed and involved in future care and support. If it is considered necessary, the individual may need to be referred for psychiatric assessment.

Completion of records

KUS 3, 4

If an accident, injury or dangerous incident has occurred you need to follow the required procedure for reporting these. Your organisation should have procedures in place for making records either on an incident form or in an accident book. You must comply with the Reporting of Injuries, Diseases and Dangerous Occurrences Regulations 1985 (RIDDOR). This legislation requires that all accidents, no matter how minor, which occur in the workplace are recorded in an accident register, and this is a requirement of the Health and Safety at Work Act 1974. If an individual incurs any injury all of the details will need to be recorded as follows:

- Full details of the individual.
- Date and time of the injury or accident.
- The nature of the injury/accident.
- Briefly what happened.
- The action taken.
- The signatures of all parties, including witnesses and contact telephone numbers, should be obtained.

KUS 3, 4

A report must be made in the individual's care plan with details of what happened, the action taken and the outcome. The details recorded must be maintained in a safe, secure place and kept available for inspection if required. In accordance with the national minimal standards as described in the Care Homes Regulations 2001, Regulation 37 requires that if an individual living with a registered care service sustains serious injury as a result of an incident then this must be reported to the Commission for Social Care Inspection (CSCI). It is essential that you follow the requirements of the Data Protection Act 1998 and ensure the confidentiality of information, both written and verbal (see unit HSC31 for more details).

Discussions at team meetings

Handover meetings or team meetings are an ideal time for you to reflect on your feelings relating to abusive and aggressive incidents in the workplace. Alternatively, you may wish to speak to your manager or supervisor in private. It is your right to have feelings, not everyone will cope with situations in the same way and no two people will feel the same way about a situation. Do not be ashamed of your feelings, everyone has them! You may have handled many situations involving behaviour of this kind, and you possibly dealt with them without experiencing any problems. However, some situations may affect you more than others and some will undoubtedly have a big effect on you.

KUS 5

You may find that other colleagues have been involved in a similar type of situation and can explain how they managed to cope with it. It is a good idea to talk to your colleagues as soon as possible. They will be able to give you the appropriate support you may need to overcome any fears or anxiety that the situation has caused.

KUS 4

Your colleagues may even have had dealings with the same individual, and if so they should have made records of this. It is essential that this information is shared with other members of the care team so that the matter can be discussed fully. Policies and procedures on how to deal with abusive and aggressive behaviour towards the staff or individuals in your care must be reviewed regularly. Incidents of aggression and abusive outbursts are on the increase and all staff need to be trained in how to deal with them. Your contribution to the organisation's practice in dealing with these incidents will be invaluable. You may feel that in some way the care setting itself contributed to the incident and you may have suggestions on how this can be improved to avoid reoccurrence. All incidents must be reviewed to see if there are common factors or triggers. Some may be isolated incidents while others may reoccur frequently. The team needs to look at all issues surrounding the incidents and consider whether they could have been avoided and if staff could have handled the situations differently or better.

KUS 1, 2

When assessing the risks of reoccurrence it is important to be non-judgemental and avoid discriminating against an individual who has been aggressive when considering the control measures to be put in place. If the situation involved a relative or other visitor, could they have been given more help and support from the care staff to deal with any problems they had? Did they have just cause to be angry?

It is only by discussing and reviewing incidents of abusive and aggressive behaviour in the workplace that improvements can be made towards preventing them from happening again. It is important to recognise that not all incidents can be prevented. If you remain alert to what is going on around you and are familiar with the physical and emotional problems of the individuals you are caring for and of any possible issues or opinions which may be concerning them, you will play a large part in reducing the occurrence of abusive and aggressive incidents.

Dealing with an incident

Aysha is 24 years old. She is currently working as a care assistant in a residential home for older people. She has had some previous experience in care work but has only recently started working in this home. She gets on well with the staff and thinks that she will enjoy working here.

One day she is working on the late shift. Everyone has had their evening meal and some individuals are sitting in the lounge watching television. It has been a busy day with a new resident arriving and one going to hospital after a fall. One or two individuals have been a bit edgy as a result of all the activity. Aysha had noticed that they seemed to be arguing with each other earlier in the afternoon about which television programme they wanted to watch, but they seemed to sort it out without any problem.

Some visitors arrive and two individuals start bickering again. One asks to be moved out of the lounge into another room. Aysha says that there is no other room available. This appears to anger one of them and he becomes abusive and aggressive towards the other individual. Despite their relatives trying to calm them down, the argument becomes quite heated. Aysha tries to get them to be quiet as it is upsetting the other individuals in the room. One of them begins shouting and becomes abusive and aggressive towards Aysha. The individual tells Aysha to get out of the room and to get someone who knows what is going on. At this point Aysha goes to get her manager.

Once the incident is sorted out, Aysha goes to see her manager again. She says that she is particularly upset about what happened, and asks to talk about it. Her manager says that she is busy and it will have to wait until the following day.

➤ *How do you think Aysha dealt with the situation?*

➤ *How could she have handled it better?*

➤ *Why was Aysha upset about what happened?*

➤ *Do you think that the manager was wrong to have dismissed the incident and told Aysha to wait until the next day to discuss her feelings? Explain your answer.*

➤ *What effect may this have on Aysha, or in fact any other colleague who was involved?*

➤ *What records should Aysha have completed following the incident?*

Key points – reviewing incidents of abusive and aggressive behaviour

- It is best to review incidents of abusive and aggressive behaviour as soon as possible in a calm and supportive manner.
- Encourage individuals to examine their own behaviour, and offer time and space so that they can reflect and address the reasons for it.
- Provide reliable contributions to team meetings and to the review of such incidents and offer suggestions about how best to handle them. Contribute to discussions relating to specialist help which may be required.
- Recognise personal feelings which have developed as a result of the incident and seek advice and support from someone able to help you to deal with them.
- Complete all necessary documentation and store it according to your organisation's requirements.

Unit HSC336

Are you ready for assessment?

Contribute to the prevention and management of abusive and aggressive behaviour

This unit is about how you positively contribute to preventing abusive and aggressive behaviour. It is about how you communicate in an appropriate manner with different individuals and encourage a meaningful exchange of views and information without discrimination or oppression. It is also about how you deal with incidents of abusive and aggressive behaviour taking appropriate action to prevent any possible triggers to that behaviour, protecting those individuals who are at a direct risk and acknowledging the rights of individuals while maintaining their safety. It is about how you work with others and contribute to reviewing incidents of abusive and aggressive behaviour as well as managing your own feelings.

Your assessment will be carried out mainly through observation by your assessor and this should provide most of the evidence for the elements in this unit. If your assessor is unable to observe you directly then you may be able to use the testimony of an experienced colleague acting as an expert witness. You will need to discuss this with your assessor. Evidence of your knowledge and understanding will be demonstrated through observation, your assessor examining work products, e.g. reports, minutes of meetings, as well as through answering oral and/or written questions.

You need to be aware when planning assessments that this unit also relates to some core and optional units, in particular HSC31, HSC32, HSC35 and HSC335, and so you may also be able to evidence performance criteria for these. If direct observation would be intrusive or difficult to pre-arrange you will need to consider alternative evidence-gathering methods, e.g. expert witness testimony.

▶

Direct observation by your assessor

Your assessor or an expert witness will need to plan to see you carry out the performance criteria (PCs) in each of the elements in this unit. The performance criteria that may be difficult to meet through observation are:

- **HSC336c PC 4**

Other forms of evidence

You may need to present other forms of evidence in order to:

- Cover criteria not observed by your assessor.
- Show that you have the required knowledge, understanding and skills to claim competence in this area of practice.
- Ensure your work practice is consistent.

Your assessor may also need to ask you questions to confirm your knowledge and understanding and ensure that you can apply this to your practice.

Preparing to be observed

You must make sure that your workplace and any individuals and key people involved in your work agree to you being assessed. Explicit, informed consent must be obtained before you carry out any assessment activity that involves individuals or which involves access to confidential information related to their care.

Before your assessments you should read carefully the performance criteria for each element in the unit. Try to cover as much as you can during your observation but remember that you and your assessor can also plan for additional sources of evidence should full coverage of all performance criteria not be possible.

Check your knowledge

- Describe how you would communicate with individuals in a manner which encourages an open exchange of views and information.
- Why could the environment be a factor in abusive and aggressive behaviour, and what could you do about it?
- How could you minimise possible triggers to abusive and aggressive behaviour?
- How could you protect individuals at risk?
- What constructive action could you take to minimise abusive and aggressive behaviour whilst maintaining effective working relationships?
- What policies and procedures are available for handling abusive and aggressive behaviour in your organisation?
- Why is it important to call for immediate help and assistance?
- What records should you complete and why should these be kept safe and secure?
- Why should individuals be allowed to review and evaluate the incident?
- Who might the individual need to be referred to?
- How would you manage your own feelings about the incident?
- Why is it important to share the information with other members of the care team?

Support individuals to live at home

*T*his unit is about how you can support individuals to live at home and the care you can
provide to make it possible for them to remain in their own homes for as long as
possible by accessing appropriate services to meet their needs. It consists of the following
three elements:

- **HSC343a** Support individuals to identify their personal, physical and safety needs to
enable them to live at home

- **HSC343b** Work with individuals to identify and access additional support and
resources

- **HSC343c** Support individuals to review their needs and identify changes necessary to
enable them to live at home

Introduction

KUS 1

Many individuals with health and social care needs choose to live at home, and supporting them to do this is a vital part of promoting health and social well-being. A number of laws and government policies relate to supporting individuals to live at home. For example, the NHS and Community Care Act 1990, National Service Frameworks for Older People (2001) and for Mental Health (1999) and the Human Rights Act 2000 all talk about the importance of promoting independence, person-centred care, choice and closer joint working to ensure individuals can access appropriate support to live at home.

KUS 2, 4, 19

Supporting individuals in their own home is different to working in an institution. You need to remember you are a guest in their home and demonstrate that you respect this and how this impacts on your practice. Your working relationship with individuals needs to focus on working in partnership as equals where there is mutual recognition of rights and responsibilities. You need to demonstrate your respect for their decisions even if these conflict with the views and advice of health and social care practitioners. Supporting individuals to live at home can present different dilemmas regarding individuals' choices, carers' choices and your own feelings. Ensure you access support to manage and resolve these feelings and dilemmas.

KUS 11

An individual's home becomes a workplace when health and social care workers provide support and you need to be aware that this can create tensions. You should be familiar with your organisation's health and safety, infection control and risk management policies so that you can effectively manage and resolve these as far as you are able within your role.

KUS 2

It is important that you take time to build a good rapport with individuals to enable you to understand their wishes and needs. Medical and social problems can impact on an individual in many different ways, for example their ability to be independent, their sense of identity, self esteem and self image. It is important that you are familiar with their needs and ensure appropriate and effective communication between all involved. There may be a range of resources, services and facilities within your local area that you could access to support the individual and key people. This includes financial information, local amenities, support networks and charities that can provide services. Finally you must remember that whilst providing active support, you must place the preferences and best interests of the individuals at the centre of everything you do.

Element HSC343a

Support individuals to identify their personal, physical and safety needs to enable them to live at home

Identifying individuals who need support

'There is no place like home.' How often has that phrase been uttered? Living at home is something that most of us take for granted. For many people they are born into a home, they live there until adulthood and eventually move to set up their own home with their own family. The idea that you may not be able to live in your own home does not occur to many of us. So if something happened to you and there was a possibility that you would not be able to continue living in your own home, how would you feel? No doubt you would hope that enough support was available to enable you to go home with family and friends around to help you.

This element looks at how you can support individuals to identify their personal, physical and safety needs to enable them to live at home, even if they are not totally independent. It is only through an accurate, realistic and holistic assessment of their needs that appropriate support can be accessed and provided.

KUS 14, 18

Individuals requiring help

Individuals may need support at home for a variety of reasons.

Older people

In today's society the population is very mobile. People move freely around the country or even the world to access work or for other reasons. Travel links and accessibility are vastly improved giving people more choice and opportunities. In some cultures the family unit that traditionally remained close to home about 30–40 years ago rarely exists now. Many older people find themselves increasingly isolated because their children have moved away from them. In the past the children would have cared for their parents, often taking them into their own homes, but this is not often the case now. Older people who do move to live with their children often find themselves isolated as they lose familiar social and community networks and find it hard to make new contacts. The loss of independence and social contacts can lead to a loss of identity. The increasing number of women employed in the workforce, smaller families, smaller houses and adult children remaining at home for longer are all pressures which make it difficult for families to support older relatives at home. In other cultures elders continue to be supported within the family. However, increasing social and economic pressures are also affecting more traditional cultures and they too may be unable to support older people at home. Older people are therefore one group of individuals who may need support to continue living at home if they have lost some independence.

Disabled people

People can become disabled at any time in their lives. More people are disabled following an illness or accident than have a congenital disability. Disabled children will be cared for either by their families or in care settings, but once they reach adulthood they may want to assert their independence. The same is true of those who become disabled in adulthood. It is no longer the expectation that a disabled adults' only choice is to live in a care environment all of their life. Individuals will seek to live independently in their own home and may require some support to enable them to achieve this. For these individuals transition may be more difficult as they may have to adapt to a new body image and a changed perception of how society views them.

People with mental health problems

Research indicates that one in four people will suffer from a mental health illness at some time in their lives. This could be due to the stress of modern living or because we are better at diagnosing mental health problems. As with any physical illness mental health problems can be short or long term.

In the past, people with mental health problems were placed in institutions and given no choice but to remain there most or all of their lives. They became institutionalised with few personal rights and no way to support themselves. Old Victorian mental institutions were often cold, cruel places with forced treatments and very little dignity for individuals who were regarded as inmates with no right to expect anything better. The progression to caring for people in the community means that these institutions are now closed and individuals have been rehoused in their own or small group homes. However, they may still need support both personally and physically in order to maintain their independence.

Figure 1
Institutions are a
thing of the past

People with learning disabilities

People with learning disabilities find it difficult to learn, communicate or do many everyday things. Conditions associated with learning disabilities are cerebral palsy, epilepsy and autism. They are not learning disabilities themselves, but the consequences of these conditions lead to difficulties with learning. Other things that may cause difficulty learning are brain injuries or illnesses such as meningitis. It is important not to label individuals, as disabilities will vary from being mild or moderate to severe, therefore the type of support required is individual.

People who are terminally ill

Many individuals with a terminal illness receiving palliative care may choose to spend their last days at home in familiar surroundings. As they become increasingly frail, they and those caring for them will need support so that they can remain comfortably at home.

Support individual choices

Once you have identified those individuals who need support to remain at home, you should work with them and key people to identify their strengths and skills. This will help you to identify the extra support they will need. Each individual will have a very different set of strengths and will have different needs, so an individualised approach to assessment is essential. Individuals will also have their own ideas about the type of support that they want and are prepared to accept. It is important to remember that the individual has the right to refuse help even if it would clearly be of benefit. Of the groups of people mentioned above, certain groups may well have similar types of problems, strengths and needs. Whatever their difficulty, it is of paramount importance that you identify what the individual can do and focus on this. Encourage them to be as independent as possible and support them in ways that enable them to retain their skills. Your role is one of enabling and your work practice with individuals needs to reflect this.

KUS 16

- Older people – as people grow older they may experience mobility problems. They may become fatigued easily and as a result find everyday tasks more difficult and need help with these. They may find it difficult to carry out tasks in the home such as cleaning and cooking or to attend to their personal care needs. Often older people with mobility problems will spend most of their time at home and they may feel very socially isolated. Therefore, it is important that while giving care you talk about current events, the news and local happenings – many of the people you support will look forward to your visit as much for the company as for the care you provide. Although some older people may need a high level of support it is important to remember that many older individuals remain very alert mentally. You should respect their right to make their own decisions and encourage them to do so.

- Disabled people – different degrees of disability will necessitate different types of support. Disability tends to suggest physical rather than mental health problems. Just as with the older individual, the care required may be of a more practical nature, such as around the house or with personal care. People with disabilities may have few visitors and feel isolated from contact and interaction with others, especially their own age group.

- People with mental health problems – although some individuals will have significant personal care needs, they also require emotional and social support. Even if they are physically able to care for themselves, people with mental health problems may not be aware of or understand how to meet their own needs. They may need support to feel confident about carrying out the everyday tasks that we take for granted. Some of the simplest tasks such as spending time with other people, going out shopping or to the cinema may be very challenging for them.

- People with learning difficulties – the level of support needed will vary according to the severity of the disability. It is important to try and identify the support need from the individual's perspective. A person-centred planning approach helps to identify what is important to the individual and this is increasingly being used in this area. This approach helps to focus on the individual's strengths and skills to encourage empowerment, participation and involvement.

- People who are terminally ill – the care required for individuals in this situation is often intensive, frequent and short term to allow the individual to die peacefully in their own environment according to their wishes. Although it may be difficult to focus on strengths when an individual's well-being is deteriorating, it is just as important to encourage the individual to do as much for themselves as they are able to. Maintaining some measure of control over their life in this situation helps the individual to retain their dignity and sense of self.

KUS 4, 16

Whatever the individual's circumstances and whatever your own personal view, the wishes and choices of the individual must be considered at all times. As far as possible these personal preferences need to be the basis for care and support provided even though at times financial constraints, availability of staff and resources may present difficulties.

When considering the best way to support individuals, you need to take into account their own support networks. There may be key people who can help towards

KUS 16, 17

supporting an individual and promoting their general health and well-being. Although many families are now diverse and living apart from each other, it is important to remember that this is not always the case. Transport links and access are much better than they were, and even if families do live a long way from each other they may still be very willing and able to provide support. It is important to identify and include friends, neighbours and other key people who are significant to the individual in providing support. Remember that as people live longer, the people who were once the informal carers (children, spouse, siblings etc.) are growing older themselves. It is not unusual for carers to have needs themselves and so it is important to recognise the special needs and limitations of informal carers. You must establish with them what assistance they can give and where formal support needs to be provided.

KUS 3, 4

**Figure 2
Include key
people when
providing support**

Assessing the risks

The individual will require a holistic and comprehensive assessment of their needs before any provision can be identified. You need to understand their physical, mental and social needs in order to provide adequate support to enable the individual to live at home and at the same time you must reduce any risks.

KUS 2, 4

The wishes and preferences of the individuals and the key people involved are very important. Some of their preferences may mean that an element of risk still exists, but this has to be measured against the overall well-being of the person. If the individual is aware of the risks and accepts them then there is a shared responsibility towards managing these risks more effectively. For example, a person with mental health problems may have a tendency to forget to take their medication. The danger and likelihood of this happening must be measured against the overall benefits to their well-being of encouraging them to live an independent life.

KUS 4

There are many risks associated with living at home, even for more able individuals. So for those with some form of reduced independence these risks will be even greater. Your role is to provide active support to individuals and key people in order to manage and minimise these risks.

Risks

Abuse

KUS 24

There are many forms of abuse. There are individuals who will seek to harm themselves in the form of overdose, self-mutilation or simply failing to take care of themselves appropriately. Those being cared for by others may be subject to neglect as the carers struggle to cope because they lack the skills or knowledge to provide care.

Individuals who rely on others for support or assistance may be vulnerable to people taking advantage of them or intimidating them and may not be able to prevent unwanted people entering their environment. Therefore it is especially important that identity badges are displayed when entering someone's home and that new workers are introduced by known workers. The individual you are supporting needs to be confident that you are who you say you are.

KUS 6, 15

It is also important to realise that abuse and bullying can come in all forms – physical, emotional and financial for example. Those providing care can also be the abusers, so careful attention should be paid to the relationships between individuals and family and friends so that you can recognise signs of stress or distress before they become abusive. When an individual requires support from others to manage their daily life this changes the relationship they have with those people. Previously the relationship may have been a fairly equal one with mutual support. A level of dependency on another person alters the equilibrium and the power within the relationship. Sometimes this power can be used in a positive way to encourage the individual to try new ways of doing things. Sometimes, however, the carer can misuse that power to either abuse the individual or, for example, coerce them into making decisions against their will which benefit the carer and not the individual.

Equally the individual themselves may be abusive to others as the relationship alters and the power balance shifts to the individual. For example, the dependency of the individual on the carer may create a situation where the individual exploits the carer's guilt or sense of duty to the detriment of their own well-being. Where abuse is suspected or discovered you must never jump to conclusions. You must gather and consider all of the facts.

If you think you recognise any possible symptoms of abuse, e.g. bruises, the person becoming upset easily, belongings missing from their home etc., it is essential that you tell someone. There will be policies in place for the protection of vulnerable people and those policies will help you take the right actions. For further information on abuse you should refer to units HSC35 and HSC335.

Damage and destruction

Individuals may be less able to cope with an emergency situation.

Awareness of a potential fire risk is important as fire will spread quickly and can cause significant damage, injury and even death. Are there smoke detectors, do they have batteries and are they checked regularly?

Are appliances modern and up to date? Have regular checks been carried out? Have heating appliances, gas fires, space heaters etc. been properly maintained?

Gas leaks, burst pipes, power failures are all problems which a less independent person would find difficult to manage. Are there any general maintenance problems that could pose a threat, for example loose plug fittings, exposed wires, dripping taps?

You should be prepared to identify and report any risks that could be present in the individual's home.

Danger

Personal safety and security are also risks that need to be identified and addressed. Are there adequate door and window locks? How do carers access the home without placing the individual at greater risk from intruders?

Some individuals may want to consider installing a burglar alarm or a personal alarm that they can press to call for help. It is important that individuals feel safe and secure in their own homes.

Some people will have 'key safes' that allow carers to use a key to enter, and if there are alarms you might have the codes or passwords. You need to keep information about security confidential. Make sure you keep your identification with you at all times and encourage individuals to ask for ID before admitting anyone to their home.

Injury/harm to people

All of the risks mentioned so far have the potential to injure or harm individuals, but there is also the risk of accidents in the home. It is statistically recognised that most accidents occur in the home. Older people are in the highest-risk group. The greatest risk of accident is the threat of falls, followed by injuries from burns. The cause of falls can be due to internal (intrinsic) and external (extrinsic) factors.

Intrinsic factors might be medical problems such as arthritis and osteoporosis. These may make moving around more difficult and this may mean that the older person is unsteady on their feet. In addition these conditions make the bones more susceptible to breaks. Poor eyesight is also a significant factor.

Figure 3
A spillage may
cause a fall

Extrinsic factors are those in the environment such as stairs, loose-fitting carpets/rugs poorly maintained fixtures and fittings and inadequate lighting. All of these increase the potential for the older person to fall.

Burns can be caused by sitting too close to fires or radiators or simply by touching hot objects.

Reckless behaviour

This is any other behaviour that could cause injury or harm. The likelihood of this happening needs to be assessed. This risk could come from the individual themselves or from the key people, such as family, friends or carers who are not fulfilling their role correctly, or from intruders or those who would seek to abuse or bully. The risk may be due to impaired senses of vision or hearing, lack of awareness and insight about personal abilities or the result of drug or alcohol abuse.

You need to be aware that some behaviour that is considered reckless may not be intentional and may be caused by the individual's cognitive impairment and lack of insight into the consequences of their actions. For example, they simply may not understand the danger of leaving saucepans unattended on the cooker, or of placing damp clothes near fires. Equally, if their memory is failing they may forget that they have left them there.

Range of resources, services and facilities available

KUS 2, 5, 21

There are many different resources, services and facilities in the community that individuals may be eligible to access to enable them to live at home. Your role may be simply to let individuals and key people know what is available and how to access it. You will need to agree the individual's preferred options and contribute to identifying the resources that will enable them to live at home. This can sometimes be difficult and resources will vary greatly depending on which part of the country you live in. Some services are available regardless of where you live, for example free eye tests and flu injections for those over the age of 65. The main providers of services are the health service, social services, housing services and voluntary organisations. The boundaries of provision of service are often blurred between health and social care and this can cause much confusion, resulting in a slow inefficient service. This has now been widely recognised by government bodies and as a result the National Service Framework for Older People (2001) and the National Service Framework for Mental Health (1999) have been developed. These address the needs of individuals and provide guidance on the national standards, national service models and frameworks for providing integrated services to support those needs in a variety of different settings. They emphasise the need for organisations to work together to improve the lives of those they seek to support. This can be demonstrated through, for example, the implementation of the single assessment process for older people and the joint working that results from this.

KUS 7, 8, 11, 13

Essential resources

Medical service

One of the main identified resources that needs to be available to individuals to enable them to live at home is access to medical help if required. This needs to be available 24 hours a day and may be the GP, a nurse or A&E departments. This is applicable for all individuals who require medical help.

Counselling

If an individual is not used to living at home independently then they will need a substantial amount of emotional support to build up their confidence. In particular, individuals with mental health problems who were previously living in hospitals or homes may need this kind of support in the transitional phase, that is in the period immediately after moving out of hospital into their own home. Counselling can be accessed via a number of sources, for example GP referral, psychiatric liaison nurse, community psychiatric nurse and voluntary organisations, e.g. MIND.

Helplines

It may not be possible for someone to be always available to visit an individual, but another useful source of help and support are helplines such as NHS Direct. The government is actively encouraging the use of NHS Direct as a way of relieving pressure on over-stretched services. It provides a good first contact point for identifying potential problems. Other helplines include the Samaritans, which is a nationally recognised contact point for individuals who are in distress or suicidal and need support, but there will be many other specialised helplines in your local area. It would be useful for you to collect a list of voluntary helplines which may be appropriate to the people that you care for and other key people.

Advocacy services

Advocates are impartial and independent and speak on behalf of individuals who are unable to speak for themselves. The government runs an advocacy service called the Independent Complaints Advocacy Service, which assists individuals to make a complaint about the care or treatment within the NHS. There are also many locally run and voluntary advocacy services that can be accessed by individuals if required. In your area there may be specialist advocacy services for adults with learning difficulties or mental health problems. Such services may have specially trained advocates to understand the individual's specific needs and circumstances.

Drop-in/day centres

These are a good source of support and advice and also provide opportunities to meet other people and socialise. The centres can be run by social services or independent, voluntary or charitable organisations. You need to locate these in your local area and find out what they can offer as well as the criteria for individuals to access their services. You can then consider with the individual whether the centres are appropriate and able to meet their needs.

Domiciliary care

This service provides practical assistance to those individuals who are unable to attend to their personal care needs or manage household activities such as shopping, housework, washing, cooking and ironing. The type of service provided will depend on local arrangements and eligibility criteria. Services can be provided by social services or independent, private or voluntary agencies. Age Concern, Mind, Citizens Advice Bureaux or Mencap will have information about how to access these services. Adults with learning difficulties may access this type of support as part of their supported living care package. They may be supported with practical tasks (personal care, shopping, cooking) and in developing their social skills, e.g. accessing the local swimming pool or pub to meet with friends. Depending on the type of help that is needed, care may be provided by live-in carers.

Figure 4
Mind logo

mind

For better
mental health

www.mind.org.uk

Community nursing support

District and community nurses can provide specialist nursing care at home, such as help with dressings, pressure area care, injections etc. Practice nurses can also help, but as they are often based and work within the GP's surgery, the individual must usually be able to get to the surgery to access their services. In some areas health visitors may be employed to provide help and advice particularly to older people. They may be able to give advice on topics like diet, health improvement and immunisations. There are also specialist nurses dealing with particular groups of individuals or specific health problems, for example Parkinson's disease specialists, Macmillan nurses, diabetes specialist nurses and even nurse consultants. These specialist nurses can provide advice, support and education. In some areas nursing services such as Marie Curie and 'hospice at home' support may also be available. They may provide a night-nursing service for individuals who are dying to enable them to remain at home as well as to support the family and carers.

Community alarm systems

It is essential to make sure that in an emergency an individual is able and knows how to access help. There are many types of alarm available on the market and these include smoke detectors, flood detectors and fall detectors. Most people are familiar with 'lifelines' or community alarms. They allow the individual to call for help even if they cannot reach the phone. There is usually a 24-hour response on these alarms and they are connected to a response centre who will then contact a designated family member or friend to go round to the individual's home. Recent developments in technology have seen the advent of intruder or inactivity sensors; these will detect movement or lack of movement. For example, if as part of their normal routine an individual normally gets up at 8 a.m. and no movement is detected by 10 a.m. a central control would be alerted. Similarly, if an individual goes to bed at a certain time and the detectors sense excessive movement during the night this may suggest an intruder.

Accessing resources, services and facilities

KUS 11, 12, 21

One of the major problems for individuals and key people is how to access resources, services and facilities that can be provided in the quickest and most efficient way. Services that require funding, for example, often entail the individual completing long and complicated forms. Many individuals find this frightening and off-putting and as a result they do not always apply for services and benefits to which they are entitled. In your role you may find that you need to assist individuals and key people to complete the required paperwork. Therefore you must ensure that you are familiar with the forms that are used regularly in your area. If an individual has poor eyesight, for example, you may need to read and explain the form. If an individual has trouble writing you may need to complete the form for them. In many areas there are organisations, e.g. Age Concern, Mind, Mencap, which have been funded to provide this support to individuals. Find out if this type of support is available in your area and how to access it.

KUS 5, 10

When completing forms individuals and key people will need to be encouraged to be realistic and make a true and fair assessment of their needs. This may be difficult at times as they may not recognise their limitations. They may be embarrassed or ashamed to admit that they need help. This may be especially true of an older person who has previously been independent and is proud of the fact. You must be tactful and encourage them without being forceful. This is not always easy and if necessary you should seek the assistance of a senior member of staff.

Table 1 An assessment form

Assessment information	
Clinical background	The medical problems of the individual will be relevant to ongoing care, medication and the effects of this. Is their condition chronic or is their condition likely to improve?
Personal care and physical well-being	This will include an evaluation of capabilities in the following areas: personal hygiene (washing/bathing/grooming), dressing, oral health, mobility, continence, sleeping pattern, pain, skin condition (i.e. pressure sores/other wounds).

Senses	How good is the individual's hearing, sight and general communication? Are they alert or confused? Do they have a degree of dementia or problems with communication due to depression that are making them withdrawn?
Relationships	What family or social contacts do they have and who are their key people? Do the informal carers have any special needs? What existing arrangements are in place?
Individual's perspective	What is the individual's assessment of their needs and what do they think will help them to overcome the difficulties they are experiencing? What support do they expect from services? What is realistic and how motivated are they? What do they want their life to look like (i.e. what difference do they want services to make to their present circumstances)?
Environment	Where do they live and what type of accommodation is it? Is it appropriate to their needs? Is rehousing required? Do they live alone? How easy is it for them to access shops and outside facilities? What are the general living conditions – central heating, hot water, carpets? Where is the toilet? Can they access the bath?
Safety	How safe is the individual in their own home from potential accidents, abuse, and mistreatment and from environmental danger?

All of the areas shown in Table 1 must be considered and they will determine the type and amount of care that is required. It is not your responsibility to decide what type of care is required, but it is your role to assist in the completion of documentation. You must also contribute to agreeing how and when the care provided will be reviewed with both the individual, key people and others as the circumstances of all those involved may change over time. In addition to agreeing timescales the methods for reviews must be negotiated and agreed with everyone involved.

Formal reviews generally involve the individual and those significant to them meeting face to face and at a prearranged date and time with all those providing support. Informal reviews may take place when significant changes require more urgent action. Informal reviews may involve fewer people. Reviews will generally involve the evaluation of monitoring information, both written and observed, as well as discussion. All individuals need to contribute to the review process to ensure that a realistic picture of the individual's circumstances and progress is presented to support effective decision-making. The review needs to consider the individual's progress against agreed outcomes and discuss any difficulties or concerns.

Many individuals with learning difficulties present their views and goals by making a video diary which is then shown at the review. This is an empowering way of involving the individual and ensuring their voice is heard. The individual may choose not to attend a review meeting and may ask someone else to act as their advocate.

Practical Example

Assessing needs

Maggie is 83 years old. She was admitted to the hospital ward after a fall at home. She had been lying on the floor overnight and was found by a neighbour. Maggie was in an unkempt state, thin, unwashed and had been incontinent of both urine and faeces. She had a pressure sore at the base of her spine. She lives alone but has managed independently until this admission. She is now recovering and wants to return home as soon as possible as she does not like being in unfamiliar surroundings.

➤ *What do you think Maggie's needs are?*

➤ *What personal care do you think Maggie should be offered to enable her to continue living at home?*

➤ *Which services and facilities might you access to help Maggie to continue living at home?*

Key points – supporting individuals to identify their personal, physical and safety needs to enable them to live at home

- Individuals must be given freedom to choose the care they receive.

- Build on the individual's strengths and skills to enable them to be independent.

- Identify existing support networks before providing additional support.

- Consider the risks to the individual but at the same time measure these against the individual's wishes and try to balance the risk against the benefits.

- Be familiar with the range of resources and services available in your area so that you can offer appropriate advice.

- Be aware of the processes for accessing services and be prepared to assist individuals to complete necessary documentation if they are unable to do this themselves.

Work with individuals to identify and access additional support and resources

Identifying individual needs

KUS 2

Assessing the individual's needs will enable you to identify and agree on what support they require and what resources may be available to meet these needs. Again it must be stressed that the preferences of the individual are paramount and that you cannot force support on those who do not want it. When considering the needs of individuals you could divide them into the following areas.

Social needs

The type of housing that individuals live in needs to be considered – is it appropriate for their needs? Where is the property situated and what type of accommodation is it – flat, house or bungalow? If it is a flat, on what floor is it situated and is there a working lift? Is the lift large enough to accommodate a wheelchair? Most new buildings have disability access, such as wide doors, but older buildings may not. If the individual is living in a house, are there stairs? Can the individual concerned manage the stairs; has a stair lift been considered? If not, is there enough room for a bed to be placed downstairs? What about access to the toilet? You need to discuss these issues with the individuals and gain their agreement for any changes that may need to be made. If the individual lives in local authority/housing association housing it may be possible for them to be rehoused. If they live in a privately owned house, are they willing to sell and relocate to a more suitable property, or are they able to afford to pay for adaptations that may need to be made to the house?

You also need to consider the condition of the property. Modern purpose-built properties will have many of the necessary requirements, such as central heating, modern kitchen appliances, running water, double glazing etc. Older properties may not and a considerable amount of money may have to be spent on them to bring them up to an acceptable standard. Some home improvement grants may be available to help with costs. The local housing office should be able to provide advice.

Environmental needs

Another key factor in identifying available support is the accessibility of local amenities. Does the individual live in a city, town, village or a remote/isolated area? Those requiring support may well have mobility problems which do not allow them to walk very far or, if using a wheelchair, push themselves very far. Other individuals may have anxiety problems which prevent them from venturing too far from home. It is likely that many of these individuals will have to rely on public transport or friends and family if they need to travel any distance. So it is important to know how far away they are from the local shops, post office, library and doctor's surgery. Is the individual concerned able to reach these on foot? How good are the local transport links in that area? There may be local arrangements for assisted transport for people who have mobility problems or are unable to access suitable transport, e.g. specialist taxis or dial-a-ride schemes.

Financial needs

KUS 21,
23

The eligibility criteria and the financial support available is one of the most complicated areas of claiming and providing support for individuals to live at home. Access to the various allowances and grants may vary from county to county and this can cause confusion. Organisations such as the Citizens Advice Bureau and voluntary agencies such as Age Concern and MIND employ people who are experts in these areas and will know all of the financial entitlements that individuals may be eligible to claim. So if you are unsure you should refer individuals to one of these agencies or seek advice from them yourself. Advice can also be sought directly from the Department for Work and Pensions.

Those on low incomes, who are sick, disabled, over 60 years old, caring for someone sick or disabled, or registered blind will be entitled to a variety of different benefits. The area of benefits is complex and changes frequently as government policy changes. Some of the benefits currently available include:

- Income support.
- Housing benefit.
- Carer's allowance.
- Disability persons tax credit.
- Working tax credit.
- Disability living allowance.
- Community care grants.
- Cold weather payments.
- Attendance allowance.

There are many other smaller grants and loans available for individuals with more specialised circumstances and each individual will need a proper assessment and consultation with a social worker to ensure they access all the benefits they are entitled to claim.

Some grants and loans are available from local councils to help with costs or small repairs to the home. These are most likely to apply to making access more suitable and improving insulation and draught proofing.

Physical and personal needs

An individual living at home may require support to meet a range of physical and personal needs. The needs may be related to the activities of daily living, for example getting up and going to bed, washing, dressing, cooking and cleaning. They may also have needs related to moving around their environment. An assessment of needs will identify the areas where the individual requires support, and evaluation of this information will help to determine the appropriate support needed to encourage independence and self-management. A range of resources are available to assist the individual including aids and adaptations, e.g. jar openers, bathing and dressing aids as well as domiciliary care support.

It is important that assessment is holistic and considers the whole person as they may also express needs in relation to their sexual and spiritual needs. They may feel anxious about expressing these needs and you should respond positively especially if their

KUS 6,
15, 19 ,20

expression of these needs challenges your ideas. Be aware of your responses to ensure that negative body language or expression do not cause the conversation to end prematurely. Ask open questions to help the individual to express their needs. Be conscious of your body language and show an open body posture to encourage communication. Sexual and spiritual needs are areas of an individual's life that often get overlooked. Whether this is due to cultural reserve, embarrassment, assumptions about disability, e.g. 'disabled people do not have sexual desires', age or religion, these things are often not spoken about as they are intensely private subjects. However, these are important facets of life for us all to a greater or lesser extent and areas in which the individual may require support.

In relation to sexual and relationship needs it may be appropriate to refer the individual to specialist workers, e.g. the community learning disability team, the community psychiatric nurse, their GP or a counselling service for further advice and support. It is important to discuss with the individual what support is appropriate for them in relation to spiritual needs and find out if they already have links with any spiritual or religious leader.

Health and safety needs

KUS 8

Supporting an individual at home potentially raises a number of health and safety needs depending on their circumstances. Daily living activities, e.g. getting in and out of the bath or shower, moving around their environment or cooking, may present issues if the individual is unsteady on their feet or is confused, unwell, weak and frail. Observing the individual undertaking daily living activities will enable health and social care workers to determine the appropriate support required to enable the individual to continue these activities safely. Aids, e.g. bathing and dressing aids, cooker guard, kettle pourer or adaptations (e.g. installing a hoist or stair lift) can all help to make activities safer. An occupational therapist may also be involved in providing specialist assessment and support. Some aids are readily available in larger high street chemists or via catalogues or the internet. Others may be provided by the NHS or voluntary organisations. An occupational therapist can also refer for funding on behalf of the individual for the installation of a major adaptation such as a stair lift and shower.

For some individuals, being supported at home means that contaminated waste or needles will require disposal. Individuals should be given the appropriate containers/bags to ensure this does not pose a health and safety risk.

Addressing the risks

It has been stressed that with every source of help available, the individual has to be willing to accept that help. Risk assessment is therefore extremely important to ensure that support focuses on enabling the individual to be as independent as possible as safely as possible. The home is not as controllable as a health care setting in terms of health and safety. However, for workers it becomes a workplace and legislation requires that the risks are minimised. Some adaptations to the individual's home, e.g. a hoist or stair lift, may or may not be acceptable to them and this can create tension.

If the individual does not understand or agree with practitioners about their assessed needs and there is not co-operation between everyone involved then available support may not be accepted or it may be resented. Effective negotiation and communication is needed to ensure that individuals and their families make informed choices, that their rights are promoted and they are not discriminated against in these circumstances. Sometimes the tension between individual rights and choices and health and safety risks creates a dilemma between meeting needs and managing risks. One solution to enable the individual to continue receiving support at home is for them to assume responsibility for their health and safety as well as that of care workers. If this situation arises then a legal agreement is made between the service provider and the individual and/or their carer so that the individual accepts liability for any injuries that may occur. If an individual is to live at home, even with all of the support available you still need to consider the risks that remain as it is not possible to eliminate all risks. You have a responsibility to reduce the risks as far as is reasonably practical and to provide information and support that will enable the individual to reduce the risks. This entails you making a proper assessment of the individual's home and environment and identifying the risks. The two main areas to consider will be security of the home and the potential for accidents in the home as these are the most common types of risks.

KUS 4

Security and accidents

Many individuals, especially older people, may feel vulnerable in their own home, so it is important to help them to access facilities to improve their security. There are a number of options available to improve personal safety and home security.

Crime prevention officer

The local police can offer advice from a crime prevention officer. They can give expert advice on locks, alarms and generally making your home more secure. They may also be aware of neighbourhood watch schemes that may be in place in the individual's area which can offer additional peace of mind. There are also notices available for individuals to place on their doors or windows to discourage doorstep callers and sellers.

KUS 12

Alarms

If an individual requires help in an emergency it is important that they know how to obtain that help. There are lots of different alarm systems available, from a burglar alarm system to individual personal alarms. Burglar alarms can be expensive to install and may be difficult for some people to operate. Personal alarms can be used as a deterrent or to summon help. Deterrent alarms can be carried when the individual goes out. If they are activated they let off a high-pitched sound to deter attackers. There are also community lifelines (see page 246) which can be worn around the individual's neck and they can activate this if they have had an accident in the home. For example, if an individual falls and is unable to get up they can activate the alarm, a central point will be alerted and help will be sent.

Telephones

Telephones are another way of summoning help and they add to the feeling of security. In recent years mobile phones have become very popular and this is a good way of helping an individual to feel secure especially when they leave their home. Older individuals may find some mobile phones difficult to manage as they are quite small and the keypad may be difficult to use. There are mobile phones made specifically for older people with large clear buttons and simple instructions. Cordless phones are also very useful as individuals may carry the telephone around the house with them for ease of access.

**Figure 5
Cordless phones
are useful security
measures**

Communication and support

**KUS 2,
5, 6, 20**

Once you have identified resources available and assessed the risks, then you need to ensure that relevant information is passed on to individuals and key people to enable them to access the resources they require as quickly as possible. You must find ways of checking that the information has been understood. Problems with understanding will vary greatly according to the individuals you are dealing with.

Language barriers

You must always be aware that individuals and key people may not speak English as their first language; they may have a different ethnic or national background where English is not the common language. Even if English is their first language, words may be used differently, e.g. in North America the word 'pants' refers to trousers as opposed to underwear. If you are dealing with individuals whose first language is not English you may need to access an interpreter or another family member who can speak English.

In translation some words may be misinterpreted. It is important to remember this and go over details several times to make sure everything is clear, as an informal interpreter (such as a family member) might not understand medical or professional terms and may have very different views and priorities to the individual.

A family member is not always the best interpreter due to conflicts of interest and family relationships. Also remember that it may be best to use an interpreter to help preserve a person's dignity and confidentiality.

Poor sensory perception

Individuals and key people may have some form of sensory deficit. They may have a hearing or visual impairment or speech difficulties. When supporting individuals it is important to remember that they are probably able to understand what you are saying but have difficulty either taking the information in or responding to it appropriately/ verbally. You need to establish what their preferred form of communication is and make sure that others involved are also aware of the best way to communicate.

Poor cognitive understanding

KUS 6

If the individual or key people have cognitive problems, that is, difficulty understanding and interpreting information, you will find that their understanding varies. This is especially true of individuals with depression and different forms of dementia. You will need to be patient and take time to reinforce information by giving it several times and in slightly different ways to ensure that the individual has understood what you have said. You and the individual may find it helpful to have a friend, family member or even an advocate involved, so they can offer additional support and reassurance to the individual.

Support

There are different kinds of support that can be accessed for individuals and key people with communication and/or language difficulties.

KUS 6

If the individual is registered blind you may be able to access information in Braille or on tape. Many official documents can be obtained in Braille, but if not you must be prepared to read official forms to individuals and complete them on their behalf. Official forms are also printed in many different languages to allow ease of access.

If individuals have sight problems they may need simply to be referred to an ophthalmologist or optician for an eye test. These tests are free for a number of individuals particularly if they are already in receipt of other benefits. If an individual is housebound then you may be able to arrange a home visit from an optician.

Speech and language therapists also work in the community. If speech problems exist and might benefit from the input of a therapist, this service can be accessed through a GP referral. Speech and language therapists may also be able to provide a number of aids which would help with communication and writing such as picture boards.

Managing affairs and risks

You must identify the resources available to assist individuals and key people to develop skills to help them manage their domestic, personal, social and financial affairs. The needs assessment will include consideration of these needs and identify what support, if any, is required to enable them to live at home. The individual may be finding domestic tasks difficult or impossible to do without help and so practical assistance may be required. Alternatively many domestic tasks may be carried out by their carer and practical support of this kind may enable the carer to continue their caring role.

KUS 13

Under the Carers (Recognition and Services) Act 1995 a carer who provides regular and substantial care (e.g. a family member) is entitled to an assessment of needs in their own right. Although there is no direct entitlement to receive services they may be able to access respite care to enable them to continue caring and to maintain their own interests and activities. The local authority social services department can provide a carers assessment form or it may be available online. The carer may need to complete this. The carer may also be entitled to a range of benefits to support them in their caring role and may require advice and support to complete these. These benefits may enable them to pay for additional support, specialist equipment or the additional costs of caring, e.g. meeting special dietary requirements.

If the carer is employed it may be vital to the family income for them to continue working, and this should be taken into consideration when identifying needs and planning care. If the individual has children then the whole family situation will require careful consideration and this may include involving colleagues from children's services especially if children are acting as the individual's carer.

The individual, their carer and/or family may require emotional support too. Social workers and health visitors can provide support to the whole family both on a practical and emotional level. If the individual is dying then specialist hospice workers can support the family to prepare for what is going to happen and through bereavement.

The role of practitioners is to enable the individual to retain control of their life for as long as they are able and this may include supporting them to develop new skills and coping strategies. It may also include exploring with them and others what specific risks the individual encounters. For example, the individual may work with an occupational therapist to assess their risk of falling when bathing or moving around their home. The occupational therapist would be able to identify what support was available to meet their needs and minimise risks, e.g. aids and adaptations and grants to meet any financial cost. Aids and adaptations are the starting point and you need to work with others to enable the individual to adapt to doing things differently and utilise new coping strategies to minimise the risk of accidents.

Statistics show that most accidents occur in the home, particularly among the older population. These may not necessarily be fatal accidents but may require some kind of health care intervention. The older individual living at home is more vulnerable for a number of reasons. Their vision and hearing may be failing and they are not as quick to react as a younger person. Equally, from a physical point of view, a disabled person may find it difficult to deal with a potential danger. For example, if they are confined to a wheelchair and knock over an ashtray with burning embers they may not be able to pick it up.

Fire

One of the greatest dangers in the home is the potential for fire. Nowadays homes have many electrical devices and gas appliances which may pose a risk.

Kitchen

The most dangerous room in the house is probably the kitchen. It is fitted with the most electrical and gas appliances. New appliances are usually fitted with safety notices and have sealed-in plug sockets. You can advise individuals where to place appliances for ease of use and also for safety. Electrical items should not be too near the water supply. Items such as tea towels and cleaning cloths should not be left near the cooker. It is important to keep these areas clean because a build-up of grease and fat may mean that fire is a greater risk. If individuals are unable to clean properly themselves due to their disability then you need to consider getting a domestic cleaner to assist them. There are many types of adaptive equipment – such as timers to turn off the cooker after a specific period of time – that can be very useful for people to help them retain their independence.

Electrics

In older buildings the electric wiring may need to be checked and updated. If necessary you may need to arrange for an electrician to come and do this. There are also some basic steps that you can take to help prevent electrical appliances and wires becoming a danger. Plugs should be checked to make sure no wires are exposed, sockets should not be overloaded and plugs should not be placed under rugs or carpets. If there are a lot of plugs for one socket you should advise the individual to obtain a proper adaptor. If lights start to flicker you should replace the bulbs. Regular safety checks of electrics are essential to prevent the danger of a fire. Circuit breakers may be a useful safety precaution. Electric blankets and portable heaters pose a particularly high risk of fire and special attention needs to be paid to ensure these are safe and are used safely.

**Figure 6
Plug sockets
should not be
overloaded**

Furniture

All modern furniture should carry a fire-resistant permanent label, although older furniture may have been made when fire resistance was not a high priority and therefore may not have a label. You should be particularly careful if buying furniture through second-hand stores and make sure they meet these requirements. If obtaining furniture from charities, they will usually only supply items that display fire-resistant labels, but you should always check.

Cigarettes, matches and lighters

Lots of domestic fires are started by cigarettes that are not correctly extinguished. You cannot prevent individuals smoking, but you can ensure they have adequate ashtrays and use lighters rather than matches, and you should encourage them not to smoke in bed and to empty ashtrays regularly when ashes are cool.

Smoke alarms

Warning devices are available to detect the presence of smoke – they do not prevent the spread of fire but may give individuals time to escape. Smoke alarms are relatively cheap and are readily available from supermarkets and DIY stores. Ideally a smoke alarm should be placed on the ceiling of every room of the home. Test the batteries weekly to make sure they are working. Reaching up to the alarm may be difficult, in which case you could arrange for someone to do this for the individual or fit a long-lasting battery. In most areas the fire service will come and check (and replace) smoke detector batteries free of charge. All you need to do is call and make an appointment. The advice is to change batteries at least once a year.

Have a plan

In addition, it is important that people, especially those with mobility or sensory problems know what they would do if there is a fire. Having a plan, an escape route and a planned meeting place are all sensible steps that can help to keep the individual safe.

Although you cannot prevent a fire occurring, you can help individuals to take the above precautions, identify the risks and make sure they know what to do if a fire occurs. You can contact the local fire brigade and arrange for the fire prevention officer to visit and give advice on safety precautions.

Accessing support

KUS 10, 19, 20

In order to access appropriate support the individual and key people may ask you to assist them to complete a range of documents and forms. These could be forms to access funding for adaptations to their home, for example Disability Living Allowance (under 65 years old) or Attendance Allowance (over 65 years old) forms to access government benefits. There may also be forms related to local services, e.g. disabled parking or leisure-centre membership. Official forms can be daunting for many individuals due to the way they are laid out or the questions asked, or the individual may feel too unwell to complete them. As you have a good knowledge of their circumstances you are well placed to help them with this task. They may require support in actually writing the responses or in understanding the questions asked. Ensure that you reflect their own words when completing forms and do not present their situation from your perspective.

Managing changes

KUS 17,
22

It is important that you work with individuals and others to deal with changes to the individual's health, finances, social or legal position.

Regular assessment and review of the risks, needs and support required is essential if the individual is to remain living at home. Managing changes that may be needed requires discussion between all parties involved. That includes the individual, their family or key people and the care team. This may be on a relatively informal basis, through visits to the individual's home, or it may require a more formal approach through an organised meeting such as a case conference. At this meeting all individuals involved in providing care are invited to attend for a general discussion about the care needs. Of primary importance at such a review, whether it is formal or informal, are the wishes of the individual receiving care. If necessary an advocate should also attend to represent the individual's views and wishes if they have difficulty doing this themselves.

If the individual becomes terminally ill or incapable of making decisions due to reduced mental capacity, it may be necessary to review the legal position. In some cases it may be necessary to consider taking out a Power of Attorney. This is a document whereby one person gives another person or persons the power to act on their behalf with regard to their property and financial affairs.

This means that the individual can appoint a relative or other key person to manage their affairs if they become mentally incapable. It is a legal document and individuals should be advised to take legal advice before setting this up so that they fully understand the implications of what they are doing.

Individual's social and financial positions may also change. Key people who were providing support may no longer be able to do so, and you may need to look for help in other ways. If individuals are claiming financial benefits you should be aware of any changes in the eligibility criteria and how this may affect individuals and key people. The health and financial, social and legal positions of individuals and key people need to be reviewed at agreed timescales to ensure that adequate care and support is being provided.

When working with individuals and key people it is important to agree timescales for reviewing their situation and circumstances. At first, as new services are being introduced, reviews may take place frequently, e.g. every 4–6 weeks, to ensure that any problems are being identified and resolved early. As the situation becomes more settled then reviews may occur every 6–12 months although monitoring will continue and if needs or services change then a review can be undertaken when required. In some circumstances the situation may remain unsettled with changes occurring frequently, e.g. if the individual is deteriorating, dying or if their medical condition is unstable. You may be involved in providing information that informs both the monitoring and review processes. This could be through observation and care plan recording or more formal reporting procedures. To be effective monitoring and review processes must be agreed by all involved.

Figure 7
Power of Attorney document

Court of Protection
Enduring Powers of Attorney Act 1985
Form EP2
Application for Registration

EP2V1APGO

IMPORTANT: Please complete the form in <u>BLOCK CAPITALS</u> using a <u>black ballpoint pen</u>. Place a clear cross 'X' mark inside square option boxes ⊠ – do not circle the option.

Part One – The Donor

Please state the full name and present address of the donor. State the donor's first name in 'Forename 1' and the donor's other forenames in full in 'Other Forenames'. Name of Residence should be completed with the name of the nursing/care home or hospital where the donor resides, if applicable.

Mr   Mrs   Ms   Miss Other
☐   ☐   ☐   ☐   ☐
Place a cross against one option ⊠

If Other, please specify here:

Last Name:

Forename 1:

Other Forenames:

Name of Residence:

Address 1:

Address 2:

Address 3:

Town/City:

County:

Postcode:

Donor Date of Birth:

D D M M Y Y Y Y

If the exact date is unknown please state the year of birth

Please do not write below this line - For Office Use Only

Produced in association with the
Public Guardianship Office

© Crown Copyright 2005

Provider details

Billy is a 25-year-old man with learning difficulties who has been living in residential care and has expressed a desire to live more independently in the community. He is able to manage his personal care independently, but he lacks social and life skills and the confidence to live alone.

➤ *What housing choices are available to Billy?*

➤ *How would you help Billy to consider all of the options available?*

➤ *How could you help him develop the necessary life skills to manage on his own?*

➤ *What benefits may he be able to access to help him?*

➤ *What support groups can Billy access to help him?*

Key points – identifying and accessing additional support and resources

- You must identify the individual's social, environmental and financial needs.

- Work with the individual to identify options to meet these required needs.

- Consider the security risks to the individual and give guidance on how to manage these.

- Make sure the proper precautions have been taken to reduce the domestic risks to the individual.

- Develop communication skills to deal with all types of communication differences.

- Include key people in the review and management of change.

- Establish regular methods and timescales to review and evaluate the care package.

Support individuals to review their needs and identify changes necessary to enable them to live at home

Reviewing individual needs

KUS II, 22

Even though you make plans and assess individuals according to needs, their situation will always change, and this may be for the better or at times for the worse. You should know how to access information and advice that might be useful when reviewing any changes. If information is readily available the process for monitoring and reviewing individual's needs will be more efficient and the services can be adapted and changed in response to new situations. Changes may mean increasing, reducing or withdrawing care. The frequency of reviews will depend on the individual's needs, the support being provided and the stability of the situation. The reviews needs to be done on a continual basis to allow individuals to remain living at home.

Reducing facilities and services

When an individual first moves to independent living or has been assessed and requires a package of care, this may be fairly extensive with a lot of support from various practitioners. The purpose is to keep the individual living in their home. If the individual's condition improves once they have received additional input then after an agreed time the services can be reviewed and a gradual withdrawal agreed. Every individual will differ in confidence and ability, and reducing services and facilities must be negotiated to ensure individuals' preferences and wishes are considered whilst minimising risks. The timing for the withdrawal of services is also crucial and must be negotiated with all those involved – the individual, the identified key people and the care team. It is important that any reduction in care support does not lead to a loss of confidence in the individuals and key people involved. Stopping all support at once may cause the individual to relapse if they are not ready to cope totally independently. Some services may never be withdrawn, such as personal care, if the individual has a permanent disability which is never likely to improve.

Increasing facilities and services

It is also possible that the individual's condition will deteriorate and therefore the care package will need to be reviewed and increased in order to meet the increase in their support needs. The ease with which this can happen will depend on the changes to the individual and whether these relate to their health, financial, social or the legal situation. If resources and support need to be increased this may significantly change the financial situation and funding. The individual may not be entitled to any further benefits and may not be able to afford to pay for additional support through their own funds. This may mean a full review of the individual's care and support needs and service provision.

Palliative care

The individual's condition may deteriorate to such an extent that they become terminally ill and palliative care is required. If this is the case then the whole package will need to be reviewed. The individual has the right to choose where and how they spend their last days, and many will opt to remain in their own home. Factors which need to be considered are as follows.

Choices of treatment

What choices are available to the individual? This could be a change in drug therapy or a more intense treatment requiring a period of hospitalisation or attendance for treatment at a day unit.

Pain and distressing symptoms

Symptoms of illness can cause more distress than the illness itself. Incontinence, diarrhoea and nausea in particular can be very upsetting and are sometimes the result of the medical treatment received.

Spiritual care

The religious and cultural beliefs of the individuals need to be considered. Those with a strong faith may wish to have regular visits from spiritual leaders or to access places of worship. Those with no previously declared faith may in these circumstances seek solace in religion or faith. Life-changing events can lead individuals to reassess their views and you need to be sensitive to this possibility and not make assumptions.

**Figure 8
Consider the
religious and
cultural beliefs of
individuals**

Alternative therapies

Alternative treatments other than general medication are now recognised as having genuine therapeutic effects when used to complement traditional medical treatments. There are many different treatments, but for example acupuncture, massage and reflexology can all be used as a form of pain relief.

Bereavement support

The individual, their family or key people may need support to come to terms with the process of diagnosis, dying and death. It is a time of great emotional distress when the wishes of the individual and the family may conflict. All those concerned will grieve for their loss. There may be feelings of guilt, bitterness, anger or estrangement – at many levels this can be a very difficult time. The individual may grieve for the loss or their life or body image, and they may take some time to come to terms with what is happening.

Social/financial care

The practical care which has to be provided to the individual will naturally increase, even though this may be only for a short time. It is essential that you ensure the comfort and dignity of the individual and support their carers and family to enable them to focus on the individual.

Identifying and implementing changes

KUS 5, 12, 20, 22

You will need to provide additional information to individuals and key people involved about where to obtain extra resources and facilities. Ensure that you help individuals and key people to identify any extra resources that could give them added support and agree who will be responsible for accessing the available support. The individual may wish to do this themselves or may ask you to do it on their behalf. The local authority in your area will provide details about care services and there should also be information at places like doctor's surgeries and libraries and on the internet. Voluntary organisations or the Citizens Advice Bureau also have a lot of information about extra support and facilities, particularly within the local area. Libraries also provide internet access. Some resources are free, e.g. some voluntary organisations provide a bus service to the local supermarket or a reduced-rate fare. This may assist if individuals are having difficulty going to the shops. Once you have determined and collected the relevant information you should discuss with individuals and key people which services, facilities and resources they may wish to access and if necessary accompany them. You need to ensure that the individual and key people give permission for you to share relevant personal information with other potential service providers. Once they have consented to information sharing you need to pass on the relevant details to ensure that the individual can access and receive support from those organisations. The information being passed to each organisation may be different depending on information-sharing agreements and the type of service being provided. For example, you might share a lot of information with a service provider about the individual's overall needs, but you may give limited or specific information to someone running a support group. The individual and key people may ask you to support them to initially access new services, facilities or support groups. They will be able to tell you how they wish you to do this, e.g. staying with them during their first visit or taking them to the location beforehand so that they know where it is.

Additional resources

Table 2 is a list of the types of service and facilities that may be available in your area. You should check to see if they are accessible for the individuals and key people that you work with and make notes about where to access them. You may find other useful contacts that are not mentioned in the table.

Table 2 Services and facilities that may be available in your area

Mobile shop (selling basic groceries)	Mobile library service (provides access to reading materials)
Community equipment services (continence advisers, wheelchairs)	Respite care
Taxi (specialists who deal with disabled needs)	Bus timetable (local bus numbers and times for amenities, doctor's surgery etc.)
Disabled badge holder/parking (apply for eligibility)	Mobile hairdresser (visit in own home)
Free training courses (for over 65s and those on benefits, low incomes)	Internet shopping (may be helpful if unable to reach shops)
Reading tapes for the blind	Volunteer help (some organisations visit people in their own homes to help with basic household chores, gardening etc.)
Pet therapy	Community dental service
Chiropody	Health visitors
Lunch clubs and social clubs	Day centres
Pick-up prescription service	Macmillan Cancer Relief (provide palliative care service)

Evaluate changes and risks

Whenever possible you should work with others involved to agree any changes to resources, support, services and facilities. Changing services and resources may involve working with a different provider if the service being provided did not meet the individual's needs or the equality or quantity of care was not as agreed. It may also mean increasing or reducing services. The individual and key people will have provided information through the monitoring and review processes to support proposed changes.

Any change will involve a re-evaluation of risk. It is possible that by removing resources you will increase the risk to the individual. The risk must always be measured against the wishes of the individual and be respectful of their right to choose. A new risk assessment should be completed with the individual and other key people (if appropriate) and the implications discussed. It is important that the individual is fully informed and able to make an informed decision about the level of their care. If the individual is unable to make a decision due to their condition then a Power of Attorney (see page 260) could be used and decisions discussed and made with the designated person. In some cases individuals may have made a living will. A living will must be made while the individual is of sound mind. Its purpose is to make clear what type of medical care and/or intervention an individual would like to receive in the event of them being unable to make this clear themselves due to deterioration in their capacity to consent to treatment. At the present time it is not enforceable by law, but it gives a strong indication of the individual's wishes regarding treatment. This in turn may help to evaluate the type of changes that should be implemented.

In some cases individuals may not accept or recognise the risks to them and insist that care be withdrawn. These adults may be considered to be at risk. In the same way that an 'At Risk' Register exists to protect children in vulnerable environments, some areas of the country have set up an adults at risk service. You should check locally to see whether your social service provides this.

Figure 9
A care plan for an individual at risk

NURSING MANAGEMENT OF THE CLIENT AT RISK OF SELF-HARM

DATE	NAME:	REVIEW DATE/TIME
PROBLEM	Method of coping with stressors is to engage in self-harm behaviours	
GOAL	To assume responsibility for ensuring his/her physical safety To learn coping strategies	
ACTION	Keep a diary of thoughts, feelings and action and discuss these with named carer. To contact care staff if feel compelled to self-harm. Attend occupational therapy to develop coping strategies and relaxation skills Identify friends who can provide ongoing support	

Vulnerable adults would be those who are at risk due to age, physical disability, learning disability, mental health problems or sensory/cognitive impairment. If an individual is found to be living in a situation where they could be in danger from physical, financial or sexual abuse, neglect or physical injury, the situation should be investigated. If the situation cannot be resolved a conference can be called and a specific care plan can be developed. The risks to the individuals are highlighted and arrangements made to deal with emergency situations if they occur.

Report on changes

KUS 7, 9

Accurate record keeping and reporting of procedures is essential. You must be aware of your organisation's procedure for recording and reporting on care given. If you are responsible for visiting and providing care to individuals in their own home you must always record accurately on the individual's care plan the care given. This is especially important to ensure the continuity of care and that relevant information, e.g. regarding a change or a problem, is passed to other workers. You should also know the signs and symptoms that would give cause for concern and what should be reported to senior staff. If there seems to be deterioration in an individual's condition this should be reported to the care manager.

You must be aware that documentation should be completed accurately and legibly, and that many individuals may have access to it. Use proper terminology and spelling, and state the facts objectively without using any bias or judgemental terms. For example, you would not say someone was 'filthy' – you would say the person needed to be washed. Your organisation will have specific procedures for completing documentation and you must be aware of these. The individual has the right to access information about themselves and you must be aware of this. Try to complete written documentation with the individual concerned, then they will be aware of what has been written. It is a misconception that recording documents are the property of the different organisations that provide them – these documents actually belong to the individual and should be treated with respect.

Records are also confidential and you must always remember that every individual has the right to confidentiality. If they discuss issues with you then you must not discuss

**Figure 10
Records are
confidential**

these openly with other staff unless you have the individual's permission to do so. However, you should document discussions. If an individual asks you to keep a secret and you agree to this it could put you in a very difficult position, for example you have a responsibility to report actual abuse or suspicions of abuse. In these circumstances it is best to refer the matter to the care manager or senior staff. If you feel the individual is in danger, you must report this information but let them know that you are going to inform your manager.

Reviewing needs

Emma is a 45-year-old woman with multiple sclerosis (MS). Her partner left six months ago and she is now living alone for the first time in her life. She lives in a two-bedroom first-floor flat. She has been able to work flexible part-time hours from home for the past three years and wants to continue this. When she is well she manages her personal care but needs help to get in and out of the bath. When she has a relapse she needs more support with most daily living activities. Her partner supported her with personal care when needed and undertook all of the domestic tasks. Since the relationship ended Emma has become depressed and her MS symptoms have worsened, which has made it increasingly difficult for her to manage alone. Her parents want her to move in with them. Emma does not want to lose her independence. However, she is finding it difficult to manage daily living tasks, has lost weight and has not been out for the past two months. Her flat requires some modification to enable her to remain there.

➤ *What practical help can you offer Emma?*

➤ *What services may she be able to access?*

Key points – supporting individuals to review their needs and identify changes necessary

- Care packages must be monitored and reviewed regularly.
- Services and resources may need to be increased and on occasions reduced.
- There are special support packages available for individuals who are terminally ill.
- Make use of services offered by the Citizens Advice Bureau and voluntary organisations.
- There are a number of extra resources and services available; you must know how to locate these.
- Some adults are vulnerable living alone and may need special care.
- Accurate recording and passing on of information is essential to ensure continuity of care.

Unit
HSC343

Are you ready for assessment?

Support individuals to live at home

This unit is about how you support individuals to live at home. It is about how you identify the individual's personal, physical and safety needs and how you support them to identify and access appropriate support and services to meet those needs. It is also about how you work with individuals and key people to review their needs and identify any changes that may need to be made to enable them to continue living at home.

Your assessment will be carried out mainly through observation by your assessor and this should provide most of the evidence for the elements in this unit. If your assessor is unable to directly observe you then you may be able to use the testimony of an experienced colleague acting as an expert witness. You will need to discuss this with your assessor. Evidence of your knowledge and understanding will be demonstrated through observation, your assessor examining work products, e.g. reports, minutes of meetings, as well as through answering oral and/or written questions.

You need to be aware when planning assessments that this unit also relates to the core units, in particular HSC31, HSC32 and HSC35, as well as some optional units, and so you may also be able to use evidence performance criteria for these.

You need to take in to account that you may need to be observed in the individual's home. Therefore you need to explain about the assessment and seek their permission for your assessor to visit. If their visit would be intrusive you will need to consider alternative evidence-gathering methods, e.g. expert witness testimony.

Direct observation by your assessor

Your assessor or an expert witness will need to plan to see you carry out the performance criteria (PCs) in each of the elements in this unit. The performance criteria that may be difficult to meet through observation are:

- HSC343b PCs 5, 6

Preparing to be observed

You must make sure that your workplace and any individuals and key people involved in your work agree to you being assessed. Explicit, informed consent must be obtained before you carry out any assessment activity that involves individuals or which involves access to confidential information related to their care.

Before your assessments you should read carefully the performance criteria for each element in the unit. Try to cover as much as you can during your observation but remember that you and your assessor can also plan for additional sources of evidence should full coverage of all performance criteria not be possible.

▶

Other types of evidence

You may need to present other forms of evidence in order to:

- Cover criteria not observed by your assessor.
- Show that you have the required knowledge, understanding and skills to claim competence in this area of practice.
- Ensure your work practice is consistent.

Your assessor may also need to ask you questions to confirm your knowledge and understanding and ensure that you can apply this to your practice.

Check your knowledge

- How can you ensure that the carer is supported in their caring role?
- How can you empower individuals when making decisions?
- How and where would you access information and support for individuals you are supporting?
- What is the current legislation that supports individuals to live at home?
- How can living at home affect an individual's sense of identity, their self-esteem and self-image?
- How can you implement plans to manage risks?
- Where would you access advice on financial planning?
- How can you balance individual preferences and ensuring safety?
- How do you deal with discrimination that may occur when individuals attempt to access services?

Support individuals to retain, regain and develop the skills to manage their lives and environment

*T*his unit covers the support given to individuals to enable them to identify the skills they need to manage their lives and environment. The skills they require could be related to preparing food, eating and drinking, dressing, bathing and washing, mobility (including getting in and out of bed), navigating the environment, or cleaning the environment. It is also concerned with supporting the individuals to retain some of the skills they already have, and helping them to regain or develop any other identified skills that they feel they need. The unit also looks at the evaluation of these skills. You will need to be aware of the codes of practice and conduct and the standards and guidance relevant to your role and the roles, responsibilities, accountability and duties of others when supporting the individuals to retain, regain and develop their skills.

The unit contains three elements:

⌣ **HSC344a** *Support individuals to identify the skills they need to manage their lives and environment*

⌣ **HSC344b** *Support individuals to retain, regain and develop the identified skills*

⌣ **HSC344c** *Support individuals to evaluate the use of the skills in managing their lives and environment*

Introduction

KUS 12

KUS 2, 7, 19

The government Green Paper 'Independence, Well-being and Choice 2005', and the government report 'Improving the Life Chances of Disabled People 2005', as well as research by health and social care organisations such as The Kings Fund, have all emphasised the need to provide support and services to individuals to enable them to be as independent as they can for as long as possible. In order to be independent, individuals may need your support to retain, regain and develop the skills necessary to manage their lives and environment. It is essential that they are given the appropriate support, advice and guidance to help achieve this. You should be able to give individuals help and assistance to encourage them to do as much as possible for themselves and maintain some of their independence. All individuals need to be enabled to maximise their own potential and independence regardless of their physical or mental abilities.

The individual's preferences, beliefs and wishes must always be taken into account in relation to any personal, social, cultural or religious needs, and you must avoid any discriminatory practices against any individual in your care.

Although we talk about equality of care and treating everyone the same, you need to remember that all individuals are different, they are unique. You need to recognise the essential differences between individuals and consider the concept of equity. Equity is a better term to use than equality – it is more about fairness than sameness. All individuals are entitled to suggest what they think is the best course of action for themselves, and they need to be enabled to discuss this openly without feeling under pressure. They need assurance that all information disclosed will be kept confidential and only used on a need-to-know' basis. Information will have to be shared with the appropriate services and facilities and with other care workers to enable a suitable package of care to be devised for the individual.

It is important that the individuals in your care are given the opportunity to demonstrate their current skills and abilities. By working with the individual you will be able to find out what these are, and if you have built up a good rapport they should feel confident in performing these skills with your support. You need to undertake ongoing monitoring and assessment of the individual to measure their ability to perform the activities for daily living. Be aware that someone may have the occasional bad day when they need more assistance than usual, but you will be able to determine their strengths and weaknesses and endeavour to work on these.

**Figure 1
Encourage
individuals to
perform everyday
tasks**

Encourage individuals and key people to join in with any discussions about the individual's ongoing care. Welcome any contributions that they make about other skills that they feel will help the individual to achieve some degree of independence. Targets must be agreed with the individual, their carers and the care team, and these should be reviewed when the situation changes.

Support individuals to identify the skills they need to manage their lives and environment

KUS 2, 5

You need to work with colleagues and service providers to identify the possible options for individuals and any risks that have to be managed. By discussing these options with the individual, their carers and others involved, agreement on the best options to meet their needs and requirements can hopefully be reached. At the same time the likelihood of any risk of danger, harm or abuse arising from anything or anyone associated with these options will need to be discussed with the individual, their carers and others supporting them. A clear, concise explanation needs to be given to everyone concerned regarding any perceived risks. It is essential these risks are reduced and managed before any final decisions on the options available to the individual are made. A comprehensive risk assessment must be carried out for each option chosen, and this should be explained to everyone involved. If individuals are unsure about any activity or skill, any necessary training needs to be given so that everyone has a clear understanding of how they can avoid the risk of danger, harm, injury or abuse to the individual or to themselves.

Risk assessment

KUS 8

The Management of Health and Safety at Work Regulations 1999 state that employers have to assess any risks which are associated with the workplace and work activities.

There are five key questions in relation to risk assessment:

- What is the purpose of the risk assessment?
- Who is competent to assess the risk?
- Whose risk should be assessed?
- What should be assessed?
- When should the risk be assessed?

The employer must take into account all activities that happen in the workplace including dealing with aggression and violence. Once the risk assessments have been carried out, actions need to be taken to apply risk control measures that will reduce the identified risks. You must check that a risk assessment has been carried out before you perform any task in the workplace as this will protect both you and the individuals. Always seek help and advice from your manager or supervisor if you are uncertain about a particular risk assessment. If you consider that there have been any changes in the condition of the individual or in the environment, which means that the task is no longer safe for you to perform, it is your responsibility to seek advice before taking any action.

KUS 5, 7, 8, 19

It is far easier to undertake risk assessments in a care setting than in the individual's own home. In a care setting the individual is a guest in your environment, in the individual's home you are a guest in their environment. The individual may not be

KUS 2, 4

aware of the risks and you will need to point these out and explain the possible dangers. Although your employer will still be able to carry out some risk assessments to protect the individual, their carers and other people including you, the actual layout of furnishings and other equipment in the home is really the individual's own choice. Advise the individual and their carers of any health and safety risks. Always report your concerns to your manager or supervisor and never put yourself in any danger of harm or injury.

**Figure 2
Carry out a risk
assessment of the
individual's home**

KUS 1, 2,
5, 7, 8, 19

Communication of needs

All individuals have a right to make their own choices and decisions about their lives and environment. In order for them to be able to make the right choices they must be given the full range of options, including any advantages and disadvantages. Make them aware of their options by presenting them in a format that they can understand easily. This may include the use of the individual's preferred spoken language, the use of signs, symbols or pictures, writing, objects of reference and other non-verbal forms of communication. If the individual or their carers need to use sensory equipment you should ensure that these are available and are in good working order. You may find that the individual requires the help of an interpreter or translator or the support of an advocate, and this must be arranged as soon as possible.

You must take into account each individual's personal preferences, religious and cultural beliefs, their language, any age-related needs and any special needs or requirements. The individual needs to be supported in making their choices, and these must be respected. It is important that the information given by everyone involved is consistent to avoid any confusion which could lead to the wrong decisions being made and potential relationship breakdown.

You need to encourage and support individuals to communicate their needs, preferences and beliefs about the skills they need to manage their lives and environment. It is important that you have good communication skills when talking to the individual, listen carefully to what they say and make sure that you have heard them correctly, reflect what you heard back to the individual. This will give the individual the opportunity to either confirm that you have heard correctly or to clarify what they said. By communicating in this way with the individuals and their carers you will be able to build up a good relationship and a good rapport with them. Encourage them to discuss any problems or concerns they may have. If these are not sorted out then they may have a detrimental effect on how the individual is able to cope. Even though everyone is different, we all have similar needs and requirements to enable us to meet our basic day-to-day living needs. Everyone will have different views and priorities regarding their needs, preferences and beliefs, and will have their own thoughts and opinions about what they require to be able to meet these needs. It is important that they are given the opportunity to communicate these to everyone who is concerned with their ongoing care so that the appropriate support networks can be set up to provide advice, guidance or any training they may require.

Identifying the individual's current skills

KUS 21

The individual and their carers will need your support to identify their current skills and abilities. They may need advice on how they can build on these to meet their current and future needs. You may already be aware of the abilities of some of the individuals you support, especially if you have known them for some time. The individual may not be aware of the skills they already have as they may have lost their confidence, and so your contribution will be beneficial in identifying these. Monitoring these skills is necessary to ensure the individual will be able to manage their daily activities without any problems. Help the individual to undertake self-care as much as possible. Whenever possible involve the carers with some of the activities in order to build up their confidence when helping the individual to manage their lives and environment effectively.

What you must not do

KUS 2, 8, 14

You may consider that sometimes it is much quicker and easier for you to undertake the activity for the individual, but this will not help to build up their ability and confidence in performing the activities for themselves, and neither will it increase their self-esteem and self-worth.

**Figure 3
Help individuals
to undertake
activities**

Prioritising their needs

Individuals will require your support to identify and communicate their needs and priorities in terms of the skills they **need**.

Needs are categorised under the following headings:

- Personal and social care.
- Cultural and religious.
- Physical health.
- Mental health.
- Financial.
- Access/transport.
- Accommodation.
- Education/employment/leisure.
- Needs of carers.

Individuals may perceive their needs in a different way to yourself and other colleagues. They may not be able to prioritise these appropriately, and may not be sure of the skills they need to help them manage their lives in the short or medium term. It is important for you to focus on these time periods in relation to this unit, for example during the short term the individual may require more support from you in helping them to develop the necessary skills to meet even their basic daily living activities. For instance, the individual may have been involved in an accident and have sudden disability due to trauma. They may not be able to perform the skills which they normally took for granted, like personal hygiene, toileting, dressing, eating and drinking. They will find it very strange to have someone else doing these things for them and may feel embarrassed, angry and frustrated. They may gradually recover from their disability and be able to perform the activities for themselves with assistance. They may make a full recovery and be able to get on with their life just as it was before the accident.

KUS 2, 5, 16, 18, 19, 20

You might be caring for individuals with learning disabilities and you will need to work with the individual, their carers and other care providers to develop a programme of care specifically designed to help them perform the activities they need in order to maintain some form of independence. Their access to learning skills will need to be discussed and agreed with everyone involved. You will need to help some individuals to learn to communicate by using objects of reference or a picture exchange communication system (PECS) or other forms of non-verbal communication. Their abilities and achievements will need to be monitored on a daily basis.

You may be caring for individuals with mental health problems such as phobias associated with depression or obsessive compulsive behaviour, or individual's with bipolar disorder. This is an illness, commonly known as manic-depressive illness, characterised by swings in mood between the opposite extremes of severe depression and over-excitability. The needs and requirements of the individuals will vary according to their condition, and their capabilities will fluctuate. You will need to reassure them and give them all the help you can to encourage them to participate.

KUS 16, 20

You may work with individuals with dementia or Alzheimer's disease which in the early stages involves short-term memory loss, becoming more severe as the disease progresses. Both the individual and their family will need support during this time. It will be very distressing for them to see someone they know and love change so much.

Whatever the individual's physical, mental or emotional condition they will have specific needs. You need to work with the individual, their carers and key people to assess the skills required to help them manage their lives to the best of their ability. Any worries or concerns must be taken into consideration and resolved. Give the individual all the reassurance and assistance you can to help them to feel confident and comfortable in performing the required skills. Find out where you can access records and information to support your practice when assisting the individuals and their carers to retain, regain and develop the necessary skills. Ask your manager or supervisor for assistance if necessary.

As the individual and their carers become more able and confident in performing the agreed skills, further assessments and discussions should take place to decide what other skills need to be developed in order for them to manage their lives in the medium term. Be conscious of the fact that retaining, regaining and developing new skills to manage their lives and environment can affect the individual's sense of identity, their self-esteem and self-image. They may no longer feel in control of their own life.

Consider what additional support the individual may require from other service providers, and ensure that this is available as required. Ask your manager or supervisor for assistance if necessary. You need to ensure that the needs of the individuals reflect their strengths and aspirations as well as those of the key people in their lives. Any worries or concerns that the individual has must be taken into consideration when identifying and prioritising the skills they need to enable them to manage their lives and environment. Depending on the physical and mental ability of the individual, these skills may need to be modified to suit their immediate requirements.

Additional and specialist support

Some skills that the individual needs to develop may require additional/or specialist support. For example, an individual who has had a stroke may have lost their speech. They will need to work with the speech therapist to help them regain it. They may need to work with the physiotherapist to help them to learn to walk again. Individuals who have been diagnosed as diabetic will need to learn the skills required to help them manage their diabetes. They will need to learn how to give their insulin injections, check their blood sugar levels and understand the diet they should follow. Once the necessary skills have been identified, the individual can be referred to the appropriate people who can provide this additional or specialist support. You need to work alongside these people in helping them to motivate and encourage individuals in developing their new skills. After all, the individual is likely to feel more confident if they are supported by someone they know. It may be a skill or procedure that is completely new to them and they will need a lot of extra support in order to achieve it. You may be asked to continue working with the individual between sessions, for instance doing exercises or encouraging practice of certain activities. In this situation the specialist practitioner can help you to learn what to do and how to encourage the individual. The individual might think they are not able to learn any new skills, and they may feel like giving up. They will need a lot of additional and specialist support to help them to regain some of their confidence and mobility. Let them know that everyone is there to help them, and that in the long term it will be beneficial for them and will help them to achieve their independence.

Special procedures and equipment for assessment

Where special procedures and equipment are required for assessment, you need to explain to the individuals and their carers what this involves. If they are aware of what will happen, any anxiety can be minimised and they will be able to co-operate fully.

Assessment

KUS 8, 21

It is important that you understand that a needs-led assessment fits resources to people – not people into services. The NHS and Community Care Act 1990 states that all assessments must be focused on the needs of the individuals and their carers irrespective of what resources are available.

Individuals are continuously assessed on their **ability** to manage their lives and environment and their **capability** to do so. These assessments should be carried out in partnership with the individual and their carers and other key people.

An assessment of the individual will enable a measurement of their ability to perform activities for daily living. It may be necessary for special procedures and equipment to be used for the assessment. If this is the case then you will need to explain to the individual and their carer what this involves so they are fully aware of what is happening. For example, the individual may have had a hip replacement and need to be assessed by the physiotherapist when walking and going up and down the stairs using crutches. They will need to negotiate these successfully before they can go home. An individual with learning disabilities may be assessed to see if they can manage to live in their own home. An older person may be assessed using a stairlift to get up and down the stairs at home. Or an individual with a deteriorating illness such as Parkinson's disease or multiple sclerosis may be assessed to see if their condition has changed and their abilities decreased.

KUS 10, 11, 14, 22

If you are involved in the assessment process you need to be familiar with any special procedures or equipment and have received the appropriate training. Never use any equipment you are not trained to use, and always ask for assistance if unsure. There may be guidelines or procedures that you need to follow when you are carrying out an assessment. You can check this with your manager or supervisor. If you are involved with the actual assessment of the individual, ensure that you make an accurate record of this using the correct documentation. Report your findings to your manager or supervisor so that information can be disseminated to the appropriate people and any special procedures or equipment can be made available. As with all other personal information your records need to be kept in a safe and secure place and confidentiality must be maintained. Be aware of how you can access, review and evaluate information about the training you need in order to use aids and equipment and to train others in their use.

Agreement on the skills identified

You must agree with the individuals, key people and others the skills that the individual needs to enable them to manage their lives and environment. These skills need to be monitored to ensure that they reflect the individual's choice and enable them to achieve

KUS 15

and/or maintain independence. Individuals and carers who require ongoing care and support must be given the names and contact numbers of the services and key people who will provide further help and assistance as required. You need to answer any questions that individuals may have and check they have understood your responses. The individual and their carers will need to be given advice on how they can assess their changing needs, and how they can access training, aids, equipment and resources to carry out the agreed outcomes and skills. See that the individual can demonstrate the necessary skills competently. Any changes in the individual's physical or mental health, or any changes relating to their carers or the environment, need to be reported and recorded as these will affect the individual's ability to safely manage their lives and the environment. A further assessment will need to be carried out to ensure that the individual is not at risk, and changes should be made accordingly. You must take into account any underlying factors affecting the health, well-being and behaviour of the individual and their ability and capability to achieve their targets. Take a holistic view of the individual, their lives and environment. Anything preventing the individual from achieving their goals needs to be discussed with everyone involved and measures should be taken to overcome the obstacles. It is important to recognise when the individual or others are placing limitations on the individual's ability to gain new skills due to their age or disability, e.g. not encouraging the individual to learn to cook or use technical aids. You have a responsibility to challenge this type of discrimination as it may limit the individual's independence and autonomy.

KUS 13, 20

KUS 1, 6

Support individuals to manage their life and environment

Margaret is 62 years old. She is married and lives at home with her husband who has a full-time job. They have two daughters who are both married and live nearby. Margaret is a housewife and is very house-proud. Until recently she has managed to undertake most of the housework herself and has been able to prepare a hot meal for her husband on his return home from work. For many years Margaret has suffered from arthritis which causes her a lot of pain and discomfort. Some days are worse than others. She is now finding it more difficult to undertake some of the tasks around the house, even some of her personal hygiene requirements, and as a result she is becoming rather depressed.

One day when Margaret was trying to vacuum the carpet she slipped on a rug and fell. Fortunately she was not seriously hurt and apart from some minor bruises she felt alright. Margaret's husband was quite concerned and suggested that Margaret made an appointment with her doctor the following day. Margaret's doctor prescribed some different medication and suggested that she could possibly do with some help in the home and that some minor adaptations or alterations could be made to her home in order for her to maintain her mobility and independence.

An assessment of her ability to cope with daily living and other activities was carried out and some suggestions were made regarding suitable adaptations to the kitchen. Margaret was shown a leaflet with specialised equipment, crockery and cutlery that would help her to manage. It was also suggested that some minor adaptations could be made to the bathroom such as bath and

▶

hand rails, and special taps that would make it safer and easier for her to carry out her own personal hygiene. Margaret was also told that there were other people who could help her to manage her life and environment. Margaret began to feel that she was no longer in charge of her own life or her environment. She became concerned that these other people would take over, and that she would lose her independence.

➤ How can Margaret be encouraged to communicate her needs, preferences and beliefs about the skills she requires to manage her life and environment?

➤ How should Margaret's family and other key people help her to accept these changes?

➤ What options do you think might be suitable for Margaret and her family, and what risks may be associated with these?

➤ What do you think Margaret's priorities might be?

➤ What type of additional and/or specialist support will Margaret require?

Key points – supporting individuals to identify the skills they need

- Work with others to identify the possible options available for individuals and assess any risks.

- Encourage and support the individual in communicating their preferences and beliefs about the skills they require.

- Assist the individual to prioritise their needs for managing their lives and the environment in the short term and the medium term.

- Identify the skills which will require additional and/or specialist support.

- Explain to individuals the need for any special procedures and equipment and what this involves.

- Agree with the individual, key people and others the skills that the individual needs to manage their lives and environment.

Support individuals to retain, regain and develop the identified skills

Element HSC344b

Once the necessary skills have been identified, individuals and their carers will still need support from you. They may be facing some big changes in their lives and they will have to make some very important choices and decisions. They will need to know that whatever they decide there will be plenty of support available to help them cope. As a rule, individuals learn the various skills they need to manage their lives and environment as they grow and develop from childhood to adulthood. Sometimes these skills are taken for granted because we have used them so often that they become second nature to us. When changes occur in our lives we occasionally find that these skills are not quite as strong as they used to be, or they may have been lost altogether. We may be encouraged to regain those skills or to learn new skills to help us manage our most basic needs and requirements. This can be very difficult, and depending on our circumstances we might find it simpler to just give up and let someone else do things for us. Individuals in your care may be faced with these dilemmas, and they will need your support to adapt to their changed circumstances.

Active support

KUS 2, 5, 19

You need to provide active support to enable individuals to take as much responsibility as possible for developing new skills, regaining and retaining former skills and making the best use of their current skills and abilities. You need to put the best interests of individuals at the centre of everything you do. Enable them to take responsibility (as far as they are able and within any restrictions placed upon them) to make and communicate their own decisions about their lives, actions and risks. You can give active support to the individual by encouraging them to do as much as possible for themselves in order to maintain their independence and physical ability. You can do this by reassuring them and helping them to stay motivated and enthusiastic. Some individuals will be able to pick up new skills without any real problems whereas others may not.

KUS 4, 5, 7, 17, 19

You need to be aware that the carers and other key people in the individual's life may not have undertaken a caring role before. The carer may be a son or daughter caring for an elderly parent, in which case there will be a role reversal. Find time to discuss their thoughts and feelings, and help them as much as you can. Carers have a right and a need to be adequately supported by the care services. They might find some activities embarrassing or may be unsure of others. For example, they need to be aware of infection control issues such as how to control the spread of infection. Advise them about correct hand washing before and after carrying out any activities or procedures with the individual. If they are assisting with personal hygiene or changing dressings, they should be informed how to dispose of waste safely and in the correct disposal bags and containers. Make sure they know why they should wear protective clothing and gloves. Alternatively they may need to be aware of the importance of the correct storage, handling and preparation of food, and basic hygiene procedures should be explained to them. You may find that the carer feels under pressure to do everything right for the individual. Remember that most of us think that no one can look after us better than we can. It is important that good standards are maintained at all times, and carers and key people need to be aware that they cannot force their own standards onto the individual they are caring for.

You will need to have a great deal of patience and understanding with the individual and with their carers to help them overcome any concerns they may have in learning and developing new skills. The individual needs to take some responsibility for themselves and their future well-being. Help them understand the long-term benefits and the satisfaction they will achieve from reaching their goals through their own efforts.

Work with the individuals and help them to use their current skills and abilities and to develop these further to meet their needs. They may be surprised that they still have these abilities, and this may encourage them to develop more skills to help them achieve or maintain some independence.

**Figure 4
Some individuals will be able to carry out certain activities using their current skills and abilities**

There may be some skills that the individual needs to regain, and by helping them to attempt these you will discover what they can do and what else they need to achieve. You may be caring for an individual who has just learned to carry out their personal hygiene activities, but they are still having difficulty getting dressed. Their carers may find it difficult to assist them and the individual may become impatient and unco-operative. When personal activities are involved consider the individual's beliefs and preferences in order to protect their privacy and dignity and to avoid humiliation and embarrassment for either the individual or their carer. You may be working with an individual who is just getting used to using a motorised wheelchair. They may have managed to achieve some manoeuvres but are having difficulty with others and are becoming agitated and depressed. It is essential that you do not push the individual or

KUS 2, 4, 5, 7, 17, 19

**Figure 5
There may be some skills that the individual needs to regain**

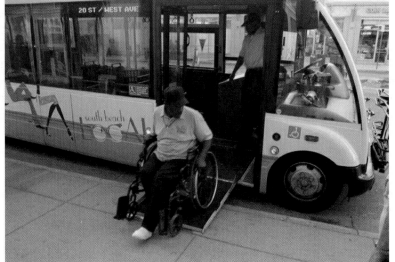

their carers to learn the skills they need. You need to keep the individual motivated and maintain their confidence, give them good feedback on their achievements. Often power and influence can be used and abused when supporting individuals to retain, regain or develop new skills – this must be avoided. Keep the individual motivated and maintain their confidence, give them positive feedback on their achievements.

The individual will need far more support from you if they are developing new skills. Make sure that you can demonstrate these skills to the individual and that you can give them adequate guidance and explanation about how to perform the skills and the reasons for them. If you are unsure then you will need to speak to your manager or supervisor so that the appropriate people can be involved in teaching the individual new skills. Remember, these new skills are for the benefit of the individual in being able to manage their lives and environment, so they need to know what they are doing and why they are doing it.

Figure 6
You may need to seek advice from your manager or other colleagues before demonstrating new skills to an individual

Agree goals with individuals

It is essential that you agree **goals** with individuals that will enable them to work at their own pace to acquire, regain and retain skills that are essential to their daily living.

Goals are individual and will depend on several factors including age, physical or mental condition, ability and capability, chosen language, level of understanding, culture, religion, beliefs and preferences. The records and case notes should outline what action needs to be taken and what assistance the individual requires. Individuals will each have their own pace of working and their own level of understanding, and these will need to be considered when you are assisting them to regain and retain the skills that they need.

Learning styles

KUS 10, 13

You will need to assess the individual's personal learning style. This is relevant when teaching new skills as well as when you are encouraging individuals to regain skills. Learning styles and preferences can be assessed by means of a questionnaire or by discussion. In 1982 Honey and Mumford developed a theory based on four learning types. These are as follows.

 Activists

Activists like to be involved in new experiences. They are open-minded and enthusiastic about new ideas but get bored with implementation. They enjoy doing things and tend to act first and consider the implications afterwards. They like working with others but tend to hog the limelight.

Activists learn best when they are:

- Involved in new experiences, problems and opportunities.
- Working with others in group tasks, role-playing.
- Being thrown in at the deep end with a difficult task.
- Leading discussions or meetings.

Activists learn less when they are:

- Listening to long explanations.
- Reading, writing or thinking on their own.
- Absorbing and understanding data.
- Following precise instructions to the letter.

Reflectors

Reflectors like to stand back and look at a situation from different perspectives. They like to collect data and think about it carefully before coming to any conclusions. They enjoy observing others and will listen to their views before offering their own.

Reflectors learn best when they are:

- Observing other individuals or groups.
- Able to review what has happened and think about what they have learned.
- Doing tasks without deadlines.

Reflectors learn less when they are:

- Acting as a leader or role-playing in front of others.
- Doing things with no time to prepare.
- Being thrown in at the deep end.
- Being rushed or worried by deadlines.

Theorists

Theorists adapt and integrate observations into complex and logically sound theories. They think problems through in a step-by-step way. They tend to be perfectionists who like to fit things into a rational scheme. They tend to be detached and analytical rather than subjective or emotive in their thinking.

Theorists learn best when they are:

- Put into complex situations where they have to use their skills and knowledge.
- In structured situations with clear purpose.
- Offered interesting ideas or concepts even though they are not immediately relevant.
- Able to question and probe ideas behind things.

Theorists learn less when they are:

- Participating in situations which emphasise emotions and feelings.
- Taking part in an activity that is unstructured or the briefing is poor.
- Doing things without knowing the principles or concepts involved.
- Out of tune with other participants, for example individuals with different learning styles.

Pragmatists

Pragmatists are keen to try things out. They want concepts that can be applied to their situation. They tend to get impatient with lengthy discussions and are practical and down to earth.

Pragmatists learn best when they are:

- Able to see an obvious link between the topic and the task/skill.
- Able to try out techniques with feedback, e.g. role-playing.
- Shown techniques with obvious advantages, e.g. saving time.
- Shown a model they can copy, e.g. in a video, DVD or diagram.

Pragmatists learn less when they are:

- Unable to see an obvious or immediate benefit.
- Lacking practical guidelines on how to do it.
- Faced with an event or learning that is all theory.
- Unable to see the apparent value to the learning – not everyone learns best from formal training.

Learning preferences

Some individuals develop a preference for a particular learning style, whilst others may be able to achieve a more holistic approach to learning. Many people think of learning in terms of memorising facts, but this is not the case. Much of the skill and knowledge that enables individuals to lead a happy successful life is learned practically through personal experience, rarely do individuals learn from experiences which just happen to them. One of the first principles of learning is being motivated to learn. Individuals need to be actively involved in trying to learn something through practice.

KUS 2, 8, 13

Rather than giving the individual too much to learn at once which could be over-powering, you need to break it down into smaller component parts or chunks so that they can learn a little bit at a time. They need to be able to take things one step at a time. Give them praise and encouragement as they achieve each step. Check with them when they are ready to move on to the next step. By using this method the individual will feel that they are actually getting somewhere and as they achieve each step they will begin to see and feel the benefits. They may feel more comfortable performing some skills or activities than others. Explain that you are willing to demonstrate these and give them all the support they need to achieve them.

You may find it necessary to repeat something several times before the individual is able to grasp what you are trying to convey. The skill may come easily to you, but the individual may find it more difficult to grasp, and you may need to think of different ways to help them to achieve it. If the individual uses a different language then you will have to arrange for an interpreter or translator to be present when demonstrating the skill to the individual. You should also be aware of any cultural restraints that may exist in relation to the individual or their carers when they are performing or assisting the individual with these skills. For instance, some cultures have very strict preferences relating to personal hygiene, showering and toileting. If an individual is unable to perform these activities it will be very embarrassing for them to have someone else deal with them. They would not be happy about someone of the opposite sex or even someone younger than themselves undertaking these tasks for them. It is important that you recognise any differences and deal with these accordingly. If you think that you may have a problem with this then you need to seek the help and advice of your

**Figure 7
An interpreter
might need to be
present if there is
a language barrier**

manager or supervisor. Remember to maintain privacy, dignity and respect with all individuals at all times.

Identifying appropriate methods

You need to identify the appropriate **methods** that will enable individuals to build on their strengths when developing, regaining and retaining the skills important to their daily living, and to enable them to achieve their agreed goals. Take into account the individual's personal learning style as previously discussed. You may be working with an individual who prefers to watch you doing an activity or performing a skill first of all before doing it themselves. Alternatively, they may feel confident to try it out first, and just need your reassurance and encouragement to complete it.

Individuals each have their own ways and their own strengths in dealing with life and situations. Encourage them to build on these strengths to help them regain or retain their current skills and abilities. Ideally they should be able to do this for themselves, but it may still be necessary for you to help them with the assistance and support of their carers and key people.

KUS 5, 15, 19

You need to talk to other members of the care team, the individual and their carers in order to obtain their thoughts and opinions on the type of support that may be required. It is important to agree a definite action plan so that everyone is aware of their role and responsibility in supporting the individual to achieve their goals. Several methods may be suggested and the individual and key people may need support to select the methods they think are most likely to enable them to progress. This will depend upon the individual's physical, emotional or mental condition and the support available to them.

Some individuals may need a lot of support to help them progress, whilst others may need very little. It may be necessary for some individuals to take it slowly and learn a bit at a time. Alternatively, others may just want to get on with it and see how they progress. Whichever method is selected the situation will need to be monitored and reassessed if changes occur. It is important to maintain health and safety and minimise risk. However, some risk is a crucial element of life, and it has been said that a life without any risk in it is no life at all.

You may be caring for a young adult who has sustained a physical disability resulting in them being in a wheelchair. They may not have lost any of their mental ability and will be able to decide for themselves the activities and skills they need to progress and achieve their goals. The individual may wish to continue living at home and might have a job which they wish to return to. Their choices and preferences must be respected.

As a result of their illness or disability some individuals may not be able to return to their usual type of work and may need to be retrained for another job. Not only will they have to deal with the change in their physical or mental health, they will also have to cope with learning new skills to enable them to earn a living and maintain some of their independence. They may be able to access re-employment or re-enablement programmes in the community. The individual and their carers and key people will need plenty of support during this time to access the appropriate facility that will meet their particular needs.

Relevant legislation

KUS 1, 8

You need to recognise that the individual has a right to more than simply being looked after. The Chronically Sick and Disabled Persons Act 1970 makes provision for the welfare of individuals with disabilities. It gives local authorities a positive duty to provide amenities and services recommended under the Act. These duties include:

- To establish the numbers of disabled persons in their area in order to determine their needs and publicise services.
- The duty to provide the following services (where they are satisfied there is a need):
  - practical assistance at home
  - help with radio and television
  - library, recreational and educational facilities
  - assistance to take up facilities outside the home
  - assistance with travel to/from their home to these services
  - meals in the home and elsewhere
  - holidays
  - aids and adaptations to the home
  - a telephone and any special equipment necessary to enable the person to use the telephone
  - additional facilities designed to secure greater safety, comfort or convenience at home.

Although this Act applies to all ages, in practice it is often difficult for people over the age of 60 to achieve registration under the Act, and in practice you may find that many services are not provided. Although the above services may be widely available, each authority is able to decide whether there is a need for them to be provided in their area.

Other Acts you need to be aware of (relating to adults)

Disability Discrimination Act 1995

The Act is designed to prevent discrimination against individuals with disabilities in the areas of employment, access to education and transport, housing and obtaining goods and services. Employers and landlords must not treat a disabled person less favourably than a non-disabled person. New transport facilities must meet the needs of disabled individuals, and colleges, shops and other services must ensure that disabled individuals can use their services.

Disability Rights Commission Act 1999

This Commission has the power to conduct formal investigations and to serve no-discrimination notices, make agreements and take other action to prevent discrimination against individuals with a disability. The Commission can also give information to individuals who believe they have experienced discrimination.

Mental Health Act 1983

This Act forms the framework for service provision for individuals with mental health problems or learning disability. There are provisions within this legislation for social services departments to assume responsibility for individuals who are so mentally impaired that they are not able to be responsible for their own affairs.

National Health Service and Community Care Act 1990

This Act ensures that individuals in need of care are appropriately assessed and have rights of complaint. The Act allows for service-purchasing by authorities and sets out responsibilities for all care agencies, both statutory and independent, to work colla-boratively. You need to be aware that if an individual is suitably involved and empowered they may well begin to complain more, and those who do not complain at all may have such low expectations or low self-esteem that they will accept anything.

The safety and efficiency of equipment and materials

To prevent any danger, harm or injury to the individual, you must check the safety and efficiency of any equipment and materials before, during and after use in accordance with the Health and Safety at Work Act 1974. You need to understand your responsibilities regarding health and safety. This will be explained either in the organisational policy or your contract of employment.

Health and Safety at Work Act 1974

All care settings are covered by this Act and it places the responsibility for all aspects of health and safety on employers and employees (see unit HSC32 for more details).

Figure 8
Make sure aids and equipment are safe to use

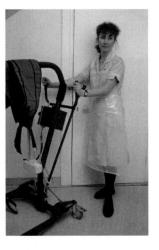

It is your responsibility to ensure that any equipment or materials to be used by the individual are fit for the purpose. Check that everything is in good working order and that it is safe for the individual to use. If you are unfamiliar with some of the equipment or materials used, it is your responsibility to speak to your manager or supervisor and ask for someone who is appropriately trained to take over. You must never put yourself or the individual at risk. Always check that the equipment or materials are safe during use. If either you or the individual feel that there is something wrong, you must stop the activity immediately and ask for help, for example when using the hoist to move an individual from bed to a chair or into the bath. Do not leave the individual unattended at any time whilst they are using equipment or materials. After use you need to check the equipment again to make sure it is clean and still in good working order, and replace everything in the correct place. If you find any faults or problems with any of the items used they will need to be withdrawn from use, correctly labelled and reported to your manager or supervisor to prevent harm or injury to anyone.

Promoting safety

KUS 3

Whenever an individual and their carers are undertaking any activity you need to support them in ways that promote the safety, involvement and confidence of all involved, and consider any cultural and spiritual beliefs and preferences so that the activities are undertaken in ways that promote good standards of care. Some of the activities could relate to preparing food, eating and drinking, dressing, bathing and washing, mobility (including getting in and out of bed), navigating the environment or cleaning the environment. It is important that the individual's personal preferences and beliefs are taken into account, but at the same time the carer's preferences and beliefs should also be considered. Encourage the individual and anyone involved in the activity to talk to you about any worries, issues or concerns they may have. Give appropriate reassurance, remembering that you cannot promise anything that is outside your authority or responsibility to provide. If you feel that there may be particular implications then you need to seek advice from your manager or supervisor. The individual's overall safety is of paramount importance and you have a responsibility to promote that.

KUS 14, 17

Before starting an activity you need to check that everyone understands what they are doing and feels confident doing it. The individual may not have carried out the activity for themselves for a while, or it may be a completely new activity which they need to learn. If their carers are helping with the activity, it may be the first time that they have assisted another individual and it might feel strange to them. Involve them in the activity so that they can become more confident. Make sure that you deal promptly with any questions or concerns and respond in a way that the individual understands. Let them know that you will give them all the support they need and that they should not be embarrassed to ask for help. The individual may be learning to use aids to help them get dressed or to help them to eat and drink, or they may be learning to walk with crutches or a walking frame, or even to use an electric wheelchair to assist their mobility. Demonstrate the activity slowly, give them adequate coaching to enable them to learn the activity or skill and talk them through the different stages, repeating any they are not sure about. Encourage the individual and their carers to be aware of any safety aspects that relate to the activity or the equipment or materials they are using, and make sure that the appropriate training has been given.

KUS 2, 5, 9, 19

Whatever the activity, it is important that you recognise and adhere to any cultural or spiritual beliefs and preferences. For example, some cultures prefer to wash under running water so they would prefer a shower rather than a bath. In that case, there would be no point explaining how to run the bath water. These are very important aspects of an individual's life and so they should be respected and not discriminated against. Always make sure that the individual and their carers are comfortable under-

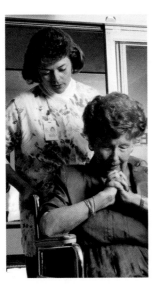

taking the activity, and if you have any concerns about their ability to carry out any aspect of it then you should ask them if they need further explanation or if they need someone to show them again what they need to do. Never force the individual to perform an activity that they are having difficulty with or that they feel they cannot do. That would seriously affect their confidence and they might just give up and not want to try again.

Giving constructive feedback

The more you work with individuals the more you will be able to recognise their determination in wanting to do things for themselves. You will know the ones who may need more encouragement and motivation and those who want to run before they can walk. You will also recognise the individuals who do not want to try to do things for themselves at all. In that case the individual and their carers may need to undertake the activity together. They will need to learn to trust each other in order to work together. You should give them the appropriate advice and support, without taking over, and recognise their success. Give the individuals and their carers **constructive feedback** on their achievements and progress. This will give them more encouragement to continue.

Receiving constructive feedback, praise and encouragement motivates the individuals to progress. Very rarely do people give praise where it is due, and when we receive praise it helps us to feel better about ourselves and increases our motivation. Try to find out just what motivates the individuals in your care.

Individuals may respond to regaining, retaining or developing skills differently. They may have feelings of loss, frustration, anger or depression. All of these feelings will need to be responded to differently as they will impact on their motivation, and so clear and understandable feedback is essential. Always remember to give constructive feedback and not destructive feedback!

Modifying your approaches

You will need to modify your approaches if an individual becomes distressed, is in pain or communicates their wish to stop or change the activity. Their ability to cope with retaining, regaining or developing the skills they need will depend on their physical or emotional condition. They may carry out some activities but become uncomfortable or distressed during others. Assessment is ongoing by observing the individual during activities. If you feel that the activity is causing them some pain and discomfort then the activity should be stopped. The individual may not actually tell you they are in pain, and it will be up to you to recognise the signs. They may cry out in pain or discomfort or their facial expression may indicate that they are in pain. They may also become distressed, which in turn can make them frustrated or even angry. If that is the case it will prevent them from carrying out the activity effectively. They may even tell you that they want to stop the activity, or ask you if there is an easier way to do it. They may be frustrated by their new limitations or they may tire easily. You need to listen to what they are saying and let them know that you will speak to your manager or supervisor and see if the activity can be modified so that they can manage it more easily.

Seeking advice and support

It is essential that you seek advice and support from others where any safety issues have arisen. No matter what the activity or the care being given, it is essential that you report any concerns about safety issues. Concerns need to be recorded accurately and legibly using the correct documentation, and you must date, sign and print your name. These records need to be given to your manager or supervisor so that the appropriate action can be taken to deal with the issues. Never put yourself or the individuals in your care at risk from any harm or injury as a result of inappropriate safety measures.

If you experience any conflict between yourself, the individuals, their carers or key people then this needs to be dealt with calmly and as soon as possible to prevent the conflict from escalating. Try to find out what the problem is by asking everyone concerned. It may be something quite simple that you can deal with yourself or you may need to ask your manager or another colleague for advice and support.

The individual may not want to continue with the activity or they may be in distress or pain. If this is the case you should sit and talk to the individual and find out what the problem is. They may just need more encouragement or instruction from you, or they may need some medication for pain or discomfort. If they are in pain or distressed they will not be able to concentrate on the activity and may become upset or angry and not want to be bothered. You will need to be patient with the individual and with their carers and give them time to learn and develop the new skills.

Support to regain and retain skills

Mohammed is 25 years old. He has a wife and three small children – two daughters and one son. He can speak English fairly well, but his wife speaks only a little. Mohammed works for a manufacturing company as a fork-lift truck driver. He was involved in an accident at work causing the fork-lift truck to tip over, and heavy pallets fell on top of him. Mohammed was seriously injured and was admitted to hospital.

Mohammed has been diagnosed with minor brain damage. It has affected his speech and he has reduced movement in his legs. His wife and other members of his family are very supportive of him, and they have told him that they will help him as much as they can.

After a period of time in hospital, it was decided, following discussion with his wife and family and other care providers, that Mohammed would be transferred to a unit for younger disabled individuals for care and rehabilitation. He has been receiving physiotherapy on a regular basis and has started to use a wheelchair to help his mobility. He can understand what is being said to him, but sometimes he gets angry and frustrated because he is not always able to communicate effectively. His family is pleased that he will be discharged from hospital, and his wife has said that she would eventually like him to come home.

➤ What active support will you need to provide for Mohammed?
➤ What goals should be set with Mohammed?
➤ How will you identify which skills Mohammed will be able to regain or retain?
➤ How will Mohammed's family be able to help him manage, and what support will they need?

Key points – supporting individuals to retain, regain and develop identified skills

- Provide active support to the individual and encourage them to take as much responsibility as possible to use their current skills and abilities and to develop new ones.
- Agree the goals that the individual will need to work to in regaining, retaining and developing skills that are important to their daily living.
- Identify the methods that will enable the individuals to build on their current strengths, and support individuals to select the most appropriate methods that will help them to progress. Modify these if the individual is in pain or distress or asks to stop the activity.
- Ensure the safety and efficiency of equipment and materials before, during and after use.
- Give constructive feedback to the individuals and their carers.
- Seek advice and support from others where any safety issues or conflicts arise.

Support individuals to evaluate the use of the skills in managing their lives and environment

Element HSC344c

Agree criteria

You need to work with individuals, key people and others to agree the criteria for evaluating the effectiveness of the activity and methods used. You may be asked to take part in evaluating the effectiveness of the skills and activities that the individual has developed to help them manage their lives and environment. It is possible that you were involved in teaching the skills to the individual and to their carers and that you were happy with their progress. It is important that there is agreement on the specific criteria that will be used to monitor and review the individual's ongoing progress, and that everyone involved works to the same criteria. Everyone involved should refer to the individual's care plan and the care outcomes that were agreed. The individual, their carers and other key people need to contribute to the discussion, and their opinions, reflections and suggestions must be considered. Information and reports need to be available from key people and others involved in supporting the individual so that progress can be evaluated and to ascertain whether or not changes need to be made to benefit the individual.

Highlight extra support

You need to work with individuals, key people and others to assess their progress and highlight where extra support is needed. Some individuals may have made good progress with the support of their carers and key people, and their confidence and ability may have improved sufficiently to enable them to manage their lives and environment. Other individuals may not have progressed quite so well and might be struggling to cope. Perhaps there have been changes to their health and/or family circumstances due to illness or other problems. This may have affected their daily lives and their environment. All of these things can interfere with the individual's ability to make effective progress. Depending on their circumstances, they may have been too embarrassed or afraid to ask for extra help and support. Make it clear that they can seek help from other people or services. The extra support they need may be for a short period of time or it may be required over a longer period. The individual or their carers may be in a position to let you know the type of extra support that they think they need. They need to be given the appropriate advice and guidance to meet their needs.

Review future needs

The ongoing support needs of the individual need to be planned according to their personal circumstances and health and social care needs, and you should work with the individual and others to review these. The individual may need to learn new skills to help them manage their daily activities and their lives, and you should provide support and reassurance to achieve this and to maintain their independence as far as possible. You will need to review their future needs too. For example, whether or not the individual will be able to continue living at home with the help and support of the services and facilities available to them, or whether they may require residential or nursing care. Ideally the individual needs to be supported to live at home and manage their lives and environment as long as they possibly can if this is their preference. Although providing ongoing help and support to the individual and their carers is very exhilarating and rewarding when you see them making progress, there may come a time when they no longer need you, and you may go through a kind of bereavement and feel lost. You need to accept this and move on – there are others who need you!

Identify new skills now and in the future

You need to work with individuals and others to identify any new skills that they need to acquire to meet their changing needs and circumstances both at the present time and in the future. As previously mentioned this will depend on the changes that have happened either with their health needs or personal and social circumstances. By working with the individual and their carers you will be able to identify how the individual is progressing, and you will be able to encourage them to develop new skills. It is possible that the individual or their carers will let you know when they are ready to learn new skills. Encourage their motivation and enthusiasm. Alternatively, other service providers may feel that the individual would benefit from learning new skills to improve their mobility and independence. If you feel that the individual's physical or mental health needs have changed and they are struggling to carry out the activities needed to manage their daily lives, you must report this to your manager or supervisor so that a further assessment of the individual's needs and the skills they require can be arranged. If the individual's support networks and personal circumstances have changed, you must report this to your manager or supervisor to avoid putting the individual at risk of harm.

The individual's rights should always be considered. They have the right to:
- Be respected.
- Be treated equally and not discriminated against.
- Be treated in a dignified way.
- Privacy.
- Be protected from danger and harm.
- Be cared for in the way that they choose.

- Access information about themselves.
- Communicate using their preferred methods of communication and language.

Ensuring a co-ordinated approach

You will need to work with others to ensure that a co-ordinated approach is used to identify and meet the individual's short-, medium- and long-term needs. Everyone who is involved in the individual's care will have a different perspective on what they think the individual's needs are. There should be regular meetings between the service providers to assess what the individual's needs are likely to be over a specific period of time and to prioritise and agree how these are to be achieved. The individual and their carers need to be involved in these discussions in order that their requirements can be met. Several different service providers may be involved in the care of the individual, such as the physiotherapist, occupational therapist, medical staff, nurses and health visitors, and social services. Some individuals will require the support of a lot of people whereas other individuals may not need quite so many. Whatever the situation, there needs to be a co-ordinated approach so that the most effective care and support can be given. The care plan needs to show the outcomes for the individual and the different stages of involvement for each of the care providers. Everyone has an important part to play in the care of the individual and it is essential that everyone works together to avoid duplication of care.

Recording and reporting

You must record and report on actions, processes and outcomes, in accordance with confidentiality agreements and legal and organisational requirements in line with the Data Protection Act 1998 (see unit HSC31 for more details).

All information about the individual, whether it is written or stored on a database, must be kept safe and secure and stored in a locked cupboard or office. You need to understand and adhere to confidentiality requirements for information relating to individuals in your care. Everyone working in the health and social care fields is expected to work within the guidelines on confidentiality, and individuals need to be assured that any information held about them is confidential. You need to be aware of and familiarise yourself with your organisation's requirements.

Support individuals to evaluate the use of skills to manage their lives

Jane is 46 years old. She lives at home with her husband and two young daughters, Karen and Kathryn. Jane's husband Bob, who is 52, suffered a mild stroke a few months ago and was admitted to his local hospital for treatment. He made quite a good recovery. He had a slight limp and weakness down one side, but he felt that he was ready to go home. Bob had been working with the occupational therapist who had assessed his ability to carry out activities relating to his daily living and his ability to walk. Bob and his family had been involved in discussions about the skills he needed to regain and develop to enable him to manage at home. They all agreed to help him as much as they could. Once he felt confident to use the skills identified he was discharged home.

Bob has been at home for a few weeks now. One of the community staff visited him. She found that he was struggling to get upstairs to use the bathroom, and he said he was finding it difficult to make himself something to eat and drink at lunchtime. He said that his wife had a part-time job in the mornings and the girls were at school. Bob said the family was helping him when they were at home, but that Jane was beginning to feel very tired as she was responsible for looking after him, taking the girls to school and going to work. He said that Jane was becoming depressed because she felt she was letting him down. She had asked him not to tell anyone. He asked if there was anything else that could be done to help him improve his ability to cope in order to take some of the pressure off Jane.

➤ *Who would need to be involved in evaluating the effectiveness of the activities performed by Bob?*

➤ *What extra support might Bob need?*

➤ *What new skills might Bob need to acquire to help him meet his changing needs and circumstances?*

➤ *Who should be involved in the discussions regarding Bob's short-, medium- and long-term needs?*

➤ *Why did Jane tell Bob not to tell anyone that she was depressed?*

➤ *What extra support might Jane need?*

➤ *What actions should be taken and what records should be made?*

Key points – supporting individuals to evaluate the use of skills in managing their lives and environment

- Agree, with the individual and others, the criteria for evaluating the effectiveness of the activity and the methods used.
- Assess their progress with the individual and others and highlight where extra support may be needed.
- Work with the individual and others to review their future needs and the skills they require to meet changing needs and circumstances.
- Ensure that a co-ordinated approach is used to identify and meet the individual's short-, medium- and long-term needs.
- Record and report on actions, processes and outcomes, and maintain confidentiality agreements according to legal and organisational requirements.

Unit HSC344

Are you ready for assessment?

Support individuals to retain, regain and develop the skills to manage their lives and environment

This unit is about how you support individuals to identify the skills that they need to manage their lives and living environment. It is about how you work with individuals, key people and other practitioners and services to support individuals to retain, regain and develop the identified skills. It is also about how you support individuals to evaluate the use of those skills in managing their lives and living environment.

Your assessment will mainly be carried out through observation by your assessor and this should provide most of the evidence for the elements in this unit. If your assessor is unable to observe you directly then you may be able to use the testimony of an experienced colleague acting as an expert witness. You will need to discuss this with your assessor. Evidence of your knowledge and understanding will be demonstrated through observation, your assessor examining work products, e.g. reports, minutes of meetings, as well as through answering oral and/or written questions.

You need to be aware when planning assessments that this unit also relates to the core units, in particular HSC31, HSC32 and HSC35, and other optional units so you may also be able to evidence performance criteria for these.

You should take into account that you may need to be observed in the individual's home. Therefore you need to explain about the assessment and seek their permission for your assessor to visit. If their visit would be intrusive you will need to consider alternative evidence-gathering methods, e.g. expert witness testimony.

Direct observation by your assessor

Your assessor or an expert witness will need to plan to see you carry out the performance criteria (PCs) in each of the elements in this unit. The performance criteria that may be difficult to meet through observation are:

- **HSC344a PC 6**
- **HSC344b PCs 8, 9**
- **HSC344c PC 6**

Other types of evidence

You may need to present other forms of evidence in order to:

- Cover criteria not observed by your assessor.
- Show that you have the required knowledge, understanding and skills to claim competence in this area of practice.
- Ensure your work practice is consistent.

Your assessor may also need to ask you questions to confirm your knowledge and understanding and ensure that you can apply this to your practice.

Preparing to be observed

You must make sure that your workplace and any individuals and key people involved in your work agree to you being assessed. Explicit, informed consent must be obtained before you carry out any assessment activity that involves individuals or which involves access to confidential information related to their care.

Before your assessments you should read carefully the performance criteria for each element in the unit. Try to cover as much as you can during your observation but remember that you and your assessor can also plan for additional sources of evidence should full coverage of all performance criteria not be possible.

Check your knowledge

- Describe how you would identify possible choices for individuals and any risks that have to be managed.
- Why would it be necessary to identify the individual's current skills and abilities?
- How would you identify skills that need to be developed for which additional and/or specialist support would be required?
- Why would it be necessary to explain to individuals why special equipment or procedures are being used for assessment?
- Describe how you would provide active support to assist individuals in developing new skills.
- Why is it important to set goals with the individual?
- Why should you give constructive feedback to the individual about their progress and success?
- What action would you take if conflict occurred between you and the individual or key people?
- Why should there be specific criteria for evaluating the effectiveness of an activity and the methods used?
- What is the reason for evaluating the effectiveness of an activity?
- How can their changing needs and circumstances affect the progress of the individual?
- What records should you make, and who would you report to regarding actions, processes and outcomes?
- Why is confidentiality of information important?

Plan, agree and implement development activities to meet individual needs

This unit is about planning, agreeing and implementing development activities to meet the needs of the individual. These may be intellectual activities or activities that help individuals to regain their skills, enable them to keep fit and mobile, and help them to interact with others.

The unit has three elements:

- **HSC351a** *Identify and agree development activities to meet individual needs*
- **HSC351b** *Plan and implement development activities with individuals and others*
- **HSC351c** *Evaluate and review the effectiveness of the development activities*

Introduction

Use of development activities

Development activities are wide ranging, as shown in Figure 1.

**Figure 1
The different types of development activity**

Physical: games, walking, horse riding, sports, dancing

Creative: arts and crafts, cooking, drama, poetry, gardening, music

Social: bus trips, barbecues, entertainment, music, reminiscence, cultural activities

Intellectual: table games, quiet games, reading, meetings, reality orientation therapy

Individual: reading, massage, aromatherapy, tacticle therapy

Spiritual: visits from religious leaders, e.g. priest, Imman, Rabbi, or attending religious services, e.g. Mass

Development activities play an important part in health and social care settings. They help to promote the individual's physical, social, emotional, intellectual and spiritual needs. They can be used on a daily, weekly or occasional basis and will form part of the individual's care plan. They are used to empower and stimulate the individual.

KUS 1, 2, 11

The individual experiences choice in deciding to participate in as many or as few of the activities as they wish. In this way decision making and participation are promoted. The individual can expect to enhance and improve their quality of life through development activities. They can be fun to undertake, bringing together individuals in a care setting and creating a friendly and enjoyable environment.

Each development activity should be planned and discussed with the individual before it is commenced. During these discussions cultural and religious values can be incorporated and promoted according to the individual's preferences.

Afterwards a full evaluation of the activity should be carried out to see how it has met the needs of the individual. It is also important to find out if they enjoyed the activity and felt it was beneficial as this will help you to decide whether to repeat the activity. Development activities are suitable for all individuals.

Activities can be planned to help in the retention of skills and abilities, e.g. using computers, cooking. They can also provide stimulation and interest, e.g. puzzles, art and craft and visits.

KUS 10, 11

Activities can also be used with individuals who are recovering from ill health, for example physiotherapy can improve **fine** and **gross motor skills**. Alzheimer's disease can improve, with a reduction of behavioural symptoms. Some activities, e.g. dancing, can also slow down the progression of symptoms. Activities can help during recuperation from illness by reducing boredom and providing stimulation.

Cycle of development activities

In some care settings it is the same person who assesses, develops, implements and reviews development activities. In other settings different aspects of the process will fall to different staff. You need to check the policy and procedure in your setting to ensure that the individual receives good quality care.

No matter what the procedure, in order to produce development activities that meet the needs of the individual it is important that the full cycle takes place.

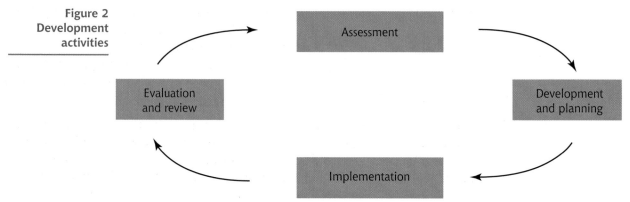

Figure 2
Development
activities

Element HSC351a

Identify and agree development activities to meet individual needs

Identify development activities

It is your role as a carer to support individuals to identify and communicate their needs and preferences about their development activities.

Communicate needs and preferences

The individual is central to the identification of a development activity. By focusing on their needs and preferences you can meet the needs identified in the care plan. Individual needs are shown in Figure 3.

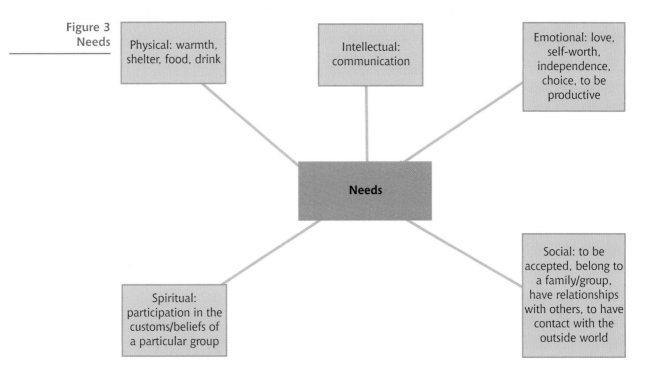

Figure 3
Needs

Ask the individual what their needs are and listen carefully in order to identify them. You should communicate with the individual using their preferred language. If any support is required this should be provided, for example support with spoken language, use of signs, symbols, writing, objects of reference, communication passports, non-verbal forms of communication, computers or an interpreter. Further information can be found in unit HSC31.

KUS 1, 2

Some individuals may not be able to identify their needs and preferences, e.g. individuals with limited insight. In this case the individual's needs would have been identified by others such as family, friends and carers. You may also consult specialist practitioners, e.g. physiotherapists and occupational therapists, to identify needs.

Assessing is about finding information in order to plan development activities that serve a purpose for the individual. Any assessment is likely to reflect the contributions of:

- The individual.
- Other members of staff.
- Family members and other carers.
- Practitioners involved in running the activity.

Always try to keep the individual central to the process – you can ask them to complete a self-assessment audit. Other methods of assessment include:

- Observation of the individual.
- Designing an assessment framework.
- Using assessment methods designed by a professional, e.g. **Bereweeke**, **Portage** and the Personal Record System (Schlesinger and Whelon).

It is also important to take account of the individual's interests and previous recreational activities when identifying developmental activities. Again this can be achieved through active listening and consultations with others. If you know what the individual's interests are, you are more likely to pick a suitable activity that they wish to participate in.

KUS 1, 2

Developmental activities should promote care for individuals in a manner and in an environment that maintains or enhances dignity and respect. You should therefore recognise the individuality of each participant. You need to offer choice of activity in relation to each plan of care. You could encourage the individual's participation by supporting them to interact with members of the community. Emphasise the individual's strengths and abilities as this will help the individual to feel confident and competent in what they do.

It is also important that cultural and religious factors are taken into consideration when planning activities. For example, some cultures do not allow certain foods to be eaten or women to participate in activities with men.

When preparing information on the activity and when instructions are given you need to be aware of the language needs of individuals.

Range of development activities

KUS 10

It is important that you identify development activities that meet the needs of the individual. There are a wide range of activities that can be grouped according to the type of development they are enhancing.

Intellectual activities

These can include any activity that uses thinking and reasoning skills. Intellectual activities play a large part in our lives as we are thinking and reasoning all of the time.

**Figure 4
Intellectual
activities**

Puzzles

Crosswords

Card games

Jigsaws

Reminiscence

Games: chess
and other
board games

Reading

Computers

The benefits of intellectual activities for the individual can be an improvement in thinking and concentration. An individual's attention span may also be increased and memory can improve. Problem-solving skills can also improve and this is important for adults who are regaining lost abilities.

Intellectual activities can also support the development of language skills, which will be important for people who are maintaining and recovering existing vocabulary. By improving language skills the individual is able to express feelings, experience increased confidence, maintain relationships and problem solve.

Physical activities

These are activities that involve the use of gross motor or **fine manipulative skills**. Using muscles the individual can maintain strength and increase fitness. They assist the individual to keep fit and mobile.

Physical activities provide the individual with many benefits. The **cardiovascular system** is improved as the heart rate increases and the heart becomes stronger. The **respiratory system** is also affected as exercise increases the breathing rate and more oxygen is taken in. Physical activity can also affect the digestive system by toning muscles, controlling appetite and improving bowel function. Social skills can be

**Figure 5
Physical activities
provide many
benefits**

Armchair
aerobics

Games, e.g.
skittles, bowls,
basketball,

Music and
dance

Gardening

Walking

Swimming

improved as communication and friendship are encouraged. There is also an emotional benefit of taking part in physical activities. They can increase happiness and allow for self-expression.

Other activities, for example doing jigsaws or completing crafts, can help with fine motor skills. These can also be intellectually stimulating and can enhance the individual's social life, for example dancing.

Social activities

Social activities are important as individuals can establish new relationships and maintain existing ones. They can help individuals to participate and interact with others. Social activities can include interactions with family and friends as well as groups. By maintaining good relationships individuals can raise their self-esteem and self-image and develop a sense of identity. Social needs are identified by Maslow as being important in order to reach self-actualisation (see unit HSC31). Social activities can also help to support an individual's communication skills and sensitivity towards others. Encouragement and support to gain social skills may be required to help individuals who have lived alone for a period of time.

Figure 6
Social activities

Drama

Quizzes

Music and dance

Meals together

Team games

Discussions

Emotional activities

These activities can improve well-being and help to release emotions and feelings. This also reduces stress and can strengthen an individual's sense of identity which can help to develop self-confidence and self-fulfilment.

KUS 4

It is important not to make assumptions about appropriate development activities based on age, gender or culture, e.g. assuming that older people would not be interested in computer-based activities or that younger people are not interested in traditional board games.

Emotional activities

Creative writing

Music and dance

Reminiscence

Arts and crafts

Drama

Pottery

Information and range of support

There are various sources of information that you can access about development activities. This will help you to explain to the individual and key people what the activity is, the reasons for doing it, how to access it and the resources required.

Local sources of information

KUS 8, 9

Some organisations will provide information on a number of activities, for example the Citizens Advice Bureau, the local council, the healthy-living centre or health centre. There may also be an information point for activities such as craft workshops or leisure centres and these can often be found in local libraries, charities, healthy-living centres, town halls, civic centres and tourist information centres. Staff at these places can also help you find the information that you require or can recommend where it can be obtained.

Specialist groups

Sometimes the individual will require information on a specific issue. Specialist groups can help to provide the information, for example about art courses, walking groups, specific cultural activities and groups. There are also specialist organisations that can provide information for individuals with a specific medical condition, for example Mencap, Age Concern, the Autistic Society, Alcoholics Anonymous and Narcotics Anonymous. The contact address and telephone number for these organisations can be found in the telephone directory, at the local library, Citizens Advice Bureau or council's voluntary services.

The internet

The internet can provide up-to-date information on a range of activities. This information may list the benefits to the individual and the group that the activity caters for, contact details and resources required by the individual. However, you will need access to a computer and internet facilities. Local libraries can provide this resource. You should also be aware that not all information published on the internet has been checked and therefore you should verify information before you give it to the individual. This can be achieved by using reliable websites, for example those of the government, universities, professional journals, research organisations etc. You can also help individuals and others to access information via the internet. This will help them to become self-managing and will increase their knowledge or even teach them new skills. The care setting should ensure that there are appropriate controls in place especially when you are supporting vulnerable adults. This will include having policies in place regarding internet use and access.

Once information has been obtained it should be stored where details can be accessed. This may be in a file or electronically in a central office computer. It is important that the information is kept up to date and is still relevant for the individuals in your care setting.

KUS 2, 12, 14, 15

Active support

When you are identifying development activities you should encourage the individual to be as self-managing as possible to encourage and maintain their independence. This should start with the individual identifying needs and preferences for accessing information on the activity. If this is not possible you may have to make arrangements to access the information on behalf of the individual.

You should encourage individuals to undertake activities that are designed to meet the interests and the physical, intellectual and social well-being of the individual, as identified in the assessment.

You should assess how much support and supervision the individuals are likely to require during the activity. This needs to include an analysis of the skills and abilities required to take part in the activity. You should have the appropriate level of support available to the individual so that the individual is safe and independence is encouraged. A risk assessment is also required to ensure the activity can be undertaken safely. This will include consideration of the number of individuals undertaking the activity at one time and the amount of support required. Consider the environment used and the resources required. You may have to consider altering the activity so that the risks are reduced. In this way you are promoting the health and safety of the individual and minimising the potential for harm.

Communication needs

The individual should be encouraged to communicate their needs and preferences using their preferred method of communication. This could be signs, symbols, pictures, writing, objects of reference, communication passports or technology. You need to refer to the individual's care plan to identify communication and other specific needs that require consideration before, during and after activities.

You should also be aware of the individual's preferred spoken language. The assessment of need and identification of development activities should take place using this language. It is important that all information is provided using the preferred language and communication should be facilitated through an interpreter if necessary. You will have to agree and make practical arrangements with everyone involved in order to implement the development activity (see also unit HSC31).

Resources for activities

In identifying the development activity preferred by the individual it is important to identify the resources required. This can include:

- Room/space for the activity, e.g. a large room for dancing.
- Staff to help with the activity, e.g. staff to support and partner individuals.
- Equipment required, e.g. CD player.
- Money to buy resources, e.g. the CDs.
- Specialist help, e.g. a dance instructor.
- Time required to complete the activity, e.g. an afternoon per week for one hour.

Inform your line manager of the resources required and make arrangements to run the activity. It is important to plan and prepare an alternative activity just in case your plans have to be changed. Individuals will be disappointed if things do not go ahead as planned, e.g. if you run out of resources or time. You need to have a plan of how the activity can be run in an alternative way, for example a different craft using the same materials but which takes less time.

KUS 3,
12, 15

Drawing up a plan

Once the individual's needs have been identified a plan can be drawn up. This can introduce the types of activities that will promote and enhance needs.

Using this plan you can discuss available alternatives with the individual and others. This will help you to select the activities that will meet the needs identified. Then you can plan the resources required for the activity and the timescales involved.

Roles and responsibilities

Clarify with your manager your own role and responsibilities in supporting the individual and others involved. You will then be able to relate your work to the legal requirements and codes of practice that relate to your area of work.

Legislation

KUS 1, 5, 6, 7

The provision of development activities is inherent in the guidelines for the care of individuals in a variety of care settings. This has been identified in the Care Standards, Essence of Care 2003, Residential Homes Registration and Inspection Standards 2004, NHS Plan 2000, Care Standards Act 2000, National Minimum Standards in Care Homes for Older People 2000 and Regulation of Care (Scotland) 2001. The Human Rights Act 1998 requires all action to be interpreted through the European Convention on Human Rights 1950. The Human Rights Act 1998 promotes choice, freedom of access and expression of religion.

Planning development activities

With support from others involved, you should identify the individual's needs. A review of the activity will include progress in attaining the personal outcomes identified by the individual and any agreed action regarding rehabilitation or specialist services.

KUS 12, 16

It is important to follow the roles and responsibilities laid down in organisational policies and procedures when identifying development activities for individuals. Different members of staff and practitioners will have different roles.

Others who may be involved in identifying development activities to meet individual needs can be those who work in your organisation or are provided by organisations other than your own, as described below.

Nurse

Nurses will ensure that the individual's recreational and leisure needs are identified. They will help to develop a plan of care with identifiable and realistic goals. This plan should be developed in conjunction with the individual.

Key worker

The key worker can help to identify the needs and preferences of individuals. They can help to identify and agree development activities to meet these needs. They will help to gather information about these activities and to identify the resources required. The key worker will also be responsible for recording and reporting the development activities identified.

Physiotherapist

The physiotherapist has a key role in the mobility of individuals. They are involved in the assessment of mobility needs and can improve the health and function of the individual in activities, for example swimming, sports and walking.

Occupational therapist

The occupational therapist is involved in the treatment of illness, both physical and mental, by way of activity. A large part of their work is with individuals who have a physical or learning difficulty. They work either one to one with an individual or in groups. Their aim is rehabilitation and the ability to complete activities of daily living. They will be involved in the assessment of needs and identification of activities to help improve skills, for example cooking. They can also advise about aids and adaptations required by the individual to complete the activity, for example adapted cutlery.

Diversional therapists

They recognise that leisure and recreational experiences are the right of all individuals. Diversional therapists promote involvement in leisure, recreation and play. This is achieved through reducing barriers to participation and providing opportunities for the individual to participate in activities. They can help with decision-making and participation when developing activities.

Specialist therapists

These are therapists who use specialised activities to promote the physical, social, emotional and intellectual needs of individuals. The following are specialist therapists.

Drama therapists

Drama therapists use drama to tell their own story to achieve relief of symptoms, reduce emotional symptoms and increase personal growth. They use theatre arts, puppetry, role play, pantomime and mask work. They help to identify needs such as isolation, and help to develop coping skills. The individual can express feelings and develop relationships. Drama therapy can be used with adults, the elderly and individuals with physical/learning disabilities, mental health problems and substance abusers.

Dance therapists

Dance therapists assess the individual and identify activities that use movement as a process that furthers the emotional, intellectual, social and physical integration of the individual. These can take place through classes, workshops and performances in a variety of settings, for example care homes and theatres. Dance therapy can be used with adults and those with physical and learning disabilities.

Music therapists

Music therapists can help individuals with self-expression and communication. This can help facilitate positive changes in behaviour and emotional well-being. Music therapists work in a wide range of care settings including hospitals, schools, day centres and community settings. Music therapy is used with individuals who have a wide range of needs including physical and learning disabilities, psychological disorders and sensory impairments. Many of the activities are improvised and suit the needs of the individual.

Arts therapists

Arts therapists use art materials to facilitate self-expression and reflection. Art therapy can offer the individual a chance to express their thoughts and feelings. Art therapists have a good knowledge of art processes and their relationship to healing. They can help individuals in residential and community settings, e.g. child and family centres, adult mental health, learning disabilities, prisons, palliative care and hospitals.

Recording

Once you have the individual's agreement to the development activity, record the discussion between yourself and the individual and also any discussions between practitioners. The views of the individual and others should be recorded. The plan needs to be dated and signed and entries must be easily identifiable.

Further information on record keeping can be found in element HSC31d.

Practical Example

Identifying development activities

Mr Clarke is a 70-year-old man who has been admitted to a nursing home. He has a history of Alzheimer's and often displays behavioural symptoms of agitation, anger, frustration and depression. He also wanders around the care setting and goes into other people's rooms.

You have spoken to his family and they have told you that Mr Clarke used to enjoy cooking, music and gardening. He had served as an engineer in the army and was keen to keep fit. He was a member of the local walking club and also enjoyed visiting art galleries.

You can remember attending a study day that explained the benefits of development activities in reducing behavioural symptoms and enhancing remaining skills. It was suggested that it is best to focus on the individual's previous interests and that activities should be done on a regular basis (perhaps the same time every day) to introduce routine and increase the individual's sense of stability.

➤ *What needs are identified?*

➤ *How would you carry out assessment of these needs?*

➤ *How do you feel development activities could help?*

➤ *What development activities could you suggest?*

➤ *What practitioners would need to be involved?*

➤ *What information would you record in the care plan?*

Key points – identifying and agreeing development activities

- Individuals should be involved in identifying needs and preferences for development activities.
- There are many different activities to support physical, social, emotional, intellectual and spiritual development.
- Development activities should focus on the abilities of the individual.
- Use different sources of information to find out about development activities.
- Identify your roles and responsibilities and those of others.
- Record and report information in a way that promotes confidentiality.

Plan and implement development activities with individuals and others

Plan development activities

Following assessment and identification of the development activity, you should be involved in the planning process. Careful and comprehensive planning will ensure that the activity works well and any unexpected occurrences are managed. You will also be able to plan any support that the individuals may require to carry out the activity.

By planning the activity you will be able to think in detail about the points shown in Figure 8.

Figure 8
Assess, identify and plan the development activity

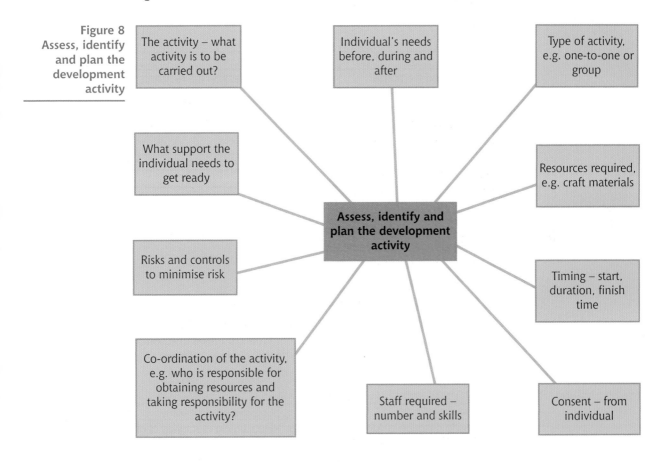

Activity Plan

Activity: Reminiscence on Childhood

Number of Adults: 10

Setting: Sitting Room Residential Home

Preparation Time: 1 hour

Activity Time: 1 hour

Staffing	Overall Aim
2 Care Assistants 1 Member of staff from museum	To enable the residents to remember their childhood
Materials	Specific Objectives
Video of childhood memories Television and video Items from museum e.g. toys	At the end of the session the residents will talk about their childhood The residents will be able to create a memory book

Areas Of Learning & Development	
Physical Development	
To use hands when using holding objects Use hands and fingers when compiling memory books	
Personal, Social & Emotional Development	Creative/Aesthetic Development
Recounting memories of childhood	Creating memory book Writing phrases to accompany pictures Writing down memories
Language Development	Cognitive development
Using terms to describe childhood e.g. games played, school	Recounting memories of childhood
Spiritual Development	

Implementation

Introduction To Activity

Development Of Activity

Conclusion Of Activity

Health & Safety Issues

Evaluation

How did the activity meet your objectives?

What was the value of the activity to the individual's development?

Evaluate your own role in the activity.

How could this activity be improved?

How could this activity be extended?

Co-ordination with others

KUS 12, 15, 16

If the activity requires the co-ordination of different members of the care team or specialist staff, for example a drama therapist, ensure that you have communicated with them in advance.

This will involve:

- Clarifying the **objectives** of the activity, e.g. what needs the activity will meet.
- Listing the goals/outcomes to be met, e.g. painting a picture.
- Breaking the activity down into individual tasks, e.g. selecting subject, preparing canvas, choosing paints.
- Giving details of the individuals involved, e.g. art therapist, individual.
- Communicating the needs of the individual, e.g. fine motor skills, emotional and social needs.
- Stating the date and time that the activity is to be carried out.
- Deciding the length of the activity, i.e. how long it is expected to last.
- Arranging where the activity is to take place, for example the conservatory.
- Organising resources, e.g. painting materials.
- Getting consent, e.g. from the individual.
- Taking account of special requirements, e.g. communication needs.

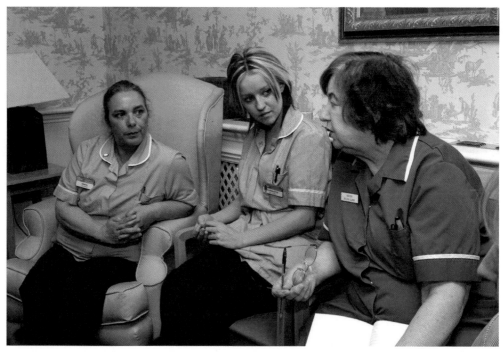

Figure 10
Co-ordinate the activity with the others involved

KUS 14

Co-operation from the individual, colleagues and others can be achieved through effective communication and consultation so that everyone is clear about their roles, responsibilities and expectations. Colleagues need to know the individual's support needs, the purpose and desired outcomes of the activity. They will be able to contribute to the evaluation and review of the activity.

Joint working has been encouraged through policy documents, such as Modernising Social Services 1998. This has enabled organisations to work in partnership to meet the complex needs of the individual. Check the policy and procedures of your organisation regarding working with other agencies, for example sharing information. You need to gain the individual's consent before sharing any information about needs.

Risk assessment

While planning the activity you need to carry out a **risk assessment**. This is carried out to identify a number of things:

- The individual's behaviour, e.g. do they have a tendency to be aggressive.
- Moving and handling issues.
- Problems with access.
- Perceived risk of the individual falling.
- Other health and safety issues, e.g. use of equipment.

KUS 5, 6

Risk assessment is a tool to enable the individual to maintain independence, empowerment, involvement and participation. Risk assessment is a careful examination of what could cause harm to people in the workplace. It also enables you to decide if steps are required to prevent accidents and to ensure good health. Risk assessment is also required by law.

All risk assessments have the same common basis, as shown in Figure 11.

Figure 11 Procedure for carrying out a risk assessment

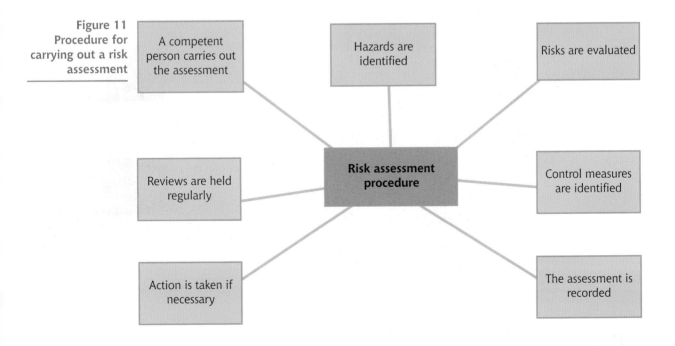

A competent person carries out the assessment

Hazards are identified

Risks are evaluated

Reviews are held regularly

Risk assessment procedure

Control measures are identified

Action is taken if necessary

The assessment is recorded

Figure 12
A completed risk
assessment form

RISK ASSESSMENT FORM

Name: Mary Robinson

Key worker: Kevin Stewart

Organisation: The Oaks

Assessment completed by: Steven Harrison

Date completed: 12.12.05

NATURE OF ACTIVITY Can be broken down into manageable sub-activities	HAZARD/S i.e. Anything associated with this activity with the potential to cause injury, disease etc	PEOPLE AFFECTED e.g Individual's, Staff, Public etc	EXISTING CONTROL MEASURES e.g. Training given, supervision, on-site training, standard operating procedures	SEVERITY	LIKELIHOOD	RISK RATING	ADDITIONAL PRECAUTIONS NECESSARY List any measures required in order to reduce the risk to 4 or less e.g PPE, inspections, systems of work etc
Mary wishes to take a bath once a week Mary wishes to undertake this activity alone	Mary is at risk of falls Mary is confused at times	Individual	Mary has been given advice about the risks of bathing Bath hoist is available for use, training has been given to key worker	3	2	6	Bath is to be filled and water temperature checked by Key Worker Bath hoist is to be used Floor is to be checked to ensure that it is dry Key worker is to check on Mary when she is bathing

RISK ASSESSMENT FORM

RISK RATING GUIDE

Severity × Likelihood = Risk Rating

SEVERITY		LIKELIHOOD	
4	Fatality	4	Probable
3	Major = Broken limb, > 24 hrs in hospital	3	Highly Likely
2	Serious = > 3 day injury/attends casualty	2	Likely
1	Minor = First Aid treatment only	1	Unlikely

I hereby give approval for this activity and am satisfied that it has been thoroughly Risk Assessed.

Signed: Su Kim

Date: 12.12.05

The activity plan should show the risks you have identified and the control measures you have put in place to minimise those risks, for example consideration of potential scenarios and how to deal with these and contingency plans, 'What to do in the event of ...'. The activity plan should include planning and agreeing with key people what action to take to minimise risks and how to deal with these, and any contingency plans that need to go into place.

Preparation of the environment

Before starting **development** activity you will need to consider the environment where the activity is going to take place.

Figure 13
Consider the environment where the activity is going to take place

Is there enough space?

Is the space/room suitable for the activity?

Does it have the correct facilities for the activity?

Is it taking place inside or outside?

What equipment do you need? Is it all ready? Does it all work?

Allow plenty of time to set up the environment. You will need to decide when to set up the equipment and how the space will be arranged. You may need to check that you have access to the environment before the activity begins and that equipment is available. Resources will need to be arranged where you have access to them.

Following the activity you should allow sufficient time to clear and restore the environment.

Individuals also need to be prepared to take part in development activities. This will include explaining the activity, obtaining consent, transport to the activity and protection of clothing (apron etc.).

Implement development activities

Roles and responsibilities

You need to be clear about your role and responsibilities and those of others when implementing the development activity. If you are responsible for carrying out the activity you should ensure that:

- Careful planning has taken place.
- The activity meets the individual's needs.
- Individuals have given their consent.
- All resources are gathered.
- Staff are informed and available.
- The environment is prepared.
- Equipment is available.
- The activity plan is available and you are familiar with it.

Support for other staff

KUS 12, 16

Your role could also be to provide support for other members of the care team during the activity. You should be clear about the role they have to play during the activity and you should be able to provide support through verbal and non-verbal communication.

If specialist staff from other agencies are involved in providing activities you need to liaise with them to ensure they have all the information they require regarding the individuals' needs and preferences. Make sure the environment is prepared and equipment obtained and that if necessary you are able to stay during the activity to support the individual and colleagues.

Support for the individual

KUS 14

KUS 13

Explain to the individual the purpose of the activity and how it will benefit them. Check that they are happy to continue and consent to undertaking the activity. You may need to support the individual during the activity. It is important that you get feedback from the individual about the activity and observe their response and engagement. Feedback and both positive and negative responses will help you to evaluate if the activity has achieved the planned outcomes. This needs to be recorded and reported according to organisational requirements. If the individual is unhappy about undertaking an activity or refuses to do it then you need to find out their reasons for this and reach a compromise. Record what happened and review the care plan and developmental activity outcomes.

Timing

Once everything is ready the activity can start. You should go through the activity plan step by step allowing enough time for each stage. The timings should be identified on the plan.

Careful timing of the activity at every stage will help it to be a success. If the activity has to be stopped because you have run out of time individuals may become frustrated and feel let down.

Changes in well-being

Development activities are used to help meet individuals' needs. It is therefore important that you assess their effectiveness in achieving this. An important part of your role is supporting individuals to communicate their feelings about their well-being, both positive and negative, that may result from participating in development activities. They may feel more confident or have made friends and that will make them feel better about their quality of life. Equally they may feel anxious about participating in the activity and this may increase their stress levels to the extent that they become distressed.

Factors affecting development

Genetics

KUS 10

Genetics can affect development as genes are a set of instructions passed from generation to generation. Genes contain the information required to make living organisms. Particular conditions result from genetic influences. Genes are carried on **chromosomes** and some illnesses and conditions are caused by a variation in these genes, for example Down's syndrome, Huntington's chorea, cystic fibrosis. These can have effects on development, such as physical growth or learning difficulties etc.

Lifestyle factors

Some lifestyle factors can influence development, for example exercise, stress, drug and alcohol abuse, diet during pregnancy, quality of diet, smoking. All of these factors can lead to more illness occurring, for example smoking has been linked to heart disease and cancer.

Socio-economic factors

Socio-economic factors have been shown to affect development as some individuals are in an environment that offers less chance of leading a healthy life. These factors include social class, housing, employment conditions, education and unemployment. Wealth and income are likely to influence housing, diet, the neighbourhood lived in and education received. In turn these things can influence lifestyle, overall health, and interests and leisure activities. Individuals may experience poor health, stress and a lack of fulfilment. Physical development can also be affected if the individual has a poor diet and therefore does not receive enough nutrients.

Social and community support

This can include health services, family/friends, community and religious groups. The support of the community can help social and emotional development and provide the individual with support. Lack of support can lead to stress as the individual will not be able to discuss difficulties and may feel isolated. This may lead them to feel stressed about their situation.

Environmental conditions

The environment can influence health and well-being and create a problem where the individual lives. This can include pollution, noise, employment conditions, education and unemployment. The environment can lead to stress, ill health and lack of fulfilment, e.g. pollution can lead to respiratory disease such as asthma.

Recording observations

Figure 14 Observe individuals doing an activity

By observing individuals you are able to:

- Review developmental progress – check against planned outcomes.
- Identify any concerns – is the activity suitable for the area of development?
- Identify any social problems – does the individual mix with others?
- Share information with practitioners – progress with activity and effects on development.
- Evaluate the effectiveness of the activity – does it meet with planned outcomes?
- Evaluate the support required by the individual – can the individual manage with the support of staff or can they manage independently?
- Report and record progress – against planned outcomes.
- Review development activities – does it work?
- Identify positive effects of the activity on well-being – does the individual feel happy?
- Identify negative effects of the activity on well-being – does the individual feel unsure about taking part in the activity?

All observations need to be recorded and reported following guidelines on record keeping set down locally and nationally. Details about the positive, negative and neutral impact of development activities on the individual's well-being need to be included as well as any changes to the activity. If any changes are required these should be agreed and implemented between you and the individual.

Confidentiality should be agreed between you and the individual and maintained, and records must be stored as recommended in policies and procedures.

Identifying and planning activities

A local supported housing scheme for individuals wishes to introduce a new programme of activities that would meet the needs of the individuals. The scheme is responsible for the care of 30 individuals with mental health issues.

You have been asked by the manager to contribute to the planning and implementing of an activity in their new programme. The manager has asked you to plan and monitor the effects of the activity. You have also been given the opportunity to identify the content of the activity.

➤ *What do you feel would be a suitable activity?*

➤ *What are the risks associated with the activity?*

➤ *What would be a suitable environment?*

➤ *Develop a plan for the activity.*

Key points – planning and implementing development activities

- A plan should be completed before implementing the activity.
- The environment should be prepared before the activity takes place.
- There are two main developmental theories (biological – development is linked to the individual's inherited genes; and learning – individuals learn their skills and responses).
- Factors affect development .
- The activity should be observed and records made.

Element HSC351c *Evaluate and review the effectiveness of the development activities*

How to evaluate and review activities

KUS 9,
12, 15, 16

Evaluation and review of the development activities is the last stage of the planning process. When writing the activity plan you need to consult with everyone involved to identify how and when the review will take place. Evaluation is an integral part of providing activities for individuals. How the activity will be evaluated needs to be planned from the beginning. This will help you to identify clear outcomes. SMART objectives or outcomes can be used to plan and evaluate activities (see Table 1).

Table 1 SMART objectives

Specific	They say exactly what is to be achieved/done, e.g. individual will make a cup of tea
Measurable	You can prove that you have accomplished the objectives, e.g. the individual has made a cup of tea
Achievable	You can accomplish the objectives but given the individual's abilities and circumstances, e.g. has some skills needs to adapt with help from occupational therapist and aids
Realistic	Can the objective be achieved in the circumstances, e.g. is making a cup of tea within the individual's capabilities?
Time related	They have deadlines, e.g. three one-hour sessions with the occupational therapist

By setting these outcomes/goals you will have something to measure progress against when you are evaluating the activity. The individual will be able to see what outcomes/goals have been met and what has not gone so well. The individual will then be able to set targets for the future based on these findings.

The content of the evaluation will depend on the activity, but it may help your practice if you can think about evaluation.

Evaluation

**Figure 15
Things to consider
before carrying
out an evaluation**

What is the evaluation to be used for?

Who will have access to the information?

How will the information be recorded?

Who is responsible for collecting all of the information on evaluation?

What evaluation methods are to be used?

How were the goals of the activity decided?

Are any other practitioners involved?

Was choice offered?

How are you going to involve the individual?

How are you going to involve family/friends?

Does the individual have communication needs to be supported?

Are other members of the care team involved?

Who should be involved?

It is good practice to consult everyone involved with the planning and implementation of the development activity. This can be:

- The individual.
- Family and friends and others significant to the individual.
- Other members of the care team.
- Other practitioners involved in the activity.

How and when will review take place?

The evaluation and review should take place as identified in the plan. This could be when the activity has been completed or at different stages depending on the activity. There may just be verbal feedback perhaps from:

- The individual/family and friends.
- Other members of the care team.
- Other practitioners.

Involvement in the review process

KUS 2, 9, 15

Support and encourage individuals to identify how they wish to be involved in the review and whether they require additional support to participate.

A detailed written evaluation may have to take place later when there is time to record findings. The developmental activities should also be evaluated and reviewed at the review meeting for the individual's care plan.

The individual

Involving the individual in feedback is essential when working in a person-centred way. They can tell you how and if the activities met their needs. Individuals can also identify if there is anything that needs improving in the activity. This will help meet needs in a more effective way and provide good quality care. It is also important to consider different ways to record feedback from the individual, for example in learning disability individuals often use video diaries to contribute feedback on their progress. These can be used at review meetings and help the individual to take an active part in their review.

Feedback from the individual can be verbal and then recorded by staff, or it can be on a feedback form. The form can be produced in the appropriate format and so that it is easy to complete in order to aid communication. The criteria on the form should be agreed beforehand and these should be appropriate to the activity.

If it is appropriate, the individual could be asked questions about the activity and their responses could be recorded. The questions should be asked in an appropriate and sensitive way. You may need to support the individual to provide feedback in the most appropriate way. All information given must be treated in confidence and recorded according to organisational policies and procedures. The individual needs to be enabled to give feedback using their preferred communication method. Provide appropriate support if there are any communication needs identified in their care plan.

Other members of the care team

Again verbal feedback should be used and this should be recorded. You can also record information on a feedback form designed for the activity. It may also be good practice to design an evaluation form together with the plan. Evaluation can then be discussed at a meeting and any changes implemented. The results of the discussion can be recorded.

Members of the care team can also complete specified evaluation forms. This could be designed as part of the personal assessment record.

Observation of the individual is an important method of evaluation and the results should be recorded. By observing the individual the effects of the activity can be noted, e.g. if the individual looks happy and is involved in the activity.

Other practitioners

KUS 9, 12, 16

Practitioners can evaluate the development activity. Again this can take place:

- Verbally.
- Through observation.
- By completing evaluation forms.
- During discussions.

Figure 16
Ways in which feedback can be obtained

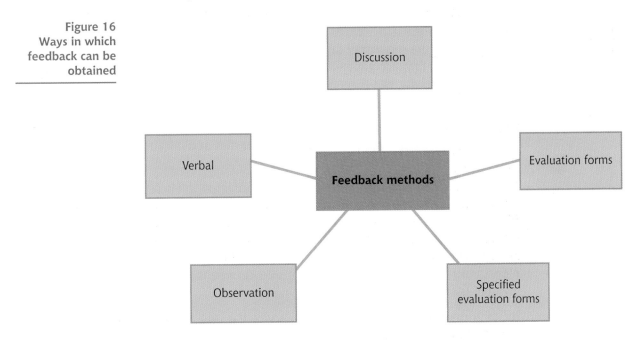

Evaluating activities

Roles and responsibilities

Make sure you know and understand your role and responsibilities regarding evaluation of activities. Check with your organisation to find out what type of information is required to measure how well the activity has met the agreed outcomes. This may include verbal or written feedback from the individual, their family and others who are significant to them. Information from specialist staff can also be used. This can include observations and written and verbal feedback. You may have to collate all of the information to enable a review of the benefits of the activity. This is particularly important if other practitioners are evaluating the activity.

You may be responsible for collecting all of the information, for observing and questioning the individual and completing the evaluation. All of the information needs to be recorded and reported according to organisational policies and procedures.

Information should be collated and evaluated against the activity outcomes for the individual. This will include the targets identified in the planning of the activity and the risk assessment, e.g. the outcome was to enable the individual to express their feelings in a poem.

Ensure that individuals receive the evaluation forms in sufficient time before the date of the review. This will also apply to the evaluation forms required from the other members of the care team and practitioners involved. All information should be in an appropriate format and meet all communication needs.

Review with individuals

You will have to use the agreed indicators (SMART outcomes) to decide if the activity was a success and the individual achieved the set targets. These targets will also give you guidance if the activity was too difficult. This may be supported by the feedback obtained from the individual and others. At this stage it is appropriate to review the risk assessment that accompanied the activity to ensure that the risks were minimised and that the activity was a success.

Before the review takes place it is important that you discuss with the individual the purpose of the review. This will enable the individual to prepare and contribute fully to the review. All communication needs should be met and information given in a format that the individual understands.

Care needs to be taken to ensure that the individual feels supported and the focus remains on their strengths and abilities, e.g. the individual can now boil a kettle and make a cup of tea. This will enable the individual to feel supported and motivated to carry out further activities to promote independence with daily living tasks, for example making shopping lists. Improvements in well-being should be discussed, e.g. the individual may feel more independent and confident about living alone if they can manage daily living tasks.

It is also worth exploring how well the service has met the individual's expectations of the activity. Depending on the purpose of the developmental activity you could ask them or observe their responses to judge whether any change has occurred. Alternatively, if the activity is designed to improve their ability to self-manage then you need to observe their daily activities and monitor if there is a change in their ability to undertake specific tasks or they are more motivated, confident or active.

The individual should be informed about how the evaluation will be used and how the information will be stored. Permission should be sought if the information is to be shared amongst other members of staff and organisations.

**Figure 17
Reviewing the
development
activities with the
individual fulfils a
number of
requirements**

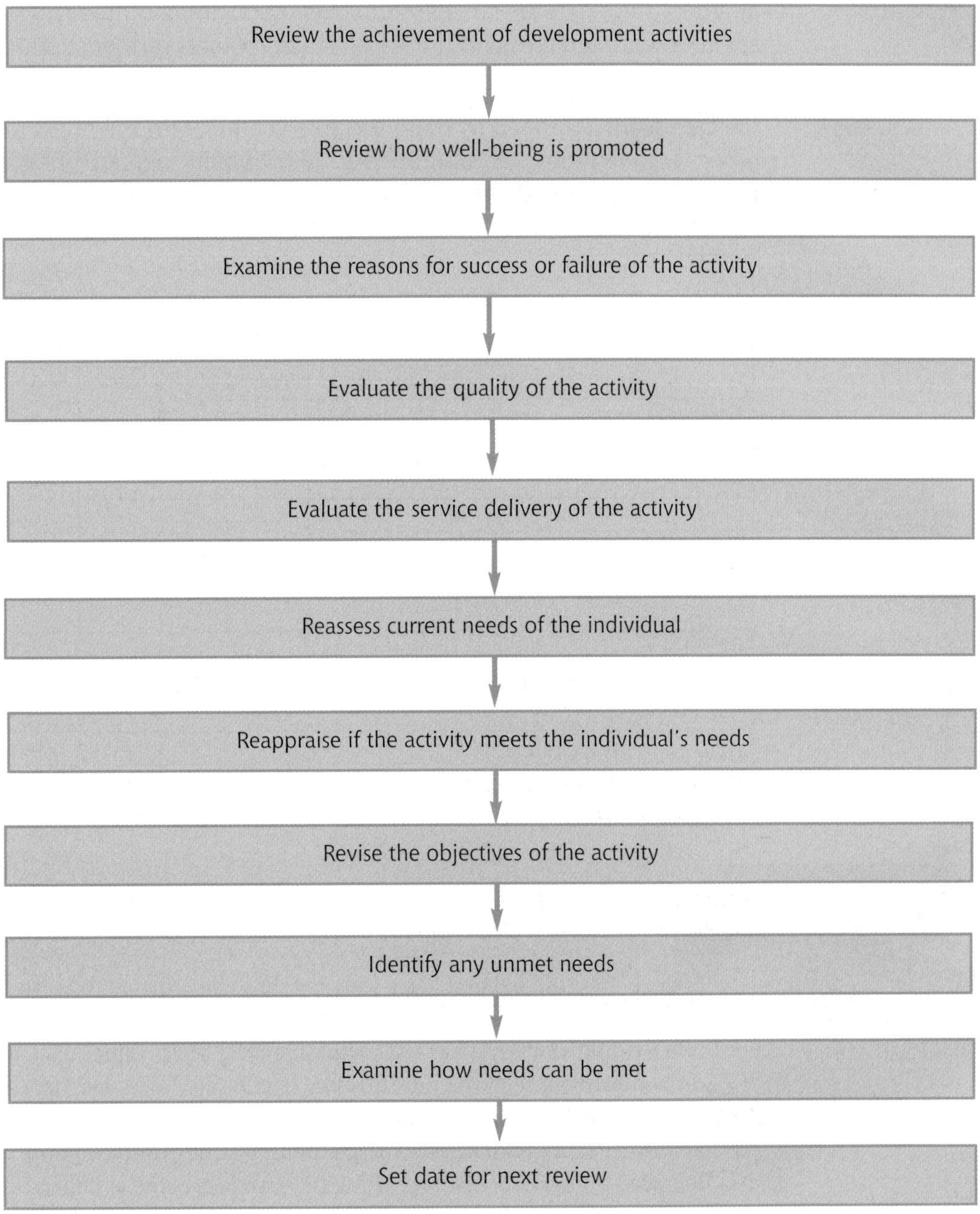

Review the achievement of development activities

Review how well-being is promoted

Examine the reasons for success or failure of the activity

Evaluate the quality of the activity

Evaluate the service delivery of the activity

Reassess current needs of the individual

Reappraise if the activity meets the individual's needs

Revise the objectives of the activity

Identify any unmet needs

Examine how needs can be met

Set date for next review

Changes in activities

You should talk to the individual and agree where the activity met their needs. If their needs have been achieved it is then part of your role to evaluate with the individual what activities would meet their current needs. This will facilitate the planning of new activities.

However, feedback and review of the activity might show that changes need to be made, and you should examine where these changes need to be made. This can occur

**KUS 2,
12, 15, 16**

at any of the stages of the activity including planning of the activity, the resources and environment required, and if the individual requires further support.

All changes need to be discussed, reported to the appropriate people and recorded in the care plan. You need to share this information with members of the care team and other organisations as appropriate and within agreed information-sharing and recording procedures and legislation.

**Figure 18
An activity
evaluation**

	What has been your level of interest?						Do you currently participate in this activity?		Would you like to pursue this in the future?	
	In the past 10 years			In the last year						
	Strong	Some	None	Strong	Some	None	Yes	No	Yes	No
Activity										
Gardening										
Sewing/needlework										
Playing cards										
Foreign languages										
Church activities										
Radio										
Television										
Walking										
Art and craft										
Golf										
Listening to music										

Practical Example

Plan and review activities

Stella is 20 years old and has a learning disability. She attends the local further education college and lives in supported living accommodation with three other young adults. At her last review meeting Stella expressed a desire to live on her own in one of the new tenancy flats in the town, like her friend Helen. An assessment of her needs identified that Stella needed to develop her domestic skills including shopping, menu planning and cooking. These are all included on her care plan activities and she does some at college and some at home with her key worker.

➤ Write SMART outcomes for a menu-planning activity.

➤ Identify the methods you would use to evaluate the activity.

➤ Give reasons why you have chosen these methods.

➤ Explain what you would do if an individual has stated that they feel the activity does not meet their needs.

➤ What changes do you feel you could make in the activity?

➤ How will these changes be recorded?

Key points – evaluating and reviewing the effectiveness of development activities

- Evaluation and review is an integral part of development activities.
- There are different methods of obtaining feedback.
- The individual is central to the evaluation process.
- All information needs to be collected, collated, analysed and recorded and the outcomes used to inform future activities.
- Well-being should be promoted.
- Changes should be negotiated and agreed.

Unit
HSC351

Are you ready for assessment?

Plan, agree and implement development activities to meet individual needs

This unit is about how you identify and agree development activities that will meet individuals' needs. It is about how you plan and then put in place appropriate development activities with the individual, key people and other practitioners. It is also about how you evaluate and review the effectiveness of those development activities in meeting the individuals' identified needs and make appropriate changes.

Your assessment will be carried out mainly through observation by your assessor and this should provide most of the evidence for the elements in this unit. If your assessor is unable to directly observe you then you may be able to use the testimony of an experienced colleague acting as an expert witness. You will need to discuss this with your assessor. Evidence of your knowledge and understanding will be demonstrated through observation, your assessor examining work products, e.g. reports, minutes of meetings, as well as through answering oral and/or written questions.

You need to be aware when planning assessments that this unit also relates to the core units, in particular HSC31 and HSC32, and so you may also be able to evidence performance criteria for these.

You should take into account that you may need to be observed in the individual's home, therefore you need to explain about the assessment and seek their permission for your assessor to visit. If their visit would be intrusive you will need to consider alternative evidence-gathering methods, e.g. expert witness testimony.   ▶

Direct observation by your assessor

Your assessor or an expert witness will need to plan to see you carry out the performance criteria (PCs) in each of the elements in this unit. The performance criteria that may be difficult to meet through observation are:

- **HSC351b PC 7**

Other types of evidence

You may need to present other forms of evidence in order to:

- Cover criteria not observed by your assessor.
- Show that you have the required knowledge, understanding and skills to claim competence in this area of practice.
- Ensure your work practice is consistent.

Your assessor may also need to ask you questions to confirm your knowledge and understanding and ensure that you can apply this to your practice.

Preparing to be observed

You must make sure that your workplace and any individuals and key people involved in your work agree to you being assessed. Explicit, informed consent must be obtained before you carry out any assessment activity that involves individuals or which involves access to confidential information related to their care.

Before your assessments you should read carefully the performance criteria for each element in the unit. Try to cover as much as you can during your observation but remember that you and your assessor can also plan for additional sources of evidence should full coverage of all performance criteria not be possible.

Check your knowledge

- What areas of development are covered by activities?
- Who should be involved in assessment of activities?
- How would you provide support to the individual when they are undertaking development activities?
- How do you set targets for development activities?
- How does the individual provide feedback on the development activity?
- How do you record and report changes to the activity plan?

Glossary

Ability Being able to do something. Having sufficient power, competence, cleverness, talent and skill to do it.

Abuse Physical, emotional and/or sexual harm that is caused to an individual and/or the failure to protect them from harm. Violent ill-treatment, speaking harshly to an individual, using harsh and vulgar comments. The violation of an individual's human and civil rights by any other person or persons.

Active listening This involves not just hearing what an individual is saying to you, but also showing that you are actually listening to what they are saying. You can show this by maintaining eye contact with the individual and by nodding and encouraging the individual to communicate. You can also paraphrase what has been said. This involves summarising or repeating what the individual has said to you, and it will check your understanding of what has been said. At the same time you can use reflective listening, which helps you to understand the feelings and emotions that the individual is communicating to you.

Active support The way that you enable an individual to take part, with or without assistance, in life activities to the best of their ability.

Advocacy The process of representing the needs of an individual, for example a person with mental health problems may use an advocate to suggest the move to a more independent living environment.

Advocate A person who will express the views, wishes and feelings of an individual, and who will speak on their behalf if they are not able to do so.

Alzheimer's disease A disorder of the brain that results in progressive physical and mental decline. Individuals may wander, suffer loss of memory, be agitated and depressed.

Ambivalence A state of feeling two conflicting emotions at the same time.

Analysing Breaking something down into its component parts to a level of detail that helps you to understand it better.

Autonomy The freedom to determine your own actions and behaviour, i.e. the ability of the individual to be independent and make their own decisions in relation to care planning.

Bereweeke An assessment method used by occupational therapists. It is used to measure activities of daily living, leisure, sensory awareness, perceptual and visual–motor integration, infant and child development, motor development, cognitive ability, psychosocial needs, social skills and disability status.

Caldicott Principles In 1997 Dame Fiona Caldicott chaired a committee which was reviewing patient-identifiable information within the NHS. The government published a report based on the recommendations of the Caldicott Committee, including the six principles that outline how this information should be handled.

Capability The quality of being capable. Competent and having the capacity and the ability to do. Having the physical or mental ability to do something.

Cardiovascular system Consisting of the heart and blood vessels.

Care management The process where the care plan is implemented and managed as agreed at assessment.

Chromosomes These are responsible for the transmission of genetic material, e.g. eye colour.

Cognitive awareness The faculty of knowing or being physically aware of something.

Cognitive impairment The inability to use memory or language in the capacity that is expected for the individual's age, due to brain damage or disease.

Connotation An idea suggested by a word or phrase. For example, the phrase 'that's cool' may refer to the temperature but can be used by a teenager to express satisfaction.

Constructive feedback Giving someone helpful information in response to something done. Useful and helpful advice.

Continuing professional development (CPD) This relates to any job-related learning that is designed to develop and improve your work practice, e.g. fire safety training or a workshop about understanding disability.

Danger The possibility of harm or abuse occurring. A state of being vulnerable to injury or loss. A person or thing that may cause injury. The likelihood that something unpleasant will happen. The danger could be imminent, in the short term, the medium term or in the longer term.

Denotation The generalised meaning of a word. For example, a bed is a piece of furniture on which to sleep.

Development How someone grows and matures. For example, physically by crawling and then walking.

Diversity The quality of being different or varied, of having a range of differences. People are diverse, they have their own unique individuality, personality and identity. Identity can be explained as a state of being a specified person or thing.

Emergency An immediate threat or danger to individuals and others.

Empowerment Gaining more control over your life. Being aware of and using personal and external resources. Overcoming obstacles in order to meet your needs and aspirations. Having your say in decision-making. Being able to challenge inequality and oppression in your life.

Equitably Providing health and social care support equitably means that you recognise and address the essential differences between individuals and groups to ensure their needs are met appropriately and they receive the same quality of care as others. Equity is an essential principle of current health and social care practice.

Fine manipulative skills The small finger movements and manipulative skills including hand–eye co-ordination, for example holding a pencil, and turning a page.

Fine motor skills Smaller actions like picking things up between the thumb and finger or wriggling the toes.

Genetics Relates to the genes inherited from our parents.

Goals The aims of the activity, e.g. to improve fine manipulative skills.

Gross motor skills The movements of the whole body and limbs, co-ordination and balance. An example would be walking.

Harm The effects of an individual being physically, emotionally or sexually injured or abused. Physical, mental or moral injury.

Hazard Anything that can cause harm. A source of danger.

Holistic This involves looking at the individual as a whole and should include physical, psychological, social and spiritual aspects.

Incident An event that requires immediate attention to avoid possible danger, but is not immediately life threatening.

Informal carers People involved in the care of the individual who are not paid workers. This can include an adult looking after an ageing parent or partner, or an adult looking after a child who has a physical or learning disability.

Interpersonal communication A process of sharing meaning, feelings and information between people. This happens through using verbal and non-verbal communication. For example, communicating with an individual to show that you understand how they feel about a change to their care environment.

Interpersonal interaction The word 'inter' means between; therefore, interpersonal interaction means action between people.

Kinesics This is defined as involving the conscious or unconscious body positioning or actions of the communicator. For example, leaning towards the individual to show you are listening to what they are saying.

Lifelong learning The term used to describe continuing learning and professional development throughout adulthood.

Methods A special form of procedure, in this case the means of achieving goals.

Need A want or requirement. The requirements of individuals to enable them to achieve, maintain or restore an acceptable level of independence or quality of life.

Objectives The aims or goals to be achieved, e.g. enabling the individual to hold a paintbrush.

Objectives of care The goals of care planning, for example to maintain continence.

Oppression To subject a person or persons to a harsh or cruel form of domination. Persecution, causing physical, emotional and mental stress.

Paralanguage Part of non-verbal communication and consists of sounds like 'mmm' and 'uh huh'. The use of pitch and tone also form part of paralanguage. Fear or anxiety can often be communicated through raised pitch.

Philosophy of care The nature of the care given. For example, the belief that care is given to promote the needs of children.

Portage An assessment system that is used with individuals who have special educational needs. Developmental levels are measured.

Proxemics Part of non-verbal communication and involves the use of personal space and touch. For example, you might comfort an individual who is distressed by moving closer and touching their arm.

Reflecting Thinking seriously and carefully about something in order to understand it better.

Respiratory system Consists of the lungs, nose, trachea, larynx and the muscles used for breathing.

Retribution Punishment or vengeance for bad deeds.

Risk The chance that someone will be harmed by a hazard. For example, a bottle of bleach is a hazard and becomes a risk when it is opened and is being used.

Risk assessment This is carried out in health care in order to judge the potential dangers that an individual and/or activity may present with a view to putting control measures in place to minimise the risk of danger and harm. It involves weighing up the chance that someone will be harmed by a particular hazard. For example, the benefits of going out for a walk against the danger of being knocked down by a car.

Socio-economic Involves both social and economic factors. For example, the amount of income earned by different social classes can affect housing, health, education and the development of the individual.

Statements of purpose These are used in care planning to match the individual's needs to services provided. For example, the need for support with washing and dressing in the individual's own home is matched to the availability of care staff in the local area, cost and access.

Stereotype A fixed opinion or view of individuals, including the way they look, the way they act, the abilities they have and what they do. A standardised idea of a type of person or thing. Stereotypes are not descriptions of real people, they are a collection of thoughts and ideas regarding habits, dress, language, attitudes and behaviour.

Values Moral principles. A person's judgement of what is important in life, for example showing respect for others.

Vulnerable adult An individual who is in need of the care services by reason of mental or other disability, age or illness, and who is, or may be, unable to take care of themselves or protect themselves against significant harm or exploitation.

Index

Page numbers in *italics* indicate figures or tables.